Preface

This book had its beginnings rather a long time ago. Two of the authors were sitting in a bar at Chicago airport on their return to the UK from a conference in Florida. When they had finished bemoaning the miserable lot of a British academic, they turned to another favourite topic of conversation; that there simply wasn't a textbook on visual perception that was quite right for the courses they taught. There were books that were excellent but too difficult for most undergraduates, there were books that were too boring and dull, and there were books that had some good bits and some bad bits. So, they resolved, as you do after a few beers, to write their own. Copious notes were scribbled on beer mats that day and, had either of the authors thought to pick up the beer mats when their flight was called, this book might have been published some years ago.

We first got together as a trio of authors in the latter years of the last century. We rented a cottage on the border between England and Wales and, cut off from the outside world from dawn until we went down the pub at night, we wrote and wrote. Initially we adopted a pragmatic, some might say lazy, guiding principle: if we three, with some 80 years of vision research and teaching between us, didn't know something, then an undergraduate studying visual perception didn't need to know it either. We have had other guidelines, too: the book has to be fun to read, it must be as up to date as we can make it, it has to look good, and nearly everything we say should be true.

We think we have achieved all these ambitions, but although we are very proud of the result, there have been disappointments and struggles along the way. Each of us has written pages of text we thought were pertinent only to have the other two authors drop our contribution in the bin. Even when we all agreed on the inclusion of a topic, we have all seen our work rewritten and trimmed down. But this process has resulted in a book in which a uniform style has emerged and we hope one that represents the best of each of us.

Visual perception is about looking at the world and seeing things. So it is something of a surprise that so many books on the subject just aren't very attractive to look at. We believe this book is one of the first undergraduate textbooks on visual perception to be published in full colour, and we hope you'll agree with us that it is the best-looking book around. Much credit for this must go to Oxford University Press. We thank Jon Crowe for holding our hands throughout the publishing process, June Cummings and Nicola Bateman for keeping our eyes on the ball and simultaneously, our noses to the grindstone. The book is lavishly illustrated, as a book on vision should be. Many of the figures have been drawn Steve Crumly and we are indebted to him for making the book look so good. Many images and photos have been supplied for the book by a host of different people and we thank them all, especially Ruth Craven at OUP for her quiet efficiency in organizing the figures: more formal acknowledgements are given on page xiii.

The writing of textbooks is generally frowned upon by our employers. Universities are measured by the quality of the research they publish, so given that we have taken time from research to write this book, we probably should thank our respective universities for their indulgence. More importantly, this book has taken time from our families and friends, and we thank them most of all.

Robert Snowden, Cardiff
Peter Thompson, York
Tom Troscianko, Bristol
April 2006

Contents

Figure acknowledgements

There are instances where we have been unable to trace or contact the copyright holder. If notified the publisher will be pleased to rectify any errors or omissions at the earliest opportunity.

Fig 0.0 Photograph courtesy of Mike Land.

Fig 0.1 Photograph: 'Hidden Dalmatian' by R.C. James reproduced from Gregory, R. (1997). *Eye and Brain*. 3rd ed. Oxford: Oxford University Press.

Fig 0.2 Photograph: 'Hidden Dalmatian' by R.C. James reproduced from Gregory, R. (1997). *Eye and Brain*. 3rd ed. Oxford: Oxford University Press.

Fig 0.3 Reproduced from Ishihara, S. (1960). *Tests for Colour-Blindness*. 15th ed, Tokyo: Handaya Company.

Fig 0.4 Reproduced from Gregory, R. (1997). *Eye and Brain*. 3rd ed. Oxford: Oxford University Press. Originally produced in Yarbus, A. L. (1967). *Eye Movements and Vision*. New York: Plenum Press.

Fig. 0.7 Reproduced from Thompson, P. (1980) Margaret Thatcher: a new illusion. Perception, 9, 383–384.

Fig 0.8 Courtesy of Peter Halligan, Cardiff University.

Fig 0.9 Reproduced from Felleman D.J. and van Essen D.C. (1991). Distributed Hierarchical Processing in the Primate, *Cerebral Cortex*, 1: 1–47 by permission of Oxford University Press.

Fig 1.0 Photographs courtesy of Mike Land.

Fig 1.5 marinewildlife © Paul Kay.

Fig 1.6 Medical illustration courtesy of National Glaucoma Research, a program of the American Health Assistance Foundation. http://www.ahaf.org/glaucoma/about/glabout.htm). Redrawn with permission.

Fig 1.7 Photograph courtesy of National Eye Institute, National Institutes of Health.

Fig 1.13 Photograph by Ralph C. Eagle. Photo Researchers, Inc. reproduced from [No author], 2003, *Photoreceptors* [online] Available from World Wide Web: http://webvision.med.utah.edu

Fig 1.15 Images C, J, and K are reproduced from Roorda, A. and Williams, D. R. (1999). The arrangement of the three cone classes in the living human eye. *Nature* 397, 520–522. All other images were made by Heidi Hofer.

Fig 1.16 Derrington, A., 2002. From the Retina to the Brain. In Roberts, D. (Ed), *Signals and Perception*. Palgrave Macmillan, The Open University, reproduced with permission of Palgrave Macmillian

Fig 1.17 Reproduced from Andrews, T. J., Halpern, S. D., and Purves, D. (1997). Correlated size variations in human visual cortex, lateral geniculate nucleus and optic tract. *Journal of Neuroscience* 17, 2859–2868

Fig 1.1.2 Photograph courtesy of Mr Richard Harrad.

Fig 2.0 Photograph courtesy of Ron Douglas.

Fig 2.8 Photograph © The Nobel Foundation.

Fig 3.0 Hadjikhani, N. and Tootell, R. B. (2000). Projection of rods and cones within human visual cortex. *Human Brain Mapping*, 9 (1): 55–63; Copyright (2000, Wiley-Liss, Inc.). Reprinted with permission of Wiley-Liss Inc., a subsidiary of John Wiley & Sons, Inc.

Fig 3.2 Andrews, T. J., Halpern, S, D. and Purves, D. (1997). Correlated Size Variations in Human Visual Cortex, Lateral Geniculate Nucleus, and Optic Tract. *Journal of Neuroscience*, 17 (4): 2859–2868, Copyright © 1997 by the society for Neuroscience.

Fig 3.4 Nicholls, J. G., Martin, A. R., and Wallace: B. G. (1992). *From Neuron to Brain*, 3d edn., Sunderland, MA: Sinauer Associates.

Fig 3.15 Source: Bruce, C., Desimone, R., and Gross, C. G. (1981). Visual properties of neurons in a polysensory area in superior temporal sulcus of the macaque. *Journal of Neurophysiology*, 46, 369–384, used with permission.

Fig 3.16 Adapted with permission from original artwork by Terese Winslow © 1999.

Fig 3.18 Reproduced from Felleman D. J., and van Essen D.C. (1991). Distributed Hierarchical Processing in the Primate. *Cerebral Cortex*, 1, 1–47, by permission of Oxford University Press.

Fig 3.2.1 Reproduced from Frisby, J. P. (1979). *Seeing*. Oxford: Oxford University Press.

Fig 3.3.1 Obermayer, K. and Blasdel, G. G. (1993). Geometry of orientation and ocular dominance columns in monkey striate cortex. *Journal of Neuroscience*, 13, (10) 4117. Copyright © 1993 by Society for Neuroscience.

Fig 4.1 'Ascending and descending turtles' © Akiyoshi Kitaoka 2002.

Fig 4.3 Redrawn from De Valois, R., Yund, E., and Hepler, N. (1982). The orientation and direction selectivity of cells in macaque visual cortex. *Vision Research* 22, 531–544.

Fig 4.11 Redrawn from Blakemore, C. B. and Sutton, P. (1971). Size adaptation: a new after-effect . *Science* 166, 245–247.

Fig 4.20 Courtesy of Michael Lewis, Cardiff University.

Fig 4.27 Reproduced from Rock, I. (1975). *An Introduction to Perception*. Basingstoke: MacMillan.

Fig 5.0 Reproduced from Ishihara, S. (1960). *Tests for Colour-Blindness*. 15th ed, Tokyo: Handaya Company.

Fig 5.3 Reproduced from Sinclair S. (1985). *How Animals See: Other Visions of our World*. London: Croom Helm.

Fig 5.4 Image Courtesy NASA/JPL-Caltech

Fig 5.5 © Bjørn Rørslett-NN/Nærfoto.

Fig 5.8 Reproduced from Douma, M., curator. (2006). Newton and the Color Spectrum, Color Vision & Art from WebExhibits, Institute for Dynamic Educational Advancement, Washington, DC. Available from the World Wide Web http://webexhibits.org/colorart/bh.html [Accessed 22 December 2005].

Fig 5.9 Copyright Dr. Roy Bishop < rg@ns.sympatico.ca > , The Royal Astronomical Society of Canada.

Fig 5.14 Reproduced from Domb, L. G. and Pagel, M. (2001). Sexual swellings advertise female quality in wild baboons. *Nature* 410: 204–206.

Fig 5.20 Based on the work of De Monasterio, F. M. & Gouras, P. (1975). Functional properties of ganglion cells of the rhesus monkey retina. *The Journal of Physiology* **251**, 167–195

Fig 5.29 Reproduced from Hadjikhani, N., Liu, L. K., Dale, A. M., Cavanagh, P., and Tootell, R. B. H. (1998). Retinotopy and color sensitivity in human visual cortical area V8. *Nature Neuroscience*, 1 (3), 235–241.

Fig 5.1.1 Photograph by Mitsuaki TAKATA.

Fig 6.0 'U-zu-maki glasses' © Akiyoshi Kitaoka 2003.

Fig 6.14 Tootell, R.B.H., Reppas, J.B., Dale, A.M., Look, R.B., Sereno, M.I., Malach, R., Brady, T.S. & Rosen, B.R. (1995). Visual motion aftereffect in human cortical area MT revealed by functional magnetic imaging. *Nature*, 375, 139–141.

Fig 6.16 'The Enigma' by Isia Leviant (1984)

Fig 6.3.1 Reprinted from Pinna, B. and Brelstaff, G. L. (2000). A new visual illusion of relative motion, *Vision Research*, 40, 2091–2096, Copyright (2000), with permission from Elsevier.

Fig 6.3.3 Reproduced from Gurnsey, R. (2002). Optimising the Pinna-Brelstaff illusion. *Perception*, 31, 1275–1280.

Fig 7.0 'Valley' © Akiyoshi Kitaoka 2005.

Fig 7.2 M.C. Escher's "Ascending and Descending" © 2006. The M.C. Escher Company-Holland. All rights reserved. www.mcescher.com

Fig 7.3 (a) ©Photodisc

Fig 7.3 (b) Photographer: Irene Timossi. Reproduced with permission from University of California, Berkeley – Sagehen Creek Field Station collection.

Fig 7.3 (c) ©Ingram

Fig 7.3 (d) Reproduced from http://www.cucco.org/

Fig 7.8 Photograph by J. R. Eyerman/Life Magazine/Time & Life Pictures/Getty Images

Fig 7.9 Image: Two Young Women Studying Stereopticon Pictures © Bettmann/CORBIS reproduced with permission.

Fig 7.15 Image courtesy of Brian Rogers, Oxford University.

Fig 7.24 (a) Reprinted from Knill, D. (1998). Surface orientation from texture: Ideal observers, generic observers and the information content of texture cues. *Vision Research*, 38, 1655–1682, Copyright (1998), with permission from Elsevier.

Fig 7.24 (b) Image courtesy of Simon Watt, University of Wales, Bangor.

Fig 7.25 (b) Reproduced from Wick, W. (1998). *Walter Wick's Optical Tricks*. New York: Scholastic.

Fig 7.26 Image courtesy of Pascal Mamassian and Dan Kersten.

Fig 7.30 Reproduced from O'Brien, J. and Johnston, A. (2000). When texture takes precedence over motion in depth perception. *Perception* 29(4), 437–452.

Fig 7.32 (a) Reproduced with permission © Exploratorium, www.exploratorium.edu

Fig 7.1.1 Image courtesy of Christopher Tyler.

Fig 7.4.1 Image courtesy of Simon Watt, University of Wales, Bangor.

Fig 7.4.2 Hillis, J. M., Watt, S. J., Landy, M. S., and Banks, M. S. (2004). Slant from texture and disparity cues: optimal cue combination. *Journal of Vision* 4, 967–992.

Fig 8.0 Baby courtsey of Claudine Crane.

Fig 8.2 Reproduced with permission from Saunders, K. *Acuity Representations* [on line]. University of Ulster. Available from: http://www.science.ulst.ac.uk/visionsci/acureps/ho_pg.htm

Fig 8.11 Photograph by William Vandivert, reproduced from Gibson, E.J. and Walk, R.D. (1960). The 'Visual Cliff'. *Scientific American*, 202 (4), 64–71.

Fig 8.12 Reprinted with permission from Pascalis, O., de Haan, M., and Nelson, C. A. (2002). Is face processing species-specific during the first year of life? *Science*, 296, 1321–1323. Copyright 2002 AAAS.

Fig 8.14 Kiorpes, L. and Bassin, S. A. (2003), Development of contour integration in macaque monkeys. *Visual Neuroscience*, 20 (5) 567–575. © (2003) Cambridge University Press.

Fig 8.16 Blakemore, C. and Cooper, G. F. (1970). Development of the brain depends on the visual environment. *Nature*, 228, 477–478.

Fig 8.18 Photograph courtesy of pedseye.com.

Fig 8.20 Photgrapher: John H. Krantz, Ph. D., Psycology Department, Hanover College, Hanover, In.

Fig 9.0 Nature Publishing Group

Fig 9.14 Simons, D. J. and Chabris, C. F. (1999). Gorillas in our midst; sustained inattentional blindness for dynamic events. *Perception*, 28 (9), 1059–1074.

Fig 9.15 SPG Media, 2006. *Air force Technology* [online]. Available from http://www.airforce-technology.com/projects/hercules/hercules3.html [Accessed 19th January 2006].

Fig 9.25 Marshall, J. C., and Halligan, P. W. (1995). Seeing the forest but only half the trees. *Nature*, 373, 521–523.

Fig 9.26 Husain, M., Mannan, S., Hodgson, T., Wojciulik, E., Driver, J., and Kennard, C. (2001). Impaired spatial working memory across saccades contributes to abnormal search in parietal neglect. *Brain*, 124, 941–95, by permission of Oxford University Press.

Fig 9.1.1 Redrawn from Corbetta, M., Miezin, F. M., Shulman, G. L., and Petersen, S. E. (1993). A PET study of visuospatial attention. *Journal of Neuroscience* 13, 1202–1226.

Fig 10.0 'Old Age, Adolescence, Infancy (The Three Ages)' by Salvador Dali (1940) © Salvador Dali, Gala-Salvador Dali Foundation, DACS, London 2006.

Fig 10.1 (a) ©iStockphoto.com/Lise Gagne

Fig 10.1 (b) ©iStockphoto.com/ Lise Gagne

Fig 10.1 (c) ©iStockphoto.com/Jody Elliott

Fig 10.1 (d) © iStockphoto.com/Kateryna Govorushchenko

Fig 10.3 Image ©2000–2006 by René Joseph. All rights reserved www. renejoseph.com

Fig 10.5 Reproduced from Thompson, P. (1980). Margaret Thatcher: a new illusion. *Perception*, 9, 383–384.

Fig 10.8 (a) Image: © Bettmann/CORBIS

Fig 10.8 (b) Image: © TRAPPER FRANK/CORBIS SYGMA

Fig 10.8 (c) Image: © Stephane Cardinale/People Avenue/Corbis

Fig 10.8 (d) Image: © Rufus F. Folkks/CORBIS

Fig 10.9 (a) and 10.10 (a) Image: © Danny Moloshok/epa/Corbis

Fig 10.9 (b) and 10.10 (b) Image: © Mitchell Gerber/CORBIS

Fig 10.9 (c) and 10.10 (c) Image: © Michael Goulding/Orange County Register/Corbis

Fig 10.9 (d) and 10.10 (d) Image: © Stephane Cardinale/People Avenue/Corbis

Fig 10.11 Chimaera Bronze statue, 4th century BC, Museo Archeologico, Florence

Fig 10.12 Images courtesy of Jason Brake and Fiona MacRae.

Fig 10.13 Courtesy of Department of Psychology, University of York

Fig 10.14 Reproduced with permission. www.mudgestudios.com

Fig 10.15 Lee, K., Byatt, G., & Rhodes, G. (2000). Caricature effects, distinctiveness and identification: Testing the face-space framework. *Psychological Science*, 11, 379–385.

Fig 10.17 – © Fox Broadcasting Company

Fig 10.19 Redrawn from Calder, A. J., Young, A. W., Perrett, D. I., Etcoff, N. L., and Rowland, D. (1996). Categorical perception of morphed facial expressions. *Visual Cognition* 3, 81–117.

Fig 10.20 Redrawn from Calder, A. J., Young, A. W., Perrett, D. I., Etcoff, N. L., and Rowland, D. (1996). Categorical perception of morphed facial expressions. *Visual Cognition* 3, 81–117.

Fig 10.21 Based on an idea by Chris Benson, University of Bristol

Fig 10.22 Based on an idea by Chris Benson, University of Bristol

Fig 10.23 Image provided by Michael Webster, University of Nevada.

Fig 10.24 Reprinted from Hasselmo, M. E., Rolls, E. T., Baylis, G. C. (1989). The role of expression and identity in the face-selective responses of neurons in the temporal visual cortex of the monkey. *Behaviour Brain Research*, 32: 203–218, Copyright 1989, with permission from Elsevier.

Fig 10.25 Image courtesy of Tim Andrews. Based on work from Kanwisher, McDermott and Chun (1997), The Fusiform Face Area: A Module in Human Extrastriate Cortex Specialized for Face Perception. The Journal of Neuroscience. 17 (11) pp. 4302–4311 Copyright © 1997 by the Society for Neuroscience

Fig 10.27 Reprinted by permission from Macmillan Publishers Ltd: *Nature Neuroscience*, 6 (6), 624–631, copyright (2003).

Fig 10.28 Redrawn from Tranel, D., Damasio, H. and Damasio, A. (1995). Double dissociation between overt and covert face recognition. *Journal of Cognitive Neuroscience* 7, 425–432.

Fig 10.29 Reprinted from *Trends in Cognitive Sciences*, 5, Ellis H. D., and Lewis M. B., Capgras delusion: a window of face recognition, 149–156, Copyright (2001), with permission from Elsevier.

Fig 10.1.1 © Photo RMN/© Hervé Lewandowski/Thierry Le Mage 'Mona Lisa' by Leonardo da Vinci (1503–1506), Musee du Louvre, Paris

Fig 10.3.1 Reprinted from *Vision Research*, 45, Hershler, O., and Hochstein, S., At first sight: A high-level pop out effect for faces, 1707–1724, Copyright (2005), with permission from Elsevier.

Fig 10.3.2 Reprinted from *Vision Research*, 45, Hershler, O., and Hochstein, S., At first sight: A high-level pop out effect for faces, 1707–1724, Copyright (2005), with permission from Elsevier.

Fig 10.3.3 Reprinted from *Vision Research*, 45, Hershler, O., and Hochstein, S., At first sight: A high-level pop out effect for faces, 1707–1724, Copyright (2005), with permission from Elsevier.

Fig 11.0 Reproduced from Aglioti, S., DeSouza, J.F.X. & Goodale, M.A. (1995). Size-contrast illusions deceive the eye but not the hand. *Current Biology*, 5, 679–685.

Fig 11.9 Image: © M. Perenin of Inserm, France. Reproduced from Milner, D. and Goodale, M. (Eds) (1995). *The Visual Brain in Action*, Oxford: Oxford University Press.

Fig 11.14 Reprinted from *Current Biology*, 5, Aglioti, S., DeSouza, J.F.X. and Goodale, M.A., Size-contrast illusions deceive the eye but not the hand, 679–685, Copyright (1995), with permission from Elsevier.

Fig 11.15 Yarbus, A. L. (1967). *Eye Movements and Vision*. New York: Plenum Press

Fig 11.16 Drawn based on data taken from Starr, M. S. and Rayner, K. (2001). Eye movements during reading: some current controversies. *Trends in Cognitive Sciences* 5, 156–163.

Fig 11.17 Redrawn from Starr, M. S. and Rayner, K. (2001). Eye movements during reading: some current controversies. *Trends in Cognitive Sciences* 5, 156–163.

Fig 12.0 Reprinted from *Current Opinion in Neurobiology*, 15, Sereno, M. I., and Tootell, R. B. H., From monkeys to humans: what do we know about brain homologies?, 135–144, Copyright (2005), with permission from Elsevier.

Fig 12.1 Source: Schmolesky, M. (2000). *The Primary Visual Cortex* [online]. Available from World Wide Web: http://webvision.med.utah.edu, reproduced with permission.

Fig 12.2 (a) Valverde, F. (2002). *The Golgi method* [online]. Available from the World Wide Web: http://www.cajal.csic.es/Valverde%20Web%2002/man.htm, accessed 31st March 2006.

Fig 12.2 (b) Reprinted from *Trends in Neuroscience*, 9, Masland, R. H. and Tauchi, M., The cholinergic amacrine cells, 218–223 Copyright (1986), with permission from Elsevier.

CHAPTER 0
A trailer to the book

The eyes of a really scary jumping spider (Metaphidippus), normally resident in California. Generally the bigger you are the better you can see (remember Little Red Riding Hood – 'what great big eyes you have, Grandma . . . '), but this furry little creature has exceptionally good visual acuity given its relatively small body size.

'I see nobody on the road,' said Alice. 'I only wish I had such eyes,' the King remarked in a fretful tone. 'To be able to see Nobody! And at that distance too! Why, it's as much as I can do to see real people, by this light!'

Lewis Carroll, *Through the Looking Glass*

An apology

We would like to apologize in advance for the content of this book. We set out not to write the definitive textbook on vision, but to write an enjoyable one. We have occasionally (well, quite often really) sacrificed what some people hold to be 'the truth' for the sake of a coherent story, and simplified some ideas to the extent that our colleagues in vision science will be outraged to see their own area of the subject being presented so frivolously or even ignored altogether. Therefore what you have here are, at best, the bare bones of vision. We hope that you will enjoy our book and that you will feel inspired to go and read a book that is more advanced but probably more boring than ours (we list some of these at the end of each chapter).

The problem

Vision appears very easy. As we glance out of the window we are met with a wealth of information. We can see that there are red berries on the bush, and that they are now ripe for the birds to eat, we can see there is a slight drizzle in the air, we can see a man and we immediately know that it is someone we have never seen before, yet we can tell that at this moment he doesn't look very happy. All this from a single glance. We do this so easily and so quickly that it does not strike us just what an amazing accomplishment each glance actually is. But let's think about this for just a moment.

Light can be thought of as lots of little balls (photons, to give them their proper name) that arrive from the sun or a light bulb, or some other source. These balls bounce off the objects around us, the trees, cars, humans, and so on, and some of them just happen to bounce in such a way that their path takes them from the object and through a tiny transparent window in our eye. Inside our eye these balls are collected and vision begins. By way of analogy we could imagine a little man with a net catching these light balls and, from the contents of his net, doing all the things that vision does – seeing colours, knowing that a car is coming towards him, recognizing his friend has a new haircut, reaching out and picking up his coffee cup . . . and a million other things. Put like this, vision appears bewilderingly difficult. This book aims to present some of what we know about how we take the contents of this net and turn it into 'seeing'.

Take a look at Figure 0.1. What do you see? The answer is probably 'not much, just a lot of spots'. However, if you continue to look at the figure for some time your impression will probably change. After a while most people have a sudden revelation that it is not just a set of spots, it's the picture of a spotty dog sniffing at the ground (for those of you still struggling, **turn the page and there is help for you in Figure 0.2**). From now on, whenever you see this figure, you will not see just spots, it will always be the spotty dog. Somehow your brain has interpreted this figure and made an object from the spots. This process is at the heart of what vision does – it is always trying to make sense of its input and telling us about the things we need to know about. Vision is active, not passive. Our eye is often likened to a camera – both have an aperture at the front, some type of lens to focus the light, and then something that absorbs the light at the back. This may not be a bad analogy for the eye itself, but it is a bad analogy for vision. Why? Because the camera doesn't have to do very much; it doesn't have to interpret the world and act accordingly – it doesn't have to produce dogs from spots. The camera never lies, because the camera doesn't have to tell us what it sees – but our visual system does. Our visual system is not there to faithfully record the image outside, it is there to give us the necessary information for us to behave appropriately.

The last phrase we used, '*necessary information for us to behave appropriately*', is actually rather important. It tells us that we see the world in a particular way not because that is the way the world is, but because that's the way we are. Let's try and clarify this puzzling statement with an example. Figure 0.3 shows what is known as an Ishihara plate. It's just a bunch of spots. No dog this time, but most of us can see the number 74 hidden in the dots. However, there are some people who can see no such number. Show it to your pet dog, or cat – you will find that they cannot see it either, though your goldfish will see the 74 with ease! Why? Surely the number 74 is either there or it isn't. The answer lies in your physiology. The colour of the spots has been subtly designed so that the difference between the 74 and its background can only be detected by animals with a certain type of colour vision. As we shall learn in Chapter 5, human colour vision is different from that of nearly all other mammals in having great ability to distinguish between the colours we

Fig. 0.1. What can you see in this picture?

call red and green. To most other mammals (cats, dogs, horses, bulls, etc.) these colours do not exist – they see them all as various shades of browny yellow (we are being rather bold here in claiming to know what it's like to be a dog, but we hope you get the gist). Likewise, the small proportion of humans that we term 'red–green colour blind' cannot see this number 74 at all; they are invariably dressed in bizarre combinations of colours and happily will put a red sock on one foot and a green sock on the other as both look the same to them, providing great amusement for the rest of us.

Fig. 0.2. Now can you see what the picture is? Look back at Figure 0.1 and you'll see the Dalmatian clearly, we hope.

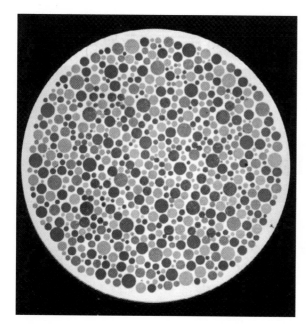

Fig. 0.3. An plate from the Ishihara test for colour blindness – can you see the number?

At night we lose our abilities to see colours completely. If you lead a sad and uninteresting life you may have this book as bedtime reading; if so, turn off the light and try looking at Figure 0.3 in your dimly lit bedroom. You will no longer be able to see the number 74. Indeed, a simple glance around the room will tell you that there is no colour anywhere. How can this be? Surely a green object will still be green even if there is not much light around? Not so. 'Green-ness' is an invention of your brain, and if there is not enough light around it cannot create this particular magic we call colour.

So why do we have an ability to see colour that our pet dog lacks? Is he adequately compensated by being able to lick parts of his own anatomy that we can't? The statement *'necessary information for us to behave appropriately'* seems to imply that there is something we do that needs this information that dogs don't do. As we shall see in Chapter 5 this may well have to do with picking ripe fruit, something of great importance to our ancestors, but an activity for which most dogs lack any enthusiasm. Quite why the goldfish should want to go picking ripe fruit we shall leave for you to consider.

Vision in action

So vision isn't there merely to form a pretty picture of the world – it's there in order for us to be able to make sense of what is out there and to interact with it, and to actively seek information about the world. If you carefully watch a person as they perform any visual task, from merely watch TV to driving a car at high speed, you will see that their eyes do not merely stand still and absorb information, instead they flick rapidly from place to

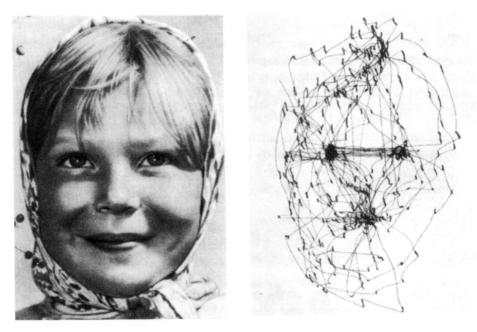

Fig. 0.4. Pattern of eye movements whilst looking at a picture.

place, in almost constant motion. If we measure eye movements carefully, we find that the eyes move about 3–4 times per second as we perform these tasks. Figure 0.4 shows the pattern of eye movements that a person made while looking at a simple stationary picture. It shows that the person looked from place to place as they inspected this figure. It also shows that the movements of the eye were not random, but each movement caused the central part of our vision to fall upon an 'interesting' part of the picture such as the eyes of the statue. The reason for this is that vision is not uniform across our field of view. Our central vision gives us really good detail of the point we are looking at. However, as we move further and further away from this point our vision gets worse and worse (see Figure 0.5). Thus at any one moment we only have really sharp vision for one small part of the world, and in order to understand what is going on we need to move our eyes around. This raises the question of how we do this – how do we decide where to look next? Given that these eye movements are highly structured to what is in the picture (Figure 0.4), it must be that we use the 'poor' information to guide these movements to the next point of interest. Clearly, if we are to understand how we see, we must also understand this active process of grabbing information from the scene in front of us.

Fig. 0.5. Acuity decreases with eccentricity. This picture has been tampered with so that it becomes more blurred away from the point of fixation (the central figure). This mimics the way our own vision loses the ability to see fine detail away from the centre of vision.

Illusions

Figure 0.6 shows a remarkable illusion that even we still find hard to accept. It looks like a picture of two tables, one long and thin and the other short and fat. However, the table-tops are exactly the same shape. Yes, that's what we said, they are the *same shape*. To convince yourself of this, trace out the shape of one and then overlay it on the other. You may be tempted to conclude that your visual system is pretty useless, as it has failed to spot that the two shapes are the same. However, that would be a mistake, because what your brain has actually done is very clever. It has turned the two-dimensional (2-D) picture on the page into the most plausible three-dimensional (3-D) objects. That is, we do not see these tables as merely lines on a piece of paper. To us they become objects, we recognize them as tables – things we put stuff on. In doing so (and we have no choice in this matter), we scale and distort these two identical quadrilaterals into one that is long and thin and one that is short and fat. As we shall see in Chapter 7, our willingness to produce three dimensions from the poorest of information can account for many illusions.

So our visual system can, and frequently does, get it 'wrong'. It does not represent the physical world correctly, because it makes assumptions about the world and uses these to give us the information we need. In the case of the tables in Figure 0.6, what is identical about these tables is their projection on the back of your eye. But we are not interested in what is on the back of our eye – we are interested in what is out there in the world. As we do not need to know about what's on the back of our eye, we do not need conscious access to it (it would be rather confusing if we did). Instead, our brain gives us a table of a certain shape, and if we need a long skinny table for our buffet lunch, this is far more useful.

Illusions therefore provide us with a means of examining the workings of the visual system. For instance, if you look briefly at Figure 0.7 you will see two pictures of a once well-known face. The pictures look pretty much alike, but if you look carefully you will see that the one on the left has been tampered with. The eyes and the mouth have actually been cut out, inverted and stuck back down. However, this change is quite hard to spot.

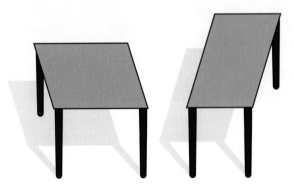

Fig. 0.6. These two table tops are identical, but do they look it?

BOX 0.1   When is an illusion an illusion?

You may notice in this chapter that we are a little coy about what we mean by the term visual illusion, so much so that we sometimes put the 'illusion' bit in quotation marks just to confuse you. At one extreme we could opine that everything is an illusion, but that would be both trite and tiresome. Perhaps it is easier to consider an example. Consider the Adelson figure (Figure 0.1.1). The two marked parts of the figure have identical luminance – that is, the same amount of black ink on the page – if you don't believe us, then take a pair of scissors and cut out these two squares and lay them side by side. You will find they are identical. However, in this 'illusion' they appear to have very different lightnesses.

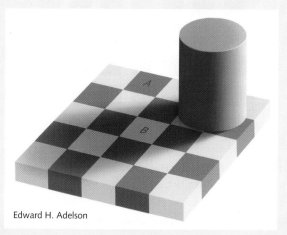

Edward H. Adelson

Fig. 0.1.1. The Adelson illusion. The two squares marked A and B have exactly the same luminance but their perceived lightness is very different. We perceive A as a dark square and B as a light square in shadow. Does this show how easily fooled your visual system is or how clever it is?

Now we could claim that this represents a visual illusion because we perceive physically identical bits of paper as being of different lightness. But in the scene portrayed in the picture the two chequerboard squares are really different – one is a black square the other is a white square – so our visual systems have given us the correct answer. Why should we regard this as an illusion? Now imagine that rather than looking at a *picture* of a cylinder casting a shadow on a chequerboard, we were looking at a *real* cylinder casting a shadow on a chequerboard. Again we would perceive the lighter square as being lighter than the darker square, but would we want to call this an illusion just because the luminances of the squares are the same by virtue of the shadow? This would be crazy, we would be calling something a visual illusion when we perceived it correctly. Because of this, illusions are fairly rare in natural scenes – though not unknown. Generally we see the world the way it is. Once we get in a completely artificial environment like a laboratory it is possible to create illusions with ease. A case in point would be the Hermann grid (Figure 0.1.2). This really is an illusion because the 'ghostly grey dots' at the white intersections do not exist in the picture, nor do they exist in any object that the picture is seeking to represent. At the end of Chapter 4 we shall make this point again. There we shall examine so-called visual illusions that depend upon the visual system interpreting 2-D pictures as 3-D scenes and, as a result, 'misperceiving' the size of objects. Arguably these shouldn't be regarded as illusions at all because the visual system is accurately representing what the picture is of.

Fig. 0.1.2. The Hermann grid. Do you see the ghostly grey dots at the intersections of the white lines? Do they really exist? What happens when you look directly at one of the grey dots? It should disappear.

Even by our definition there are some occasions when we experience illusions in the real world, but they tend to be when things are a bit weird; when driving in fog we underestimate our speed, when swimming underwater we tend to underestimate distance and hence overestimate the size of underwater objects.

Now turn the book upside-down so that the picture itself is the right way up. Now the changes become obvious and the tampered face takes on a grotesque appearance (some might argue that attempting to make Lady Thatcher look grotesque is rather redundant – we couldn't possibly comment). This tells us that there must be something different about the face when it is upside down, because we were unable to read the facial expression correctly. We are obviously used to seeing and interpreting faces which are the right way up and perhaps the neural machinery we use to do this is only designed (or has only learned) to do this for the right-way-up pictures (more in Chapter 10).

There are other sorts of visual illusions that can be used to investigate our visual senses, illusions in which we deliberately induce a change in perception by doing something out of the ordinary. For instance, we can use a technique called adaptation to temporarily alter our visual systems. You have probably had this experience yourself: you have been driving quickly down a major road for some time, and then you have to switch to a minor road where you are required to drive more slowly; you often get the feeling that everything is

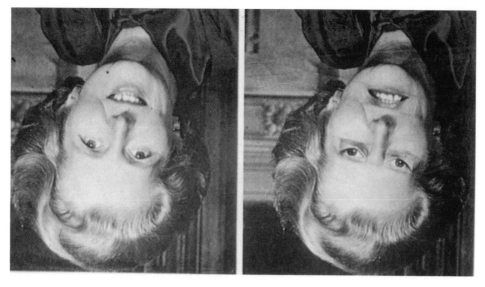

Fig. 0.7. The Thatcher illusion. Turn the page upside down to see the 'real' Lady Thatcher.

happening too slowly. The 30 mph (50 km/h) that you are now doing feels as though it is only half that. This is an example of adaptation. Something in your brain had 'got used' to the fast speed and produced this illusion. With more careful experiments in a laboratory we can use such phenomena to investigate how it is that we can sense speed in the first place, and why we get it so wrong in this situation. This in turn brings us to one of the main reasons for studying vision. If we can understand why these things occur, we might be able to do something to help. In Britain (and probably many other countries too) motor accidents frequently occur as drivers negotiate a junction immediately after coming off a motorway (freeway). The nature of many of these accidents is that the car is simply going too fast as it attempts to negotiate the transition to the minor road. One suspects the reason for this is the illusion we have just described. Drivers 'feel' like they are going slowly when in fact they are moving much more quickly. So we should be able to use our knowledge of speed perception to help. Indeed, in Britain the entrances to such junctions are often now marked by a series of lines painted across the road. We know that such marks make objects appear to move faster than if no lines are present. Hence drivers think they are travelling faster, and slow down. Road tests show that this works – and saves lives.

Damage to the system

> In any well made machine one is ignorant of the working of most of the parts – the better they work the less we are conscious of them . . . It is only a fault that draws attention to the existence of a mechanism at all.

> Kenneth Craik, *The Nature of Explanation* (1943)

Fig. 0.8. People with visual neglect often fail to copy one half of a picture.

This quote from Kenneth Craik (who, incidentally, died in a road accident) helps summarize what we have tried to learn so far and what we are about to say. It emphasizes that our visual system is indeed a 'well made machine' – so well made that it works without us being aware of its processes. However, in some individuals there appears to be some fault in the system – unfortunate for them, but fortunate for scientists. When we find such an individual we can get a glimpse of what it is like not to have some process that we take for granted. Let us illustrate this with an example. In Chapter 9 we discuss cases of visual neglect – a condition in which the sufferer seems to just ignore half of the world. Figure 0.8 gives an example of such a person doing a simple (well, simple to us) task. When asked to copy the picture of a cat she did pretty well, apart from missing out one half completely; however, she believed she had drawn the whole animal. When asked to draw a clock, neglect patients draw a circle containing all the numbers (they have not lost their intelligence – they know what a clock should look like) but they put all the numbers on the right-hand side of the dial. When they read, they only read the right-hand side of the page. When presented with a plate of food they only eat the things on the right-hand side of the plate; simply turning the plate allows them to finish the meal! It seems that they are continually pulled to the right, and things on the left fail to grab their attention.

From this information we can immediately see that there must be something in our brain that normally allows objects to grab our attention and be processed more thoroughly. Careful consideration of just what such patients can and cannot do, along with studies of just what has been damaged, allows us great insights into what the brain is doing and how it does this. Of course, we then hope to use this information to help such patients.

The list of possible visual problems caused by brain damage is huge, probably because no two cases of brain damage will ever be identical, but we shall introduce you to cases where colour or motion appear to have been affected, and to cases where, for example, a man can look at the face of his wife and have no idea who she is, although a sight of her shoes is enough to reveal her identity.

The brain

Earlier, we drew an analogy between a camera and the eye, and said that this is fine for the eye but not for vision. So where does 'vision' take place? This is a pretty hard question to answer. First, there is conscious vision, and there are theories of how and where this might arise that we shall discuss in Chapter 11. Second, there is all the visual processing that occurs without any obvious consciousness; for instance, as we walk around a room we somehow must have calculated just where the chair was and then have sent signals to our legs so that we could avoid it, but we were never conscious of doing so. Third, we know from being students ourselves many years ago that there are certain things inside the eye called **photoreceptors** that are busy changing light into electrical signals. These things have certainly got a lot to do with vision (without them we are blind), but these cells cannot be regarded as 'seeing'. So to get back to our question of '*where does vision take place*', the boldest answer we're willing to give is '*in the brain*'. Therefore, the study of vision seems to necessitate that we understand the various bits of the brain that are involved, right from those photoreceptors that initially change light into neural signals, to those areas that might give us knowledge of the mood of our friends, or allow us to steer a car along a busy road.

Figure 0.9 is a picture of the brain of a primate. As in the human brain, the cortex (the outside layer) is crumpled into many folds, so to make it easier the lower part of the picture shows the cortex as if the poor monkey had been run over by a steam-roller. To help us further, the parts of the brain that we know have something to do with vision are shown in colour. Two points can be noted. First, someone had to do a lot of colouring – over 50% of the cortex is involved in visual processing. Recently we have begun to be able to chart what areas of the human brain might be involved in visual processing. You might imagine that it would be far less – after all, we humans presumably need lots of brain for doing the things we think we do so well: reasoning, playing chess, doing hard sums, and so on. However, it appears that the amount of cortex we devote to vision is just as large as in this monkey – over half your cortex is devoted to merely seeing. If we do some very rough sums and generously give hearing 10% of the cortex, all your other senses another 10%, and probably we should allow 10–20% for moving all the bits of your body, you can see that there is hardly anything left over for doing the hard bits like chess, crosswords, and perception assignments. But that is exactly the point. Vision is easy because we have lots of brain devoted to it; chess is hard because we don't have lots of brain devoted to it. If the situation were reversed and over 50% of your cortex were devoted to chess you would, no doubt, be able to take on the most sophisticated computer in the

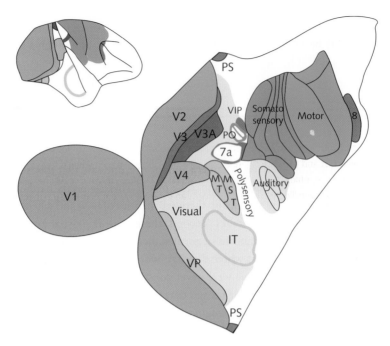

Fig. 0.9. The visual areas of the primate brain. See text for details.

world and beat it. However, computers can now beat the most brilliant of humans when it comes to chess, but no computer in the world can put up the slightest of challenges when it comes to vision. Indeed, we would happily back a humble housefly against the most sophisticated computer in a 'vision Olympics'.

We mentioned that there were two things to note about Figure 0.9. The first was the large amount of colouring-in required, the second is that different colours are used in different places to signify that there is something different about these different areas. In other words, the area of brain devoted to vision is not one homogeneous mass, but it has lots of areas (over 30 at the last count), each of which is doing something different. Just why we have so many areas, and what each of them is doing, is a major challenge for vision science. At the time of writing we believe that each might have a specialized role to play in analysing some part of the scene. As an example, we could consider the area labelled MT (a small area the size of half a pea and coloured yellow for our convenience). Examination of this area, as we shall see in Chapter 6, has suggested that it must play a large role in our perception of motion. All the brain cells inside this area seem to care about the movements of the outside world – they do not fire much in response to a static scene, but they burst into action if an object moves in a particular way. If this area is involved in our sensing the motion of objects, we might predict that if we were to destroy it then we wouldn't see any motion. It may be hard to imagine, but this does indeed appear to happen. Unfortunate individuals who have damage in this region of the brain report that their world is frozen and they are unable to tell us about the movements of

BOX 0.2 — Different senses

Figure 0.2.1 shows a table of differences between the senses. These differences are due to the different properties of the physical 'messengers' and the design of the sense organs to capture these most efficiently. You will see that different senses are good for different things. Sound can travel around corners – light cannot. So we can use sound to tell us that there is something hidden behind a bush. Light is particularly good at telling us about the detail of something which is far away – it travels fast and therefore there is normally little delay between when it leaves the object and arrives at our eye, unless we're looking at some distant galaxy, in which case the delay could be anything up to a few billion years. But it requires an **imaging system** to make sure that different rays hit different receptor cells – otherwise you can't distinguish different rays, and you would lose information about detail. That may not be too tragic – you can move around even if your vision is very blurry, and simple animals like limpets manage without any sharp image. But if you want to spot something small or a long way away, you need good eyes; humans and hawks have extremely well-developed eyes that allow them to see things far away. So, how good your eye needs to be at resolving fine detail depends on (a) how far away you need to see stuff, and (b) whether you're sophisticated enough to have a brain that can handle all of the information the eye sends it. In general, the larger the creature, the faster it can move, and the bigger its brain can be. Therefore, large creatures tend to have well-developed eyes, and brains, and good ability to resolve fine detail. Remember Little Red Riding Hood: 'What big eyes you have, Grandma', she says to the wolf, who replies 'All the better to see you with'. If only she had asked 'What colour is my Riding Hood, Grandma?' she might have discovered the truth; wolves are red – green colour blind . . . Nocturnal animals, such as cats and owls, need to catch what little light there is if they are to use vision successfully; therefore they have big eyes but their ability to see fine detail isn't very good. Hence the expression 'blind as a cat'. Many of these animals rely on other senses such as hearing, ultrasound, or smell.

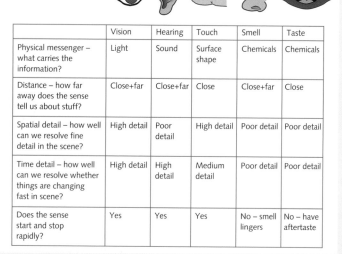

	Vision	Hearing	Touch	Smell	Taste
Physical messenger – what carries the information?	Light	Sound	Surface shape	Chemicals	Chemicals
Distance – how far away does the sense tell us about stuff?	Close+far	Close+far	Close	Close+far	Close
Spatial detail – how well can we resolve fine detail in the scene?	High detail	Poor detail	High detail	Poor detail	Poor detail
Time detail – how well can we resolve whether things are changing fast in scene?	High detail	High detail	Medium detail	Poor detail	Poor detail
Does the sense start and stop rapidly?	Yes	Yes	Yes	No – smell lingers	No – have aftertaste

Fig. 0.2.1. Some properties of our major senses.

objects. There are also individuals who seem to have lost other very specific abilities, such as the ability to see colour, or depth, or faces, or emotional expressions, and many more besides. But we are getting ahead of ourselves. We shall return to these cases in the various chapters that consider these specific abilities.

So we have a simple notion that each of these areas is devoted to some aspect of our visual sense. This simple idea serves as a good starting point for considering the various aspects of vision, but is probably far too simple. After all, if the shape of a London bus is processed in one part of the brain, its red colour in another part, and its speed in yet another, how do we put all the bits back together again to create the percept of the big red bus speeding towards us? Fortunately the various visual areas of the brain are actually richly interconnected and they must work in concert to produce 'vision', but the details of how this miracle is achieved remain one of the great challenges to neuroscience.

The study of vision

The study of vision is a multidisciplinary affair. In this book you will come across experiments and ideas drawn from anatomy, ophthalmology, biology, psychology, physiology, physics, neuroscience, neuropsychology, and even computer science and philosophy. Indeed, we hope that the readers of this book will also come from a wide variety of such disciplines. This has advantages and disadvantages. In order to really understand vision we believe that all these approaches are required – each brings with it a different level of explanation. However, mastery of any one of these disciplines is difficult enough without having to know them all. The study of vision has many practical implications that we have already hinted at. One can see the obvious medical benefits that study of disorders of vision can have, and deeper understandings of problems like glaucoma and amblyopia are of benefit to many millions around the world. Vision is also a microcosm of the rest of the brain, and the findings here serve to inform many other problems such as how we can recover from brain damage and how to build prosthetics to take the place of a damaged system. We have also mentioned that the findings can be used to make our world a better place. The design of aircraft cockpits and cars, of road-markings and fire-escape exit signs, of advertisements and warnings can all benefit immensely from a knowledge of what people can see, where they look, and how it all works. In our world of TV and virtual reality, being able to present a person with the information that is needed through their visual sense is vital. Our knowledge of what is used (and what is not used) for a task or a particular percept allows us to compress images so that the minimum amount of information can be sent without the quality of the image being compromised.

The study of vision therefore has much to offer from an applied viewpoint. However, it can also be studied simply because it is there, in front of us, almost every wakeful moment – and so seems to dominate our conscious lives.

● READINGS AND REFERENCES

There are many, many books on visual perception that will give you far more detail on the subject than this book does. Amongst them are Palmer (1999) and Wandell (1996) which provide an account of vision from a psychological perspective. Hubel (1988) provides a more physiological perspective. Many find the book by Tom Cornsweet (1970) very easy to read and informative. For coverage of the 'higher' aspects of vision, the books by Martha Farah (2000) and by Milner and Goodale (1995) are excellent. Finally, recent research has begun to look more at how vision is used, as well as how it is done, and the book by John Findlay and Iain Gilchrist (2003) provides a perspective from this angle.

Papers on specific issues

Illusions Some of the classic old illusions are well described in Ittelson and Kilpatrick (1951) and Gregory (1968). For a more up-to-date approach and more reference to the underlying neural structures see Eagleman (2001).

Multiple visual areas For an overview of these areas in both humans and non-human primates see Tootell *et al.* (1996).

● POSSIBLE ESSAY TITLES, TUTORIALS, AND QUESTIONS OF INTEREST

1 Do you see what I see?

2 When is an illusion an illusion?

3 Consider two very different animals of your choice. How and why do their visual systems differ?

4 Why do we have many different areas of the brain devoted to vision and not just one large one?

References

Cornsweet, T. N. (1970). *Visual perception*. London: Academic Press.

Eagleman, D. M. (2001). Visual illusions and neurobiology. *Nature Reviews Neuroscience* **2**(12), 920–926.

Farah, M. J. (2000). *The cognitive neuroscience of vision*. Malden, MA: Blackwell Publishers.

Felleman, D. J. and Van Essen, D. C. (1991). Distributed hierarchical processing in primate cerebral cortex. *Cerebral Cortex* **1**, 1–47.

Findlay, J. M. and Gilchrist, I. D. (2003). *Active vision : the psychology of looking and seeing*. Oxford: Oxford University Press.

Gregory, R. L. (1968). Visual illusions. *Scientific American* **219**, November, 66–76.

Hubel, D. H. (1988). *Eye, brain and vision*. New York: Scientific American Press.

Ishihara, S. (1960). *Tests for colour-blindness*, 15th edition, Tokyo: Handaya Company.

Ittelson, W. H. and Kilpatrick, F. P. (1951). Experiments in perception. *Scientific American* **185**, August, 50–55.

Milner, A. D. and Goodale, M. A. (1995). *The visual brain in action*. Oxford: Oxford University Press.

Palmer, S. E. (1999). *Vision science: photons to phenomenology*. Cambridge, MA: MIT Press.

Tootell, R. B. H., Dale, A. M., Sereno, M. I., and Malach, R. (1996). New images from human visual cortex. *Trends in Neuroscience* **19**, 481–489.

Wandell, B. (1996). *Foundations of vision*. Sunderland, MA: Sinauer Associates.

Yarbus, A. L. (1967). *Eye movements and vision*. Plenum Press, New York.

CHAPTER 1
The first steps in seeing

Which animals can you identify from their eye alone (answers below)? Eyes appear to have evolved on many occasions and come in a variety of forms (the most obvious distinction being between the single eyes such as our own and the compound eyes of such creatures as insects). However, you might also note that even within a type of eye there are many variations. For example, in single eyes the shape of the pupil varies greatly. Our human pupils are round, but those of the cat are more oval to allow it to close to a smaller size than ours. In other animals (e.g. geckos) the pupil is a slit that when closed becomes just three small holes in a line and thus can shut out far more light than our own.

Answers (from left to right, top to bottom): (a) robber fly, (b) jumping spider, (c) ogre-faced spider, (d) Gigantocypris (deep-sea crustacean), (e) horsefly, (f) scallop, (g) Histioteuthis (squid), (h) Dilophus (fly), (i) Tridacna (giant clam).

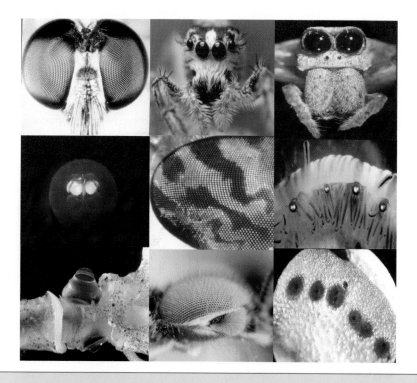

CHAPTER OVERVIEW

Even without having read any of this book, it seems likely that you have realized that
the eyes are rather important for seeing. Close them and vision disappears. But what
actually goes on inside these squishy little spheres? Early scientists cut a hole in the
back of a bull's eye and were astonished to find that the eye produced a small upside-
down image of the world. They concluded that they had solved 'vision'. Unfortunately
they had not (which means lots more reading for you!). After all, who is looking at this
upside-down image? If we have a little man in our head looking at the image, how
does he see? Does it matter that the image on the back of our eye is upside-down? In
this chapter we explain what the eye actually does and what happens when things go
wrong with it. It turns out that the back of the eye, called the **retina**, is a far outpost of
the brain; it is an intricate web of nerve cells that turns the light entering the eye into a
set of electrical signals. These messages begin a remarkable journey that turns light
from the world into the phenomenon we experience as vision.

The eye

There is good evidence that the eyes are important for vision. Close your eyes and you can
see rather little. Poke your eyes out with a pointed stick and you will see even less. So if we
want to trace the visual pathway then the eyes seem a good place to start. Figure 1.1
shows a front view of a human eye and Figure 1.2 a cross-section through it. The first
thing to notice is the **cornea**, the transparent window through which light enters the eye.
The cornea is curved and acts as a lens; in fact it is the main lens of the eye. (Three-
quarters of the eye's focusing power comes from the cornea, and only a quarter from the
bit of the eye we call the 'lens'.) The purpose of these pieces of optical equipment called

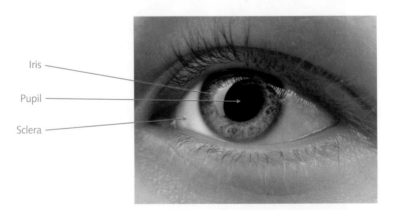

Iris

Pupil

Sclera

Fig. 1.1. Front view of the human eye.

lenses is to focus light on to the retina (the cells at the back of the eye – we'll tell you about these later).

Lenses have two important characteristics; they have at least one curved surface, and they are made of stuff through which light travels more slowly than through air. This means that light gets bent when it hit the surface (just as a stick appears bent when it is half in water). Figure 1.3 shows why. Imagine you are driving a car along a tarmac road beside a sandy beach (position A). All four tyres have an even grip on the road and the car travels in a straight line. When the right-hand front wheel hits the sand (position B) the car will turn towards the right as the left-hand wheel will still be gripping the tarmac while the wheel in the sand will lose traction and move forward more slowly. Once the car is completely in sand (position C) it will once again travel in a straight line, much more slowly, but its direction of motion will have been bent by the tarmac/sand edge. Exactly the same thing happens when light hits the cornea. Light travels at different speeds through different materials and it goes faster through air than through your cornea. How much bending takes place depends on the nature of the materials on each side of the boundary. When you open your eyes under water, everything looks very blurry. Light

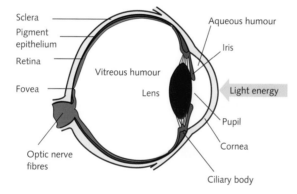

Fig. 1.2. Horizontal cross-section through the human eye.

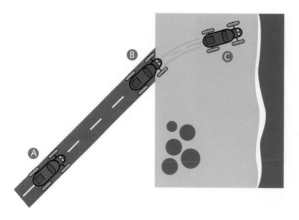

Fig. 1.3. Why light gets bent when it passes from one material into another. See text for details.

travels at similar speeds through water and cornea, so little deflection of the light takes place and you are unable to focus the world on to your retina (Figure 1.4a). Wearing goggles re-establishes an air/cornea boundary and, sure enough, we can see clearly again (Figure 1.4b). Fish, which don't usually wear goggles, tend to have much more bulging eyes to compensate for the small degree of deflection between water and the lens (Figure 1.5).

Behind the cornea is the anterior chamber filled with **aqueous humour**, a watery liquid that flows from the ciliary body, through the delightfully named zonules of Zinn, through the pupil, and into the anterior chamber. From here it passes through the trabecular meshwork and leaves the eye down the (we're not joking, honest) canal of Schlemm (Figure 1.6) – anyone trying to think of a name for a rock band need look no further. The canal of Schlemm actually runs in a circle just beneath the border of your iris (the coloured bit) and the white of your eye (called the sclera). The pressure of the aqueous humour is very important. In someone with glaucoma, a disease in which the pressure becomes too high, retinal damage and blindness can result (Figure 1.7). When you go the optician to have an eye examination you will probably have the pressure of your aqueous humour

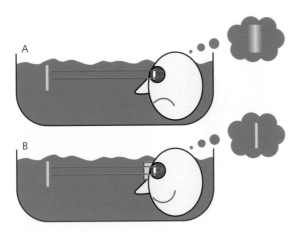

Fig. 1.4. Why things look blurry when you open your eyes under water. Light travels at a similar speed in water and through the cornea, so the cornea fails to act as good lens. The solution is to wear goggles, which re-establish an air/cornea boundary.

Fig. 1.5. Why don't things look blurry to fish? The answer is they have really bulging corneas that can bend light more than ours. This fish is a moray eel. Don't get this close to one and certainly don't annoy one. They have been known to attack humans, though apparently they can be quite friendly once they are used to you.

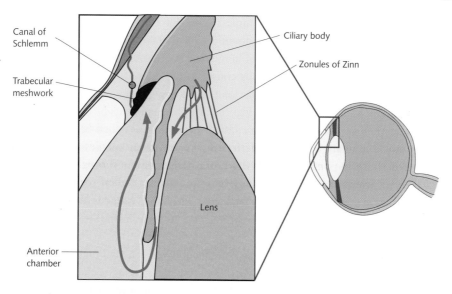

Fig. 1.6. In the commonest form of glaucoma the aqueous humour drains through the trabecular meshwork but gets clogged in the canal of Schlemm. This is called 'open angle' glaucoma because the angle is clear. In 'closed angle' glaucoma, a much rarer condition, the blockage seems to be in the trabecular meshwork.

Fig. 1.7. How the world might look to someone with glaucoma. Much of peripheral vision may be lost without the patient realizing it.

checked by having a puff of air blown against the cornea. This air puff is calibrated to distort the surface of the cornea by a set amount. If the cornea doesn't move enough, it suggests the pressure is too high. In the same way, when you blow up a balloon you can check the pressure by gently squeezing the balloon to feel how much 'give' there is.

Next we come to the iris, a structure that provides an adjustable aperture and is the coloured part of the eye. When light levels are high the iris constricts and the pupil – the hole in the middle of the iris – gets smaller, limiting the amount of light passing through; when the light is dim, then the iris relaxes, allowing more light through. This seems like a neat way of regulating the amount of light reaching the retina – and is used in cameras to the same purpose, but as the area of the pupil when fully dilated is only 16 times bigger than when it is fully constricted, this isn't a lot of use. The range of luminance that the visual system can deal with, from the dimmest lights that can be detected up to intensities that will start to damage the retina, is about 10 000 000 000 : 1. How the visual system actually deals with such a wide range of luminance is discussed in Chapter 2.

It turns out that sometimes our pupils constrict and dilate for reasons other than in response to the incoming light level. It has long been known that women with large pupils are considered more attractive by men (Figure 1.8). This explains why deadly nightshade, which causes the pupils to dilate when applied to the eyes, is called belladonna (which mean 'beautiful woman' in Italian). The pupils dilate when one is excited, and it is claimed that showing pictures of naked women to heterosexual men – or pictures of naked men to heterosexual women – produces pupil dilation. Of course you get the responses you would expect from homosexual men and women as well. There is, apparently, one curious sex difference; pictures of naked sharks induce pupil dilation in men and pupil constriction in women.

Pupil dilation can of course reveal your excitement when you might wish to conceal it – hence the gambler's eye-shade to prevent his opponents gaining a clue the poker face intends to conceal. It is claimed that jade dealers have long examined the pupils of prospective customers – pupil dilation will push up the asking price, in the knowledge that the customer is interested. (The solution to this is to take off your sunglasses just as the jade dealer presents you with a piece of jade; your pupils will constrict in the bright light and a bargain is assured.)

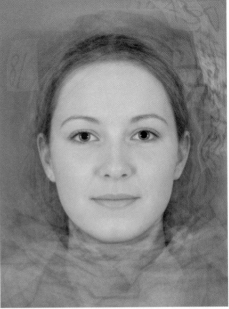

Fig. 1.8. Do big pupils make a woman look more attractive? Some drugs, for example deadly nightshade (belladonna), dilate the pupils.

Keen photographers will know that pictures taken with a small aperture have a greater depth of focus than pictures taken with a large aperture. (One of the neat things about a pinhole camera is that everything is in focus, regardless of how far away it is.) The same is true for us – when our pupils constrict, our depth of focus increases. This is quite important as we get older, as you'll discover on the next page.

Beyond the iris we reach the **lens**. Although the lens has less power than the cornea, it has one great advantage: it is adjustable. The lens is held between the zonules of Zinn. Contraction of the circular ring of ciliary muscles relaxes the zonules, so the lens gets fatter and we have more refractive power. This is what is required when we need to focus on a close object. When we want to focus on things further away, we need the lens to be stretched into a skinnier shape and this is achieved by relaxing the ciliary muscles (Figure 1.9). For this system to work correctly you need to get a few things right. First, you need to have your cornea of the appropriate curviness to focus light on the retina. Another way of looking at this is to say that you need to have your eyeball the right length for your optics. The point is that the power of the lens system must be appropriate for the size of your eyeball. Figure 1.10a shows just such an eye; the light rays from distant objects that reach the eye are near parallel and need little bending to bring them to a focus on the retina, so the lens gets pulled into a skinny shape by the ciliary muscles. Close objects send diverging rays to the eye, which need to be bent more to bring them into focus, so the ciliary muscles relax, the lens goes fat, and the light is bent more. If your eye works like this then your vision is said to be **emmetropic** and you're very lucky. If, however, your optics are too strong for the length of your eye – or your eye is too long for your optics, it comes to the same thing – then you are **myopic**. This is a fancy way of saying you're short-sighted (Figure 1.10b). Distant things are blurred because they get bent too much by the

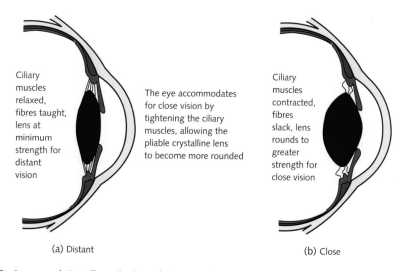

Ciliary muscles relaxed, fibres taught, lens at minimum strength for distant vision

The eye accommodates for close vision by tightening the ciliary muscles, allowing the pliable crystalline lens to become more rounded

Ciliary muscles contracted, fibres slack, lens rounds to greater strength for close vision

(a) Distant

(b) Close

Fig. 1.9. Accommodation allows the lens of the eye to become more rounded when looking at close objects, by contracting the circular ciliary muscles and relaxing the zonules of Zinn: (a) distant vision, (b) close vision.

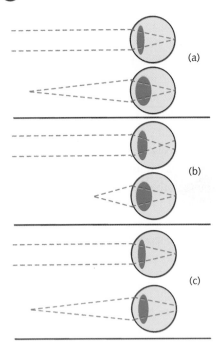

(a)

(b)

(c)

Fig. 1.10. Matching the lens system to the size of your eyeball is critical: (a) emmetropic vision – both near and far objects can be focused on the retina; (b) short sight – the strong lens focuses close objects on the retina but distant objects are brought to a focus in front of the retina; (c) long sight – the weak lens is adequate to focus distant objects but is not strong enough for close objects, which are brought to a focus behind the retina.

optics but very close objects, which only come into focus after a lot of bending of the light, will look sharp. The opposite condition, in which the lens is too weak (or the eye too short) is called **hypermetropia**, or long-sightedness (Figure 1.10c). Distant objects that need little bending to be focused can be dealt with OK, but close objects can only be focused behind the retina.

You don't need to be a genius to see that both myopia and hypermetropia can be helped by putting lenses in front of the eyes. A hypermetrope has a weak lens and needs extra power, so needs a converging lens to add to the existing optical system. A myope needs a diverging lens to reduce the power of the optical system. These lenses can be put into frames that balance on the bridge of the nose and are held in place by struts that hook around the ears. Crude, but effective.

As we get older the lens loses its natural elasticity (and so does much else in the body, believe us). This means that when we relax our ciliary muscles the lens does not move as much as it should and our **near-point**, the closest point we can focus on, moves away from us. This is called **presbyopia**, and it's time for reading glasses.

In Figure 1.11a we see the eye of a normal young person, able to change the shape of the lens to accommodate distant and close objects. In Figure 1.11b we see what happens with age; the lens now shows little or no accommodation and, if distant objects are still reasonably well focused on the eye, near objects will look blurry as the ability of the lens to change shape has been lost. In Figure 1.11c we see the solution to the problem, a lens to help seeing close objects – reading glasses. The extent of the loss of accommodation is

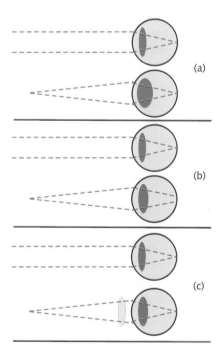

Fig. 1.11. Presbyopia, the effects of ageing on our lens: (a) the emmetropic vision of Figure 1.10a; (b) inability to focus on close objects as the lens becomes inelastic. The solution (c) is to wear reading glasses.

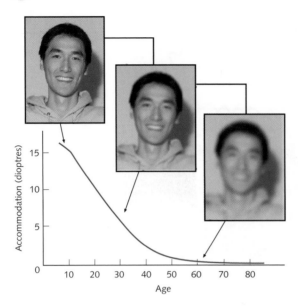

Accommodation (dioptres)

15

10

5

0

10   20   30   40   50   60   70   80

Age

Fig. 1.12. The accommodative power of the lens changes with age. The elasticity of the lens declines from birth onwards. Even fit young students are already well down the perilous slope towards reading glasses.

quite frightening – by the age of 30 you have lost around half of your focusing power and by 55 there is nothing much left at all (Figure 1.12).

The main cavity of the eye, behind the lens, is filled with a gelatinous substance called the **vitreous humour**. This keeps the eyeball in shape and the retina pinned to the back of the eye. If the vitreous humour shrinks (and it does in old people) then the retina can become detached and may need to be spot-welded back with a laser.

Eventually we reach the **retina**, the light-sensitive layer at the back of the eye. This is the important bit and the start of real visual processing. Figure 1.13 shows a cross-section of the retina. Light approaches from below in this view, and the light-sensitive photo-pigments are to be found in the outer segments of the **photoreceptors** near the top of the picture. So the light must travel through a good deal of neural gunge before reaching the receptors. This seems an odd arrangement, as if we designed a camera and then put the film in the wrong way round. One reason for this strange arrangement may be that the process of transduction – the turning of light energy into electrochemical energy within the nervous system – is an operation that requires a good deal of energy, and that energy must be supplied by the blood supply. Clearly, blood can be delivered more easily to the back of the eye than to the surface. Interestingly, the octopus has a retina in which the receptors are at the front rather than at the back of the retina. Perhaps this shows that our own arrangement is an accident but, as we manage to see quite well despite all the gunge in front of our receptors, it was an accident not worth correcting. Actually, we still have a certain number of blood vessels that lie on the surface of the retina and, although we are normally unaware of them, we can make them strikingly visible (see Box 1.1). Notice that another penalty for having an 'inverted' retina is the presence of a blind spot in each eye

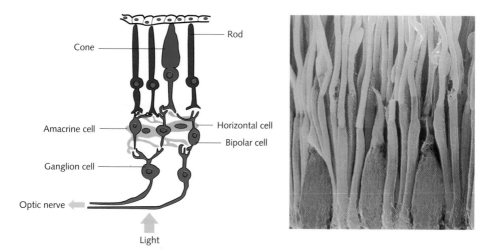

Fig. 1.13. A cross-section through the retina. Note that light would come from the bottom of the figure and would have to pass through the retina before reaching the photoreceptors. The photo, a scanning electron micrograph of primate retina, shows what the rods and cones really look like.

BOX 1.1   Seeing your own blood vessels

If our retinas are covered with blood vessels that lie between our receptors and the outside world, why can't we see them all the time? There are two key reasons; first, the blood vessels don't move and the visual system is notoriously poor at detecting anything that is stationary (or 'stabilized') on the retina. Second, the light reaching the retina is sufficiently diffuse for shadows not to form on the receptors (see Figure 1.1.1). We can overcome these problems quite easily and then we can see the shadows of our own blood vessels. Follow these instructions carefully and make sure you carry out step 2 before step 3:

1 Take a piece of stiff paper or card
2 Make a small hole in the card with a drawing pin
3 Close one eye and raise the card to the other
4 Jiggle the card slowly around close to the surface of the cornea while looking at a well-illuminated blank surface.

You should see a pattern of shadows that resemble the veins on a leaf (see Figure 1.1.2); these are the shadows of your retinal blood vessels. Note that there is one area where there are no shadows – the point where your vision is focused. This is because there are no blood vessels covering the retina at the fovea, the area of our vision where we have our highest acuity.

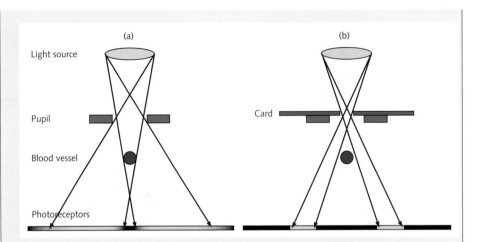

Fig. 1.1.1. (a) As the blood vessels are small in comparison to the size of the pupil, and are quite distant from the photoreceptors, they cast little shadow. (b) The introduction of a small aperture – the pinhole in the card – will result in a shadow of the blood vessel falling on the photoreceptors.

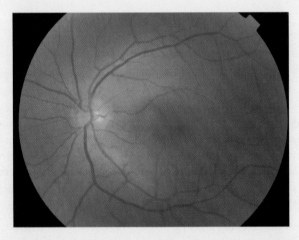

Fig. 1.1.2. The pattern of blood vessels over the retina, as seen through an ophthalmoscope. Note that the fovea (centre right) is free of blood vessels and the optic nerve head or 'blind spot' (centre left) is clearly visible where the blood vessels converge and leave the eye.

where the neural bundle passes through the rest of the retina (see Box 1.2). If a creature only had one eye this would be bad news as predators could learn to creep up on it from the blind direction. Having two eyes with blind spots pointing different ways solves this problem. Perhaps this is why, as a rule, animals have two eyes, exceptions being copopods (which are small plankton-like things and not a breakfast cereal) and the cyclops (the

BOX 1.2 **The blind spot**

Each of our eyes has a blind spot – the region where all the stuff gets in and out of the retina and therefore has no photoreceptors – and therefore no vision.

Figure 1.2.1 should help you to see your blind spot (or not see if you see (or not see?) what we mean). Close your left eye, and look at the upper green star with your right eye. One of the numbers should completely disappear! If you move your head back and forth (no sniggering) you should find that a number nearer to the star disappears when you are closer to the page. King Charles II of England (the one who hung out with Nell Gwynne, the girl with the oranges) used to play a little parlour game where he lined up the heads of people in his court with his blind spot, and thus saw them apparently beheaded. He was clearly interested in such matters since his father, Charles I, had been beheaded in a rather more permanent way.

Fig. 1.2.1. Seeing the blind spot.

Now move your head until the number 3 disappears and then look at the lower green star. You should find that the gap in the line disappears – but what is more it is replaced with a green line! So what is going on? It seems that some 'filling in' process must occur. The blind spot takes on the characteristics (such as average colour and brightness) of the area around it, and can even extrapolate the existence of lines. Two hypotheses may explain what is going on. The easiest explanation is that as we can't see in this spot we automatically see what is around it by default. Alternatively there may be some active process that extrapolates what is seen around this spot and expands it to cover the blind spot.

The same lack of awareness of a blind spot occurs if for some reason some part of a retina stops working (as can happen as a result of retinal detachment). Although there is now an extra 'blind spot' (known as a scotoma), the person is often unaware that there is no vision in that part of the visual field. In fact, this can be rather bad news. Patients with glaucoma (see p. 23) can lose most of their peripheral visual field, but are often unaware of this until the loss is pretty much total. How come? Nobody is quite sure but it does seem that brain processes try so hard to 'fill in' missing information that the person with glaucoma is unaware that their visual world is disappearing.

most famous of these, Polyphemus, ended up with a somewhat larger blind spot that he bargained for.)

Once the light reaches the outer segments of the receptors, neural processing can begin. The receptors are connected to bipolar cells and these in their turn synapse with retinal ganglion cells. The ganglion cells are important, for it is their axons that carry information from the eye on its journey towards the visual cortex. Connecting across the retina laterally are two further cell types – horizontal cells at the point where the receptors synapse with the bipolar cells and amacrine cells where bipolar cells synapse with the ganglion cells. For our purposes we need to know little about bipolar, horizontal, or amacrine cells, but we do need to know a little more about receptors and ganglion cells.

The photoreceptors

There are ten things you should know about the photoreceptors:

1 There are two types of photoreceptor in the human eye, rods and cones. The outer segments of the rods are generally rod-shaped and the outer segments of the cones are generally cone-shaped (Figure 1.13).

2 All our rods are basically the same; they all contain the same photopigment (the stuff that absorbs the light) in their outer segments. This is called rhodopsin. Rhodopsin is purple in colour and is known (not unreasonably) as 'visual purple'. Of course the colour of an object tells us about the light reflected from it rather than the light absorbed by it. Rhodopsin reflects much red and blue light (hence the purple), but it absorbs green light preferentially.

3 Cones come in three main sorts, often (wrongly) called red, green, and blue. So-called 'red' cones contain a photopigment that is most sensitive to long wavelengths of light, 'green' cones are most sensitive to middle wavelengths of light, and the 'blue' cones to shorter wavelengths. So we should call the cones 'long-wave', 'middle-wave' and 'short-wave', but this only complicates things so we'll call them red, green, and blue. It is because we have three cone types that we have colour vision. This is covered more fully in Chapter 5.

4 Rods respond very well to extremely dim light and are therefore very useful in dim conditions – i.e. at night. As the light level increases, so does activity in the rods. Because rods are so sensitive, they will be responding as much as they can when the light is still quite dim, so they are completely useless in full daylight. Cones, on the other hand (well, not really on the other *hand*), are much less sensitive, hence are not used under dim conditions but are the ones responsible for most of our daytime vision. We have all had the experience of going into a dark cinema from a bright day and found ourselves groping in the dark before sitting in a stranger's lap. Some minutes later we can look around and see quite clearly. When we enter the dark cinema there is not enough light to get our cones going, and we have to rely on our rods. Unfortunately our rods have just been outside in bright sunlight and are completely bleached. It takes some minutes in the dark for the rods to recover their sensitivity. When only rods are active we call our vision scotopic,

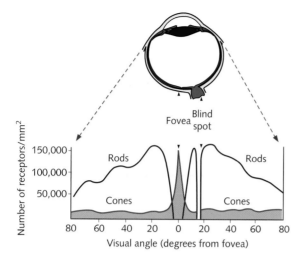

Fig. 1.14. The distribution of rods and cones across the retina. Note that, although cones are most densely packed in the fovea (around 150 000/mm²), even in the periphery there are still several thousand per square millimetre.

when it is so bright that the rods cannot function we call our vision photopic, and the region in between when both receptor types play a role is called mesopic. The issue of light and dark adaptation is covered further in Chapter 2.

5 Rods are most sensitive to green light, whereas the cone system overall is most sensitive to yellow light. Next time you are given a red rose in moonlight (and this will be sooner for some of you than for others) note the relative brightness of the red of the flower and the green of the foliage. You should notice that the red of the petals looks very dark and the green of the leaves looks relatively light. Next morning compare the flower and the foliage again as the rose lies in the morning sunshine filtering on to your pillow; now the red flower will look lighter than the green foliage. This is known as the Purkinje shift. Don't mention this fact to your loved one if you want to receive red roses in the future. If you think the Purkinje shift is just slushy nonsense, then perhaps you will be more interested to know that in World War II night pilots were briefed in rooms illuminated by red light. This ensured that their rods, insensitive to the long wavelengths, were not being bleached and were, therefore, ready to spring into action the minute Biggles and his chums left the briefing room for the dark of the airstrip and their waiting crates.

6 Photoreceptors are not evenly distributed across the retina. Cones are heavily concentrated in a central area known as the fovea (Figure 1.14). When you look straight at something, it is imaged on the fovea. Rods are completely absent from the central fovea and are most densely packed some 12–15° into the periphery (Figure 1.14). This explains why, when you look at extremely faint stars, they disappear when on the fovea but can be seen in the near periphery.

7 There are no blue cones at all in the central fovea – blue cones are rather strange things (and are only understood by rather strange people) and somewhat unlike either red or green cones. Interestingly, people with normal colour vision can have very different numbers of red and green cones (Figure 1.15).

8 Ganglion cell axons and blood vessels leave the eye at a point known as the **blind spot** or **optic disc**. This region, situated about 12–15° into the nasal retina, is devoid of all receptors and consequently we are blind in this area (see Box 1.2).

9 Congenitally colour-blind people have a problem with either their red or green cones. One of these cone types may be completely missing, or it may be weaker than is normally the case. Colour blindness is dealt with in detail in Chapter 5.

10 er... that's it.

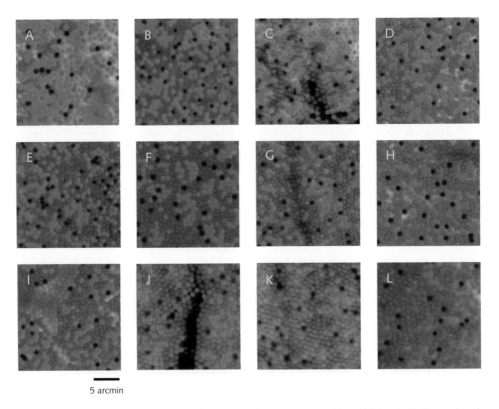

5 arcmin

Fig. 1.15. Images of the cone mosaics of 10 subjects with normal colour vision, obtained with the combined methods of adaptive optics imaging and retinal densitometry. The images are false-coloured so that blue, green, and red are used to represent the blue, green and red cones respectively. (The true colours of these cones are yellow, purple, and bluish-purple.) The mosaics illustrate the enormous variability in red/green cone ratio: the ratios are A, 0.37; B, 1.11; C, 1.14; D, 1.24; E, 1.77; F, 1.88; G, 2.32; H, 2.36; I, 2.46; J, 3.67; K, 3.90; L, 16.54. The proportion of blue cones is relatively constant across eyes, ranging from 3.9 to 6.6% of the total population. Images were taken either 1 or 1.25° from the foveal centre. For 2 of the 10 subjects, two different retinal locations are shown. Panels D and E show images from nasal and temporal retinas respectively for one subject; J and K show images from nasal and temporal retinas for another subject.

The retinal ganglion cells

The last layer of cells in the retina is known as the **retinal ganglion cells** (see Figure 1.13). We shall deal with some of the properties of these cells at length in Chapter 2. Here we shall simply note that they come in two varieties – large and small. We shall call the large ones **M cells** (M for magnocellular) and the small ones **P cells** (P for parvocellular). These cells differ not only in their size but also in their properties. Careful study has revealed that P cells distinguish between signals coming from the red cones and those coming from the green cones. So, for instance, some P cells will be excited by the red cones and inhibited by the green cones. The M cells don't seem to care about this distinction, and mix them up. Therefore only the P cells appear to carry the information about colour. On the other hand, the M cells appear much more suited to carrying information about the dynamic aspects of the world such as movements and flicker. Studying these cells is quite difficult, as they are all intermingled in the retina. But one thing we do know is that both types of cells send their signals to the next visual structure, the **lateral geniculate nucleus (LGN)**, but do so in such a way that all the M cells project to one bit of the LGN and the P cells project to other bits. The grouping of these cells allows us to lesion them selectively and discover what they do, something that we can't do in the retina. We shall therefore pick up this story again shortly when we get to the LGN.

Beyond the eye – the optic nerve

The optic nerve leaves the eye at the blind spot and begins its journey to the cortex which, curiously, is about as far from the eyes as it's possible to get and still remain inside the head. The main pathways are shown in Figure 1.16. First the optic nerves from the two eyes converge at a point called the **optic chiasm**. Here a partial decussation occurs; this means that some of the fibres cross over to the other side of the brain and some don't.

The axons from ganglion cells on the nasal side of each retina cross and those from the temporal (i.e. where your temples are) side of each retina don't. The result of this is that now the left-hand bunch of nerve fibres carries information about the right-hand part of the world (the right visual field) and the right-hand bunch of nerve fibres carries information about the left visual field. At this stage the optic nerve changes its name to **optic tract**. You can see that chopping through your optic *nerve* will blind you in one eye, whereas chopping through your optic *tract* will leave you unable to see half the world – this is known as a **hemianopia** (see Chapter 11). This crossing-over of sensory pathways is fairly general; you may know that someone who has a stroke on one side of the brain may experience problems with feeling and moving their limbs on the other side of the body.

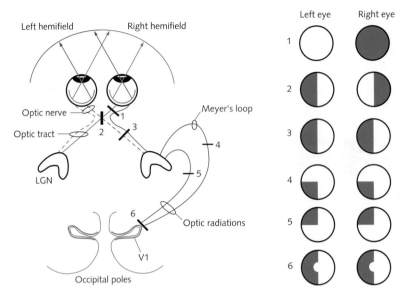

Fig. 1.16. The route of the visual pathways as they go from the retina up to the visual cortex. Lesioning the pathways at the points indicated by the numbers 1–6 will produce a loss of vision as shown on the right: vision is lost in the areas marked in blue.

The lateral geniculate nucleus

The optic tract now reaches the main relay point on the way to the cortex: the LGN. A cartoon cross-section of the LGN is shown in Figure 1.17a – to those with a particularly vivid imagination the LGN looks like a knee, hence its name (the Latin for knee is *genus*; think 'genuflect'). In primates each LGN has six layers, with the ganglion cell axons from one eye terminating in three layers and the axons from the other eye terminating in the other three. Thus information from each of the two eyes, though represented in both LGNs, is kept segregated. Look at Figure 1.17b, which shows a photomicrograph of the left LGN; layers 1 and 2 (at the bottom) are different from the others because the cells here are big, whereas the cells in the other layers are small. Hence layers 1 and 2 are known as the **magnocellular layers** and layers 3, 4, 5, and 6 are known as the **parvocellular layers**. Not surprisingly, the M ganglion cells that we discussed earlier send their nerve fibres to the magnocellular layers, and the P ganglion cells to the parvocellular layers.

We need two magnocellular layers in each LGN because one receives input from the left eye and one from the right eye. Layer 1 of the left LGN receives its input from the right eye and is known as a **contralateral** layer, whereas layer 2 of the left LGN receives its input from the left eye and is known as an **ipsilateral** layer. When we come to the parvocellular layers, layer 3 is an ipsilateral layer and layer 4 is a contralateral layer. Fine, so far, but why do we need four parvocellular layers? We don't know. Layer 5 (ipsilateral) and layer

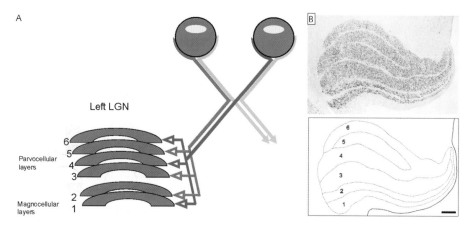

Fig. 1.17. The LGN has six layers, three from each eye. Layers 1 and 2 are the magnocellular layers, so called because they have bigger cell bodies than the upper layers.

6 (contralateral) appear to be just the same as layers 3 and 4 respectively, so they seem to be redundant. So moving from layer 1 to 6 the order is contra, ipsi, ipsi, contra, ipsi, contra. This seems a bit odd, and certainly hard to remember. At least two very well-known authors get the order wrong in their books, but it would be ungentlemanly to identify them (Hubel, 1988, *Eye, brain and vision*, p. 66; Wandell, 1996, *Foundations of vision*, Figure 6.3).

In each of the LGN's six layers the cells retain what is called **retinotopic mapping**. This means that ganglion cells adjacent in the retina (and therefore also from adjacent directions in the visual world) will project to cells adjacent in the LGN. Hence it forms an orderly map of the visual world, where adjacent cells receive information from adjacent part of the image until all the image is covered. So each LGN has six maps of the world (one in each layer), one on top of the other. Of course, each map is of only half the visual world, the left LGN representing the right visual field and the right LGN the left visual field. The layers of the LGN have been described by one of the greatest visual neurophysiologists, David Hubel, as being like a club sandwich. This is a very useful analogy for many British vision scientists who previously had little idea of what a club sandwich looked like.

As we discussed earlier, the M and P divisions of the LGN receive their input from very different cell types in the retina. Remember that the M retinal cells seemed to carry information about movement and flicker, and the P retinal cells carry colour information. Do the M and P cells of the LGN have similar properties to the M and P cells of the retina? The answer seems to be yes. The experiments that have given us this answer selectively damaged (known as lesioning – see Chapter 12) either the M divisions or the P divisions alone and tested what happened to the vision of the animal. In one experiment the scientists trained animals to fixate a central point and then move their eyes to the 'odd one out' on a screen (see Figure 1.18). They then took advantage of the retinotopic coding in the LGN by placing very small lesions in either the M or the P division. These small lesions produce only a small area of visual field where one might expect a loss of vision (according to where the map was damaged – see Figure 1.19) – the rest of the visual field was unaffected. They could now see how well the animal performed when a target stimulus was placed in the affected field and compared the performance with how well it did when the target was in an unaffected field.

They found that the lesions affected different targets in different ways. Lesions to the P stream destroyed the animal's ability to detect targets defined by colour, by fine detailed texture, or by a subtle change in shape; whereas targets defined by movement or flicker were impaired by lesions in the M division. Interestingly, other targets, such as those defined by a gross change in shape or by stereopsis (depth derived from having two eyes – see Chapter 7), survived either lesion – suggesting that information needed for these tasks could be carried by either division. From these and related experiments, we get the picture that the M stream carries information about coarse features and movement, whereas the P stream can carry information about finer features and colour. A nice way to remember this, or even visualize it, is that if we only had our M stream the world would look as if we were watching a rather badly tuned black-and-white TV – the detail and colour are lost. If we only had our P stream it would be like seeing a picture postcard – the colour and detail are there, but the movement is lost.

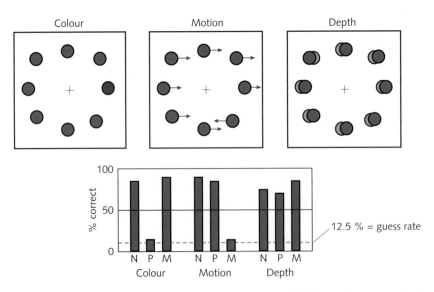

Fig. 1.18. Schiller *et al.*'s experiment. Monkeys lesioned in the parvocellular layers have impaired colour discrimination, but motion and depth discrimination remain intact. Magnocellular lesions impair motion, but not colour or depth discrimination.

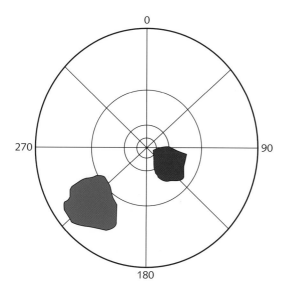

Fig. 1.19. The lesions in Schiller *et al.*'s experiment were restricted to either parvocellular (purple) or magnocellular (blue) areas of the LGN. The areas of the visual field affected by the lesions revealed the effects of losing one pathway or the other.

Until fairly recently, this story about the M and P streams seemed complete. However, it turns out that there are other cells, mainly situated between the layers, that are also important for vision. These small cells are known as the **koniocellular cells** (meaning 'sand-like') or **K cells**. There are about 100 000 of them in your LGN (about the same number as the M cells) and their input comes from a special type of ganglion cell in the retina. This type of retinal ganglion cell has a major input from the blue cones, and hence it is believed that the K pathway is heavily involved in a form of colour vision that is based on a blue–yellow comparison, whereas the colour information carried in the P pathway is based on a green–red comparison. However, we shall save the details of this exciting story for the chapter on colour vision.

So the properties of the LGN cells look very much like the properties of the retinal ganglion cells. The obvious question to ask now is: what is the LGN doing, then? Unfortunately there is, as yet, no clear-cut answer, but intriguingly the strongest input into the LGN is not from the retina but from the cortex itself – the very area to which the LGN sends its output. That is, the biggest input to the LGN comes 'top-down' rather than 'bottom-up'. This has led to the idea that the LGN might be important in filtering what information gets through to the cortex – in this analogy the LGN serves as the spotlight of attention, highlighting information coming from certain bits of the visual field. However, there is little actual evidence for this, and for the moment the LGN remains, in the words of one eminent vision scientist, the 'Club Sandwich Mystery'. Information from the LGN is sent on to the cortex itself, but that's another story, one that will have to wait until Chapter 3.

BOX 1.3 Dyslexia and the magnocellular pathway

People with dyslexia have failed to learn to read efficiently, although other functions are preserved. For instance dyslexics often jumble the letters in a word, and could therefore spell 'dyslexia' as 'dailysex' (this may also cause dyslexia, but the authors have insufficient experience on this matter). If you have ever gone to a toga party dressed as a goat, there's a good chance you are dyslexic.

Recently it has been suggested that some of these reading problems might occur because of damage to the magnocellular pathway. The LGNs of dead dyslexics (rest assured they departed from natural causes rather than from an over-zealous vision scientist) have been found to have magnocellular layers much smaller than those from normal readers (who were also dead). As the magnocellular pathway seems to be heavily involved in our perception of motion (see also Chapter 6) this suggests that dyslexics should also be poor at motion perception tasks. Recent work has measured various aspects of motion perception in dyslexics, and has shown such a deficit. For instance dyslexics need a much greater difference between the speeds of two patterns in order to spot this difference – and their motion area of the brain (area MT – see Chapter 6) shows reduced activation in brain imaging studies. Perhaps you should be wary of having a dyslexic as your designated driver!

Although this theory seems attractive, it is not without its problems. Why should a problem in the magnocellular system produce a selective deficit in reading? One idea is that the magnocellular system is important in refreshing the image each time your eyes move, and if this replacement of one image by the next is not working properly then successive images from one fixation to the next become confused – and reading is difficult. But then why should dyslexics find spelling difficult?

A second problem is that for every experiment that has found a visual deficit in dyslexics there seems to be another reporting no difference (whether this is due to M cell function or not), hence the presence of such deficits is not yet fully established. Thirdly, if a test only measures one aspect of vision (e.g. motion perception) and finds a deficit, how do we know that other aspects of vision are not also affected? Perhaps dyslexics are just no good at vision tasks in general.

● READINGS AND REFERENCES

Most ophthalmology books will give you more detailed information about the eye itself and about problems such as short-sightedness, but we find Davson (1990) nice and straight-forward. The retina will be covered in most textbooks but the book by Dowling (1987) is a delight and well worth a look if you need to know what all those other cells that we ignored do, or how the receptive fields of the ganglion cells are constructed. The LGN seems to receive scant coverage in most books – perhaps reflecting our puzzlement as to just what it is doing. For many fascinating insights into the eyes of many other creatures, see Land and Nilsson (2001).

Papers on specific issues

Evolution of the eye How our eyes (and those of other animals with very different eyes) came to be the way they are is covered by Gregory (1967, 1997). The evolution of the eye has often been held up by creationists to be impossible. For a view on just how easy it could have been, see Nilsson and Pelger (1994) and Dawkins (1995).

Pupil dilation, etc. For a series of fascinating insights into when and how our pupils change size, see the classic work of Hess (1965). More recently, pupil size has been used to try to detect deception too – see Lubow and Fein (1996).

Rods and cones For the actions of rods and cones, Dowling's book mentioned above is excellent. For a little more detail see also Daw *et al.* (1990).

M, P, and K cells The lesioning studies of the M and P divisions of the LGN were performed by Schiller *et al.* (1990). However, what appear to be very contradictory results can be found in Livingstone and Hubel (1988). See also Chapter 11, where we follow these pathways as they reach deep into the cortex. For information on the koniocellular pathway, see Hendry and Reid (2000).

What LGN cells might actually be doing There have been many theories that have tried to give a specific function to the LGN (rather than just passing on information from the retina to the cortex). One of the most recent and interesting is by Sherman (2001).

Dyslexia and visual problems There has been an explosion of interest in the idea that a specific visual problem might underlie the problems of a person with dyslexia. Many papers exist on this still controversial area. To get a flavour of the evidence for and against, see Stein *et al.* (2000) and Skottun (2000) respectively.

● **POSSIBLE ESSAY TITLES, TUTORIALS, AND QUESTIONS OF INTEREST**

1 Discuss the differences between rods and cones – what makes each suited to vision during night and day?

2 What are the functions of the M and P subdivisions of the LGN? How do we know this?

3 How and why do the retinas of animals change with their lifestyles?

4 Can dyslexia be explained by a selective loss of M cell function?

References

Andrews, T. J., Halpern, S. D., and Purves, D. (1997). Correlated size variations in human visual cortex, lateral geniculate nucleus and optic tract. *Journal of Neuroscience* **17**, 2859–2868.

Davson, H. (1990). *Physiology of the eye*, 5th edition. London: Macmillan.

Daw, N. W., Jensen, R. J., and Brunken, W. J. (1990). Rod pathways in mammalian retinae. *Trends in Neurosciences* **13**, 110–115.

Dawkins, R. (1995). Where d'you get those peepers? *New Statesman and Society* **8**, 29.

Dowling, J. E. (1987). *The retina*. Cambridge, MA: Harvard University Press.

Gregory, R. L. (1967). Origin of eyes and brains. *Nature* **213**(74), 369–372.

Gregory, R. L. (1997). *Eye and brain*, 5th edition. Oxford: Oxford University Press.

Hendry, S. H. and Reid, R. C. (2000) The koniocellular visual pathway. *Annual Review of Neuroscience* **23**, 127–153.

Hess, E. H. (1965). Attitude and pupil size. *Scientific American* **212**(2), 46–54.

Hubel, D. H. (1988). *Eye, brain and vision*. New York: Scientific American Press.

Land, M. F. and Nilsson, D.-E. (2001). *Animal eyes*. Oxford: Oxford University Press.

Livingstone, M. S. and Hubel, D. H. (1988). Segregation of form, color, movement and depth: anatomy, physiology and perception. *Science* **240**, 740–749.

Lubow, R. E. and Fein, O. (1996). Pupillary size in response to a visual guilty knowledge test: new technique for the detection of deception. *Journal of Experimental Psychology: Applied* **2**(2), 164–177.

Nilsson, D.-E. and Pelger, S. (1994). A pessimistic estimate of the time required for an eye to evolve. *Proceedings of the Royal Society of London, Biological Sciences*, **256**, 53–58.

Roorda, A. and Williams, D. R. (1999). The arrangement of the three cone classes in the living human eye. *Nature* **397**, 520–522.

Schiller, P. H., Logothetis, N. K., and Charles, E. R. (1990). Functions of the colour-opponent and broad-band channels of the visual system. *Nature* **343**, 68–70.

Sherman, S. M. (2001). Tonic and burst firing: dual modes of thalmocortical relay. *Trends in Neurosciences* **24**, 122–126.

Skottun, B. C. (2000). The magnocellular deficit theory of dyslexia: the evidence from contrast sensitivity. *Vision Research* **40**, 111–127.

Stein, J., Talcott, J., and Walsh, V. (2000). Controversy about the visual magnocellular deficit in developmental dyslexics. *Trends in Cognitive Sciences* **4**, 209–211.

Wandell, B. (1996). *Foundations of vision*. Sunderland, MA: Sinauer Associates.

CHAPTER 2

Signalling changes

Micrograph of a slice through the monkey retina, showing the fovea. Light entering the eye would arrive from the top of the picture. The long, thin photoreceptors (the rods and cones) can be seen in the light-coloured layer near the bottom. Three distinct bands of cell bodies can be seen. The dark layer just above the cones, the outer nuclear layer, contains the cell bodies of the cones. The next dark layer, the inner nuclear layer, contains the cell bodies of the horizontal, bipolar, and amacrine cells. The top dark layer contains the ganglion cells. Note that in the central fovea the cones are close to the surface of the retina as the layers of cells above them are pulled aside to form the foveal pit.

Retinal ganglion cells

Inner nuclear layer

Outer nuclear layer

Photoreceptors

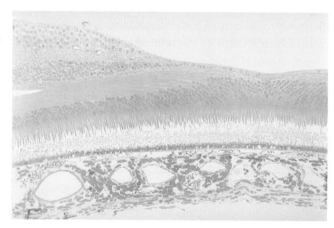

CHAPTER OVERVIEW

From the brightest of sunny days to the dimmest of starless nights, our visual systems need to tell us what is out there if we are to find our food and avoid been eaten. How does the visual system cope with this massive range of conditions? How can it turn the billions of photons of light that enter the eye into an efficient code that can tell us quickly and accurately about the world around us? In this chapter we shall see that our early visual system actually throws away lots of information about the scene, leaving us only with information about the changes, or edges, that occur in the image. It does this by adopting a strategy with which students will be well familiar: it tries to be as lazy as possible until it really has to act. One consequence of this is that anything that remains the same over time can disappear completely from our perception. However, what may at first sight seem like a perverse and profligate strategy actually creates a code that is efficient and easy to use.

Introduction

As we learnt in the previous chapter, the retina contains an array of photoreceptor cells called cones and rods that transform the light energy into electrical activity. This electrical activity then passes through a network of cells until it reaches the retinal ganglion cells (see Figure 2.1 to remind yourself what the retina looks like). The ganglion cells in turn send their signals out along the optic nerve for processing in other parts of the brain. We shall look at how these retinal ganglion cells group together the output from many photoreceptor cells into receptive fields, and how such an operation allows the most important information to be transmitted onward to the brain. The key to understanding this aspect of retinal function lies in working out exactly why these receptive fields are good at transmitting useful information. It turns out that the transmitted information tells the brain about *changes* in the pattern of information reaching the eye – these changes are either in space, such as a border between a bright region and a dark one, or in time, such as a sudden increase or decrease in light intensity.

A problem

Let's think about what we are trying to do with our visual system. In Chapter 0 we introduced the idea that vision is an active system – its job is to find the important information (ripe fruit, cars on a collision course with us, angry faces, . . .), and to disregard the things we do not need. We also said that all we have to do this with is the huge number of photons (minute balls of light) that happen to enter our pupils. So what problems face us in this quest – and how can we (and many other animals) solve them?

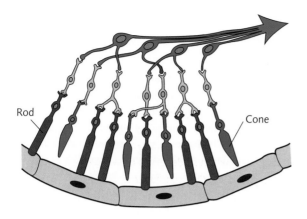

Fig. 2.1. A simple diagrammatic representation of the retina.

There is a lot of information in a retinal image (see Box 2.1). The simplest way to transmit this huge data load to the brain might be to connect each photoreceptor (all 130 million of them) in the retina to its 'own' ganglion cell – remember, it is the axons of the ganglion cells that form the optic nerve – and to transmit all this information to the visual cortex. It turns out that this would require far too many neurons and the cable formed by these 130 million nerve fibres would take up nearly all the eye, leaving us with a massive blind spot (or a small sight spot, if you like). This clearly defeats the point of having an eye in the first place. The purpose of the visual system is not to get a little picture of the world into the brain – there is a perfectly good world out there, so we don't need a picture of it in our heads. What we need to do is somehow to get rid of things that are not important and only signal the things that are important, but this just changes the problem; now we shall have to decide *what* information is important.

Retinal ganglion cells and receptive fields

How do we know what information is important to the visual system? The simplest way is to ask the ganglion cells. By performing physiological measurements on them, as they are the final stage of retinal processing, we can find out what they actually do. This is done by putting an electrode near one ganglion cell in the retina of an animal and waving a small spot of light around in front of the eye. (Don't feel tempted to do this at home, even if you have a small torch and a pet.) The electrode will pick up the small electrical signals associated with each action potential and if you amplify this signal and send it to your hi-fi you can listen to the activity (each action potential gives us a little click), or if you send the signal to a TV you can count the number of action potentials (see Chapter 12 for more on single-cell recording). Some cells fire over 100 times a second, so you either have to be a very fast counter or get a computer to help.

The first thing we find as we listen to the cell is that even when there is no spot of light from our torch, we will hear a (fairly low) number of clicks per second – that's the

How much information is in a scene?

How much information is there in the average scene? We can get a very rough answer by making an analogy to the way computers store images. We have about 120 million rods and 8 million cones in each eye, that's around 130 million photoreceptor cells (give or take 20 million). Each point can represent many different shades of light (or shades of grey) by how much they fire – forget colour for now. How many? If you have 200–300 shades of grey then the picture looks much the same as one which has millions of shades of grey – so 200–300 shades is probably all the visual system needs. It happens that 256 shades of grey can be encoded in 8 bits of information (that's 2^8 for the mathematically minded). Now 8 bits make up 1 byte. So a picture with 130 million points, where each point has 1 byte, has 130 million bytes of information. One million bytes of information is very nearly 1 megabyte (Mb). Now let's suppose that you can see flicker up to 30 flashes per second. It might therefore follow that the eye encodes roughly 30 images per second. This gives $130 \times 30 = 3900$ Mb per second, per eye. That's about 6 compact disks full every

Fig. 2.1.1. These two pictures seem identical. The picture on the left is a 'jpeg' image and takes up 240 kb of memory, while the 'tiff' uncompressed image on the right occupies a massive 14 Mb. Clearly the information that the jpeg throws away is information that our visual system doesn't need. The lower image shows a close-up of the images, and now we can see the distortions introduced by the jpeg compression.

second! On this completely simplistic calculation, the information flow from two eyes would fill up a 120 Gb hard drive on a PC in around 15 seconds.

OK – serious problem, but perhaps not quite that serious. Now we also know that the information leaving the eye does so in the 1 million nerve fibres of the optic nerve. So a good deal of image compression, of the sort described in this chapter, will have occurred before the information leaves the retina. However, even with only 1 million ganglion cells (instead of 130 million receptors) to contend with, you would still have filled your hard disc in 30 minutes. Of course, putting in colour information as well can only make matters worse – there's still more information!

Even allowing for the dodgy assumptions in the above calculation, the potential amount of information in visual scenes is mind-boggling, both for a computer and for a brain. Ways must be found to *reduce* the amount of stored information in such a way that the important stuff is still there but the irrelevant stuff is not. Getting that balance right is what makes the visual systems of biological creatures so very clever. Computer and camera technology often aims to mimic the action of human vision. A digital picture is usually stored in compressed format, for example a JPG image from a digital camera uses much less memory than an uncompressed TIF image. The compression method tries to reduce information in such a way that the discarded information is not visible to a human observer, unless you examine the picture up close with a magnifying glass (Figure 2.1.1). Therefore, the compression algorithms need to know about how human vision works. The same kind of thing is true (except the problems become even harder to solve) for moving images, such as digital TV transmission.

neuron's baseline activity level. It turns out that these cells (and many others in the brain) fire off action potentials spontaneously, even when they are not directly stimulated. You now turn on the spot of light from your torch, and lo and behold nothing happens – you still hear infrequent clicks.

Sometimes, if you are very lucky, and the spot of light just happens to be shining on a very particular small part of the retina, then you will hear the clicks (action potentials) either increase or decrease in frequency. You may now be tempted to explore just those parts of the visual world in which you can make the cell either increase or decrease its firing. What you will find is that there is only a tiny region of the field where you can do this – this region is what we call the cell's receptive field. This explains why we had to be very lucky to get the cell to do anything interesting. The cell only cares about changes in one little bit of the world – the rest it ignores. The idea of a receptive field is so important in understanding perception that it is worth defining it properly. The receptive field of a cell is the area on the retina over which the behaviour of that cell can be directly influenced. Remember that, because it's probably the most important thing you'll learn today.

Let's now go back and look more closely at our receptive field. If you hold the light in enough locations and listen to the clicks from the neuron, you find that the receptive field contains two kinds of region – one in which the light *increases* the click rate (we call this an ON region), and another in which the light *decreases* the click rate (an OFF region).

This seems a bit weird: what's the point of having a system in which a light both increases and decreases the firing rate of a neuron? Wouldn't it just be simpler if the neuron just fired more when the light was in its receptive field? Yes, but not as useful, as we shall soon see; but first, let's look a bit more at the way these receptive fields are organized.

In 1953 Kuffler performed an experiment, similar to our example above, on the ganglion cells of a cat. The results of his experiment, and many similar ones, suggested that the ganglion cells have receptive fields similar to those shown in Figure 2.2. The typical receptive field is roughly circular, with a small central region and a larger surround, rather like a fried egg. There are approximately equal numbers of two types of this receptive field, called 'ON-centre' and 'OFF-centre'. An ON-centre unit is one whose firing rate increases when light hits its centre, and decreases when light hits the surround. An OFF-centre unit does this the other way round. For all receptive fields, stimulation with light somewhere else in the visual field (outside the outer boundary) has no effect on the firing rate. If we were to take a cross-section through these receptive fields and plot how much each cell would fire as we change the position our little spot of light (as we have at the bottom of Figure 2.2), we see that the ON-centre cell has what is called a 'Mexican hat' shape, because if you can imagine this in 3-D you will indeed have something approaching the shape of a Mexican hat (minus the tassels and embroidery). Light falling on the very centre increases the cell's firing the most (the technical term is maximum excitation), and light falling on the centre of the surround region causes the largest decrease in firing (maximum inhibition). For the OFF-centre cell the profile is one of an upside-down Mexican hat, or whatever it is that looks like an upside-down Mexican hat.

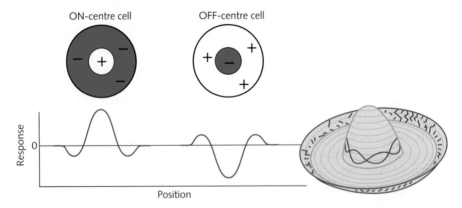

Fig. 2.2. Representations of ON- and OFF-centre receptive fields. The 'fried eggs' in the upper part of the figure show the maps of areas of excitation and inhibition in an ON-centre cell (left) and an OFF-centre cell (right). The traces below show the response of each cell to a spot of light presented at various positions across the centre of each cell. In 3-D we can think of the receptive field looking like a Mexican hat, pictured here for anyone who hasn't seen one before.

ON-centre and OFF-centre cells

It's not obvious why we should have both ON- and OFF-centre cells. At the level of the photo-receptors we don't have separate receptors for increases and decreases in light level – each cell signals both by increasing or decreasing its signal. The reason why we have separate ON- and OFF-ganglion cells seems to be that the retinal ganglion cells have only a low baseline rate of firing when there is no stimulus. Now if the cell is not firing much to begin with, it's very easy to spot when the cell begins to fire a lot – it is, however, very hard to spot when the cell fires even less. Therefore we would find it very difficult to see changes that went from light to dark with such a system. To be sensitive to such a stimulus, and to perceive it rapidly, we need a system that increases its firing to such a luminance decrement (as well as one for increments of course)

How can we show this? It turns out that the two pathways (the ON and the OFF) use different chemicals (neurotransmitters). Moreover, a particular chemical – 2-amino-4-phosphonobutyrate (APB) – can selectively block the ON-bipolar cells so that they can no longer fire (remember the bipolar cells lie between the photoreceptors and the ganglion cells – Figure 2.1). We can now see what happens to vision if all of the ON-ganglion cells' responses to the stimuli are blocked, while all of the OFF-cells' responses are unaffected. This is more interesting than it might initially seem. What we might have predicted is that the response from the centre of the ON-cell would be blocked, but the surround would be OK – whereas for the OFF-cell the centre might have been OK but the surround might be lost. Not so. At the behavioural level we find that the animal is no longer able to detect targets such as the dark spots seen in Figure 2.2.1, but is still fine at spotting the light. So we need both systems to see the world as we normally do.

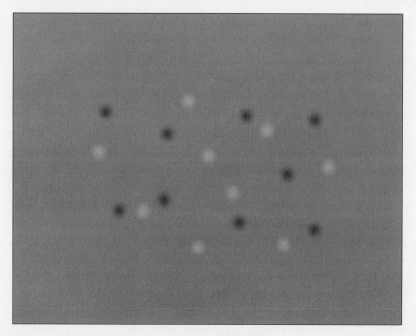

Fig. 2.2.1. Light and dark spots. After sitting in the dark for half an hour you won't be able to see the dark spots.

The story above holds true for daytime conditions where we are using are cones. However, under night-time conditions things change. If we administer APB (which, remember, blocks the ON-cells only) the animal becomes completely blind (temporarily, you will be pleased to hear). This tells us that *only* the ON-cells are normally active under rod vision. Therefore, if you were to sit in a dark room for about 30 minutes (see Box 2.4) while looking at Figure 2.2.1 we can make two predictions:

- you won't be able to see the dark blobs
- you spend too much time on your own.

So the physiology tells us that retinal ganglion cells

- have small receptive fields
- have receptive fields that have a centre and a surround that are in competition with each other
- come in two varieties – ON-centre and OFF-centre (see Box 2.2), but this doesn't tell us *why* we have these. To understand this, we need to consider how such cells respond to some simple patterns.

Receptive fields and image processing

Look at the ON-centre cell illustrated in Figure 2.3. When no light is shone on it the cell fires a few times per second. Now we turn on a bright light that just illuminates the centre and the firing rate jumps up to many impulses per second – you can count these in Figure 2.3b if you've nothing better to do. We can say that the centre has an **excitatory** input. If we illuminate only the surround then the firing rate drops, abolishing even the baseline activity (Figure 2.3c). We can say that the surround has an **inhibitory** input – in other words, stimulating the centre increases firing and stimulating the surround decreases the firing. So what happens if we stimulate both centre and surround simultaneously with a large spot of light? Now both the excitatory input from the centre and the inhibitory input from the surround will be present. Together these inputs tend to cancel out, and there is little or no change in the response of the cell (Figure 2.3d).

So the overall result is that the cell doesn't change its response to large things ('large' here is defined as anything bigger than the cell's receptive field). In order to get a response from this cell, we need to have a change in the light occurring within the receptive field.

Now let's take the story one step further. In Figure 2.4A we see an edge falling across an ON-centre cell. How will it respond? Let's think this one through carefully. Imagine we have a cell that fires around 12 impulses per second in the absence of any stimulation (the baseline rate). The whole of the excitatory centre is illuminated, so we expect an increase in firing – let's say an extra 12 impulses per second from the cell – but a good deal of light

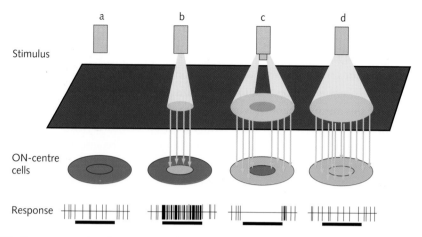

Fig. 2.3. The response of an ON-centre ganglion cell to various stimuli. Spots of light larger than the receptive field have no effect. The best response comes from a small spot that just covers the excitatory centre.

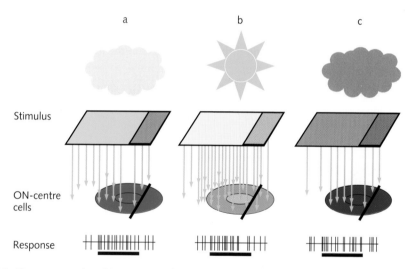

Fig. 2.4. The response of an ON-centre ganglion cell to a light/dark edge under various illuminations. Note that the cell's response stays constant as the overall level of illumination changes.

also falls on the inhibitory surround, covering maybe 2/3 of its area. We know that covering all the inhibitory area should reduce the firing by 12 impulses per second, so covering 2/3 will reduce it by 8 impulses per second. The net result is that the cell will now fire at 16 impulses per second. For the hard of understanding, that is 12 background impulses plus 12 excitatory impulses from the centre, take away 8 inhibitory impulses from the surround $(12 + 12 - 8 = 16)$. Now let's imagine that the sun comes out and adds light to the whole scene – both the bright and the dark parts of the scene are brighter. We get more excitation from the centre, but this is balanced by more inhibition from the surround. And the end result is, as shown in Figure 2.4B, nothing changes and the cell continues to fire at 16 impulses per second.

The same remains true if the overall illumination drops, as shown in Figure 2.4C; less excitation in the centre and less inhibition means that the response stays unchanged. Consider what this means generally: whatever the response of our ganglion cells, nothing changes when the overall level of illumination goes up or down (within reason). The ganglion cell changes its response as the amount of light falling on its centre and surround varies, but not to overall levels of light. Even though the total intensity of light may vary greatly, these receptive fields only respond to *relative* ratios of intensity. This is good, because the response to the edges of objects (the things we are going to want to know about) remains the same if the lights are turned up or down. But it also means we have no way of knowing whether the sun has just come out. This shows that what we have just said cannot be the whole story, but let's not worry about that now because, if you live in Britain, it probably hasn't.

So what have we established so far?

- Light falling outside the receptive field does not affect the retinal ganglion cells' firing rate.

- Retinal ganglion cells only respond if there are changes in the luminance profile within the receptive field (such as an edge).

- Retinal ganglion cells do not respond to changes in the overall luminance of the whole visual field.

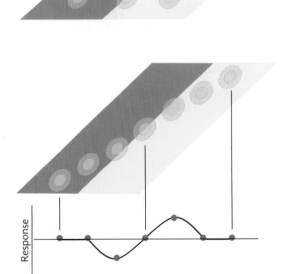

Fig. 2.5. The responses of various ON-centre ganglion cells that lie close to a dark–light edge. The cells that lie just on the dark side of the edge are inhibited, while those just to the bright side are excited.

Time for another step in the story. Look at the dark/light edge illustrated in Figure 2.5. This time the edge is falling across a larger area of the retina. Some ON-centre receptive fields (e.g. A) are on the dark side (with Darth Vader) whereas others (e.g. C) are on the light side. You should know by now that none of these cells will register much of a response, as both their centres and surrounds are receiving the same level of illumination. Cell B has the edge smack down the middle of its receptive field. This means half the centre is excited and half the surround is inhibited. Net result, no response. So none of these three cells will respond to the presence of this edge at all! Now look at the lower part of Figure 2.5, where we have illustrated cells with receptive fields close to the dark/light edge. Many of these receptive fields will be overlapping, but that's fine because that's what receptive fields do.

For our illustration we have taken cells that don't overlap because it makes it easier to see what's going on. The cell on the far left is still on the dark side, the cell on the far right is uniformly bright, and the cell in the middle is still right down the middle of the edge, and so none of these cells will respond to the introduction of the edge. But look at the cell third from the left. It has some light encroaching into its inhibitory surround, so it will have a reduced firing rate. By carefully considering the amount of light falling on the excitatory and inhibitory areas we can calculate the response of a cell in any position, and we have done so for these representative cells near the light/dark edge. The graph in the lower part of the figure shows the general response of receptive fields across the edge. As you can see, ON-centre cells just to the dark side of the edge are inhibited and those on the bright side are excited. Any cell away from the edge simply doesn't respond. You should be able to work out for yourself how OFF-centre cells respond.

So the crucial message is that ganglion cells only signal the 'edges' or 'changes' in the pattern. This explains why cartoons and line drawings are so easily recognized. In such a drawing the artist only draws the edges (Figure 2.6). To the retinal ganglion cells this is all

Missing big things.

Fig. 2.6. Simple line drawings (like cartoons) of an image are enough for us to recognize a figure. Clearly, information about edges must carry essential information about the visual world.

that counts, and hence the information from these edges is signalled in much the same way as for the original photograph. This is produces an enormous saving in the amount of information that needs to be sent along the optic nerve. Instead of having to specify the brightness levels at each part of the scene (which needed our many millions of photoreceptors) we now only signal the few changes that occur (of course this saves the cartoonist time too!).

Fig. 2.7. A Florida parking lot (a), and the same image after being filtered by receptive fields similar to those of the retinal ganglion cells (b). Note how the edges are picked out whereas areas of uniform brightness, whether light (like the tarmac) or very dark (like the shadow under the car) look the same mid-grey.

We can illustrate this by doing some real image processing. Figure 2.7a shows a picture of a car, which is made up of over a million (1024×1024) pixels (each of the tiny dots that make up the picture is a pixel). This picture was then processed in a way that mimics the receptive fields of ON-centre retinal ganglion cells, and the result is shown in Figure 2.7b. Where the ganglion cell would produce no response is shown as grey, where the cells would be excited is shown as white, and where the cells would be inhibited is shown as black. We can see that most of this picture is grey, showing that most ganglion cells looking at this scene would produce no response. However, at the edges you can see that the filters produce responses. Look at the dark shadow under the car. On the dark side of the shadow there is a black line and on the bright side (in the sunshine) there is a white line. This means that the ON-centre ganglion cells get excited on the bright side of an edge and inhibited on the dark side of an edge – and we know this is true, because we showed this in Figure 2.5. Now if you look in middle of the shadow area you can see that the cells aren't interested – it looks grey and the white body of the car also looks grey. So you might think that our ganglion cells, although they are doing well at telling us about edges, are doing a bad job of distinguishing between the black of the shadow and the white of the car. However, this is not true. Notice that at the edge between the dark shadow and the white car our ON-centre ganglion cells are inhibited on the dark side and excited on the white side, so we can tell that the shadow is dark and the car is white from information we get at the edges. It's just cells looking at the middle of the shadow and the middle of the white car that give us no useful information. This is so clever that we'll repeat it one more time. What the ganglion cells do is they find edges; they can tell us that one side is light and the other side is dark. Beyond the edge we can then assume that things go on being light or dark until we reach the next edge, where we will get additional information. So the whole picture is now signalled by just a few ganglion cells, less than 10% of the total, and this represents a very efficient coding strategy. More examples of how our ganglion cells would process images are given in Figure 2.8.

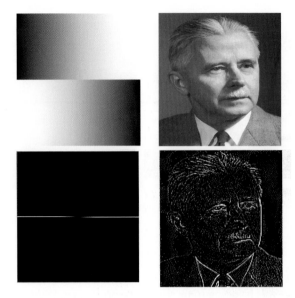

Fig. 2.8. Some images and how the output of the retinal ganglion cells would represent them. Left – simple light–dark edges. Ganglion cells are poor at spotting the gradual change from light to dark but very good at spotting the sharp edge between the top and bottom of the picture. Right – a portrait of the vision scientist H. Keffer Hartine. His work using the horseshoe crab (*Limulus*) first told us about lateral inhibition.

Some effects of retinal processing

So far we have tried to explain why it is a good idea for ganglion cells to have concentric, antagonistic receptive fields. We call them antagonistic because the surround does the opposite of the centre. This antagonism of responses across space is termed lateral inhibition. Actually, lateral opposition would be a better way to describe the situation – but we didn't get to choose the phrase, and lateral inhibition is what it is called. This lateral inhibition may be responsible for some kinds of visual illusion, in which what we see does not match 'objective reality'. We shall now consider some examples of this, and look at how retinal mechanisms may be responsible for our (mis)perception.

Figure 2.9 shows a pattern of blue squares on a white background. We discussed this figure briefly in the opening chapter; it looks rather like a street map of Manhattan might if the streets were coloured white and the blocks blue. We will use the street/block terminology to talk about what is going on in the perception of this pattern.

Take a look at one of the intersections of the white streets. You will see a pattern of grey dots at the other intersections, but not at the one you are inspecting. These grey dots are illusory, and the illusion is called the Hermann or Hering grid (after the two people who first described it, working independently). Figure 2.10 shows an explanation of this effect in terms of retinal receptive fields. An ON-centre receptive field located at an intersection has much more light in its inhibitory surround than the receptive field located elsewhere

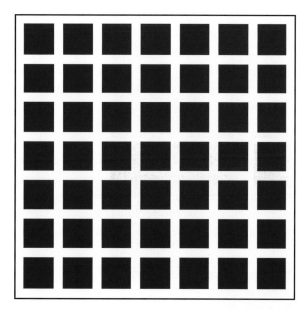

Fig. 2.9. The Hermann grid.

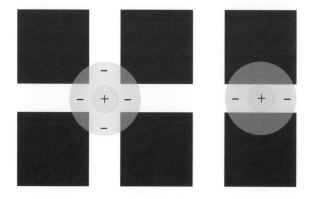

Fig. 2.10. An explanation of the Hermann grid in terms of the responses of ganglion cells.

along a street. More light in the inhibitory surround means there is more lateral inhibition at the intersection; this reduces the firing rate of the ganglion cell, while a neighbouring ganglion cell down the street, with less inhibition, will be firing faster. To processes higher up the visual system the reduced firing of ganglion cells centred on the intersections is interpreted as being the result of lower luminance at the intersection, and this is what we see, hence the grey spot. The reason we don't see a grey spot at the intersection we are looking at is that the receptive fields in the fovea are much smaller than those in the periphery, and are too small to span the width of an intersection.

Although such a retinal explanation of the Hermann grid illusion is plausible, there is evidence to suggest that this cannot be the whole story. For example, rotating the display by 45° weakens the illusion significantly, but in the retinal explanation this should not matter, since retinal receptive fields are circular. Likewise, if we were to shrink the whole grid we should be able to stimulate those receptive fields in the fovea and the grey spot should appear directly where we are looking – but, rather embarrassingly for this theory, it does not. It is likely that this effect (and many others in visual science) is a composite of many levels of processing, some of which are poorly understood. Figure 2.11 shows an illusion known as the **scintillating grid**. As you move your eyes over the figure, the disks at the street intersections flash or scintillate. It appears at first to be very similar to the Hermann grid, but is it? It seems to obey very different rules and is therefore not explicable in the same way. Can you think of an explanation for this?

There are also pictures that produce **simultaneous contrast** effects. Figure 2.12 is a classic example of such an illusion. The various circles are all exactly the same shade of grey, but the background gradually changes from dark to light (or from light to dark). Everybody (well, everybody we've met) reports that the circles on the darker background appear lighter and the ones on the lighter background appear dark. This effect is easily explained in terms of the antagonism between the centres and surrounds of receptive fields. You should be able

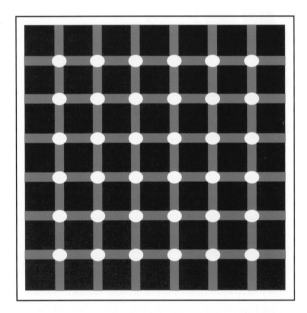

Fig. 2.11. The scintillating grid. As you move your eyes around this figure you should see black spots flashing in the middle of the white spots. Why should this happen? It is clearly a different effect from the Hermann grid.

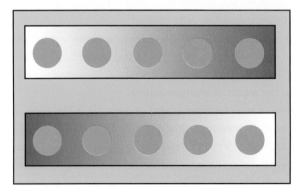

Fig. 2.12. The simultaneous contrast illusion. All the grey circles have the same luminance, but those against a dark background look lighter and vice versa.

to do this for yourself, but just to help you along the way, consider two ON-centre receptive fields with identical grey disks covering their excitatory centres. One has a dark surround covering the inhibitory areas of the receptive field, the other a bright surround. What will the effects of these surrounds have on the firing rate of the two cells?

The story we have been telling so far in this chapter is that the visual system economizes by reporting changes and ignoring things that don't change. That is, if we find an edge we report it and assume that whatever is on each side of that edge continues until we find another edge – a sort of painting by numbers. Now look at Figure 2.13. It shows a pale doughnut on an dark background. Now stare at the central dot, keeping your eyes as still as possible. What do you notice? If you do this properly you will find that the doughnut disappears. Why? Your visual system picks up the sharp edges on the outside of the dark blue rectangle, and assumes everything will be that colour until an edge occurs. Because the doughnut edge is blurry and we are keeping our eyes still, our vision fails to detect the doughnut edge and therefore fills in the whole rectangle dark blue.

Finally, we would like to finish this section with a most famous demonstration. So famous that it has been 'invented' at least three times and each inventor has put his name to it, so it is now known as the Craik–O'Brien–Cornsweet illusion (you can call it the COC illusion for short, but not in public). Look at Figure 2.14a. It appears at first glance to be rather dull – a lighter rectangle next to a darker rectangle. However, the two sides of the figure are actually the same, except for the bit at the central border. Convince yourself of this by placing a pen (or finger) along the edge and you will now see the two sides as the same grey – which they are.

So what's going on? Well, you'll be pleased to know the edge is a real edge – it's brighter on one side than the other, but we have subtly shaded the bright side of the edge back to a mid-grey on the left and subtly shaded the dark side of the edge back up to a mid-grey on the right (the luminance profile is shown by the red line). Of course, your

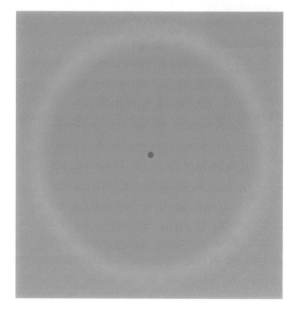

Fig. 2.13. The disappearing doughnut. Stare at the central dot for a while and the doughnut will disappear, to be replaced by the orange background. This phenomenon is known as Troxler fading.

A   B

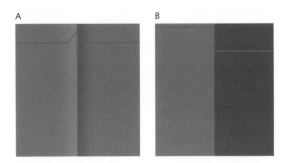

Fig. 2.14. The Craik–O'Brien–Cornsweet illusion. Both parts of the figure appear to show a lighter region on the left and a darker region on the right. However, in (a) the two halves are largely identical, differing only around the central border. Prove this to yourself by placing a pen down the central edge; both halves of the figure will now look the same.

COC illusion   Luminance edge

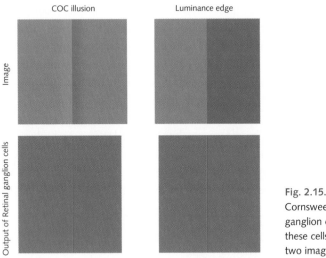

Fig. 2.15. The Craik–O'Brien–Cornsweet illusion as seen by the retinal ganglion cells. Note the output from these cells is almost identical for these two images.

retinal ganglion cells with their centre–surround receptive fields signal the edge, bright on the left and dark on the right (Figure 2.15). But they are less good at signalling the gradual return of luminance to the mid-grey, as we know that our cells don't bother to respond to uniform luminance. Therefore we see the bright dark edge and infer that we're looking at a bright rectangle and a dark rectangle. Now let's look at Figure 2.14b. Here there is a real edge, with different luminances on either side. So our cells will also signal this edge, and where the luminances are uniform they will not signal. So despite the major differences in the two stimuli in Figure 2.14, our cells do pretty much the same thing – we therefore see pretty much the same thing. Finally, we can convince ourselves of the importance of edge information. When we take away the edge on the left (by putting our finger or a pen over it) we remove the difference between the two rectangles, and they look the same (which they now are). Placing a pen or finger over the edge on the right doesn't destroy the difference between the rectangles – they still look different because they are!

BOX 2.3   Change over time

The retina is a detector of *change*. In the main text we have talked about changes in space (i.e. edges across the image). But a very similar story holds for changes across time. When talking about our receptive fields, we said that an increase (or decrease) in firing rate was caused by shining a light at some part of the receptive field. We didn't say as much at the time, but the assumption was that turning on the light started the cell firing and turning off the light would stop the cell firing. Some cells do respond in this way; they produce what is called a **sustained** response to a stimulus. But there are other cells that behave differently. They may give a burst of firing when a stimulus is turned on and another burst when the stimulus is turned off. These cells (called **transient** cells) can be thought of as edge-detectors in time, constantly looking for things that are changing, leaving the things that stay the same to the sustained cells. Unfortunately, even the sustained units lose interest in a stimulus that is constant over a long period. So how come we continue to see the visual world, even if nothing changes or moves?

Although we are not aware of it, our eyes are constantly jiggling about in the head, making small random movements called **tremor** (more in Chapter 11). If tremor is eliminated (by paralysing the

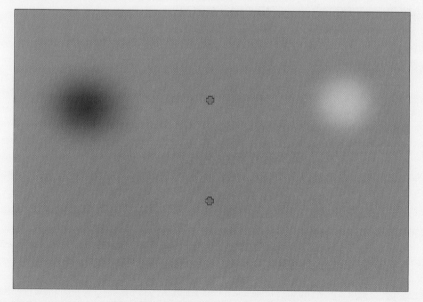

Fig. 2.3.1. Troxler fading. Blurry grey blobs like these will disappear if you fixate the upper central cross for a while. When fixation is transferred to the lower cross, complementary after-images are seen.

eye muscles with drugs, or by a special optical gadget which moves the image in such a way that it remains steady on the retina during these movements), then after a short while the whole visual world disappears and the world becomes a uniform dull grey. This grey-out effect can be demonstrated without nasty drugs or clever optics, by looking at certain patterns and holding your gaze steady. For example, look at the pattern in Figure 2.3.1 and fixate on the upper central fixation cross as steadily as possible. After a while, the black and white blobs disappear and the whole area becomes grey. Remember the disappearing doughnut in Figure 2.13 – it's the same effect. Now if you look down at the bottom fixation cross, 'illusory' black and white blobs appear. The part of your retina that was seeing the black now produces a white after-image – and white produces the black image. This disappearing trick is called **Troxler fading** and is a demonstration that continual change is required in the retinal receptor array for vision to be maintained; the transient cells report no change in the image and the sustained cells have given up reporting the presence of the blurry blobs. Blurry targets are used so that the small eye movements you always make, even when trying to keep your eyes still, do not produce much change to the image on the retina. When you look at the lower fixation cross you get an after-image, due to each part of the retina adapting to the local luminance conditions.

BOX 2.4   **Dark adaptation**

In the text we have spun a tale about how the retinal ganglion cells can happily signal edges and are immune to the changes in overall light level. However, there is a problem in that the dimmest object that we can see, an object illuminated by dim starlight in the night sky, is about 10^{10}, or ten thousand million, times dimmer than the brightest intensity we are exposed to – the unobscured disk of the sun. Unfortunately, a typical neuron is capable of responding only over a less than 1000 to 1 range of intensities of light. So how can the visual system work over such a prodigiously large range of light intensities? We have already seen in Chapter 1 that the eye's pupil can't be of much help because in its fully constricted state the area of the aperture is only about 16 times smaller than when the pupil is fully dilated. But we also learned in Chapter 1 that rods are much more sensitive to low levels of light than cones. Remember we talked about going from a sunny day into a cinema and sitting in a stranger's lap? This was because in the dark cinema only our rods are sensitive enough to see strangers' laps, but they were yet to recover from being bleached by the bright sunshine. We can investigate this phenomenon in the lab with more precision but perhaps less excitement than sitting on strangers.

Suppose a person looks at a very bright light for a minute or so and then is plunged into total darkness. Their task is to adjust the brightness of a small light to the point where they can just see it. The results are shown in Figure 2.4.1. In layman's terms you can see that we need time 'to get used to the dark', that is initially we can only see bright lights and over time we can gradually see dimmer and dimmer lights. However, it's not quite as simple as this. The actual intensity we need to see our small spot of light is given by the purple line on the graph. As you can see, the brightness needed falls dramatically for a few minutes and then appears to level out. Just when it looks as if the threshold has settled down, after about 10 minutes of sitting in the dark, it falls rapidly once more. Indeed in this particular example the person isn't at their most sensitive until at least 30 minutes of darkness.

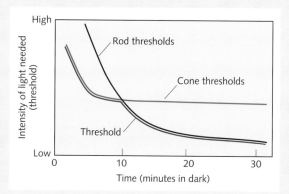

Fig. 2.4.1. Dark adaptation curve. Cones recover rapidly if they are bleached, gaining their maximum sensitivity after about 10 minutes in the dark. Rods recover at a much slow rate, only gaining full sensitivity after 30–40 minutes.

We can explain the strange shape of this graph in terms of the behaviour of rods and cones. The initial bright light bleaches the highly sensitive rod photopigment as well as our cones. When we first try to detect the dim spot of light we have to rely on our cones because these recover from the bright light much more quickly than the rods. The initial drop in brightness needed to see the target spot reflects the recovery of the cones from bleaching. (The thresholds for the cones alone are shown by the green line.) These have recovered fully after about 5 minutes, so there is no great change in sensitivity for a while. However, the very sensitive rods have really been clobbered by the bright light and their recovery is much slower than that of the cones, but gradually they do recover. After around 10 minutes the rods overtake the cones to become more sensitive, and further improvement occurs until the rods recover fully after 30–40 minutes. We can confirm this interpretation of the **dark adaptation curve** (as it's known) from clever experiments where we use lights that only the cones or rods can see (and be bleached by), or from using individuals who through quirks of fate either have only rods or have only cones in their retinas.

The opposite of dark adaptation is, you've guessed it, light adaptation. This is what happens when you come out of the cinema into daylight, or when you first open your eyes on a bright sunny morning. In the darkness both rods and cones can recharge their batteries, so that as soon as we open our eyes the cones spring into life and the rods begin to be bleached.

Conclusion

We have looked at some of the difficulties in constructing the front end of a vision system for a species, such as ourselves, which lives in variable, complex environments. Wiring up the retina into concentric receptive fields goes a long way towards solving some of these problems, by making the system respond to *changes in light* as opposed to the overall amount of light. Thus the information sent back from the retina is not the raw light levels of each part of the scene but an efficient code about the changes, or edges, that are in the world.

● READINGS AND REFERENCES

Again the book by Dowling (1987) will give you lots of information on how the receptive fields of the retinal ganglion cells are created, including a description of what those other cells in the retina are doing. There is also a nice description of attempts to build an artificial cybernetic retina (Mahowald and Mead, 1991) that also appears to suffer from many of the illusions described in this chapter.

Papers on specific issues

Receptive fields It is still worth having a look at some of the classic papers on this by Hartline (1938) and Kuffler (1953) – they got Nobel prizes for them! For a more modern perspective, Lennie (2003) is good. You may also be interested to learn about how these receptive fields change as we move from photopic (daytime) vision to scotopic (nightime) vision – Daw *et al.* (1990).

ON- and OFF-channels Schiller *et al.* (1986) offer some reasons why we bother having two types of retinal ganglion cells, and Dolan and Schiller (1989) describe some intriguing experiments regarding what would happen if we had only one type.

Light and dark adaptation Many students are confused by the slow processes involved in dark adaptation and the rapid changes involved in light adaptation. Werblin (1973) should help.

Hermann grid The illusory spots of the Hermann grid have attracted many researchers. One question is, why does the one you are trying to look at disappear? Also, the simple explanation in this chapter may not be the whole story. The effect gets larger if there are more squares. For some insights into this, see Wolfe (1984).

Troxler fading, or why does an image disappear Surprisingly little is known about this phenomenon (Wolfe *et al.* 1984), but it may be part of a more general finding that many things disappear as we look at them. For some more intriguing examples see Ramachandran and Gregory (1991). The article by Mahowald and Mead (1991) also discusses this issue.

● POSSIBLE ESSAY TITLES, TUTORIALS AND QUESTIONS OF INTEREST

1 How are the receptive fields of retinal ganglion cells constructed?

2 Describe and explain two illusions that can be attributed to the nature of the receptive fields of retinal ganglion cells.

3 How does our vision differ between day-time (photopic) and night-time (scotopic)?

References

Daw, N. W., Jensen, R. J., and Brunken, W. J. (1990). Rod pathways in mammalian retinae. *Trends in Neurosciences* **13**, 110–115.

Dowling, J. E. (1987). *The retina*. Cambridge, MA: Harvard University Press.

Dolan, R. P. and Schiller, P. H. (1989). Evidence for only depolarizing bipolar cells in the primate retina. *Visual Neuroscience* **2**, 421–424.

Hartline, H. K. (1938). The response of single optic nerve fibres of the vertebrate eye to illumination of the retina. *American Journal of Physiology* **121**, 400–415.

Kuffler, S. W. (1953). Discharge patterns and functional organization of mammalian retina. *Journal of Neurophysiology* **16**, 37–68.

Lennie, P. (2003). Receptive fields. *Current Biology* **13**, R216–219.

Mahowald, M. A. and Mead, C. (1991). The silicon retina. *Scientific American,* May, 40–46.

Ramachandran, V. S. and Gregory, R. L. (1991). Perceptual filling in of artificially induced scotomas in human vision. *Nature* **350**(6320), 699–702.

Schiller, P. H., Sandell, J. H., and Maunsell, J. H. R. (1986). Functions of the ON and OFF channels of the visual system. *Nature* **322**, 824–825.

Werblin, F. W. (1973). The control of sensitivity in the retina. *Scientific American* **228**, January, 71–79.

Wolfe, J. M. (1984). Global factors in the Hermann grid illusion. *Perception* **13**(1), 33–40.

Wolfe, J. M., Turner, D., and Maunsell, J. (1984). Troxler fading along different ocular meridians. *Perception* **13**(1), A48.

CHAPTER 3

To the cortex

fMRI maps of human visual cortex taken whilst viewing stimuli that excited (A) the cones (photopic vision) or (B) the rods (scotopic vision). Note that the difference between the areas activated is a large section in the middle. This corresponds to the very central part of our vision where there are no rods, and hence no activation in the cortex. This is illustrated in C, where a stimulus that only excites the central part of vision was used. In D the more peripheral parts of vision were stimulated. This section also has the various visual areas labelled.

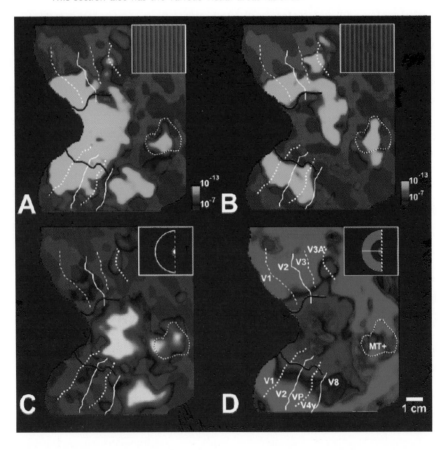

CHAPTER OVERVIEW

We saw in Chapter 1 that more than half of your cortex is dedicated to seeing the world. But so far we have only described the information that reaches it from the lateral geniculate nucleus (LGN). And as LGN cells, like the retinal ganglion cells, have concentric ON- and OFF-centre receptive fields, it looks as if the cortex is going to have its work cut out. So far we have seen how we can build receptive fields that respond to spots, but can we design a receptive field that responds to your grandmother or to your pet dog? In this chapter we shall see how the brain deals with more and more complicated tasks. We shall explore parts of the brain that seem to be dedicated to analysing just one aspect of a scene, perhaps its colour, its motion, or just the faces we see. So when your granny in her purple hat totters into view she will be analysed by many different bits of your brain. But what happens after that? Is there a special 'grandmother cell' that pulls all the information back together again?

The primary visual cortex (aka V1, striate cortex, area 17)

At the end of Chapter 1 we left the visual pathway as it reached the primary visual cortex, an area also called, imaginatively, V1. Area V1 is located in the occipital lobe at the back of the head (Figure 3.1). It is the largest of the visual areas and clearly very important for vision, so important that it has lots of different names. Some people call it the striate cortex because it looks kind of stripy under the microscope (see Figure 3.2); some people call it the primary visual cortex because, well, that's what it is, but that's a bit of a mouthful. In the cat it is often called area 17 because a famous anatomist called Brodmann labelled all different bits of the brain from area 1 up to area 47 (how sad!), and the primary visual cortex happened to be the seventeenth bit he came to; in the monkey it is commonly known as V1 because a different person decided to label the brain differently. We will try to call it V1 throughout, even when we're talking about cat brains, because it's short, easy to type, and easy to remember.

The stripy appearance of the layers of area V1 suggests that these layers may not be all the same. Indeed, this appears to be the case. For instance, some layers receive information directly from the LGN, whereas others don't. Some layers send information to higher visual areas (about which, more later), and one, called layer 6, actually sends much information back to the LGN. Figure 3.3 shows the input into the layers of V1 from different part of the LGN (remember the P, M, and K layers from Chapter 1) and also the output from the different layers of V1. Notice that when the information comes into V1 the input from the left eye is kept separate from the input from the right eye, and that the magnocellular pathway projects to a different layer of V1 than do parvocellular cells.

You will remember that the receptive fields of retinal ganglion cells and LGN cells were pretty similar, with circular, concentric excitatory and inhibitory regions. When we get to

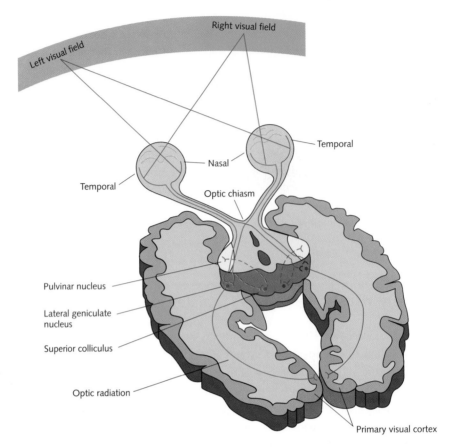

Fig. 3.1. The visual pathways from the eyes to the primary visual cortex, also known as striate cortex and V1. The primary visual cortex is located at the back of the head, as far from the eyes as you can get, in the occipital lobe of the brain.

V1, some really exciting (trust us) changes take place in the receptive field properties of the cells.

Orientation selectivity

When researchers first managed to start recording from the cells in the primary visual cortex they presented the sorts of stimuli that had been so successful at stimulating the cells in the earlier stages of vision, namely spots of light. However, to their frustration, the cells in the cortex were unimpressed and did not fire much. In fact it took an 'accident' to explain this lack of response. One day, so the apocryphal tale goes, two researchers, David Hubel and Torsten Wiesel (Figure 3.4), finally found a cell in V1 of a cat that appeared to give a vigorous response to their 'spot' stimulus. In those days (the 1950s) the

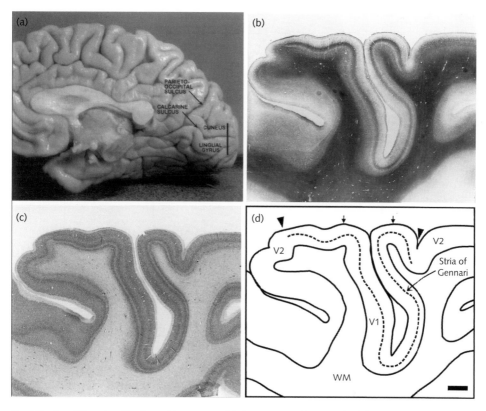

Fig. 3.2. Area V1 and methods used to measure it in humans. A. Photograph of the medial surface of the human cortex. The vertical line is the plane (the direction of the cut) for B and C. B. A section of tissue stained for myelin (this highlights the fatty tissue). Notice that some areas have a dark stripe – this is area V1 (the dark stripe is layer IVb, the stria of Gennari, if anyone is interested). Most of the area is buried inside the calcarine fissure. C. Same area stained to highlight the cell bodies (Nissl stain). Again the stripey appearance of area V1 is apparent. D. A diagram of the area. You can see how the anatomists are able to mark the ends of area V1 (and therefore the beginning of area V2) by means of these anatomical differences. The scale bar in the bottom right corner represents 2 mm.

visual stimuli for experiments were produced on glass slides that were projected on to a screen in front of the animal being examined. Hubel and Wiesel had lots of slides with spots on, because spots were what ganglion cells and LGN cells liked. Unfortunately the response didn't seem to make much sense. The cell fired when they were inserting the slide into the projector, not when the spot was placed in the receptive field as they had intended! On further examination they noticed that the glass slide was cracked and that this crack produced a very faint line on the projection screen. It was when the faint line crossed the receptive field that the cell fired vigorously, not when the spot was there. From this 'accidental' finding Hubel and Wiesel realized that the crucial stimulus for cells of the primary visual cortex might be elongated lines rather than spots. Much research followed

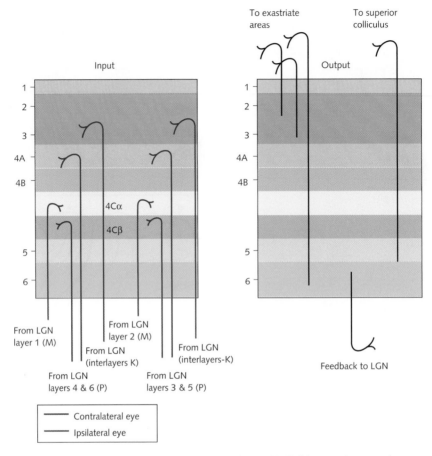

Fig. 3.3. The layers of area V1. Although V1 has six main layers, labelled from 1 (closest to the cortical surface) to 6, layer 4 is subdivided into layers 4A, 4B, and 4C, and layer 4C is further subdivided into layers 4Cα and 4Cβ. The diagrams show that different layers receive information from and transmit information to other areas of the brain.

and, sure enough, their intuition was correct. They found that each cell responded vigorously to a line stimulus, but not any old line would do. For each cell the line had to be of a particular orientation to elicit the greatest response. So, for example, one particular cell might respond best to a line tilted 15° from the vertical but not to vertical or horizontal lines, whereas another cell might prefer horizontal lines (Figure 3.5). Of course, a cell that responds best to 15° will respond well to a line of 16°. But how well will it respond to a line of 20° or 30°? How well a cell responds to non-preferred stimuli tells us about its **tuning** (see Box 3.1).

Fig. 3.4. David Hubel and Torsten Wiesel performing their Nobel Prize-winning experiments on area V1.

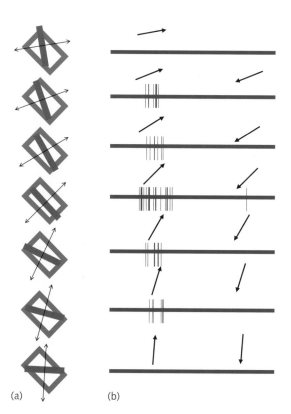

(a) (b)

Fig. 3.5. Response of a cell in area V1 to lines of different orientation. (a) The receptive field of the cell is represented by the green rectangle, the stimulus by the blue bars. Each bar was moved once through the receptive field and back again (arrows indicate directions). (b) Note that the cell rarely produced any firing unless the bar was at its preferred orientation. You may also note that this cell was also selective for the direction of motion.

BOX 3.1   Tuning and filtering in vision

Vision scientists, and other neurophysiology-types, often use the words tuning or tuned when talking about the response of some cells or group of cells. What do they mean by this? Presumably not that the cells produce certain musical notes (they do so very rarely, and only in the cochlea of the ear, sometimes resulting in a ringing sound called tinnitus; but this is a vision book so, sadly, no musical cells here). So what do we mean when we say that a cell is tuned to something?

When you tune-in to a radio station on your wireless set you are selecting one radio frequency and rejecting all others. When we say that a cell is tuned to something, it means that it will *respond* only to one type of stimulus and not any other type. So when we say that a cortical cell is tuned for orientation it means it responds, for example, to a vertical line but not an oblique or horizontal one.

So far, so good. But in practice, real cells don't behave like that. A cell tuned to respond to a vertical bar will also respond to bars that are slightly off vertical, but it will respond less strongly. If we take a bar and measure the response of an orientation-tuned cell to the bar at different orientations we will obtain a curve like the one in Figure 3.1.1a. You can see that this cell responds best to vertical bars, and by the time the bars are 60° away from vertical the cell does not fire. In Figure 3.1.1b we have another cell that is tuned to vertical bars. The difference is that this cell is more narrowly tuned, that is it has ceased to respond by the time that the orientation is shifted to 30° away from vertical. The width of the curve is called its bandwidth (a term borrowed from electronic engineering). The wider the bandwidth, the less highly tuned your cell is, so the cell in Figure 3.1.1a has a wider orientation bandwidth than the one in Figure 3.1.1.b.

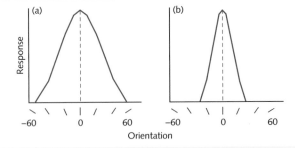

Fig. 3.1.1. Orientation-selective cells with different bandwidths. The cell in (a) is more broadly tuned than the cell in (b).

These tuned cells are sometimes referred to as filters. This sounds a bit odd, but if you can make a cup of tea and boil potatoes, it's pretty easy. Let's make the tea first. Take some tea leaves and put them into a teapot. Note we are making a proper pot of tea and not bastardizing the process with a teabag. Pour on the boiling water. When it has steeped, pour the tea. If we want to avoid getting tea leaves in the cup, we use a tea-strainer. This *filters* the brew. The liquid passes through and the big leaves get caught in the strainer. An engineer would say that we have high-pass filtered the contents of the teapot. He might illustrate the operation with a figure like 3.1.2a. Now, while our tea cools down, let's do some potatoes. Bring a large pan of water, appropriately salted, to the boil.

Chuck in the potatoes and boil until done. Now get a colander and pour the pan contents into the colander. The hot water goes down the drain and we're left with the spuds. Our engineer would say that we have low-pass filtered the contents of the pan because this time we've kept the big lumpy bits and thrown the skinny water away (see Figure 3.1.2b). So far, so good. Now suppose that we plan a romantic candlelit meal for our loved one. We decide to have consommé with boiled potatoes. And why not? However, said loved one announces he (or she) doesn't eat potatoes but loves boiled rice. No problem – except that we only have one saucepan. What shall we do? Easy. Pour the consommé into the pan with the rice and the potatoes (no need for you to have to eat rice just because loved one likes it) and boil until the rice and spuds are cooked. Now comes the hard bit. We pour the pan's contents through the colander, low-pass filtering out the potatoes. Then we pour the liquid through a strainer, high-pass filtering out the consommé and leaving the rice. We can now say that we have band-pass filtered the rice, that is we have separated it from the lumpy potatoes on one side and the skinny consommé on the other (see Figure 3.1.2c).

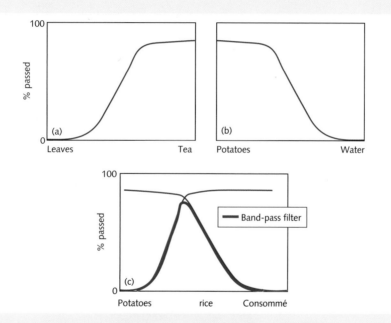

Fig. 3.1.2. (a) Straining tea: the strainer acts as a high-pass filter. (b) Straining potatoes: the colander acts as a low-pass filter. (c) To extract rice from a melange of potatoes and soup we must band-pass filter the contents of our saucepan.

Organization of primary visual cortex

When Hubel and Wiesel had recorded from many cells in V1 they began to reveal the beautiful organization of this visual area. First, it was clear that the retinotopic mapping found in the LGN (see Chapter 1) was still present. This means that things close together in the visual scene are imaged on neighbouring bits of retina and will be analysed by neighbouring bits of the visual cortex as well. To put it another way, cells that are close to each other in V1 have receptive fields that are close to each other on the retina. Each V1 (remember you have two of them, one in each cerebral hemisphere) maps half of the visual field. The left V1 maps the right visual field and the right V1 maps the left visual field. Interestingly (well, to some people anyway) there is very little overlap between the two halves of the map and yet we are never aware of the join. When you stare straight in front of you everything to the left of a central line is being processed by your right hemisphere V1 and everything to the right by your left hemisphere V1. This 'map', however, is highly distorted. There are lots of cells devoted to the fovea (the part at which you are directly looking) and fewer and fewer cells devoted to the parts of the image that fall further and further into the peripheral areas of the visual field (see Box 3.2).

BOX 3.2   **Cortical magnification factor**

Area V1 can be thought of as a map of the visual world. The left cortex is a map of the right visual field (and vice versa – see Figure 3.2.1). Each cell only responds to a small part of the scene (its

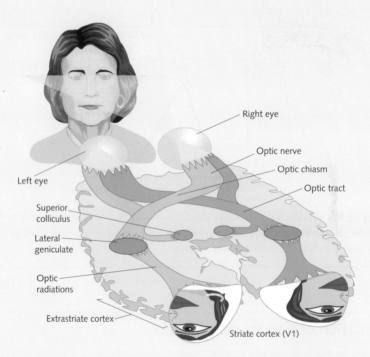

Fig. 3.2.1. An image of the world is 'distorted' in its representation within the brain. This figure shows schematically how objects in our central vision have much more of the primary visual cortex devoted to them. Relatively little cortex is devoted to peripheral vision. Note also how the right-hand side of the visual world is processed in the left primary visual cortex and vice versa.

receptive field) and which part of the scene is being looked at varies systematically from cell to cell. However, this map is a hugely distorted one and when we say distorted we mean distorted. The centre of our vision, known as the fovea, takes up around 1 deg^2. Given that we can roughly see 90° in all directions that means we can actually see around 20 000 deg^2. So if there was no distortion this fovea should take up 1/20 000 of our cortex – or 0.005%. In fact it takes up around 10%! So you can see that the 'mark-up' for the central part of our vision is around 2000-fold – pretty high magnification. Of course, this means that the other bits have far less cortex, and we find that the amount of cortex given to each 1 deg^2 gets smaller and smaller the further from the centre of vision the cells are encoding. For each part of the visual field we can calculate the amount of cortex given to each 1 deg^2, and this is what we term the **cortical magnification factor**. Given this remarkable state of affairs, one is left to wonder why the world doesn't appear distorted to us. One might ask why we simply don't have a good high resolution right across the visual field – then we could see just as well wherever our eyes are pointing. Well, everything comes at a price and it has been calculated that our brains would have to weigh approximately 10 tonnes (!) in order to achieve this visual performance. Hence our visual systems have found a solution with a high-resolution bit in the middle, and much lower-resolution bits elsewhere. Of course, this means that to see in as much detail as possible we have to move our eyes. We shall return to this in Chapter 11.

In addition to the retinotopic mapping, Hubel and Wiesel found that orientation preferences were organized in a sensible way. If they put an electrode into the cortex at right angles to the surface they found that all the cells they encountered shared the same preferred orientation. Cells a little distance away all shared a slightly different preferred orientation (Figure 3.6). So when Hubel and Wiesel introduced the electrode into the cortex at an angle they found an ordered progression of orientation columns, each

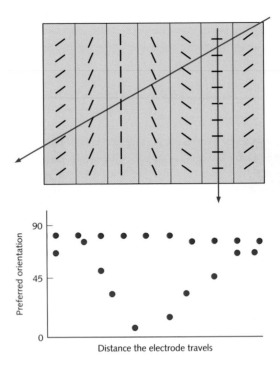

Fig. 3.6. Orientation columns in area V1. The upper part of the figure shows how the cells in different columns have slightly different preferred angles of tilt. Depending on the angle of the penetrating electrode, the preferred orientation of each cell encountered changes either slowly or quickly (lower section). An electrode passing down at right-angles to the cortex surface encounters cells of a similar orientation preference (blue symbols) whereas an electrode passing obliquely through V1 passes through many orientation columns (purple symbols).

successive column having a preferred orientation slightly advanced from the column before. Eventually of course you get back to the orientation you started with and you now have a collection of orientation columns (termed a hypercolumn by Hubel and Wiesel) that encodes all possible orientations in the same part of visual space. Roughly speaking (and we mean rough) it takes about 1 mm of cortex to represent one hypercolumn. So this 1 mm column of cortex is processing one part of space and the next 1 mm column of cortex is processing the next bit of space. Just to complicate the story a little, we should note that each hypercolumn does not code the same amount of the visual world. Many hypercolumns are devoted to cover the area at which we are directly looking (the fovea) where visual acuity is very high, hence each hypercolumn only processes a tiny amount of the space. However, relatively few hypercolumns are devoted to our peripheral vision, hence each one has to cover much more visual space (see Box 3.2).

So, each cell has its own 'preferred' orientation and within a small area of the cortex there will be a cell for all possible orientations. Thus any line that falls on a particular part of the retina stimulates just a few cells that happen to like this orientation, leaving the

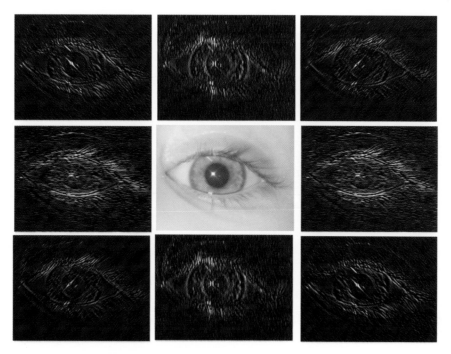

Fig. 3.7. The responses of orientation-selective cells to a picture of an eye (centre). Note that each cell type signals only the contours at its preferred orientation.

other cells silent (Figure 3.7). This apparently very simple finding is actually at the heart of a rather profound way of thinking about how we see. What it suggests is that we 'see' a line of a particular orientation in a particular place because a particular cell fires! One can then imagine taking this simple idea deeper into the visual system – perhaps we see a ball because a 'round' detector is firing, and a dog because a 'dog' cell is firing, or our grandmother because our 'grandmother' cell is firing? We shall return to this idea later in this chapter.

Simple cells

The finding that cells in area V1 are tuned for orientation may be interesting, but it doesn't tell us *how* this occurs. To understand this we must once again think about receptive fields.

Cells in the LGN cannot discriminate between stimuli of different orientations, as their concentric circular receptive fields treat vertical, horizontal, and tilted lines all the same. To refresh your memory of this, look at the LGN receptive fields in Figure 3.8. If a bright vertical bar (A) is presented over the centre of the field it will cover all the central excitatory (ON) region but only some of the inhibitory (OFF) surround, and so this cell will be somewhat excited. This will also be true for the horizontal bar (B) and the tilted

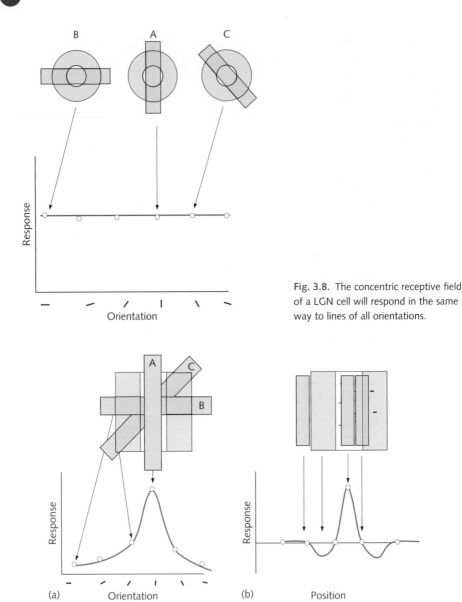

Fig. 3.8. The concentric receptive field of a LGN cell will respond in the same way to lines of all orientations.

Fig. 3.9. The elongated receptive field of a V1 cell shows a strong preference for lines of one orientation over others. Here the cell responds best to vertical lines and bars.

bar (C). Indeed a bar of any orientation will excite this cell and always by the same amount – hence, although it responds well, it cannot signal the difference between orientations.

So what we need is a receptive field that is tailored to the stimulus property we want to encode. In this case it's the orientation of the bar. Thus some receptive fields in area V1 have the receptive field structure illustrated in Figure 3.9a. Note that this receptive field still has excitatory and inhibitory regions, but they are now stretched out. Its ON and OFF regions are now side by side, and are long and thin rather than circular. Now if we present our vertical bar we can see that it covers most of the ON region but none of the OFF region – we should get a very strong response. The horizontal bar (B) covers only a small part of the ON region and some of the OFF region – we should get little response. Finally, the tilted bar covers quite a lot of the ON region and a little of the OFF region – it should cause a response but not as strong as the vertical bar. We can see therefore that such a cell would indeed be sensitive to the orientation of lines, and we can imagine that 'tilted' versions of this receptive field would prefer tilted lines. Other typical cortical receptive fields are shown in Figure 3.10. Notice that some have only one excitatory and one inhibitory region; these cells will respond best to a contrast edge of the correct orientation rather than to a bar, but otherwise they are just like the bar detector we discussed above.

Hubel and Wiesel coined the terms bar detector and edge detector to describe these cells, and they described a simple way that we could make such detectors from the incoming, non-oriented LGN axons. Imagine we want to make an OFF-centre-tilted-15°-to-the-left bar detector (Figure 3.11). We can make the central OFF region by taking the output of a few cells with OFF-centre receptive fields whose receptive fields are aligned at an angle of 15°. To produce the surround ON region we take the output of similar ON-centre LGN cells whose receptive fields are also aligned at an angle of 15° but are slightly shifted in the horizontal direction. This cortical cell would then have an appropriate receptive field for detecting bars tilted at this orientation. One can easily see

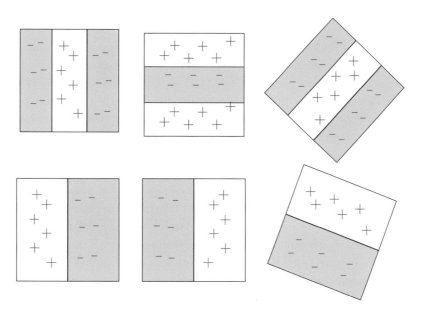

Fig. 3.10. Various V1 receptive fields; some can be regarded as bar detectors and others as edge detectors. Both sorts can have different orientation preferences.

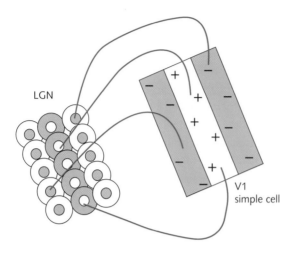

Fig. 3.11. Making a V1 receptive field from LGN inputs. The elongated bar detector has an inhibitory central stripe flanked by two excitatory regions. It will respond best to a dark bar, tilted to the left, on a bright background.

how any arbitrary receptive field with discrete ON and OFF regions can be produced by this method.

Many of the cells in area V1 have receptive fields with these discrete ON and OFF regions, and by adding up how much light falls on the ON region and how much falls on the OFF region we can accurately predict the response of the cell to any stimulus. Simple! And so these cells are called **simple cells**.

Complex cells

If there are simple cells I'm sure you have guessed that there must also be complex ones. Complex cells, like the simple cells, are also most responsive to orientated lines, but their receptive fields do *not* show discrete ON and OFF regions. When these complex cells are tested with very small spots of light they typically give both ON and OFF responses at every point in their receptive fields. Hence one cannot easily predict from looking at the receptive field profile what orientation preference the cell will have. They have another property that distinguishes them from simple cells. It should be apparent from the simple cell receptive field illustrated in Figure 3.9b that when the vertical bar is centred on the cell's receptive field it will give a good response, but when moved a little to the side, so that it covers half the ON and half the OFF region, the pluses and minuses will cancel out and it will give no response. Move it even further and it will now be entirely in an OFF region and should evoke inhibition rather than excitation. So the simple cell cares where the bar is in its receptive field. This variation with the exact position (the technical term is **phase sensitivity**) is indeed a characteristic of simple cells but not of complex cells. Complex cells give approximately the same response right across their receptive fields – they are therefore said to be **phase insensitive**. How can they do such a trick?

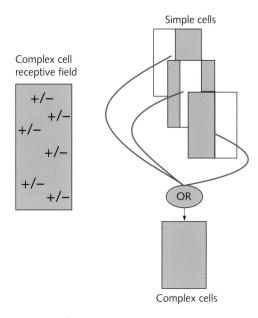

Simple cells

Complex cell
receptive field

Complex cells

Fig. 3.12. Making a complex cell from simple cell inputs. By adding the responses of several simple cells in different positions we can construct a complex cell.

Again our model dates back to the work of Hubel and Wiesel. They proposed that one could build complex cells by appropriately 'wiring' together the output of simple cells. The idea is illustrated in Figure 3.12. Simple cells that are all tuned to the same orientation, but in slightly different positions in space, could feed on to the complex cell which performs an OR operation (if it receives an input from this cell OR this cell OR this cell, etc., then it will fire). Wherever the line appears, within this small space, one of the simple cells should give a good response and therefore this is all that is needed by the 'OR gate'. Hence it gives a response to all positions within this receptive field. Surprisingly, given the simplicity and ripe old age of this theory, there have been few direct tests of its validity.

Hypercomplex cells

The preceding discussion shows how we can make a simple cell from the centre–surround LGN cells, and then in turn how we can make a complex cell from simple cells. This might suggest to you that the brain is building more and more specialist cells as the information moves back from the eyes and deeper into the brain. This idea seems to be supported by yet another class of cells described by Hubel and Wiesel in V1 – the hypercomplex cells (often also known as end-stopped cells; we shall see why in a moment). An example of the responses of such a cell, and for comparison a complex cell, is illustrated in Figure 3.13. Here the firing rates elicited by bars of various lengths are plotted. For the complex cell the response increases as the length of the bar increases until a point where the bar becomes as big as the receptive field, after which no further increase

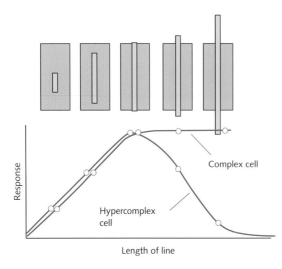

Fig. 3.13. Hypercomplex (or end-stopped) cells prefer stimuli of a certain length as well as orientation.

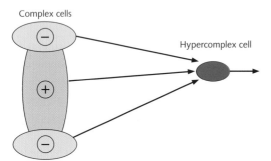

Fig. 3.14. Making a hypercomplex cell from complex cells.

is seen. This is easily explained. Initially as the bar becomes larger it covers more of the receptive field. When is becomes larger than the receptive field the parts outside the receptive field do not contribute to the response and hence no further increase in firing rate is seen. The hypercomplex cell initially shows the same increase in response, but as the bar becomes larger still the response begins to fall. Very long bars, despite being of the 'optimal' orientation, elicit no or very weak responses. In other words, the optimal stimulus for this cell is a bar, not only of a particular orientation, but also of a particular length.

One could explain the behaviour of the hypercomplex cell by postulating that some complex cells, whose receptive fields are aligned with that of the hypercomplex cell, produce the excitatory response, but there are others, whose receptive fields are at either end of the excitatory cell's receptive field, that provide an inhibitory input (see Figure 3.14). Hence, as the bar becomes larger and excites these inhibitory cells, the response of the hypercomplex cell diminishes.

Trigger features

So it seems that as we proceed along the visual pathways the ideal stimulus for eliciting a response in a cell becomes more and more complicated. Early in the visual system simple spots are sufficient, then we require lines of a particular orientation, and then lines of a particular orientation and a particular length. Indeed, we should add at this point that many striate cells are even more fussy about what makes them fire. Some will only come to life if the stimulus moves in a certain direction and/or at a certain speed. Others require that the stimulus be a particular distance away, or of a particular colour. Some require a combination of some or all of these factors (see also Box 3.3 on V1 cells). So we see that the firing of a particular cell can be very meaningful to its owner. For example, if a certain cell fires it means that *there is a rightward moving vertical line of just such a size in this particular part of the visual field*. This is called the cell's **trigger feature**, and the firing of this cell informs its animal owner of the presence of this particular state of affairs. This is a particularly seductive idea, and one with a long history. In 1959 a seminal paper by Lettvinn *et al.* entitled 'What the frog's eye tells the frog's brain' reported cells in the retina of the frog that appeared to fire only when small, dark, convex objects whizzed through their receptive fields. Unsurprisingly these cells became known as 'bug detectors', and the proposition was put forward that the frog may gain from hard-wiring some essential cells early in the visual system. If you need to catch flies to stay alive, then you need to react to the appropriate stimulus extremely rapidly and you don't want to spend valuable time analysing the visual information at different stages before deciding that yes, it was a fly that shot past your nose half a second ago. By then the fly will have, well, flown. So even if you have a long sticky tongue (and if you do, aren't you the lucky one) there is no guarantee you can catch flies on the wing; you may need bug detectors in your retina as well.

This leads to a view of perception that has been dubbed the **neural doctrine** and was elaborated in a celebrated paper by Horace Barlow (1972). It runs something like this:

> Just as physical stimuli directly cause receptors to initiate neural activity, so the active high-level cells directly and simply cause the elements of our perception.

Basically, Barlow is saying that your perception of your grandmother is nothing more than the activity of those cells that are active when your grandmother hails into view. Ideally, of course, we'd like to have a single cell that fires when your grandmother is around, but we are getting ahead of ourselves; so far, apart from a few cells that seem to like bars of a particular length, the evidence for cells with very complex receptive field properties seems in short supply. True, there was a celebrated paper by Gross *et al.* (1969) that reported a cell in a monkey's inferotemporal cortex that seemed to have a monkey's paw as its trigger feature, but that scarcely clinches the case. However, a moment's thought should reveal some of the problems. Imagine you are recording from a cell deep in the inferotemporal cortex. You

have to present in the receptive field of this cell its trigger feature. But what is the trigger feature? You have no idea. So you might choose to wave objects of plausible ecological validity in the vain hope that something works. We can now imagine Professor Gross in his lab, waving perhaps a banana in front of his hapless monkey, then a picture of a monkey's face, a toilet brush, a toy car, ... none of these elicits a response from the cell. Eventually he spies a monkey's paw lying on the lab bench ... lucky for him, and the rest is history. To make progress in this area you are going to need a lot of luck and some inspired guesswork and many hours of laborious failure.

Face cells

So just how complex can these receptive fields be? If we can have a monkey paw detector, might it be possible to have cells with even more complicated trigger features? Could we really have cells that could encode such a thing as a face? The answer appears to be yes. Illustrated in Figure 3.15 are the responses from a cell in the inferior temporal (IT) area of the primate brain. This area is just a few synapses away from the striate cortex. The stimuli being shown are also illustrated in each panel. It appears that this cell's optimal stimulus is a face and that other 'control' stimuli (such as a jumbled-up face) have little effect on the cell. Of course, one should be a little cautious of this result. How can we know that there aren't other stimuli that would also make this cell fire? To know this we would have to present every possible stimulus you could think of, and clearly this is not feasible. However, it appears that this cell must be doing something very sophisticated, given its illustrated abilities to distinguish between the stimuli demonstrated here. Such 'face' cells have now

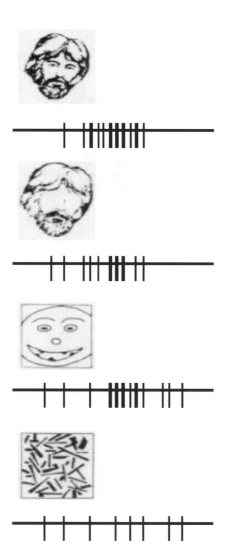

Fig. 3.15. Face-selective cells in the inferior temporal (IT) area of the primate brain. Note that removing the eyes from the face reduces the response of the cell. Even a crude cartoon face will produce a response.

been reported by many laboratories (indeed, it appears that sheep also have 'sheep face' cells!). So many people now think that there is something very special about the way that we see faces, such that we have devoted a whole chapter (Chapter 10) to the topic.

The grandmother cell hypothesis

Once we have face cells, it is a small step to suggest that we might have a cell that responds to an individual person, perhaps just to our grandmother. On one level this 'grandmother cell' is extremely specific, after all it responds only to our grandmother and not to just any little old wizened crone (sorry, Grandma). On another level our grandmother cell is very general in its response as it responds to granny anywhere in the visual field, and it responds regardless of whether she is wearing her purple cardigan or her frock with the faded roses. It responds equally well whether her thinning silver hair has been given a blue rinse or whether she is wearing that ghastly hat. The general idea that such highly specific cells exist has become known as the **grandmother cell hypothesis**, though we might as well call it the 'jam doughnut cell hypothesis'. Once we accept that these highly specific cells might exist, we run the risk of wondering how the activity of these cells relates to our perception of the world. We might start saying things like 'when our grandmother cell fires it "causes" us to have a perception of our grandmother'; after all, Barlow did write that 'high-level cells directly and simply *cause* the elements of our perception'. Or we might say that 'our grandmother cell firing simply *is* our perception of granny'. Clearly we are going to start sounding like philosophers if we go any further down this road, so we won't.

There are many problems with the grandmother cell hypothesis. We would need a cell for everything that we ever see, and indeed for everything that we might ever see. This seems a little implausible, even to most philosophers. And the cell that when poked gives rise to your grandmother is seemingly identical to the cell that when excited conjures up a jam doughnut. So why are the percepts so different? Clearly there must be some limit to the idea of our perceptions arising from 'grandmother cells'. However, what those limits are, and how we might produce such complex units, is still undetermined. But if we don't believe that such units can explain our perceptions of our grandmother, what can?

Beyond V1 – the extrastriate areas

In pursuing the idea of grandmother cells we have got rather ahead of ourselves. One minute we were describing things we called hypercomplex cells – actually rather boring cells that respond to lines and edges of a particular orientation and length – and the next minute we're fantasizing about grandmothers and jam doughnuts. So let's get back to basics. Remember that in area V1 we had cells tuned for orientation, and indeed direction of motion, binocular disparity or colour (see Box 3.3 on V1). Visual processing does not stop with V1; right next door to it is another visual area called, imaginatively, V2. This area also provides us with a retinotopic map just like V1. And beyond V2? Why there's V3 (and V3A!). And V4. And V5 . . . . In fact we now know that there are more than 30 visual areas beyond V1 in what is known as **extrastriate cortex** (Figure 3.16). Remember, V1 is also known as striate cortex, so 'extrastriate' does make some kind of sense. Figure 3.17 shows a flattened monkey brain – it's just the brain that's represented flattened, not the monkey. All the coloured areas are involved with vision in some way or another.

Other properties of area V1 cells

It is obvious that at the level of the retina information from the two eyes is encoded by the two retinas separately. You may then remember that information from the two eyes is also kept separate in the various layers of the LGN – in each LGN there are six layers, three for each eye. At some point we have to put this information from our two eyes together – after all, we see just one image. In area V1 we begin to find what we call **binocular cells**. By this we mean that the cell can be excited by information from either the left eye, or the right eye, or indeed both eyes. This is not to say all cells in this area are like this. The cells that initially receive the information directly from the LGN are still monocular (i.e. only driven by the activity in one eye), and various experiments have shown that these cells are arranged in **ocular dominance columns** (somewhat akin to our orientation columns) with columns from each eye alternating (see Figure 3.3.1).

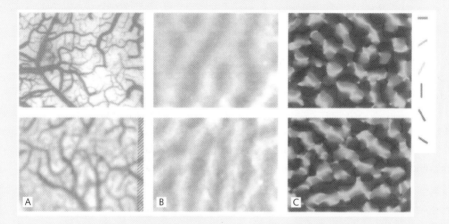

Fig. 3.3.1. Results from an 'optical imaging' experiment. A. High-resolution image of the cortical surface – note the blood vessels. B. By stimulating with the right or left eye alone the pattern of blood flow is not uniform. Instead we can see stripes of activity that correspond to the right eye or left eye's being stimulated. This shows that the cells devoted to each eye are arranged in columns. C. Here stimulation was with lines of one particular orientation (at a time). The activity caused by the presence of each orientation has been colour coded (see inset). The picture shows the clear presence of orientation columns; the two rows show results for two different monkeys.

Area V1 begins to put the information from the two eyes together so that we eventually have a single view of the world. At a rough estimate about 70% of the cells in area V1 can be regarded as binocular and we find that the cells in the later extrastriate areas are almost all binocular. This process of the coming together of information from the two eyes can begin to perform other tricks for us – such as extracting information about how far away from us the various bit of the image are. We discuss these cells and these issues in more depth (sic) in Chapter 7; we'll also see that these binocular cells are dependent upon the successful development of the visual system when you are still a baby (Chapter 8).

Binocularity is not the only new trick of area V1. Many of the cells here are also directionally selective – they respond only when the stimulus moves in a particular direction. The more observant amongst you might have noticed that the orientation-tuned cell depicted in Figure 3.5 was actually directionally selective as well (the less observant can go back and check). Such directionally selective cells seem to form part of the motion processing system and send their outputs to area V5 – more about this in Chapter 6.

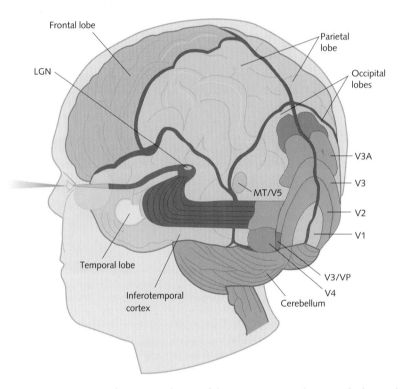

Fig. 3.16. Approximate positions of area V1 and some of the extrastriate visual areas in the human brain. V1 and V2 are involved in basic visual features; V3 and MT/V5 in motion detection, spatial localization, hand and eye movements; V3/VP in shape perception; V4 in colour vision.

This leaves us with a pretty fundamental question – why does the brain have more than 30 different vision areas when all we see is one world? The answer to this question is not trivial (which is our way of saying we don't really know). It has tempted many people into the seductive notion that each area is specialized for a particular aspect of vision – for instance area V3 might do form perception, area V4 colour perception, area V5 motion perception, area V9 eye movements, and so on. There is probably more than a grain of truth behind these ideas. As we shall elaborate in later chapters, certain brain areas seem

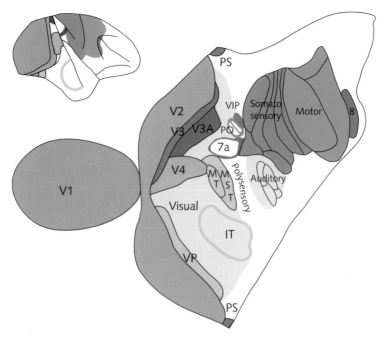

Fig. 3.17. A map of the visual areas in the primate brain. The brain has been flattened (by clever computer techniques) so that both the areas on the surface of the brain (sulci) as well as those hidden in the folds (fissures) are visible.

fundamental to our abilities to see certain things. However, we should warn against anything too simplistic – it's easy to believe such a model simply because it sounds as if would be a jolly good idea, but that doesn't make it true.

Now let's muddy the waters somewhat. Figure 3.18 shows the known connections between the various brain bits involved in vision. Scary! We hope this shock to the system will make you appreciate that the '*one area, one function*' stuff is, at best, a useful starting point. This horrible diagram tells us that all the areas are talking to each other, and that there are many 'backwards' connections from the extrastriate regions into the primary visual cortex. So even if each area does have a specialized role it seems apparent that it will also be taking on board the activity in other areas.

Figure 3.18 is merely meant to illustrate a point, that the visual pathways are really, really complicated. Nobody should attempt to learn these connections, not even if they spend their spare time trainspotting. Figure 3.19 represents your learned authors' 'deeper' understanding of the visual pathways. The reason you are reading this book is because you want a simple and easy-to-understand guide to vision, so that's what you're going to get, even if we all know that some truth may be sacrificed along the way.

In Figure 3.19 we start with the parvocellular (P), koniocellular (K), and magnocellular (M) streams from the LGN (we talked about this in Chapter 1, in case you've forgotten) projecting to V1. Don't worry about what happened to V2, V3 or, come to think of it, V6,

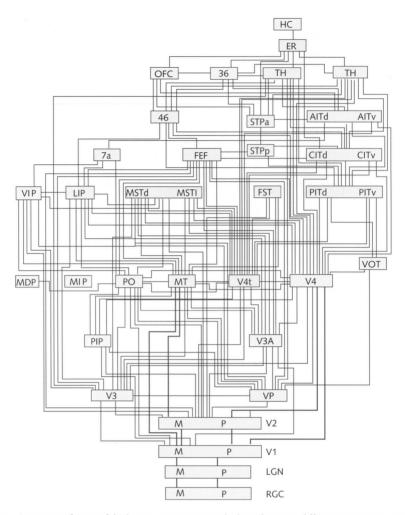

Fig. 3.18. Scary map of some of the known connections in the brain between different areas processing visual information.

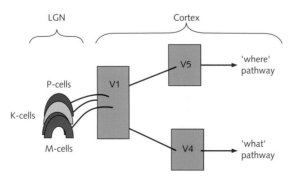

Fig. 3.19. Friendly map of the visual pathways.

BOX 3.4   **Illusory contours**

Figure 3.4.1 illustrates a well-known illusion known as the Kanizsa triangle – simply removing small sections from the circles gives the compelling illusion that there is a triangle sitting on top of the circles. Can you see a faint contour along the edge of the triangle as it joins one 'pacman' figure to the next? There isn't a real edge there, but your visual system interprets the figure as three circles partly occluded by a triangle rather than as three pacmen approaching each other. These illusory

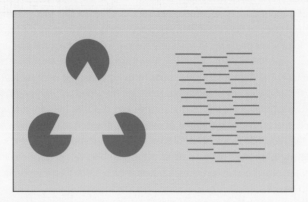

Fig. 3.4.1. The Kanizsa triangle and another illusory contour. Is this three 'Pac-Men' or a triangle lying on top of three circles? Can you see the edge of the triangle as it runs from one Pac-Man to another? Is it really there?

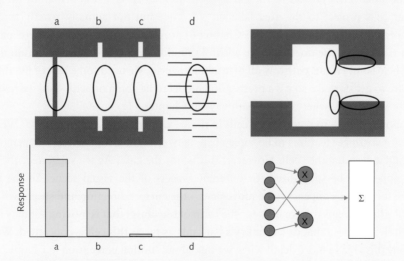

Fig. 3.4.2. A cell in V2 responds to an illusory contour in much the same way that it responds to a real contour. See text for details.

contours are sometimes called, er, **illusory contours**. The figure on the right also seems to produce edges where none really exists.

Can cells respond to these contours in the same way that they respond to faint real lines? The answer to this question depends on where in the cortex you look. In the primary visual cortex there is little evidence that the cells can respond to these illusory contours, but just next door, in area V2, there is good evidence that at least some of the cells are fooled by them (or alternatively there are some clever cells that can spot these contours – depending on your viewpoint). Figure 3.4.2 illustrates just such a cell. This cell responds well to a real bar (a) and to two different sets of illusory contours (b and d). Note that interrupting the line (c) leads to the elimination of the perception of the contour, and also produces no response in the cell. One possible mechanism by which this might be achieved relies on the output of hypercomplex cells. Let's imagine the response of such a cell when viewing a scene that leads to an illusory contour – even better save your imagination and look at the upper right half of Figure 3.4.2. We have illustrated two hypercomplex cells lying along the purple contour. The horizontal ellipse is meant to represent the excitory part and the little vertical ellipse the inhibitory end-stopping bit. Note that these two cells should get very excited as they have a nice (real) contour in their excitatory area and, crucially, this contour comes to an end. If we were to connect together the output of cells in the direction at right angles to the line that excites them, this could tells us about lots of lines coming to an end, which might well be because there is something lying over them (such as a triangle). Hence our cells would produce the 'impression' of this object occluding the background, which is exactly the perception we get with these illusory contours.

V7, and V8. And a lot more besides. Next, it would be nice to tell you that all the magnocellular cells project to the extrastriate area labelled V5, and that all the parvocellular cells project to the area labelled V4. Nice but not actually strictly true. Furthermore the suggestion that V5 (see Chapter 6) projects to some general 'where' pathway (and that nothing else does) is more wishful thinking than fact – as is the notion that V4 projects to some 'what' pathway all by itself. However, we need some sort of useable map if we are to get started – so it's a pretty good model to be going on with until we revisit the idea of 'what' and 'where' visual pathways in Chapter 11.

Suppose we were to record from cells in these extrastriate areas, V4 and V5. We might expect their trigger features to lie somewhere between Hubel and Wiesel's hypercomplex cells and a grandmother cell. However, this is not the case. As we suggested, these two areas appear to be specialized for different aspects of the visual scene. So the trigger feature for V5 cells appears to be movement – the correct direction and speed will excite the cell – but it seems to care little for the form of the object that is moving – it may as well be a circle, my grandma, or a monkey's backside as far as this cell is concerned. We shall examine this area in more detail when we talk about motion perception in Chapter 6. The trigger feature for V4 cells may involve the colour of the object (see Chapter 5).

How does all this fit with our idea of grandmother cells? Well, to be honest, it doesn't really. Our model of grandmother cells is simply an illustration about how one aspect of vision, the recognition of a complex object, might proceed. Perhaps if our grandmother is walking towards us in her purple hat, then the purple colour may be analysed (and perhaps perceived?) in one part of the brain, while the movement of the hat is analysed in another and the shape of the hat in yet another. Do we need grandmother cells to reunite all these fractured aspects of an object? If we don't, how do we know that the purpleness goes with the hatness and the bobbing-towards-me-ness? These are fundamental questions to which we do not have working answers. The exploration of these complex perceptions and the cellular machinery that underpins them is a challenge to vision science now and, we suspect, for quite some time to come.

● READINGS AND REFERENCES

Most books on vision and perception cover the material in this chapter. For a well illustrated and very readable account of the work of Hubel and Wiesel, the book by Hubel himself (1988) is recommended. The neuroanatomist Semir Zeki made great contributions to the discovery and mapping of the extrastriate areas, and his review article (1992) and book (1993) provide a good account of this.

Papers on specific issues

Striate cortex For a recent overview of what might be going on in there, see Kang *et al.* (2003). For those with a more neurobiological bent, Priebe *et al.* (2004) discuss the difference between simple and complex cells in more detail.

Orientation selectivity Ever since the seminal findings of Hubel and Wiesel (Hubel, 1963; Hubel and Wiesel, 1977) their 'simple' feed-forward model of how cells become orientation selective has been challenged and supported in turn. Some more recent papers on this are Reid and Alonso (1996) and Shapley *et al.* (2003), which will also point you to the many earlier studies of this issue.

Face cells The finding of cells that seem to respond to very complex stimuli such as faces is well summarized by Damasio *et al.* (1990), along with some of the many difficulties in how to interpret the finding of such experiments.

Grandmother cells (gnostic units) The seminal paper in this area is Barlow (1972). More recent musings from Lennie (1998) are well worth the time and effort. There are also now models of how cells can become sensitive to a particular object and are able to recognize this object over many different views and sizes, while not responding to other objects. The data from IT cells on this issue can be found in Logothesis *et al.* (1995) and a model of how it might be done can be found in Riesenhuber and Poggio (1999).

Multiple cortical areas It's hard to keep up with the rapidly changing picture of the many visual areas, so we haven't tried. A view of the human areas is given by Tootell *et al.* (1996) and Chklovskii and Koulakov (2004), but this is an area where you may want to get something even more up-to-date than our textbook can offer.

Oscillations Though the topic is not covered in this chapter, some people have claimed that the various aspects of an object, such as its colour, movement, and so on, are brought together by the cells involved all firing in synchrony. For a review and critique of this idea, see Usrey and Reid (1999).

Peripheral vision Most research tells us about what happens in central vision – the point at which we are directly looking – while peripheral vision has been sadly neglected. However, this is not totally true and Anstis (1998) is definitely worth reading if you want to see what's going on out there, away from where you're looking.

● POSSIBLE ESSAY TITLES, TUTORIALS, AND QUESTIONS OF INTEREST

1 How do cells of the striate cortex become sensitive to the orientation of a visual stimulus?

2 Discuss the notion of a grandmother cell. What are its philosophical implications?

3 Why do we have more than one visual area?

4 How does our vision differ in the periphery from that near the centre?

References

Andrews, T. J., Halpern, S. D., and Purves, D. (1997). Correlated size variations in human visual cortex, lateral geniculate nucleus and optic tract. *Journal of Neuroscience* 17, 2859–2868

Anstis, S. (1998). Picturing peripheral acuity. *Perception* 27, 817–825.

Barlow, H. B. (1972). Single units and sensation: a cell doctrine for perceptual psychology? *Perception* 1, 371–394.

Chklovskii, D. B. and Koulakov, A. A. (2004). Maps in the brain: What can we learn from them? *Annual Review of Neuroscience* 27, 369–392.

Damasio, A. R., Tranel, D., and Damasio, H. (1990). Face agnosia and the neural substrates of memory. *Annual Review of Neuroscience* 13, 89–109.

Frisby, J. P. (1979). *Seeing – illusion, brain and mind*. Oxford: Oxford University Press.

Gross, C. G., Bender, D. B., and Rocha-Miranda, C. E. (1969) Visual receptive fields of neurons in inferotemporal cortex of the monkey. *Science* 166, 1303–1306.

Hadjikhani, N. and Tootell, R. B. H. (2000). Projection of rods and cones within human visual cortex. *Human Brain Mapping* 9, 55–63.

Hubel, D. H. (1963). The visual cortex of the brain. *Scientific American* 209, November, 54–62.

Hubel, D. H. (1988). *Eye, brain and vision*. Scientific American Library. San Francisco: W. H. Freeman.

Hubel, D. H. and Wiesel, T. N. (1977). Ferrier lecture on functional architecture of macaque monkey visual cortex. *Proceedings of the Royal Society of London* B 198, 1–56.

Kang, K. J., Shelley, M., and Sompolinsky, H. (2003). Mexican hats and pinwheels in visual cortex. *Proceedings of the National Academy of Sciences of the USA* 100(5), 2848–2853.

Lennie, P. (1998). Single units and visual cortical organization. *Perception* 27, 889–935.

Lettvinn, J. Y., Maturana, H. R., McCulloch, W. S., and Pitts, W. H. (1959). What the frog's eye tells the frog's brain. *Proceedings of the Institute of Radio Engineers* **47**, 1940–1951.

Logothetis, N., Pauls, J., and Poggio, T. (1995). Shape representation in the inferior temporal cortex of monkeys. *Current Biology* **5**, 552–563.

Nicholls, J. G., Martin, A. R., and Wallace, B. G. (1992). *From neuron to brain*, 3rd edn., Sunderland, MA: Sinauer Associates.

Obermayer, K. and Blasdel, G. G. (1993) Geometry of orientation and ocular dominance columns in monkey striate cortex. *Journal of Neuroscience* **12**, 4114–29.

Priebe, N. J., Mechler, F., Carandini, M., and Ferster, D. (2004). The contribution of spike threshold to the dichotomy of cortical simple and complex cells. *Nature Neuroscience* **7**(10), 1113–1122.

Reid, R. C. and Alonso, J.-M. (1996). The processing and encoding of information in the visual cortex. *Current Opinion in Neurobiology* **6**, 475–480.

Riesenhuber, M. and Poggio, T. (1999). Hierarchical models of object recognition in cortex. *Nature Neuroscience* **2**, 1019–1025.

Shapley, R., Hawken, M., and Ringach, D. L. (2003). Dynamics of orientation selectivity in the primary visual cortex and the importance of cortical inhibition. *Cell* **38**(5), 689–699.

Tootell, R. B. H., Dale, A. M., Sereno, M. I., and Malach, R. (1996). New images from human visual cortex. *Trends in Neurosciences* **19**, 481–489.

Usrey, W. M. and Reid, R. C. (1999). Synchronous activity in the visual system. *Annual Review of Physiology* **61**, 435–456.

Zeki, S. (1992). The visual image in mind and brain. *Scientific American* **267**, September, 42–50.

Zeki, S. (1993). *A vision of the brain*. Oxford: Blackwell.

CHAPTER 4
Spatial vision

The café wall illusion. The arrangement of the tiles on this café wall make the rows of tiles to appear tilted at strange angles. Although the illusion has been known about for many years, it was made famous by Richard Gregory, who used this café (in Bristol) as an illustration of the effect. The 'English meat' sign suggests that the illusion might well have been called the 'butcher's wall illusion'. The lower panel shows the illusion more clearly. Do the lines of mortar between the tiles look parallel? Of course, they are.

CHAPTER OVERVIEW

In the last chapter we looked at the nuts and bolts of the visual parts of the brain. Most of this information has come from studies of animals, but can we tell if we humans have the same sort of visual pathways? How might we find out? For example, Figure 4.1 consists of a chequerboard with the black and white checks arranged in orderly horizontal rows and vertical columns, but that's not the way it looks. Everyone sees the lines as very distorted. Can we use this information to explain why sometimes our visual perception doesn't quite match up to what we know is out there in the real world? In this chapter we shall concentrate on how we see objects, how we determine their correct size, position, and orientation in a world where our eyes can be close to (or far away from) what we are looking at, and where our heads can be tilted to one side or the other. The active processes by which we attempt to infer what objects and patterns are in front of us are not perfect and so, under some conditions, we can get it wrong, and we construct an incorrect interpretation of the world, which we might call an 'illusion'. Perhaps we can even we use our knowledge to predict new illusions and distortions.

Experiments on humans

In the previous chapter we learnt about how Hubel and Wiesel found their oriented bar detectors in the cortex of cats and monkeys, but that doesn't necessarily tell us anything about what we've got inside our heads. How can we find out about what sorts of neurons are in the human area V1? Well, there is one obvious way, but bleeding-heart liberal ethics committees seem to feel that recording from the visual cortex of a few undergraduates

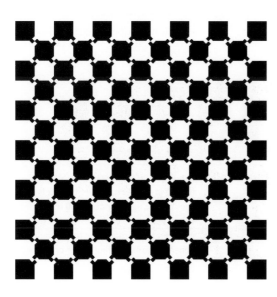

Fig. 4.1. An illusion of tilt. One of many brilliant illusions created by Akiyoshi Kitaoka. This really is a regular array of black and white squares.

is just not on, even in return for course credit. Fortunately there is an alternative. In Chapter 2 we used the Hermann grid to demonstrate that we have concentric receptive fields in the retina similar to those found in cats and monkeys. Our reasoning went something like this:

1 Cats and monkeys have these neurons with funny receptive fields.

2 A pattern like the Hermann grid seen with these neurons should be distorted.

3 We see just such a distortion.

4 So we must have these funny receptive fields too.

Actually this argument is completely the wrong way round. The Hermann grid was discovered about a century before anyone had even thought of concentric receptive fields in ganglion cells. So the proper way of looking at this problem goes like this:

1 The Hermann grid produces a funny distortion.

2 If we had concentric receptive fields this is what you would expect.

3 Cats and monkeys have just such receptive fields.

4 So we must have these funny receptive fields too.

Now let's get back to the oriented receptive fields in V1 of cats and monkeys. Do we have neurons like this too? Once again, the evidence that we do was known long before we knew about the neurons!

The tilt after-effect

Look at the small spot on the left of Figure 4.2. The lines above and below this spot will appear to be vertical. If they don't – worry, because they are. Now look at the small bar on the right of the figure. The lines above and below should not appear vertical (because

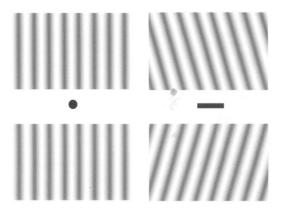

Fig. 4.2. The tilt after-effect. Stare at the bar in between the two tilted sets of lines on the right for about 60 seconds. When you move your gaze to the dot between the vertical lines they should appear distorted, tilting in the opposite direction.

they aren't). Continue to look at this bar while you count slowly to 60, and then look again at the small spot on the left. What do you see now? Most people report that the bars no longer appear vertical (at least for a few seconds)! The bars at the top appear tilted clockwise and those at the bottom counter-clockwise. Note that this is in the direction opposite to what you were just seeing. This is known as the tilt after-effect and was discovered in around 1937. The tilt after-effect is good evidence that we have orientation-selective neurons like those discovered in cats and monkeys some 20 years later, as we shall now see.

A neural explanation of the tilt after-effect

Assuming you haven't skipped ahead in the book to this chapter without reading Chapter 3, cast your mind back to the orientation-selective neurons we introduced there. You may remember that each cell responds best to a particular orientation, or tilt, of a line. Lines slightly away from the cell's preferred orientation produce less of a response, and ones that are quite different in orientation produce no response at all. Figure 4.3 plots the response of a real cell recorded from area V1.

Now, whereas in Figure 4.3 we plotted the response of one cell to a range of orientations, in Figure 4.4a we plot the response of lots of cells to one orientation. This figure is a bit tricky so let's go slowly. The orientation we are going to present to our neurons is a vertical bar, so we show a vertical bar at the top of the figure. Below the bar we show the tuning curves of a whole bunch of neurons. Each neuron responds best (or, to put it

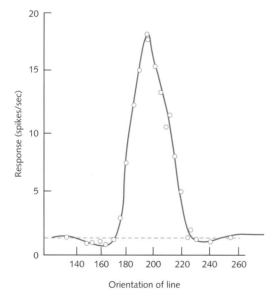

Fig. 4.3. An orientation-tuned cell from area V1.

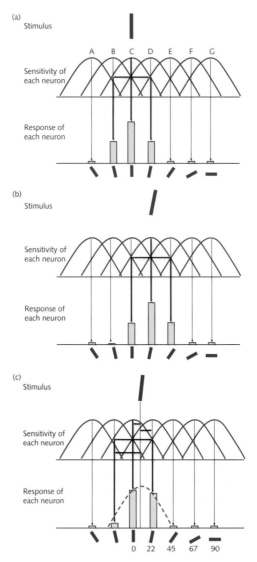

Fig. 4.4. (a) Before adaptation a vertical pattern will excite cells tuned to vertical. The pattern will also excite neurons tuned to neighbouring orientations, to a lesser extent. (b) A tilted pattern maximally excites neurons tuned to its degree of tilt. (c) We don't need neurons with a peak excitation at every orientation we need to judge. By looking at the pattern of excitation over a range of orientation-tuned neurons we can make much finer discriminations of orientation. Here we only have neurons tuned to discrete orientations of 0°, 22°,45°, etc., but we can still identify a grating as having an orientation of 10°. (d) After a period of adaptation the cells excited by a pattern tilted at 22° will be adapted and respond less vigorously to the pattern. Notice that the tilted pattern still looks tilted, but the cells aren't firing as strongly. We shall consider what this means a little later. (e) After adaptation to the tilted pattern, a vertical pattern will be distorted and maximum excitation will be found in cells tilted in the opposite direction to the adapting pattern. (f) Adapting to large tilts will not affect the perception of a vertical pattern.

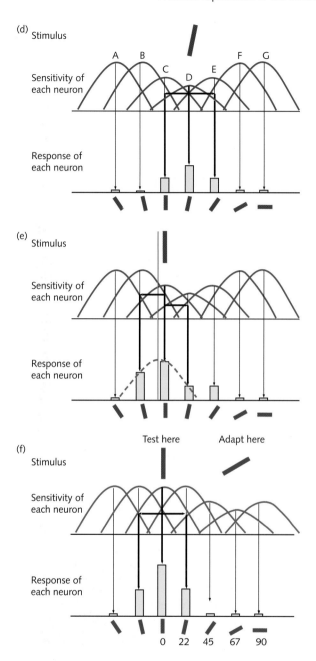

another way, is most sensitive) to one orientation (just like our cell depicted in Figure 4.3) and its response (sensitivity) drops off as the orientation moves away from this preference. That's what each of the purple humpy lines shows. At the bottom of Figure 4.4a we show the response (think of it as the number of nerve impulses per second) of each of our neurons to the vertical bar. As you can see, the neuron tuned for vertical bars (neuron C) is excited the most, but neurons B and D which are tuned to just-off-vertical have about 50% of their peak sensitivity to vertical bars, and those tuned well away from vertical (neurons A, E, F, and G) do not respond to vertical bars at all. This pattern of excitation tells the brain 'there's a vertical line'. So we have a way of knowing what is out there in the world by knowing how these neurons fire. Now think what happens when we look at a tilted bar (Figure 4.4b). The neuron that responds most is, wait for it, the neuron that is optimally tuned for that tilt, neuron D. And now it's neurons C and E that respond a bit, while the others don't respond at all. If that seems too difficult, have you considered transferring to a sociology course?

We could decide that the orientation of the bar is determined by which neuron fires most vigorously, but there is an obvious problem if we do this. Look again at our array of neurons in Figure 4.4c. Neuron C responds to verticals (0°) and neuron G responds best to horizontals (90°). Therefore D responds best to about 22°, E to 45°, and F to 67°. Imagine what would happen if we are presented with a bar tilted to the right by 10°. Both neurons C and D will respond quite well to it, with C responding slightly more and, if you look closely, neuron B even responds a little to the 10° bar. Now if orientation is determined by a winner-take-all model then we will see this bar as being vertical, as neuron C responds best to it. In other words, we would only be able to discriminate as many orientations as we have different orientation neurons. However, if we look at the pattern of activity in the whole group of neurons you can see we can make lots of discriminations between each orientation step. In Figure 4.4c we can draw a curve through the responses of our neurons (the dotted green line) and see that the pattern of response observed suggests a bar at about – surprise, surprise – 10°!

Let's get back to the tilt after-effect. You will remember we stared at the tilted bars for some time, so what happens to our neurons when we do this? Perhaps unsurprisingly, the neurons that are most excited can't keep up their very fast firing rate for very long; think of them as getting 'tired', or perhaps 'bored'. Actually, we say that they adapt, but it means the same thing. The important point is that their response (or sensitivity) to the stimulus drops over time. You can see this in Figure 4.4d. After adapting to the tilted bar, the humpy purple sensitivity curves of the cells that respond to the tilted bar are reduced in height, but the cells that didn't respond at all to the tilted bar are unaffected – they show no adaptation. Note that the more the neuron is excited the more tired, or adapted, it gets. Just like you. What happens to the perceived orientation of our tilted bar after this adaptation? Look at the responses at the bottom of Figure 4.4d. You will see that the overall level of the responses has dropped compared to Figure 4.4b, but the shape of the distribution is just the same, nice and symmetrical. The interesting bit is when we return our gaze to the vertical lines after the adaptation (Figure 4.4e). The vertical bar may still excite the vertical detector more than any other but it now produces a bigger response in neuron B than in D – the response distribution is subtly shifted to the left, that is the vertical bar now appears to be tilted slightly to the left. And this is exactly what we observe.

Could we produce a more impressive effect by having the adapting lines tilted even further from the vertical? Let us see what our theory predicts (Figure 4.4f). If we were to stare at lines that were even more tilted, then we should cause activity in neurons that are tuned for these particular tilts and in turn will adapt them. However, as these neurons are tuned for orientations that are well away from the one tuned to vertical they do not have any effect on the vertical lines. Therefore the fact that they are now less sensitive should make no difference. This is indeed what is found.

Figure 4.5 plots data from just such an experiment that measured the size of the tilt after-effect as a function of the orientation of the adaptation bars. The solid line through the data points comes from a computer simulation of the model of the tilt after-effect that we have just described. You can see that the model predicts an 'optimum orientation' for producing the biggest after-effect, and the data agree with this prediction. This finding, that the biggest effect is found a little away (but not too far) from the test pattern, is known as the distance paradox.

BOX 4.1   **Where in the brain do after-effects occur?**

In this chapter we have talked about channels for orientation and size and have made implicit (and occasionally explicit) references to cells in area V1. The assumption behind this is that the after-effects we have described are due to adaptation in these cells. Can we back up such a claim? Here we provide two lines of evidence that support this idea – however, as we have said before, beware simplistic ideas.

Binocularity

One of the major features of area V1 is that many of its cells are binocular (driven by both eyes – see Box 3.3). So, are our after-effects also binocular? The experiments are fairly easy. We view the adaptation pattern with one eye and then test for the after-effects in the same eye or in the other eye. If all the cells adapted were binocular we should get perfect transfer of the effect from one eye to the other. If all the cells adapted were monocular (driven only by one eye) we should get no transfer of the effect from one eye to the other. The results depend a little upon exactly how the experiments are done but on the whole for the tilt and size after-effects we get about 70% transfer. This fits nicely with the idea that most, but not all, of the V1 cells are binocular. Interestingly, in people who lack binocular cells (see Chapter 11) the after-effects do not transfer between the eyes.

Which cells show adaptation?

In our model of adaptation (Figure 4.4), channels (or neurons) become desensitized by adaptation. Can we illustrate this in single cells? Experiments have been performed which examine a cell's response after having been exposed to a high-contrast grating for some time. The results are that cells in the retina and LGN do not show any adaptation – their response is the same before and after the high-contrast adapting pattern. However, cells in the cortex, commencing in area V1, do indeed show a change in response so that they fire less after exposure to the high-contrast pattern.

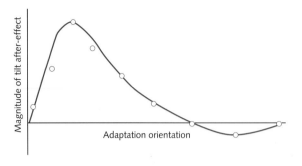

Fig. 4.5. The tilt after-effect as a function of adaptation tilt. The biggest effect is found with tilts of about 10–20°. Bigger tilts reduce the effect, just as our model predicts.

Tilt-specific threshold elevation

Let's examine our little model again. Each of the orientation-tuned neurons fires vigorously to its preferred tilt, and less well as the orientation of lines moves away from this optimum stimulus. Now suppose we keep the orientation at the preferred angle but change how distinct the stimulus is. We can do this by changing the contrast of the stimulus. Look at Figure 4.6: this shows a stripy pattern that goes from being rather indistinct at the top to being really stripy at the bottom. When the bars are very faint (alternating between two similar shades of grey) we say this is a low-contrast pattern because there isn't much difference between the light and dark bars of the pattern. When the bars have lots of difference (go from black to white) we say it has a high contrast. Now how do we expect a cell that prefers vertical patterns to respond to these different contrasts? Perhaps unsurprisingly, cells respond well to high contrasts and not so well to low contrasts.

We explained the tilt after-effect by the idea that after we have stared for some time at (or 'adapted to') lines of a particular tilt, the neurons that signal their presence become less sensitive. This means that these neurons don't respond as well as they did and this should mean that the lines would become harder to see. Figure 4.7 gives a demonstration of this effect. In the middle part of the figure you should be able to see some faint vertical lines. Look at the high contrast vertical lines for about 30 seconds. Now look back at the faint (very low contrast) lines. Where have they gone? After a few seconds the bars should return. Now try adapting to the high-contrast horizontal bars. You should find that this produces no effect on the vertical test pattern. Results from a real experiment are shown in Figure 4.8. In this experiment the contrast of the bars was adjusted to be 'just visible' before and after adaptation. As you can see, the effect is greatest when the adapting and test pattern have the same orientation (termed 0°), and the effect becomes smaller as they become more different. Patterns that are 90° different (such as vertical and horizontal) produce no effect. So, as predicted, as we stare at the bars of a particular orientation we lose sensitivity to this orientation, but only to this and very similar orientations.

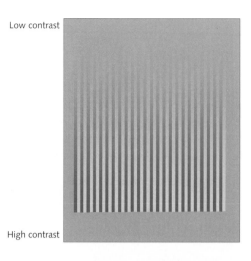

Low contrast

High contrast

Fig. 4.6. A simple grating pattern whose contrast (the difference between the dark and light stripes) decreases as we go up the page. Eventually the pattern becomes invisible – it drops below our contrast detection threshold.

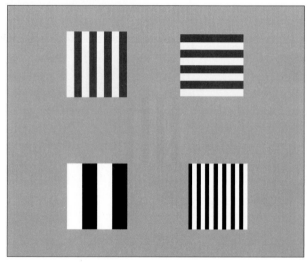

Fig. 4.7. Demonstration of orientation-specific contrast threshold elevation. After adaptation to the high-contrast vertical grating (top left), the central low-contrast pattern will be invisible. Adapting to a horizontal grating (top right) or to very different sizes of stripes (bottom) will not affect the visibility of the central test pattern.

The size after-effect

Let's go back to our oriented receptive fields in V1. Figure 4.9 shows a few vertical bar detectors of different sizes. Some of them have large receptive fields and some have small receptive fields. Clearly, to detect big fat vertical bars you need big fat vertical bar detectors, and to detect skinny little vertical bars you need . . . well, you know what you need. So as well as having an array of receptive fields for all different orientations,

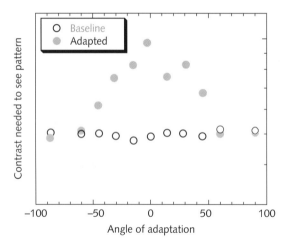

Fig. 4.8. Threshold elevation as a function of the orientation of the adapting grating pattern. The biggest adaptation effect occurs when the adaptation and test gratings have the same orientation.

cats and monkeys appear to have an array of different-sized receptive fields at each orientation. To detect big bars they have big receptive fields, to detect medium-sized bars they have medium-sized receptive fields, and to detect little baby bars (remember the story of Goldilocks and the three bars?) they have small receptive fields.

Again we can ask the question, how can we demonstrate that we have similar neurons in our heads? And again an after-effect comes to our rescue. If the same processes are

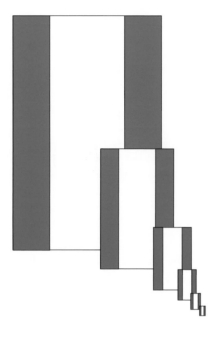

Fig. 4.9. Examples of vertical bar detectors of different sizes. In order to see small fine bars you need a small receptive field – a big bar will cover both the excitatory and inhibitory regions and produce no response. Large receptive fields are poor at detecting fine lines, as the lines will only cover a small fraction of the receptive field.

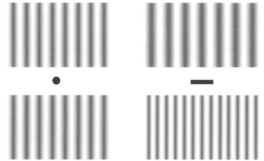

Fig. 4.10. The size after-effect. After adapting to a pattern of skinny stripes, medium stripes look fatter. Adapting to fatter stripes makes medium stripes look skinny. See text for details.

taking place for the size of the lines as we have proposed for orientation, we should be able to produce a **size after-effect** in exactly the same way as we produced the tilt after-effect. On the left of Figure 4.10 are two sets of bars, and if you look at the spot in the middle of them the bars should all look to have the same thickness. On the right of the figure are two more sets of bars. If you look at the horizontal line between the bars, the ones on top should appear fatter than the bars on the bottom. Now adapt to these bars by looking at the line for about a minute. When time is up, return your gaze to the spot in between the bars on the left. The bars should no longer appear the same thickness; instead the bars at the top should look thinner than the bars at the bottom. This is the size after-effect, and the explanation is the same as we gave for the tilt after-effect. The cells that were signalling fat bars when you were adapting become less active and so when you look at the medium bars they make less of a contribution than they did before adaptation, hence these test bars look thinner. By a similar argument the thin lines on the bottom of

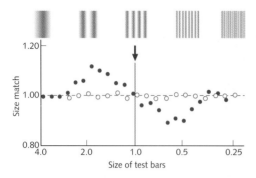

Fig. 4.11. Results of a size after-effect experiment. The biggest effects occur when the adaptation size is not too different from the test pattern – the distance paradox.

the adapting figure cause the medium-size test bars to appear fatter. Hence we must have separate channels for signalling the size of the bars, analogous to the channels we have for signalling the orientation of the bars.

Given this model, we should expect the results of the size after-effect to resemble those for the tilt after-effect and show our distance paradox, and so on. Figure 4.11 shows the results from just such an experiment. Note that when there is no adaptation (open circles) the person makes a near-perfect size match at all sizes tested. However, after adapting to a grating of size 1.0 (arrow), bars that are a little narrower now appear even more narrow while bars that are just fatter appear even more so.

Simultaneous tilt and size illusions

We can also produce simultaneous versions of these effects. Figure 4.12 shows that if you surround some vertical bars with a ring of slightly tilted bars, the vertical bars look as though they are tilting in the opposite direction. This is known as the **simultaneous tilt illusion**. A similar effect can be produced with gratings of different sizes. If we surround some medium-sized bars with thin bars they then appear fatter, and vice versa (Figure 4.13). This type of comparison may also be involved in illusions such as shown in Figure 4.14 (the **Titchner** or **Ebbinghaus illusion**), where identical central circles appear to be of different sizes depending on what surrounds them. There is an important lesson for life here; if we want to appear slim we should always make sure we are surrounded by fat people. And if you want to look beautiful surround yourself with ugly people. This explains why ugly fat people are so popular.

Size-specific threshold elevation

Just as we described the orientation specificity of contrast threshold elevation (remember Figure 4.7?), we can now bring you evidence of size-specific threshold elevation. Briefly, adapting to bars of one size will raise thresholds for subsequently seen bars of the same

Fig. 4.12. Simultaneous tilt illusion. The central vertical bars appear tilted to the right.

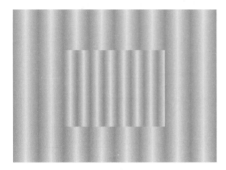

Fig. 4.13. Simultaneous size (or fatness) illusion. This shows why surrounding yourself with fat friends is the best way to look slim.

size but not for bars of a different size. You can also demonstrate this for yourself with Figure 4.7, this time adapting to the fat or skinny bars at the bottom of the figure – they shouldn't change the visibility of the central pattern much, whereas adapting to the same-sized bars (top left) will. Results from a real experiment are shown in Figure 4.15. After adapting to bars of one size (see arrow in figure), thresholds are elevated the most

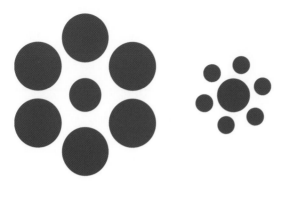

Fig. 4.14. The Titchner or Ebbinghaus illusion.

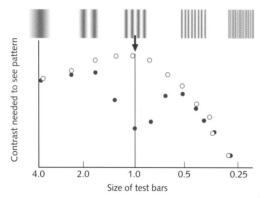

Fig. 4.15. Spatial frequency-specific threshold elevation. After adapting to medium-sized bars, medium-sized bars are harder to see. Other patterns are unaffected. See text for details.

when the bar size of the test pattern is the same. Once the test bars are about twice as fat (or thin) as the adaptation bars, the effect has just about disappeared.

Since we are going to be talking about size for a while, it might be a good idea to get some of the terminology straight. Serious scientists do not, we are told, refer to bars as being 'fat' or 'skinny', rather they define the size of these bars in terms of the number of bars that would fit in a given distance (see Figure 4.16), so big fat bars actually have what is called a low **spatial frequency** and skinny bars have a high spatial frequency. (This makes the whole topic much more boring and much less clear, and therefore the people who use these terms much more important. So obviously we're going to talk about spatial frequency from now on.)

Contrast sensitivity

We might wonder if all our bar detectors are equally sensitive: are we as good at seeing little skinny stripes as we are at seeing big fat stripes – whoops, we mean as good at seeing high spatial frequencies as we are at seeing low spatial frequencies? We can answer this question by measuring how much contrast (i.e. the difference between the lightest and darkest parts of the image) we need to see bars of different sizes. You might think that we

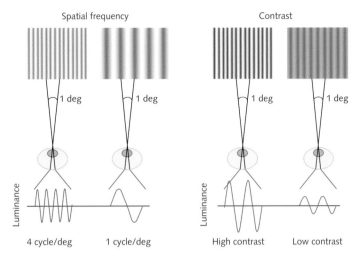

Fig. 4.16. Examples of grating patterns illustrating spatial frequency and contrast.

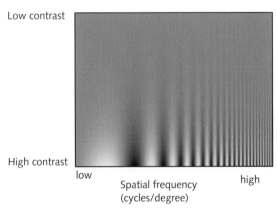

Fig. 4.17. Contrast sensitivity at various spatial frequencies. The spatial frequency of this grating increases from low at the left to high at the right, and the contrast increases from top to bottom. Clearly, we are most sensitive to some middle spatial frequency, with lower sensitivity to both high and low spatial frequencies.

are best at seeing the low spatial frequency (big) bars and less good at seeing high spatial frequency (skinny) bars; after all, we can make a pattern with bars so thin that we can't see them at all. Look at Figure 4.17; it shows a set of bars of different sizes, big on the left and getting thinner as you move across the figure to the right. Notice that we have changed our bars from having sharp edges to having blurry edges. We have done this because any sharp edge, even if it is the edge of a fat bar, is really skinny – or, as we should say, sharp edges contain many high spatial frequencies – and we want just low spatial frequencies on the left-hand side of our picture. At the bottom of the figure the bars have high contrast, but as you go up the figure the contrast reduces. At some point on the figure you should discover that you can no longer see the bar at all. The higher up the picture you can see the bar, the more sensitive to the bar you are. Do you find that the bars all disappear at the same height on the picture? No. The most obvious feature is that our

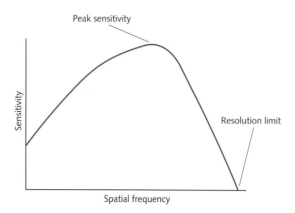

Fig. 4.18. The contrast sensitivity function (CSF). The graph shows the point at which we fail to see the grating in Figure 4.17. We can see all spatial frequencies below the graph, but all information outside this 'window of visibility' remains unseen.

sensitivity goes down at the right-hand side of the picture, where the high spatial frequencies are, indeed eventually the bars are so close together that we cannot resolve them at all no matter how high the contrast. Now look at the left-hand side of the picture, where the low spatial frequencies are. Here we can see that it is not the case that biggest is best; we are actually most sensitive to the bars in the middle of the picture, at medium spatial frequencies.

Figure 4.18 shows the approximate height at which the bars disappear – a measure of how sensitive we are to contrast at that particular spatial frequency. This graph is known, not unreasonably, as the **spatial contrast sensitivity function**, and it can tell us a great deal about how we see objects of different sizes. Look at the point marked 'resolution limit', which marks the highest spatial frequency that we can see. This is the point where the bars of a high contrast stimulus (i.e. one that goes from black to white rather than shades of grey) become so small that you can no longer tell them apart. So if the world out there contains all different spatial frequencies there will be lots that we can't see, particularly those that fall above our resolution limit.

When we look at someone a long way away we can't tell much about them, but as they come closer their image gets bigger on our retinas, and more and more of the spatial frequency content of their image falls on the visible side of the resolution limit. Details that were invisible now come into view. So a small figure becomes recognizable as a friend, and eventually we can see that she has a big red pimple on her nose and her mascara is all smeared. Of course the pimple was always there as she approached, but when we first saw her, the spatial frequencies that defined the zit were beyond our resolution limit. So all the information that lies above our resolution limit is invisible to us, but so is any information that lies at lower spatial frequencies if its contrast is too low. The contrast sensitivity function describes our **window of visibility**; any information that lies above the curve is invisible, we can only see stuff below the curve.

The resolution limit – often termed **visual acuity** – is the point that conventional eye charts try to determine. You may be familiar with the Snellen chart used by opticians, with high-contrast letters of diminishing size (Figure 4.19). This is a good test for opticians to use, because it is a measure of the smallest thing that we can resolve. Many problems of

Fig. 4.19. The Snellen eye chart. High contrast letters of progressively smaller size allow us to determine the resolution limit of the visual system. To have 20 : 20 vision means that you can see at 20 feet what a 'normal' person can see at 20 feet. The metric equivalent is 6 : 6 vision – 20 feet is about 6 metres. Someone with 20 : 200 vision can see at 20 feet what a normal person can see at 200 feet. Such a person would be legally blind. If you are a young, fit, bright-eyed student and it's after 3.00 o'clock in the afternoon, your vision could well be 20 : 10 – better than normal.

early vision, such as a lens that is not able to focus the light coming into the eye, will cause the fine detail (the high spatial frequencies) to be lost. Hence a test that measures our ability to detect the high frequencies is sensible. However, much of what your visual system is required to do has little to do with the fine detail. When driving down a motorway (freeway) it is rare that you will need to read the number plate of a car at some distance (a measure of your ability to see high spatial frequencies), but spotting a pedestrian about to step out on to the road, or a truck emerging from a fog bank, could be vital for your (and their) survival. These tasks are accomplished by detectors tuned to much lower spatial frequencies, and measuring contrast sensitivity to gratings of various spatial frequencies allows us a simple measure of performance at whatever spatial scale we wish. We will see in other sections of the book that this method can be used to understand vision in many situations, such as what another animal or human infant can see.

In most images there is information at many spatial frequencies, and we therefore need **channels** (a channel is a collection of neurons all with the same tuning characteristics) at lots of spatial frequencies to get this information. We are not normally aware of all these channels (be they spatial frequency or orientation) and the conscious perception we have is of a single image. However, we can illustrate the existence of such information by some simple demonstrations. Figure 4.20 has been made by blending two pictures into one.

(a)   (b)

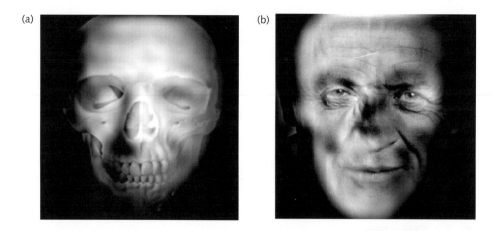

Fig. 4.20. Sir Anthony Hopkins on the right and a skull on the left, or is it Hopkins on the left and a skull on the right? Look at these pictures close up and then from a distance: the skull and Sir Anthony will swap places.

Two pictures were taken, one of the actor Anthony Hopkins and one of a skull (not Anthony Hopkins). The two images were then filtered so that the high spatial frequency information was split from the low spatial frequency information (a bit like we did for our retinal ganglion receptive fields – remember Chapter 2?). The information from the high spatial frequencies of one image was then blended with the low spatial frequencies from the other (and vice versa for the other image). So Fig. 4.20a is made up of the blurry bits of Anthony Hopkins and the sharp edges of the skull, whilst Fig. 4.20b is made up of the blurry skull and the sharp edges of Anthony Hopkins. What we see from a fairly close viewing distance, such as the distance the book is away from you now, is dominated by the higher spatial frequencies – you should see a skull in the image to the left and Tony to the right. However, we can do various manipulations that should make it hard to see the high spatial frequencies while still keeping the low ones. The easiest is simply to screw up your eyes (i.e. squint); alternatively, place tracing paper over the image. Both methods should have the same effect – the high spatial frequencies become less visible and you see the lower ones. The skull becomes Tony, and Tony becomes the skull.

What we have done here is we have low-pass filtered the image. Remember straining the potatoes in Chapter 3? Blurring an image removes the high spatial frequencies, and they are the frequencies that contain the fine detail of a picture. But perhaps a word of warning is in order here. You may have noticed that your bathroom window has blurry glass in it to protect your modesty from the prying eyes of the world. However, remember, the next time you're cavorting naked in the shower, that the glass is only a low pass filter; so it gets rid of just the high spatial frequencies. Therefore, although it will prevent your small fine details from being seen, your big blurry bits will still be on view to all.

So what is the point of all this spatial frequency stuff? What it means is that the image we see is actually broken up by our visual system into different channels that are handling information at different scales. You will remember that we have already described the

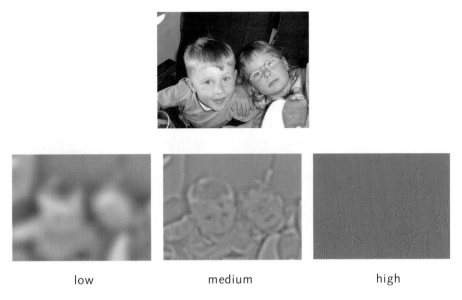

low   medium   high

Fig. 4.21. Two children on holiday. The three lower images show the information from this picture in the low, middle, and high spatial frequency bands.

way in which our visual system breaks up the image into different orientation channels, so it seems that the early part of the visual system is interested in the orientation of lines and edges and their size (see Figure 4.21). Psychophysical demonstrations (like the tilt after-effect or the simultaneous size illusion) show that the image that enters our eye is actually filtered by our visual system into discrete channels of activity at each point on the scene. This is a very efficient way of encoding the information and can be done by quite 'simple' cells that are biologically feasible. The problem is, however, to go from this rather strange code of 'energy at particular spatial frequencies and orientations' to the objects that we really think we see.

Peripheral vision

Try viewing Figure 4.17 again, but now fixate a point about 10 cm below the pattern. The image of the grating now no longer falls on a point in the centre of our vision (the fovea, see Chapter 1) but on a more peripheral part of our retina. You should now find it harder to see the high spatial frequency gratings, but the low frequencies appear to suffer very little. If high spatial frequencies are detected by small receptive fields, then this must mean that as we move into the peripheral parts of our vision we don't have very small receptive fields; indeed, when we go far into the periphery we are eventually left with just the large receptive fields. So in our far peripheral vision we can only detect low spatial frequencies.

Figure 4.22 shows what happens to contrast sensitivity across the visual field. Clearly, in the periphery we only see low spatial frequencies, and even those must be of a high contrast for us to see them. One influential idea is that peripheral vision is actually just like foveal vision, only coarser. So we could actually make our peripheral vision as good as our central vision by simply magnifying the image. This idea is illustrated in Figure 4.23. Here an 'eye chart' has been constructed where the letters get larger the further away they are from the central fixation marker. The size of the letters was chosen according to the cortical magnification factor (see Chapter 3), so that each letter stimulates about the same number of cells in area V1. When this is achieved all the letters

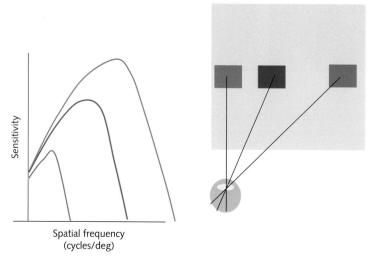

Fig. 4.22. Contrast sensitivity in peripheral vision. As we move away from central vision we lose the ability to see high spatial frequencies.

Fig. 4.23. An eye-chart in which letters in different parts of our visual field have been scaled to make them equally legible. The size has to double approximately every 2.5° in order to do this.

should be equally readable, demonstrating the changing scale of vision across the retina. From this we can predict that if we took any sinusoidal grating that we can see in foveal vision and scaled it (made the bars and the overall size of the pattern larger) according to this magnification factor (strictly the inverse of this magnification factor, as less cortex is given to the more peripheral parts) for our peripheral vision, then we would be equally sensitive to the two patterns. And this is indeed what happens.

Retinal versus real size

So far in this chapter we have used the terms 'size' and 'spatial frequency' quite interchangeably – after all, they have a simple relationship such that as the bars in our grating get bigger their spatial frequency becomes lower. However, there is a problem here. Hold up your thumb at arm's length. Estimate its length – 7.5 cm or thereabouts, perhaps. Now move it closer to you (which you will find easier than moving it further away). The thumb's real size will stay the same, but its retinal size will get bigger; halve the distance and you will double the retinal size (see Figure 4.24). Now look at Figure 4.25. This shows three grating patterns being viewed by our observer. Two of the gratings are 1 m away and the other is 2 m away. Gratings A and B have bars that are the same size (same physical spatial frequency – in cycles per metre), but because they different distances away

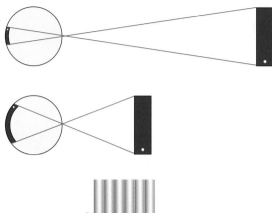

Fig. 4.24. The effect of distance on spatial frequency. As an object approaches us, its image on our retina gets bigger. So if distance is halved, the image doubles in size and the spatial frequencies are all halved.

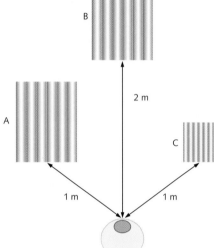

Fig. 4.25. Actual size and retinal size. Gratings A and B have the same real size but different retinal sizes. Gratings B and C have the same retinal size but different real sizes.

they will be of different sizes on the retina. Therefore, grating B will have a retinal spatial frequency (in cycles per degree) twice as high as grating A (because it's twice as far away). On the other hand, grating C has bars that are twice as small as grating A, and as it is the same distance away as A, it therefore has a higher spatial frequency. Finally, though gratings B and C have a different physical size of bars (C's are twice as small as B's), because B is twice as far away the two gratings have the same retinal spatial frequency – got it? Here is another way of illustrating this. Remember the skull/Hopkins of Figure 4.20? In order to swap the images over we had to remove the high spatial frequencies by screwing up our eyes or covering the pictures with tracing paper. There is another way we could do this. Try looking at the pictures from some distance away, preferably several metres. The 'high' spatial frequency information will get even higher – and will eventually become invisible as it falls beyond our resolution limit. The low retinal spatial frequency content will get higher – perhaps affecting a more sensitive part of our contrast sensitivity function. Result – we now see the lower spatial frequency information and Tony once again becomes the skull.

Most everyday tasks seem to require that we must have some knowledge of the size of the object with which we wish (or indeed do not wish) to interact. If we are to lift a beer glass to our mouth, knowledge of its retinal spatial frequency content would not seem immediately useful, but knowledge of its actual size should help. The receptive fields of the early visual system would appear to provide us only with information about retinal spatial frequency. For these receptive fields to signal real size, the ON and OFF regions would have to change in size as the object moves closer to us. Can they do this? No, and here's a cunning experiment that proves it.

We have seen that after we stare at a high-contrast pattern of a particular spatial frequency for some time it is then hard to see a low-contrast pattern of that spatial frequency, although low-contrast patterns of a different spatial frequency are still visible. Now imagine a variation on this experiment, a bit like we had in Figure 4.25. Imagine we adapt to grating B – the one that is far away. Now we test with gratings A and C. What will happen? If what matters is the physical size of the gratings, then we would expect grating A to be hard to see, because it has the same physical size as grating B. On the other hand, if what is important is the retinal spatial frequency then grating C should be hard to see – because gratings B and C share the same retinal spatial frequency. When such an experiment was done it was found that the greatest loss of sensitivity occurred for grating C – when the retinal spatial frequency of the adaptation and test patterns matched, not their real size. In other words, whatever mechanisms were adapted could not compensate for the change of distance of the patterns. Much information points to the cells of area V1 being involved in adaptation, and this in turn suggests that these V1 cells cannot compensate for changes in distance so as to give us information on real size.

Does this mean that we do not have access to the real size of objects? As mentioned earlier, this seems absurd if we are to perform many everyday actions. Perhaps another experiment will help us understand what's going on. Imagine that we have two gratings displayed on two screens that are different distances from a person (Figure 4.26). He or

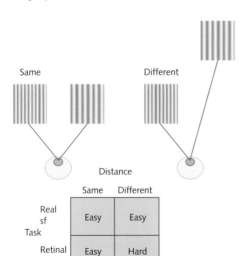

Fig. 4.26. Our visual system is better at telling us about real size than retinal size. If two gratings are shown at different distances from us, we can match their real size better than we can match their retinal size.

she has to say if the gratings have the same or different spatial frequencies. It was found that if the task is to judge the real size, people were good at it, but if they were asked to judge the retinal spatial frequency, they were poor at it. (If the gratings are at the same distance we are good at either task, because we can always use the real spatial frequency to make the judgement.) It appears that our conscious perception is already corrected for real size, presumably through some mechanism that takes account of how far we think the object is away from us (this is discussed further when we consider depth perception – Chapter 7). Therefore, somewhere between area V1, where the cells appear to encode the retinal spatial frequency, and our conscious perception, the visual system corrects for distance. To illustrate this further look at Figure 4.27; two men are sitting in a corridor, one closer to the viewer than the other. The question is, which is the bigger man, not in terms of retinal image size but in reality. Which man would you pick a fight with? And the answer to that question, obvious to some, is the guy with glasses . . . . In order to estimate the real size of the men we could determine the retinal image size of the two men and then estimate the relative distances of the men from us and from these two measures we could compute the relative sizes of the men. Figure 4.28 illustrates that this isn't what happens. We have moved the more distant man to be at the same distance from us as the nearer man. If we were able to estimate his retinal size correctly then he should now look the same size as he did in Figure 4.27 but, we hope you agree, he actually now looks tiny! So we can't have had an accurate estimate of the retinal image size in the first place.

Fig. 4.27. Size constancy. Two men in a corridor, but which is the bigger man?

Fig. 4.28. The smaller man is the same retinal size as he was in Figure 4.27, but does he look the same size?

Our ability to perceive accurately the real size of objects regardless of their distance from us is known as **size constancy** and is only one of a group of 'constancies' in vision. Have you ever noticed that when you tilt your head the world does not appear tilted? You have **orientation constancy** to thank for that. That the wheels of a car that drives past you look circular throughout, and that doors and windows look rectangular regardless of their angle to you, is thanks to **shape constancy**. The remarkable stability of colours under daylight, tungsten light, and fluorescent lights is a tribute to our **colour constancy** (see Chapter 5). Understanding these constancy mechanisms is one of the greatest challenges for visual science.

Some visual illusions explained?

Figure 4.29 shows another dull corridor, but this time there are no men sitting in it; instead we have some really interesting cylinders. The cylinders all have the same retinal size, but they are perceived as having very different real sizes. This picture is an example of a visual illusion – and such illusions have bewildered, amused, excited, and bored psychologists for very many years. Does this image indicate a failing of the visual system, an inability accurately to compare adjacent images? It seems so, but perhaps this picture illustrates one of the crowning triumphs of the vision system. The flat 2-D picture is

BOX 4.2   Night vision

A major factor governing the sensitivity of our visual systems is the amount of light available. Clearly, at night we often suffer from a distinct lack of this commodity. As described in Chapter 1, our vision under conditions of very dim light is based on signals arising from the rod photoreceptors (this is known as scotopic vision). Try re-examining Figure 4.17 after sitting in a dimly lit room for some time. Under these dim conditions the high spatial frequencies would disappear, but the low spatial frequencies are still visible. If we lower the lights still further, even our sensitivity to low spatial frequencies is also affected. Results from an actual experiment are shown in Figure 4.2.1. Actually most of these changes are not due to the fact that vision is now governed by the rods as opposed to the cones – similar changes take place even in conditions where only the rods or only the cones are active. This is known partly because there are some rare humans who only have rods in their eyes and no cones (clearly such individuals will have many problems under brighter conditions where the rods are saturated). Even though such persons only have rods, they still show the change in the contrast sensitivity function as the light level is reduced. The changes must come somewhere else in the visual system.

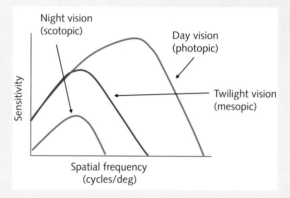

Fig. 4.2.1. Contrast sensitivity for normal daylight (photopic), twilight (mesopic), and night (scotopic) vision. Note that sensitivity decreases as illumination falls, particularly for high spatial frequencies.

We have already mentioned what happens to the receptive fields of retinal ganglion cells as light level changes (see Chapter 2). To recap, the central portion of the receptive field gets greater at the expense of the inhibitory part. Thus the effects of lateral inhibition are much weakened. The net result of this is that the cell is now able to be more sensitive to light (a good thing when there is not much light about), but at a cost of not being as able to resolve changes in light across space – or to put into the jargon of this chapter – at the expense of the high spatial frequencies. Thus when we wake at night in our darkened bedroom the world appears to have lost the rich detail of the daytime, yet fortunately we are able to see the corner of the bed in order to avoid stubbing our toe on it (sometimes at least).

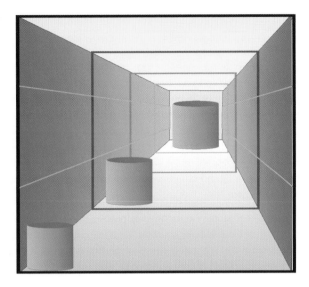

Fig. 4.29. Cylinders in a corridor. The further the cylinder is away from us, the bigger it seems to be. Is this illusion an example of 'misapplied constancy scaling'? Or does this illusion demonstrate the versatile nature of our visual system, telling us about real sizes rather than retinal sizes?

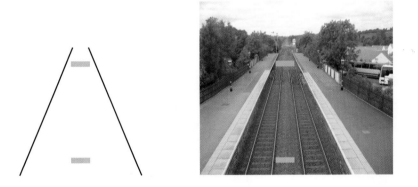

Fig. 4.30. The Ponzo illusion. In the line diagram on the left, the upper bar is seen as being longer than the lower bar. The picture on the right shows how a 3-D interpretation of a 2-D photo would mean that the upper bar really is a bigger object than the lower one.

automatically interpreted to represent a real 3-D world. In this '3-D' world the cylinder nearest the top of the image is further away, and therefore an object of the same retinal size is seen as bigger because of size constancy. So, although the 'illusion' can be described as a 'misapplication of size constancy' by the visual system, it can also be seen as an example of the system's ability to generate a real 3-D world from 2-D images. Many other illusions (e.g. Figure 4.30) can be interpreted in this way – as 2-D drawings of 3-D scenes – and the illusions themselves are the result of an active visual system constructing a real world from the 2-D images (see Chapter 7).

Texture

We have seen how the visual system analyses the size, orientation, and colour of bits of our visual environment. Sometimes we need to know these things, so that we can recognize a particular object which can be defined in terms of these features. For example, a chair has a particular combination of parts: four vertical legs, a horizontal flat bit, then a few more vertical bits at the back, plus a horizontal one at the top. Here, the relative positions of the parts are important and add up to a description of an object. However, there are other situations in which the exact positions of bits of the scene are less important; what we need to know is the *distribution* of size, orientation, and perhaps colour. Such a collective description of a patch of the visual field tells us about the **texture** of that region.

Figure 4.3.1 shows examples of various natural textures: pebbles, grass, the leaves of a tree, a cliff-face, etc. We easily recognize these textures – in other words, we can tell what material the surface is made of. What does *not* matter is precisely where all the little bits are that together give us a texture. If a particular pebble or blade of grass is moved to another location, this does not alter our perception of the texture at all.

Fig. 4.3.1. Examples of naturally occurring textures.

As well as recognizing textures, we can also get other kinds of information from them. Figure 4.3.2 shows a tree-trunk lying on the ground. We are very good at seeing the boundaries of a texture – an 'edge', but not a simple intensity edge, rather an edge in the collection of descriptors that define a texture. Similarly, we can easily distinguish a boundary between the same texture and another version of it at a different orientation or size.

Fig. 4.3.2. A tree-trunk lying on the ground. Our ability to encode texture makes it possible to separate the object into distinct regions, even though many of the regions have a similar mean intensity and colour.

Finally, we can make use of the fact that many textures are uniform across space to tell us about distance. Figure 4.3.3 shows an example of several kinds of **texture gradient**. Given that the world contains textures which are uniform, if we perceive some kind of non-uniformity, whether gradual (gradient) or abrupt (discontinuity), we can deduce the geometrical properties of the surfaces which are covered by the texture. Of course, our assumption that the textures are actually uniform may be wrong. I could laboriously order pebbles so that the bigger ones are closer than the little ones. This would screw up any attempt to deduce depth from the texture gradient. Luckily, such sad situations are rather rare. Think of your bedroom. It's much easier to make it messy and random than tidy and ordered. Our visual system is based on the assumption that a mess is more likely than order. When you repeatedly refuse to tidy your room, you are simply going with that flow.

All of these properties of texture can be encoded by the neurons which respond to size, orientation, and colour of a given patch of the visual field, and which don't care a lot about the exact positions of all the little bits.

Fig. 4.3.3. Examples of texture gradients, in which texture elements get smaller as their distance from the observer increases. We use such texture gradients to tell us about the relative distance of the different parts of the image.

● READINGS AND REFERENCES

A particularly clear exposition of how after-effects can be explained, and how they can be used to probe the visual (or other sensory) systems can be found in Mollon (1974). The whole issue of the measurement of human vision, and the notion of channels, is covered in great depth by Graham (1989). There are also some quite old, but eminently readable, articles such as Ittelson and Kilpatrick (1951) and Gregory (1968).

Papers on specific issues

Adaptation and after-effects Some classic studies in this area are those of Blakemore and Campbell (1969) and Blakemore and Sutton (1971). A more up-to-date overview can be found in Clifford (2002) or Georgeson (2004).

Contrast sensitivity Two of the more famous studies that show we process images through a series of size-selective mechanisms are Campbell and Robson (1968) and Graham and Nachmias (1971). For a simple overview, see also Campbell and Maffei (1974).

Size The classic experiment using adaptation is that of Blakemore *et al.* (1972). For another way of considering whether you can work out what size something really is, try Burbeck and Regan (1983).

Neural basis of adaptation How do cells adapt? Why do cells adapt? Try Movshon and Lennie (1979), Ohzawa *et al.* (1982), Carandini (2000), and Georgeson (2004). More recently there have been reports of adaptation taking place earlier in the visual system than previously thought; see Solomon *et al.* (2004).

Visual illusions For some explanations of illusions, try Gregory (1997) and Eagleman (2001). There will be a lot more on illusions in Chapter 11, where we consider the relationship between what we see and how we interact with things, but for now see Glover (2002).

● POSSIBLE ESSAY TITLES, TUTORIALS, AND QUESTIONS OF INTEREST

1 Describe and explain the tilt after-effect.

2 Adaptation is a common phenomenon in both humans and single cells. Does it serve any useful purpose?

3 How do we judge the size of a particular object?

4 Describe three visual illusions. What have they told us about our visual processes?

References

Blakemore, C. and Campbell, F. W. (1969). On the existence of neurones in the human visual system selectively sensitive to the orientation and size of retinal images. *Journal of Physiology (London)* **203**, 237–260.

Blakemore, C. B. and Sutton, P. (1971). Size adaptation: a new after-effect. *Science* **166**, 245–247.

Blakemore, C., Garner, E. T., and Sweet, J. A. (1972). The site of size constancy. *Perception* **1**, 111–119.

Burbeck, C. A. and Regan, D. (1983). Independence of orientation and size in spatial discriminations. *Journal of the Optical Society of America* **73**, 1691–1694.

Campbell, F. W. and Maffei, L. (1974). Contrast and spatial frequency. *Scientific American* **231**, November, 106–113.

Campbell, F. W. and Robson, J. G. (1968). Application of Fourier analysis to the visibility of gratings. *Journal of Physiology (London)* **197**, 551–566.

Carandini, M. (2000). Visual cortex: fatigue and adaptation. *Current Biology* **10**(16), R1–3.

Clifford, C. W. G. (2002). Perceptual adaptation: motion parallels orientation. *Trends in Cognitive Sciences* **6**(3), 136–143.

De Valois, R., Yund, E., and Hepler, N. (1982). The orientation and direction selectivity of cells in macaque visual cortex. *Vision Research* **22**, 531–544.

Eagleman, D. M. (2001). Visual illusions and neurobiology. *Nature Reviews Neuroscience* **2**(12), 920–926.

Georgeson, M. (2004). Visual after-effects: cortical neurons change their tune. *Current Biology* **14**(18), R751–753.

Glover, S. (2002). Visual illusions affect planning but not control. *Trends in Cognitive Sciences* **6**(7), 288–292.

Graham, N. (1989). *Visual pattern analyzers*. New York: Oxford University Press.

Graham, N. and Nachmias, J. (1971). Detection of grating patterns containing two spatial frequencies: a comparison of single-channel and multiple-channel models. *Vision Research* **11**, 251–259.

Gregory, R. L. (1968). Visual illusions. *Scientific American* **219**, November, 66–76.

Gregory, R. L. (1997). Knowledge in perception and illusion. *Philosophical Transactions of the Royal Society of London Series B, Biological Sciences*, **352**(1358), 1121–1127.

Ittelson, W. H. and Kilpatrick, F. P. (1951). Experiments in perception. *Scientific American* 185, August, 50–55.

Mollon, J. D. (1974). After-effects and the brain. *New Scientist*, **61**, 479–482.

Movshon, J. A. and Lennie, P. (1979). Pattern-selective adaptation in visual cortical neurons. *Nature* **278**, 850–852.

Ohzawa, I., Sclar, G. and Freeman, R. D. (1982). Contrast gain control in the cat visual cortex. *Nature* **298**, 266–268.

Solomon, S. G., Peirce, J. W., Dhruv, N. T., and Lennie, P. (2004). Profound contrast adaptation early in the visual pathway. *Neuron* **42**(1), 155–162.

CHAPTER 5
Colour vision

Four examples of the Ishihara plates. Each plate is made up of small circles of differing size and lightness. The colour of some of the circles differs so as to define a target number that the person must read. The changes in the lightness and size of the circles make cues other than colour impossible to use – hence this is a good test of colour perception. People with 'normal' colour vision give the responses of 57, 42, 45, and 'nothing there'. People who lack red cones (protanopes) respond '35, 2, 'nothing there', and 73', and people who lack green cones (deutranopes) respond '35, 4, 'nothing there', and 73'. Due to limitations in reproduction you shouldn't use this example as a definitive test of your vision.

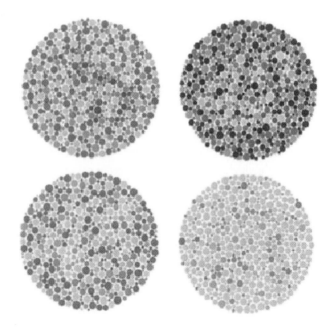

CHAPTER OVERVIEW

The world would be a lot more boring if it weren't for colour. It would be a mistake, though, to think that we have evolved colour vision just to make things look more fun. But we shouldn't take colour vision for granted, as if it must be there for all (including other animals) to see. This is simply not the case, and many of the colours we take for granted are not seen by many other creatures, or indeed by some fellow members of the human species. So why does any animal have colour vision, and why does our own human colour vision differ from that of others? In this chapter we consider the advantages having colour vision gives us, and what happens in humans when it goes wrong. Remarkably, we conclude that our own colour vision is really two colour vision systems, one that we share with many other mammals, and one that evolved far more recently, which we share only with some of our primate cousins.

Introduction

Most of us live in a world full of colours. We use colour to signal danger, to tell us to stop, to 'make a statement', and to notice the embarrassment or illness of our friends and loved ones. However, it's also clear that we can watch a black and white movie and still laugh at Laurel and Hardy, and be frightened by Jimmy Cagney (or the events in the wedding chapel in *Kill Bill*). So why do we need colour vision?

We shall start by asking 'what is colour?' and what kind of information it may convey that is useful over and above the luminance (black-and-white) information that we have considered thus far. We then go on to consider how the retina encodes colour, and what can go wrong when it does not do so in a normal fashion – the case of colour blindness. Finally, we will talk about colour processing beyond the retina and some interesting, but rare, conditions in which colour vision is affected as a result of brain damage.

What is colour, and why would you want to see it?

Colour vision (like all aspects of our vision) has evolved over millions of years. We shall take the old-fashioned view that the colour system that we have today is the result of evolutionary pressures and natural selection, but if you prefer you can call this 'God'.

Imagine a world a long time ago. In this long-forgotten world there lives a pond creature, we'll call him Percy, who has already evolved a vision system that can distinguish light from dark, but doesn't have colour vision. What useful information would Percy get from evolving colour vision? Why have so many other creatures evolved this ability?

The nature of light

Before we can answer this question of what is colour good for, we need to think a bit about light. This sounds like a job for a physicist, a proper scientist who you might expect to give you a straight answer. But no, physicists tell us that light comes along in little packets, called photons, and the number of packets arriving at any one time determines the **intensity** of the light. Light is just one form of electromagnetic radiation, and occupies only a small portion of the electromagnetic spectrum (Figure 5.1). Notice that as the wavelength changes we move from radio waves through microwaves to X-rays and gamma rays. But what is the wavelength of this radiation if it comes along in little packets, we ask our physicist. At this point the physicist mumbles, avoids eye-contact and runs hard-bitten fingernails through lank, greasy hair. In fact, most physicists will do this even if you don't ask them a hard question. However, it turns out that they have two ways of considering light; it can be thought of as a stream of photons (photons are the light version of more general energy packets called quanta) but it can also be considered as a wave energy (Figure 5.2). The distance between the peaks of the waves is termed the **wavelength** of the radiation. The wavelengths emitted can vary massively, from fractions of a millionth of a millimetre to many kilometres. There is only a difference in wavelength between radio waves (have you ever listened to a programme on long wave radio, where the waves are around 1500 m long?) and X-rays. Other parts of the electromagnetic spectrum can be used to heat up our baked beans (microwaves) and give us a sun tan and skin cancer (ultraviolet). Look carefully at Figure 5.1 and you'll notice that nestling between infrared and ultraviolet is a little strip called 'visible light'. This is the bit we are interested in.

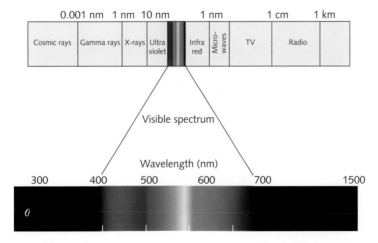

Fig. 5.1. The electromagnetic spectrum and visible light.

From the physicist's point of view, there is nothing particularly special about this visible spectrum that makes it visible – it is visible because of our physiology. If we had a different physiology we would 'see' a different part of the spectrum. So we are not being very politically correct to call the visible part of the spectrum the visible spectrum. We might be accused of being horribly species-ist. One could imagine a creature on some distant planet Zarg whose visual system is excited by the part of the spectrum we call gamma rays. Our Zargian equivalents writing their textbook on Zargian vision would presumably have a diagram where the 'visible spectrum' is over to the left side of the electromagnetic spectrum and the region we call visible would be invisible to them. Indeed, we do not have to travel as far as Zarg to find creatures that can see parts of the spectrum that we cannot. Many snakes (Figure 5.3) can sense radiation in the infrared part of the spectrum, which is produced by warm objects (such as small furry creatures). One example is the sidewinder snake, which has given its name to a type of missile that also senses infrared emissions. To the snake, the infrared radiation makes warm objects seem to 'glow' in the dark. Figure 5.4 shows just one such small furry creature glowing in the infrared. Thus, the snake can see its prey in the dark. So why can't we see in the

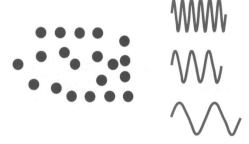

Fig. 5.2. Light can be thought of either as particles, or as a wave.

Fig. 5.3. The green tree python – a snake that uses infrared vision. Note the pit organs on its upper mandible.

infrared, if it's such a good idea? The answer is that we have warm blood, and we have blood vessels in our retina. These would glow in the dark too, and all we would see would be the glow from our own eyes. The military make night-sight devices that transform infrared radiation into visible radiation, thus allowing human bodies or hot engines to be seen in the dark.

Many birds and insects can see in the ultraviolet (UV) part of the spectrum. This allows them to see patterns, for example in flowers, which are invisible to humans and to mammals in general. Figure 5.5 shows some common flowers which, when photographed

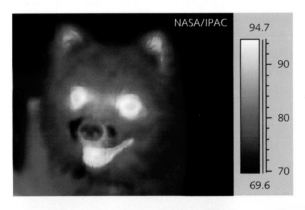

Fig. 5.4. A dog photographed in the infrared part of the spectrum. This is what a snake might see. The 'hot' bits will be the bits not covered in fur, e.g. the eyes and mouth. Note that this dog has a cold nose, a sure sign of good health.

Fig. 5.5. The flowers on the left are photographed in visible light, those on the right show the UV markings. These flowers have petally bits round the outside that reflect UV while the bits in the middle, known to biologists as the naughty bits, absorb the UV and so stand out prominently, allowing them to be detected easily by the insects they rely on for their pollination.

with film that is sensitive to UV light, have a striking pattern. This pattern is visible only to those birds and insects that see in the UV, and they are consequently attracted to the flowers. This is why you may have noticed UV lights in butchers' shops – they attract the flies, which are then electrocuted. The common bluetit (Figure 5.6) should really be called the 'ultraviolet tit' as its blue coloration is far more striking in the UV region of the spectrum (Figure 5.7). So why can't we see in the UV? The answer is that it is damaging to our eyes, and is filtered out by them. This filtering out is only partial, and therefore if we go into high-UV environments such as high mountains or tropical sunshine, we need to wear sunglasses that block UV. Birds and insects generally have shorter lives than we do, so their eyes are damaged less by UV light.

Let's look a bit closer at the bit of the spectrum that we, in our species-ist way, call the visible spectrum (we shall call it 'light' for short). Figure 5.8 shows what happens when white light (such as sunlight) is passed through a prism which splits the light so that the different wavelengths now have slightly different paths. What we see is the visible spectrum spread out before us. When this happens in nature, when sunlight is split up by little prisms called raindrops, we see a 'rainbow' of colours (Figure 5.9). At the long-wavelength end, the light appears red (not unreasonable, as it is next to infrared – *infra* is the Latin for below) and then as wavelength gets shorter, the light colour appears to go

Fig. 5.6. A pair of tits.

Fig. 5.7. A bluetit photographed in ultraviolet light. Notice how its distinctive coloration is still clearly visible in this part of the spectrum, which is invisible to us but visible to other birds.

BOX
5.1

Colour vision in different animals

It is well known that humans have three types of cone, and that implies that three lights can be mixed to produce any colour we want – the three lights have to stimulate the cones to the same extent as the desired colour.

What about other animals? First, let's think about the pros and cons of having colour vision.

As you will now appreciate, there is a large cost associated with colour vision. So what animals can we most expect *not* to bother with having colour vision? These would be:

- animals without a complex central nervous system (e.g. earthworm, limpet)
- nocturnal animals which need high sensitivity (e.g. cat, bat)
- animals living in an environment without much colour to be seen (deep-sea fish).

What about animals that do have colour vision?

Of the mammals, only some primates (monkeys and apes) have the same colour vision as we do. Other mammals, and some primates (see main text) have two receptor types, one a bit like the average of our red and green cones (thus, a 'yellow' cone), and blue cones. So, reds cannot be distinguished very well from greens. Thus, a red rag will not be much different from a green rag to a bull!

Many other animals have colour vision. Insects, birds, fish, and crustaceans (e.g. shrimps) have excellent colour vision. In the case of insects and birds, this includes a cone with peak sensitivity in the UV part of the spectrum that we don't see at all. Since one presumes that insects co-evolved with flowers, many flowers have vivid patterns that are only visible in UV radiation (e.g. celandine or bindweed; see Figure 5.5).

As we have also seen, other species, such as some snakes, can see infrared (IR) radiation, which we simply feel as heat but have no visual response to. It would be very useful for us to see IR, and in

Fig. 5.1.1. Eyes of mantis shrimp – champion of the colour vision world? This shrimp has more than 10 different types of cone.

fact the military use night-sights that work in IR so they can see the enemy in the dark. Here's a curious fact: chlorophyll (the green stuff in plants that allows carbon dioxide to be transformed into sugar during photosynthesis) reflects much light around 560 nm in wavelength, which is why it looks green to us. But it actually reflects even more in the near IR part of the spectrum, around 900 nm, to which we are blind. So grass is really IR, not green – if only we could see it. But when you walk on grass you squash it, breaking the cell walls in the stalks. This coats the grass with water. Water absorbs IR; so if someone walks on dry grass, and you look at the grass through IR night-sights such as those used by the military, you will see dark footprints on the lawn! Useful, eh?

Finally, there are some real oddities. There is a type of shrimp (mantis shrimp – see Figure 5.1.1) that has over 10 types of cone. What seems to be happening here is that this shrimp recognizes things by their spectral reflectance property – rather than putting its effort into seeing shape, it sees a totally fuzzy shape of some object that gets defined by its precise colour.

Fig. 5.8. 'White' light is split by a prism into many different colours.

through the colours of the rainbow; remember Richard Of York Gave Battle In Vain: red, orange, yellow, green, blue, indigo, and violet. Beyond violet is ultraviolet and, comfortingly, *ultra* is the Latin for beyond. Have you ever heard of indigo, though? Isaac Newton, who first showed that white light is composed of these different colours (see below), wanted to show that there are seven basic colours (like the seven notes on the piano) and needed to include indigo to make the arithmetic work.

Fig. 5.9. A rainbow over Sir Isaac Newton's house, Woolsthorpe Manor. In 1665 Cambridge University was closed because of the plague and Newton returned to his family farmhouse. It was here that he conducted investigations into the nature of light.

Our Sun emits enormous quantities of electromagnetic radiation, including lots in the visible spectrum. When all these wavelengths come along jumbled up together the light looks white, but remember that it is really a mixture of all the colours of the rainbow (including indigo). A 'green' leaf will look green to us because the leaf absorbs all the red and blue wavelengths and just reflects the green stuff. A red bus absorbs green and blue (and some of the orange and violet as well) and reflects red. So this colour business seems pretty easy; light of a particular wavelength enters our eye and we translate it into its appropriate colour. Er, well, not exactly. Remember Chapter 2 – brightness turned out to be a bit more than just the intensity of the light, and it's going to be the same again with colour. The key thing to remember now is that, as Sir Isaac Newton famously said '*the rays are not colour'd*' – colour is an invention of your brain. We will see later in this chapter just how the brain invents this colour. But, for now, let us return to our primitive creature (Percy) sploshing around the primordial swamp with the most rudimentary visual system.

A single-cone system – monochromatic vision

Our pond creature, Percy, is going to have to build his colour visual system from scratch. The first thing he will need to do is to detect the light, and we know from Chapter 1 that we can do this by having a photoreceptor. Percy is going to rely on sunlight, and although

BOX 5.2

Trichromacy, colour matching, and primary colours

Long before we were able to record from individual cones within the retina, we already knew about trichromacy. This is because of colour-matching experiments in which the observer has to mix lights in order to try to match a single wavelength of light (see Figure 5.2.1). If we only give observers one light with which to match the test light they can turn the intensity of their light up and down but it will never look the same colour as the test light. If we give them two lights (of different wavelengths) there are some situations where they can mix their two lights to match a single wavelength, but there are many other occasions on which this is impossible. However, when we give them three lights, all of different wavelengths, to mix together then they can achieve a match to any single wavelength, given time and patience. Indeed, this idea that we can simply mix together three colours to simulate any colour is essential to colour TV. If you splash a little water on to the screen (careful) and view the screen through one of the droplets which now acts as a magnifying glass, you will see that the screen is made of a series of three types of dot, one red, one green, and one blue. By varying the intensity of each of the triplets of dots any particular colour is reproduced. It must be remembered that there are three phosphors on the TV screen because we have three cones in our visual system – not because of any physical property of light. If we had four cone types then we would need four such dots, and if we had only two cone types (and some people do – see main text) then we would need only two dots. Further, it is often thought that 'red', 'green', and 'blue' are somehow special (**primary colours**). They are not – any three colours that are reasonably spread across the spectrum can be used.

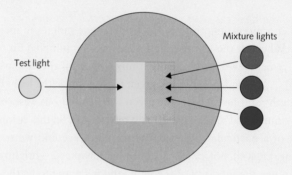

Fig. 5.2.1. Colour matching. A monochromatic yellow can be matched by a combination of red, green, and blue primaries. In this case yellow is matched by a mixture of red and green with little contribution from the blue primary.

A second confusion in making colours from other colours concerns **colour addition** versus **colour subtraction**. In the experiments described above we are mixing lights – i.e. adding. So when we add red and green light we get yellow (see Figure 5.2.2). However, if we mix together red and green paint we get something very different – sludgy brown. That is because paint works by absorbing light – i.e. subtraction. So printers often use the 'primary' colours of cyan, magenta, and yellow to make colour pictures. This often leads art students to believe that the primary colours are blue (because it looks a bit like cyan), magenta (because it looks a bit like red), and yellow (because it looks a lot like yellow). Again, these colours are used for convenience – none of them is primary to any other colour. Each subtractive primary works by absorbing one band of wavelengths. Thus, yellow paint absorbs blue light and can thus be thought of as a '– B' primary. Magenta absorbs green light and is therefore a '– G' primary. Cyan absorbs red light and is therefore a '– R' primary. So R, G, and B are primaries in both systems, but in the case of subtractive systems (paints, dyes, filters) one must put in the minus sign. So, mixing – R, – G, and – B together gives you . . . black!

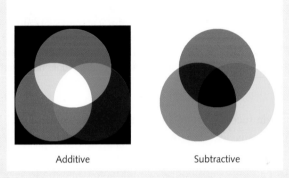

Additive   Subtractive

Fig. 5.2.2. Colour mixing.

the sun emits light of a huge range of wavelengths, most of the surface of the earth reflects light with a peak around 550–560 nm, since chlorophyll, the stuff that makes plants look green, reflects most light at that wavelength. Thus it will make sense if Percy has a photoreceptor that responds best to wavelengths around 550–560 nm. For convenience we'll call this our 'yellow' detector, and we'll put the peak of its sensitivity at 550 nm. Incidentally, to our eyes 550 nm is more a limey-green but never mind, because Percy wouldn't call it yellow or limey-green, and not just because he has no linguistic ability. Figure 5.10 illustrates to what extent a single receptor can detect the different wavelengths of light. If you look back to Chapter 1 you'll see that the photoreceptors we're talking about here are the cones, so we'll call this single receptor type our 'yellow cone'. Now this yellow cone doesn't just respond to one wavelength of light; it is sensitive to light over much of the spectrum, but is less and less sensitive as the wavelength moves away from 550–560 nm. So light of 480 nm is signalled only about half as efficiently as light of 560 nm. The same is true for light of 620 nm. Light of wavelengths under 450 nm or over 650 nm is not signalled by this cone at all.

Now this leaves Percy with a problem. What if he had two lights – one of 550 nm of intensity X, and one of wavelength 480 nm but of twice the intensity ($2X$)? Because the light at 480 nm is twice as intense, but Percy's sensitivity is only half that to a light of 550 nm, the yellow cone should respond in exactly the same manner to these two lights. So to Percy these two lights would appear identical, even though they differ in both wavelength and intensity!

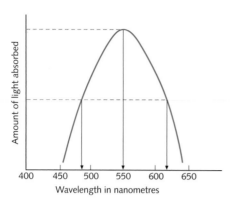

Fig. 5.10. Absorption of light by a single cone. Note that it absorbs light most efficiently at around 550 nm; by about 450 nm at the lower end and 650 nm at the upper end its efficiency falls to zero (i.e. it does not absorb any light).

A little more thought (actually quite a lot of thought for some of you) should bring you to the realization that any wavelength of light could be adjusted in intensity so as to produce exactly the same response in the cone as any other wavelength does – one whose wavelength is absorbed only very poorly would have to be made very intense, and one which is well absorbed would be far dimmer. The problem that we face here has a posh name – the principle of univariance (see Box 5.3). This means that our receptor can only vary its response in one way (*uni*-variance, get it?), that is, it can increase or decrease its magnitude of response. However, the stimulus can vary over two dimensions (intensity and wavelength). Therefore the receptor can't distinguish changes in intensity from changes in wavelength. A single photoreceptor-type always suffers from this problem. In fact under conditions of very little light (such as at night) we also only have one type of photoreceptor working – the rods – and hence we (the humans who are reading this book) also cannot tell the difference between changes in intensity or changes in wavelength under these conditions. Our solution is to simply disregard the wavelength information and 'see' an image that appears in shades of grey, and that's why we can't see colours under very dim conditions. So if Percy wants to disentangle intensity and wavelength information and his one cone type cannot do this, then the solution seems simple – get a second type of cone.

A two-cone system – dichromatic vision

What should Percy's second cone do? Clearly, this cone should be markedly different from his other cone in the wavelength to which it is most sensitive, otherwise there would be little point in having it. Since the existing cone responds best to wavelengths around 550 nm (which is a bit on the long side of the visible spectrum), Percy's new cone could respond to shorter wavelengths, which look blue to us – so we'll call this the 'blue' cone (Figure 5.11). What advantage does this give to Percy? By looking at the ratio of activity in these two cones (we shall discuss how we do this later) we can now discriminate many

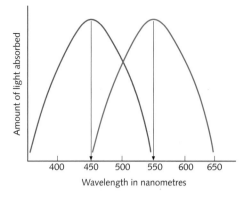

Fig. 5.11. A dichromatic system with a second cone type that absorbs light most efficiently at around 450 nm.

| BOX 5.3 | **The principle of univariance, colour vision, and domestic plumbing** |

Imagine a primitive bathroom. You will only have to imagine this if you live in the USA or Germany; for everyone else, just think of your bathroom. The bath tub has a tap (faucet) (Figure 5.3.1). You turn the tap on and cold water comes out. Turning the tap further makes more water come out. It is still cold. All this tap can do is to increase or decrease the amount of water coming out of it.

Fig. 5.3.1. One tap.

Individual nerve cells in the retina, the visual pathway or indeed anywhere in the brain are just like your cold water tap. Their rate of firing, how much they're turned on, can signal just one thing, like more or less light, just as your tap can produce more or less cold water.

Now, the sophisticated amongst you will know that it's possible to have more than just a trickle or a torrent of water; it can be hot or cold. And if you're really clever, you can get water in a whole spectrum of temperatures from very cold, through just nice and warm to scalding hot. So now you want your tap to do two things, you want it to be able to increase and decrease the amount of water and you want to vary the temperature. And you can't do that with just one tap with a twiddly knob on the top. In terms of the nervous system this demonstrates the **principle of univariance**: if your nerve cell can only increase or decrease its firing rate, it can only signal one dimension. It can't, for example, signal both luminance and wavelength information.

Back to the bathroom. The solution to getting hot water is to get a second tap (Figure 5.3.2). Now you can have hot water coming out of one (and you can write H on the top of it) and cold water coming out of the other (it's the one with C on it, unless you're in France where the hot tap is the one with C on it. You'd think they could at least get that right.)

This two-tap system works pretty well. In fact it works so well that more primitive societies don't get beyond this stage. If you want to know how much water is going into your bath, because you want to make a phone call before the bath overflows, then you estimate the amount of water coming out of the cold tap and add in the amount you estimate is coming out of the hot tap (H + C). This gives the total amount of water going into the bath. If you want to know the temperature of your bath water you calculate how much cold water is coming out of the cold tap and how much hot water is coming of the hot tap and then figure out the ratio of these two quantities (H/C). If you're really smart you'll realize that this ratio leaves us with a problem. What if we add no cold water? The ratio H/C becomes infinitely large and the bath temperature infinitely hot. If you've ever stepped into a bath when you didn't add cold water you might think this is an accurate description, but for the sticklers amongst you a better ratio for the bath temperature might be (H/(H + C). That is, the proportion of the total water that is hot.

Fig. 5.3.2. Two separate taps.

But there is an easier way and it's called the mixer tap (Figure 5.3.3). In its simplest form the mixer tap comprises a twiddly knob for the cold water, a different twiddly knob for the hot water, and one nozzle for the combined water. This system works well; the amount of water coming out of the nozzle is already the combined (H + C) and sticking your toe under this stream gives a direct measure of temperature (H/C).

Let's add just one last development to our bathroom. Suppose you adjust the hot and cold knobs on your mixer tap to get your bath or shower temperature just right, that is you're happy with (H/C), but you want to increase the total amount of water, that is you want to increase (H + C). As soon as we twiddle the hot knob to increase H we upset the fine balance of (H/C). The solution is known in the trade as a single-lever monobloc mixer (Figure 5.3.4). We now have what looks like a single tap with a lever on top rather than a twiddly knob. Pulling the lever up increases the water flow (H + C) while moving the lever to left or right alters the ratio of hot and cold water and hence the temperature (H/C). The clever thing here is that two separate controls operate at right angles (or orthogonally) to each other. Moving the lever along the x-axis changes only the temperature – the volume of water stays the same. Moving the lever along the y-axis changes the volume of water without affecting the temperature. Brilliant!

Fig. 5.3.3. Mixer tap.

Fig. 5.3.4. Monobloc mixer tap.

Why are we telling you all this? Because this is just the way your visual system encodes information about the amount of light that's out there, the luminance, and the wavelength (colour) of that light. Rather than a hot and cold tap we have red and green cones. Adding the output of these cones together (R + G) gives us a measure of the luminance, and taking the ratio of their output (R/G) tells us about colour.

forms of natural green vegetation which differ mainly in how much 'blue' light they reflect. Figure 5.12a shows a monochrome picture of vegetation; note that it's hard to distinguish some of the plants, whereas Figure 5.12b shows the colours of the picture as they would be seen by Percy with two cones. Note that many of the individual plants can stand out because of the difference in 'colour'. Also, the sky will be very different from the ground, so Percy acquires a source of knowledge about which way is 'up'; useful to an aquatic creature, and sometimes to first-year students after a heavy night's entertainment.

This simple form of colour vision is so useful that nearly all mammals (cats, dogs, even bulls) have a simple two-cone system. There are some single-cone mammals, however – nocturnal animals such as bushbabies, raccoons, and kinkajous (whatever they are) – as well as whales and seals. For a fascinating discussion of these matters, see Peichl (2005).

Now Percy has a nice colour vision system – but is there a price to be paid? Well, one problem is that we will have to get rid of some of the yellow cones so that we can put in the blue ones. However, introducing the new cone type into many retinal locations would reduce Percy's visual acuity. Acuity is the degree to which fine detail can be resolved – it's what your optician measures to determine whether you need spectacles (see Chapter 4). The more cones we can pack into our retina, the better our acuity should be, in exactly the same way that your 5 megapixel digital camera gives sharper pictures than a 1 megapixel camera. Acuity results from the brain getting different signals from neighbouring cones in the retina, but the neighbouring cones must be of the same type for a valid comparison to be possible. Consequently, the introduction of large numbers of the new blue cones into the retina would compromise acuity. So how best can Percy gain the benefits of colour vision without compromising his luminance acuity? The cunning solution to this problem is to introduce only a few of the new cones, so as not to reduce his yellow cone acuity too much. In fact Percy wouldn't have any blue cones in his fovea, the area where acuity is highest and of paramount importance. This means the acuity of his colour vision will not be very high, and inspection of Figure 5.12 shows that although the various bushes might now be more easily visible in the coloured scene, the fine detail is lost. When you were a kid you might have done some 'painting by numbers'. The lines were nice and sharp and you slopped some colour roughly into the right places. That's what this colour vision system is like (see Figure 5.13).

There's an additional and rather neat reason why there's no need to have many blue cones. Short-wave light (blue and violet) is always out of focus in the eye. This results from a defect common to most optical systems. This defect has a name – chromatic

Fig. 5.12. (a) A monochrome scene with vegetation. (b) The same scene as seen by a creature with a two-cone colour vision system.

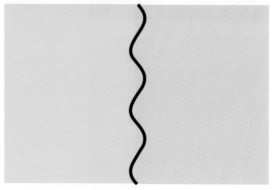

Fig. 5.13. Edwardian monochrome postcard of London, hand-coloured. If you look closely you can see that the colour is added in an approximate manner and yet, from a distance, it looks appropriate. The lower picture shows that colour information is not very spatially precise. If you stand back a little from this picture, or look slightly to one side, you will see that the colour information 'melts' into the wavy contour.

aberration – but all you need to know about it here is that it results in out-of-focus blue light. You have probably seen examples of this – a blue or violet neon sign at night usually looks fuzzy, as do those violet-plus-UV lights in dance clubs that make your underwear glow (because of agents called whiteners that are added to fabrics and washing powders to make them look brighter – you don't need to know that either). So, if the image is fuzzy anyway, you don't need many cones that respond to that wavelength because there is no fine detail to be encoded – it has all been lost in the fuzz. This does not matter – the two-colour image still allows you to distinguish the different plants in Figure 5.12, know which way up you are, and spot underwear glowing in a club (although Percy doesn't need this last bit).

Two important points have emerged from this discussion. First, that a useful degree of colour vision is possible if animals have a cone peaking at around 550 nm and another one with a peak sensitivity at shorter wavelengths, say 420–450 nm. Second, that this second cone will be inserted sparsely into the retina and therefore only respond to coarse detail. What would the world look like to this animal? Its fovea would have no colour vision, since it contains only one type of cone. In the rest of the visual field, it would have a high-acuity representation of luminance (intensity) information, and an overlay of coarse colour information that would allow it to distinguish yellowish light from bluish light.

A three-cone system – trichromatic vision

Imagine that Percy tries out his new cone for a few million years and likes it, because it allows him to make judgements about the colours of things and this helps with recognizing the objects. Let's think how he might be better (or possibly worse) off if another new cone were added to his visual system. The question is: what wavelengths should Percy's third cone respond to?

The way to think about this problem is to consider whether there is any task that is important for survival, and is impossible, or at least very difficult, with either a one-cone or a two-cone yellow–blue system. According to the vision scientist John Mollon, there is one such task: finding a cherry on a cherry-tree. More generally, finding a red or yellow fruit against a background of dappled foliage (i.e. some leaves in bright light, and some in shadow) is extremely difficult without a new type of colour mechanism. Now some of you will be thinking (as usual) of sex; surely it's worth asking whether better colour vision would help you get more, better, and more fruitful sex. And by 'fruitful' we don't mean some perversion with bananas but sex that results in pregnancy. It is worth noting that many animals, mainly primates, signal their sexual readiness by colours in their faces or on their genitals (Figure 5.14). Some female primates' nether quarters change colour dramatically through their menstrual cycle, revealing to the perceptive male when they are most fertile. So, clearly, having a good colour vision system might get you more than just ripe fruit.

Fig. 5.14. Some primates use the colour of their behinds to signal sexual readiness.

While you ponder this, consider Figure 5.15 which shows a piece of fruit hiding in some leaves – quite a normal place for fruit to be hiding. The fruit is difficult to see in both the monochrome and the yellow–blue versions of the picture, but in the red–green picture it is clearly visible. This picture is based on there being two different types of cone (which we shall term the red and the green cones) where previously there had been just the yellow cone. The way in which the yellow–blue and red–green properties of the image are worked out in the brain is considered in detail later in this chapter. For now, you should just notice that having this new cone type allows more objects to be distinguished from each other. This new, red–green, representation has another remarkable property – notice that it gets rid of the dappled shadows on the leaves. So, with this new system, the brain can work out that all these objects (leaves), which vary randomly in luminance, are actually all the same stuff, and are different from the red fruit.

In order to transform our dichromatic yellow–blue system into a trichromatic (three-cone) system, we take the yellow cone and split it into two new cone types with rather similar sensitivities (a division that happened a mere 30–40 million years ago, according to the evidence from our genes). So we now have three cone types, sensitive to short, medium, and long wavelengths of light – and these are affectionately, if somewhat inaccurately, often called the blue, green, and red cones. Figure 5.16 shows their wavelength sensitivities, as well as that of the rods. Inspection of this figure will show you that the cones' peak sensitivities are not equally spaced across the spectrum, and that the red and green cones have sensitivity peaks at very similar wavelengths. This trichromatic system, which most humans enjoy, is actually rather rare in the animal kingdom. Within the family of mammals, most of whom are dichromats, we humans share our trichromacy only with some other primates. That is not to say that you can't have more than three cone types: most birds, for example, have four different kinds of cone (including a UV-sensitive one), and there are shrimps with ten or more cone types. Delicious.

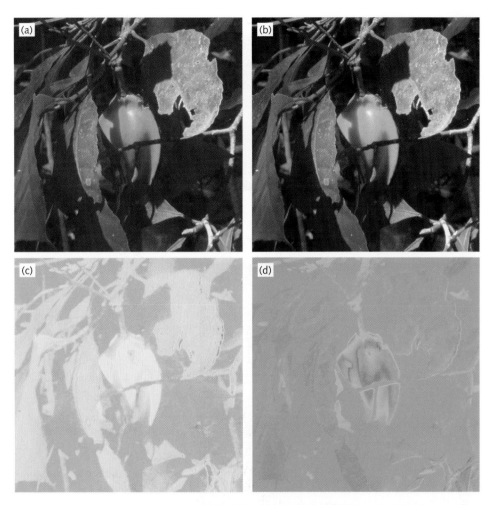

Fig. 5.15. (a) Fruit eaten by monkeys in the African rain forest. (b) The same fruit in monochrome, now harder to detect. (c) The fruit as it would appear to a dichromatic monkey. The fruit is now more visible but the dappled foliage still makes it hard to see. (d) The fruit as seen by the red–green vision system of a trichromatic monkey. Now the fruit is easily visible and the dappled foliage is now uniform.

We now have clever techniques to see the distribution of cones (and rods) in our own retina. Figure 5.17 attempts to illustrate the distribution of the cone types in the human retina (this is just a mock-up – the cones are actually far smaller than those illustrated). What we can see is that the blue cones are relatively rare compared to the red and green ones (only about 10% are blue). What's more, there appear to be no blue cones at all in the very centre of our vision (the central fovea, marked with an orange circle). As mentioned above, where blue cones are inserted we lose acuity, so it appears that at this point of highest acuity we have sacrificed colour vision in order to maintain the greatest possible spatial acuity.

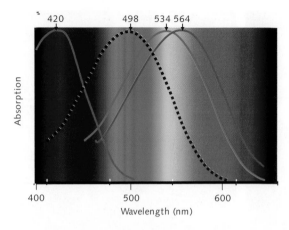

Fig. 5.16. Absorption characteristics of human cones and rods: the absorption spectra of human photopigments, that is the wavelengths that cones and rods are sensitive to, shown on a background of the visible spectrum. Notice how close together the red and green cones are in their sensitivity.

Fig. 5.17. The distribution of red, green, and blue cones in the human retina. Note the absence of blue cones in the central fovea (marked with an orange circle) and their scarcity elsewhere. Also, there are more red cones than green cones, but nobody really understands why.

Comparing activity in cones – colour opponency

So far, we have talked about the need for cones having different sensitivities to different wavelengths of light. Having such different cones allows colours of objects to be seen, but how does this ability to see colour come about? In particular, what does the brain do with the outputs from these cones to allow colour vision to work?

Let's go back to Percy in the days when he had only two types of cone, responding to wavelengths that look yellow and blue respectively. How might his brain use these cones to tell colours apart?

Suppose you have a system in which the outputs of these cones are compared. One possible way would be to compare the ratio of activity in the two cones. For example, if the yellow system were responding 10 times per second and the blue only 5 times per second, this would give us a ratio of 10 : 5, which can be expressed as 2 : 1. Now, if we were simply to double the light intensity, this would make the yellow system respond at 20 times per second and the blue at 10 times per second. The ratio would not change – it would be 20 : 10, or still 2 : 1. This ratio scheme could, therefore, tell us about the relative wavelengths in the light, irrespective of its intensity. Put crudely, this tells us the 'colour' irrespective of the 'brightness'.

Figure 5.18 depicts a scheme based on this ratio idea that seems to be a good description of what the human visual system does. This system provides us with three signals:

- A luminance signal derived by adding the signal from the red and green cones. The blue cones do not seem to provide any input to this.
- A red–green colour signal derived by dividing the output of the red cones and that of the green cones (or vice versa).
- A blue–yellow colour signal derived by dividing the output of the luminance signal (which is the addition of the red and green cones) by the output of the blue cones.

This scheme has a couple of nice points:

First, as we increase the intensity of a light, we increase the response of all cones, *but the colour ratios stay the same*. That is good, because the 'colour' hasn't changed. However, the 'luminance' signal, which derives from the sum of the red and green cones, increases as the light intensity goes up.

Second, as we change the wavelength of a light, the ratio of the two *colour* responses (the boxes called 'red–green' and 'yellow–blue') varies, but the intensity signal is relatively stable (you might argue that if we were to add in the response of the blue cones it would be even more stable – but remember that this would greatly reduce our acuity – see p. 144).

Such a scheme, which encodes colour activation by comparing the activities of the cone types, is known as opponent coding, because responses of two cone types cause opposite changes to the activity of a neuron. For example, the red–green ratio is increased by higher activity from the red cone, and decreased by higher activity in the green cone.

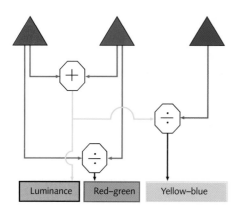

Fig. 5.18. How the outputs of the cones are compared. The outputs from the red and green are combined to form a luminance channel. The red–green system compares the output from the red and the green cones. The blue–yellow system compares the output of the blue cones with the combined output of the red and green systems.

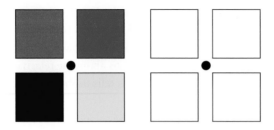

Fig. 5.19. Colour after-effect. Stare at the dot in the centre of the four coloured squares for around 30 seconds, then shift your gaze to the dot in the centre of the four white squares. What do you see?

A classic demonstration of colour opponency is the colour after-effect. If you stare at the centre black dot on the left of Figure 5.19 for about 30 seconds and then shift your gaze over to the centre of the white squares on the right, you should see that the white squares no longer appear white. Instead, each box appears tinged in a particular colour. The one in the top left should appear green. Note that when you were looking at the original picture on the left, this box was red. So adaptation to red causes white to appear green, and by the same process green causes red, blue causes yellow, and yellow causes blue. Essentially, adapting a patch of retina to a given colour reduces the sensitivity to that colour, and 'swings' each opponent channel towards its opposite extreme. You might also remember from Chapter 2 that you can get a black after-effect from adapting to white and vice versa.

An early argument, dating back to Ewald Hering in the nineteenth century, is that there are four, rather than three, 'psychological primary colours'. He pointed out that it's possible to see 'pure' yellow (which appears to contain no green or red coloration); also 'pure' red (without yellow or blue), green (without yellow or blue), and blue (without green or red), but that you never see a reddy-green or a bluey-yellow. This subjective, but generally accepted, observation is supported by there being four extreme states of the opponent signals.

Colour-opponent cells

Given this opponent colour scheme, we should therefore expect that there will be cells somewhere in the visual system that behave in this manner. For example, we should find cells that increase their response as the light excites the green cones more, but decrease their response as the light excites the red cones more (we could term this a G+/R− cell). What is the evidence from neurophysiology? Colour opponent cells have been found in many animals, and Figure 5.20 illustrates some from the LGN of macaque monkeys. In our discussion of the LGN in Chapter 2 we said that colour vision was carried by the parvocellular layers of the LGN but not by the magnocellular layers, and sure enough it is the cells in the parvocellular layers that show this red–green colour opponency. However, much more recent evidence has suggested that the blue–yellow colour signal might have its own special pathway through the LGN (and indeed even earlier) using cells located in

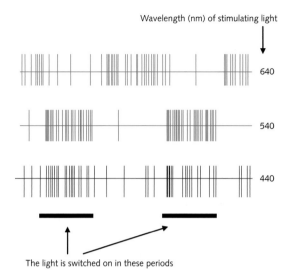

Wavelength (nm) of stimulating light

640

540

440

The light is switched on in these periods

Fig. 5.20. Response of a primate retinal ganglion cell to lights of different wavelengths. Black bars at the bottom of the figure show when the stimulating light comes on. This cell fires vigorously in response to green and is inhibited by red.

between the layers of the parvocellular system. This has become known as the koniocellular pathway and may represent a unique pathway devoted to the blue–yellow colour vision system that is quite distinct from the red–green system (see also Chapter 1).

Two-colour vision systems

So the evidence from our genes, and from recording from cells in the LGN and beyond, all points to the startling fact that we actually have two colour vision systems. The evolutionarily very old one that we seem to share with our pet dogs and cats is based on the comparison of the blue cones to the other cones, and the more recent one, found in primates, compares the output of red and green cones and may be useful in detecting such things as fruit (which may explain why your pet dog or cat shows so little interest in fruit).

How do we know that our red–green system of colour vision was developed for finding fruit in trees? In a very elegant ecological study, scientists travelled to the tropical rainforest and found that a species of monkey that lives there likes to eat a particular yellowish fruit that grows in the trees. They measured the wavelength distribution of the light coming from the fruit, as well as from the surrounding leaves. They also measured the wavelength sensitivity of the red and green cones in the retina of the monkey. They found that the spacing of the cone sensitivity curves was optimal for the discrimination of the 'fruit' signal from the 'leaf' signal. Small changes in the cone response curves would make the cones less optimal at this task. Later research, carried out by one of the authors of this book, confirmed that the other advantage of the red–green system is its shadow-removing property (see Figure 5.15). It also showed how much worse than monkeys we humans are at getting up trees – see Figure 5.21 which shows the shaky start of the first attempt at a 100-foot tree climb.

Fig. 5.21. Vision scientist climbing tree.

Colour blindness

If you have three different types of cone in your retina, red, green, and blue – and you probably do – then you are what we call a trichromat. Although this is true for most people, there are individuals who lack one or more of these types of cone and these people are said, usually wrongly, to be colour blind. Wrongly, because if you lack one type of cone that means that you still have two types of cone, which means that you can distinguish between all wavelength combinations that excite these two cones to different degrees – in other words, you can distinguish lots of colours (just like a dog, or Percy Mark 2) but you will not be able to distinguish between certain pairs of colours that are distinguishable to a normal trichromat. To have no colour vision at all, you would need to have only one type of photoreceptor and this is extremely rare. However, the partial or total lack of one cone type (leaving you with only two cones – dichromats) is less rare, and here we list the types of possible loss and their prevalence among humans.

- The total lack of red (long-wave) cones is called protanopia, and a person with such a condition is called a protanope.

- The total lack of green (medium-wave) cones is called deuteranopia, and people with this condition are called deuteranopes.

- It is also possible to suffer from a total lack of blue (short-wave) cones; this is called tritanopia and people with this condition are called tritanopes.

If you're wondering where these weird names come from it means you haven't bene-fited from a classical education; the names derive from the Greek for first, second, and third. Think *prototype, Deuteronomy* (the second book of law, although confusingly it's the fifth book in the Bible), and *triangle*.

It is also possible to have a partial loss of each cone type, in which case the person concerned is called an anomalous trichromat. If there is a lack of red cones the person is called protanomalous, whereas a partial lack of green cones leads to a deuteranomalous observer. These conditions can be genetically inherited, and the table below shows the relative incidence of these congenital conditions.

Type of deficiency	Frequency in men (%)	Frequency in women (%)
Protanopia	1	0.01
Protanomaly	1	0.03
Deuteranopia	1	0.01
Deuteranomaly	5	0.35
Tritanopia	<0.01	<0.01
Total	8	0.40

It is clear that the prevalence of congenital colour defects is much higher in men than women, and that a sizeable minority of men have some kind of deficiency.

Congenital tritanopia (lack of blue, or short-wave, cones) is much rarer and has been estimated to be between 0.01% and about 0.4% (Birch 1993), whereas the total absence of cones, called rod monochromacy, has an incidence around 0.0003% in both men and women. No figures exist for how many people have only one kind of cone, but there are rare reports of such individuals.

It is also possible to acquire a colour-vision defect; in particular, the blue (short-wave) cones are vulnerable to diseases such as diabetes (and, beware, taking drugs), and indeed colour-vision screening may give an indication of the presence of such pathologies.

What is it like to be a dichromat? A simple approximation to the answer can be seen in Figure 5.22. Here, we have removed the red and green components from a composite red–green–blue version of an everyday image, to simulate the relatively common forms of dichromacy: protanopia and deuteranopia. It should be clear why the term 'colour blindness' is a misleading one, since plenty of colours are still visible. In fact, dichromatic observers are less susceptible to certain kinds of camouflage (see Figure 5.23) that were

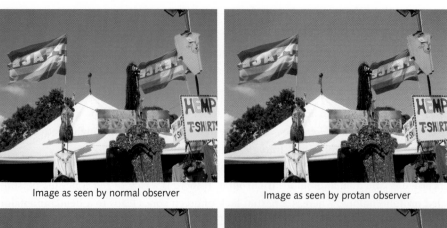

Image as seen by normal observer   Image as seen by protan observer

Image as seen by deutan observer   Image as seen by tritan observer

Fig. 5.22. Simulations of dichromacy. Notice how red colours look very dark to the protanope.

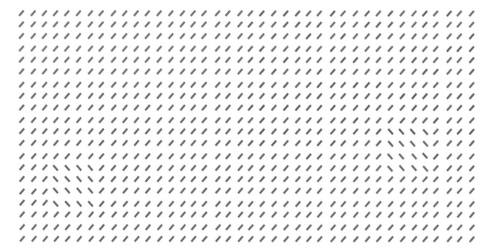

Fig. 5.23. Random colours can serve to camouflage a target. The left-tilting line segments are easily detected in the left side of this image, but when random colour is added (right-hand side) these line segments are harder to detect.

designed to fool colour-normal observers, and this resulted in the use of dichromatic people for camouflage-breaking tasks in World War II.

It is also interesting here to note a difference between New World monkeys (those found in Central and South America), as opposed to the Old World monkeys (in Africa and Asia). The Old World ones are all trichromatic, with the exception of a few 'colour-blind' individuals. However, among New World monkeys, all the males are dichromats (i.e. only have a functioning blue–yellow system). Half of the females are trichromatic, the other half being dichromatic like the males. There is only one exception to this, the red howler monkey, where all males and females are trichromatic. We do not understand much about how these monkeys with very different vision share out tasks, and exploring such issues poses a big challenge (and an opportunity for exotic holidays) to sensory ecologists.

Cortical processes in colour vision

OK – let's recap where we are (see Figure 5.24). We have established that there are three types of cone that sample the retinal image, effectively giving us three separate pictures of the world as seen by the blue, green, and red cones. We then use these three images to form another three signals that tell us about the luminance, the red–green differences, and the blue–yellow differences. This visual signal from the retina and LGN is conveyed to area V1 in the visual cortex, also known as the primary visual cortex or the striate cortex (see Chapter 3).

Throughout area V1 there are little patches of cells (termed 'blobs') where all the cells are responsive to the colour (or more accurately the wavelength) of the stimulus. These blobs are surrounded by cells that do not appear to be interested in colour at all. From these blob regions, colour information is conveyed onwards to the prestriate cortex. One of these regions, area V4, has been suggested to be particularly important in achieving the normal perception of colour. It has been claimed that in this area most of the cells are selective to particular colours – so that one cell might respond to red stimuli, but not to green, for example. Further, some of these cells also appear to respond to the colour of the stimulus rather than its wavelength. Puzzled by what we mean by this? Let us explain.

Colour constancy

We have happily ignored until now one big problem faced by the colour vision system. If the light coming down from the sky (or anywhere else for that matter) changes colour, then the whole world should change colour. After all, if you only lit your bedroom with a red light bulb then surely everything should look red? However, quite remarkably, the perceived colour of objects does not change (much) even as the light hitting them changes.

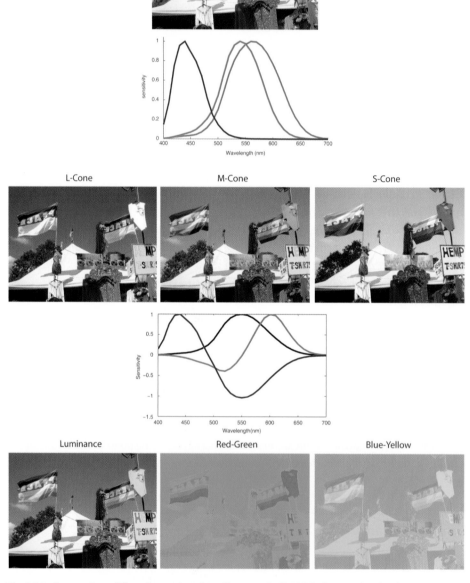

Fig. 5.24. An overview of the colour system from the cones to the LGN. See text for details.

Hence your blue shirt appears to be blue during the daytime and it also appears blue at sunset when mostly longer wavelengths are available to be reflected from it. The problem we have is that we want to know something about the shirt – its colour – but all we have to tell us about this quality is the reflected light from it, and that depends on the light that falls on the shirt, which changes all the time as we walk from daylight into a room with fluorescent lighting or into a candle-lit restaurant. Obviously we need to discount the illumination somehow if we are to get to the 'true' colour of objects.

It appears that the visual system does this by looking at lots of objects all at once. If they are all reflecting lots of long (red) wavelengths this probably means that they are being illuminated by long (red) wavelengths, and so it can compensate for this. Your blue shirt, even though it will be mostly reflecting long wavelengths at sunset, will be amongst those reflecting the least of these (and the most of the few short wavelengths that might get through). Hence it is not just the signal from the object in question that is important – your shirt is only 'blue' because it is 'bluer' than the things around it.

These principles were first demonstrated by Edwin Land. He used a patchwork of coloured papers (termed a **Mondrian pattern** after the painter who produced many a painting of patches of colour – see Figure 5.25) and lit them with different wavelengths. He found that if a single patch was presented all by itself it appeared to change colour as the light shining on it changed colour. However, when it was part of the Mondrian pattern, exactly the same patch did not change colour when the lighting was changed. This demonstrates that we need to know about lots of different patches if we are to

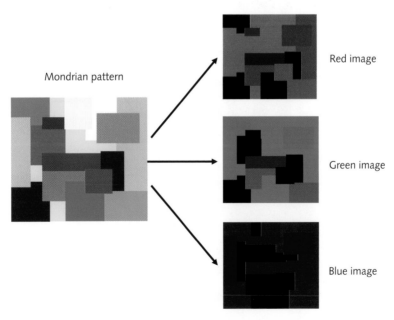

Mondrian pattern

Red image

Green image

Blue image

Fig. 5.25. A Mondrian pattern. The red, green, and blue cones would 'see' the different patches as different brightnesses.

calculate what the lighting is like, and therefore be able to discount it and achieve colour constancy. When there are lots of patches we are able to see the 'colour' of the patch rather than just the wavelength reflected, but with only a single patch we have nothing to compare this to and so we are fooled by the changes in lighting into seeing the patch as changing colour.

Back to the cortex

Exactly the same experiments can be performed on single cells – we can record from a single cell as we vary the wavelength of the light that is illuminating its receptive field. The response of cells in the early part of the cortex (i.e. area V1) changes as the wavelength of the illumination changes – they seem to think the patch is changing colour as the lighting is changing, just as we did when there was only a single patch visible. However, many cells in area V4 maintain their response even in the face of the changes in the lighting. In Figure 5.26 a V1 cell responds to the green patch, but this cell does not respond to the white patch. Likewise a V4 cell may respond to green and not to white. When a green illuminant is turned on (lower picture), the V1 cell now responds to the white patch illuminated in green light but the V4 cell, which exhibits colour constancy, does not.

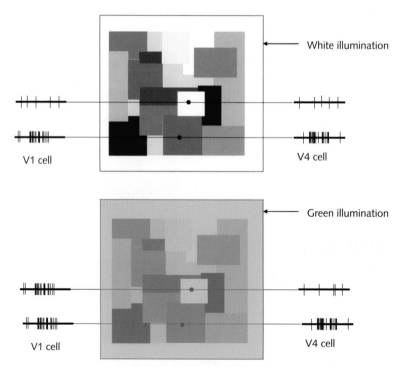

Fig. 5.26. Colour constancy in area V4. See text for details.

It can tell the difference between the colour of the surface and the colour of the light that illuminates it.

Cerebral achromatopsia

What happens if part of the colour-processing region of the extrastriate cortex is damaged, possibly as a result of a stroke? There have been rare cases of a condition known as cerebral achromatopsia, in which people with certain brain damage report that the world appears to them to consist of only shades of grey, even though they have all the normal cones in the retina. Simple tests of their colour vision reveal that they are telling the truth. Illustrated in Figure 5.27 is simple test of this. Eight possible target stimuli are presented in a circle and the observer simply has to pick the odd one out. In the left part of the figure the target is defined by colour. You will probably find this very easy, but patients with cerebral achromatopsia do not find this task easy and cannot tell us which is the odd one out. It's not that they cannot do this type of task, because when the target is defined by intensity (right part of the figure) there is no problem.

Aha – you are no doubt saying to yourself – this is because such patients must have damage in their 'colour area' of the brain, and we know that the colour area is V4, so if we were to deliberately damage area V4 we could reproduce this condition. Unfortunately (well, fortunately for the animal), when such an experiment was done in a monkey the animal still performed the colour odd-one-out task just as well as before the lesion to area V4. Clearly there is more to discover.

It seems that there is an area that is heavily involved in our conscious perception of colour, but there is evidence that it is not area V4. So where is it? Recent work looking at human brain imaging has revealed another area (unimaginatively called V8), very close to area V4, that might be what we're looking for. To locate this area, activity in an observer's brain was monitored while he viewed either a boring old black and white (luminance) grating pattern or an exciting new red–green grating. By balancing the intensities of the red and green we can eliminate luminance information (see Figure 5.28) and ensure that only colour information is present in the grating.

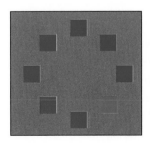 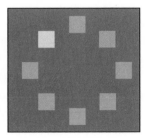

Fig. 5.27. Odd-one-out tasks. On the left the odd one out is defined by colour, on the right by luminance.

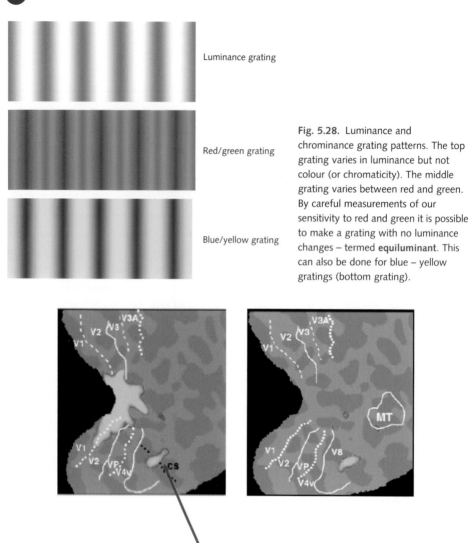

Luminance grating

Red/green grating

Blue/yellow grating

Fig. 5.28. Luminance and chrominance grating patterns. The top grating varies in luminance but not colour (or chromaticity). The middle grating varies between red and green. By careful measurements of our sensitivity to red and green it is possible to make a grating with no luminance changes – termed **equiluminant**. This can also be done for blue – yellow gratings (bottom grating).

Fig. 5.29. Left panel: Areas of the human brain activated more by coloured patterns that by luminance patterns. The area thought to be V8 is highlighted by the arrow. Right panel: Areas of the human brain activated by the colour after-effect. See text for details.

The scientists argued that any area that responded well to this latter coloured grating compared to the luminance grating must be heavily involved in colour processing. Figure 5.29 (left panel) shows that several areas were more excited by this red/green grating including areas V1, V2, and V3. However, there appears to be no such activity in area V4! Of most interest is the patch of activity just anterior to area V4 (region highlighted by arrow for readers who do not understand the word anterior). This is the area that is called V8 and is clearly activated more by the coloured grating than by the black and white one.

Interestingly, the researchers were able to show that area V8 is active even when there is no real colour information in the world. How can this be done? Well, we can use one of our old friends, the colour after-effect. Remember that when we stare at some particular coloured patch for a while (e.g. a red one – see Figure 5.19) this induces a complementary patch of colour (e.g. green, in this case). Now, by comparing brain activity when having this illusion of colour with activity when we are not having this illusion, surely we have something that reveals the site of colour consciousness? Sure enough, activity in area V8 is found under these conditions (Figure 5.29, right panel), whereas there is still no sign of activity in area V4.

Finally, you may think that there is a certain amount of confusion about whether V4 or V8 is the really important area for colour vision. And you'd be right. The position is unresolved at present, with V8 becoming more and more popular. However, for the time being just think of a V4/V8 complex; after all, these areas are very close together.

● READINGS AND REFERENCES

There are many books specifically on colour vision. The book by Mollon *et al.* (2003) contains many interesting short chapters that go well beyond the scope of this chapter.

Papers on specific issues

Why do we have colour vision? Some articles covering this, and cerebral achromatopsia too, are Bowmaker (1983), Mollon (1989), and Wolf (2002), which is a guide to Parraga *et al.* (2002). You might also take a look at Snowden (2002) to see how colour automatically attracts our attention.

Colour blindness All you really need to know can be found in Nathans (1989).

What is the colour vision of other animals like? Ever wondered what other species see? Well, try Goldsmith (1990) or Thompson *et al.* (1992). A comparison of the colour vision of many mammals can be found in Jacobs (1993).

Koniocellular pathway The finding of a unique blue/yellow pathway is quite recent and its properties are somewhat surprising – see Dacey and Lee (1994).

Brain areas involved in colour There is currently much debate over the role of various visual areas in colour vision (e.g. area V4 and V8 – see Hadjikhani *et al.* (1998).

Colour constancy For the classic early experiments see Land (1983), and for more recent work see Jameson and Hurvich (1989), Webster and Mollon (1995), and Kraft and Brainard (1999).

Cerebral achromatopsia The effects of brain damage on colour vision is well illustrated by Cowey and Heywood (1995).

● **POSSIBLE ESSAY TITLES, TUTORIALS, AND QUESTIONS OF INTEREST**

1 Why do we have colour vision?

2 Is V4 the colour centre of the human brain?

3 How does the colour vision of a colour-blind person differ from a normal person? Why is this so?

4 How can we reconcile the four-colour vision model of Hering with the trichromatic model of Young and Helmholtz?

References

Birch, J. (1993). *Diagnosis of defective colour vision*. Oxford: Oxford University Press.

Bishop, R. (1981–82). Rainbow over Woolsthorpe Manor. *Notes and Records of the Royal Society of London* **36**, 3–12.

Bowmaker, J. K. (1983). Trichromatic colour vision: why only three receptor channels? *Trends in Cognitive Sciences* **6**, 41–43.

Cowey, A. and Heywood, C. A. (1995). There's more to colour than meets the eye. *Behavioural Brain Research* **71**, 89–100.

Dacey, D. M. and Lee, B. B. (1994). The 'blue-on' opponent pathway in primate retina originates from a distinct bistratified ganglion cell type. *Nature* **367**, 731–735.

de Monasterio, F. M. and Gouras, P. (1975). Functional properties of ganglion cells of the rhesus monkey retina. *Journal of Physiology (London)* **251**, 67–95.

Domb, L. G. and Pagel, M. (2001). Sexual swellings advertise female quality in wild baboons. *Nature* **410**, 204–206.

Goldsmith, T. H. (1990). Optimization, constraint, and history in the evolution of eyes. *Quarterly Review of Biology* **65**, 281–322.

Hadjikhani, N., Liu, A. K., Dale, A. M., Cavanagh, P., and Tootell, R. B. H. (1998). Retinotopy and color sensitivity in human visual cortical area V8. *Nature Neuroscience* **1**(3), 235–241.

Jacobs, G. H. (1993). The distribution and nature of colour vision among the mammals. *Biological Review* **68**, 413–471.

Jameson, D. and Hurvich, L. M. (1989). Essay concerning color constancy. *Annual Review of Psychology* **40**, 1–22.

Kraft, J. M. and Brainard, D. H. (1999). Mechanisms of color constancy under nearly natural viewing. *Proceedings of the National Academy of Sciences of the USA* **96**(1), 307–312.

Land, E. H. (1983). Recent advancement in retinex theory and some implications for cortical computations: color vision and the natural image. *Proceedings of the National Academy of Sciences of the USA* **80**, 5163–5169.

Mollon, J. D. (1989). 'Tho' she knee'd in that place where they grew . . .': the uses and origins of primate colour vision. *Journal of Experimental Psychology* **146**, 21–38.

Mollon, J., Pokorny, J., and Knoblauch, K. (2003). *Normal and defective colour vision*. Oxford: Oxford University Press,

Nathans, J. (1989). The genes for color vision. *Scientific American*, February, 28–35.

Parraga, C. A., Troscianko, T., and Tolhurst, D. J. (2002). Spatio-chromatic properties of natural images and human vision. *Current Biology* **12**, 483–487.

Peichl, L. (2005). Diversity of mammalian photoreceptor properties: adaptations to habitat and lifestyle? *The Anatomical Record* **287A**, 1001–1012.

Snowden, R. J. (2002). Visual attention to color: parvocellular guidance of attentional resources? *Psychological Science* **30**(13), 180–184.

Thompson, E., Palacios, A. G., and Varela, F. J. (1992). Ways of coloring: comparative color vision as a case study for cognitive science. *Behavioral Brain Science* **15**, 1–75.

Webster, M. A. and Mollon, J. D. (1995). Colour constancy influenced by contrast adaptation. *Nature* **373**, 694–698.

Wolf, K. (2002). Visual ecology: coloured fruit is what the eye sees best. *Current Biology* **12**, 253–255.

CHAPTER 6

The perception of motion

'U-zu-maki glasses' by the artist/scientist Akiyoshi Kitaoka: 'U' means rabbits, 'zu' means 'figure', 'maki' means rotation, and 'Uzumaki' means spirals or swirls. Yellow represents the colour of the moon in Japan and it is imagined (though not seriously) that rabbits live in the moon and make mochi (food made from rice). Such images appear to move each time you make an eye movement. The explanation is quite complex – but here goes. There are three key things to notice about the effect. First, the patterns only move when you blink or move your eyes; second, the effect is seen best in peripheral vision; and third, the arrangement of the backgrounds of the 'rabbits' determines which way the patterns rotate. Now each time your eyes move you get a fresh image. Some parts of the image are of high contrast – they differ a lot from their background – such as the white ears on the red background. Other parts of the image are of low contrast, for example the white ears on the yellow background. Note that in the right-hand image all the high-contrast edges are on the left side of the rabbits' ears while the low-contrast edges are all on the right side of the rabbits' ears. The reverse is true in the left-hand image. We know that high-contrast information is transmitted up the visual pathway faster than low contrast and hence the motion detectors in the cortex receive signals from some bits of the image before others. The sorts of movement detectors we shall describe in this chapter respond to these signals arriving at different times as if they are detecting real motion, and when their responses are pooled together, the illusory motion is seen. Because information is pooled over large areas in the peripheral retina, the illusion is most striking there. The explanation is a bit more complicated really – but enough for now.

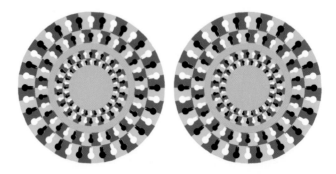

CHAPTER OVERVIEW

Imagine a world in which there is no colour. It may be dull, but it is easy enough to conceive of such a place. Now try to imagine a world in which there is no motion. This seems like an impossible task, but for a small number of individuals with brain damage their world has become devoid of such motion information. Tasks such as crossing the road or filling a glass with wine take on a difficulty (and in some cases terror) that is all too hard to appreciate. We believe that these individuals have damage in a small area of the brain that is devoted to analysing the movements of objects. In this chapter we describe how we might build detectors that could signal the direction and speed of objects in motion, and how in turn these can explain why we see movement from a set of stationary pictures such as when we watch television or go to the movies. Finally, we discuss the problem of deciding what is moving – after all, if the something appears to be moving it could be because it is moving, or it could be because we are moving. As we shall see, we do not always solve this rather important problem correctly!

Two ways of seeing movement

Movement seems (and is) vital for our perception of the world. And how we detect movement in the world is one of the greatest achievements of our perceptual systems. Let's take the easy case first. Suppose our eyes are held still and a spot of light moves across our field of view (Figure 6.1). A moving image crosses the retina and we perceive movement. No problem. (Actually quite a big problem, but we'll come back to that.) But what happens if we let our gaze follow the moving spot of light? This action is called tracking, which we achieve with smooth pursuit eye movements. Now, because the spot of light is kept on the fovea (our central vision) at all times, there is no movement of the spot across our retina – and yet we still see the spot as moving. Aha, you cry, but if the moving spot is tracked by the eye then there is still movement on the retina – of the actually stationary background moving in the opposite direction to that of the spot (see Figure 6.1). This is true (and very clever of you to spot it), but what if we can repeat the experiment, tracking a moving dot against a totally dark background? The spot still appears to move. So we must have two routes to perceiving movement, one that detects movement across the retina (we shall term this the retinal-movement system), and one that detects movements of the eyes in the head (we shall term this the eye/head movement system).

Just as we can experience movement without retinal movement (tracking the spot in darkness), we can also experience no movement when there is movement across the retina. Try moving your eyes across a stationary scene. Now as your eyes move, the scene must move across the retina; fortunately, the scene appears to stay still. So the retinal-movement system and the eye/head movement system must talk to each other to work out

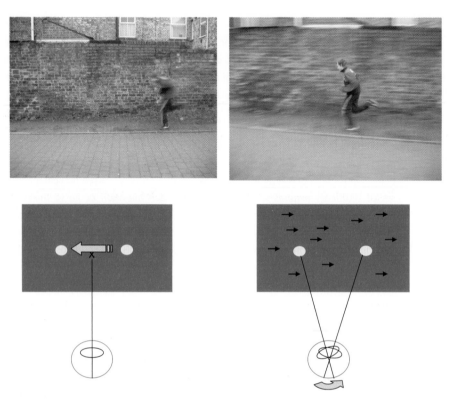

Fig. 6.1. Motion can be sensed in two ways. On the left side the viewer fixates on a stationary object and the moving object therefore moves across the retina. On the right side the viewer 'tracks' the moving object hence the moving object remains stationary upon the retina and the stationary background moves in the opposite direction across the retina. Both situations give us the perception of a moving object on a stationary background.

just what's going on in the world. This question of why the world stays still when we move our eyes was of immense interest to scientists in the nineteenth century and to two giants in the field in particular, the English physiologist Sir Charles Sherrington and the great Prussian physiologist Hermann von Helmholtz.

Basically, if we want to be able to move our eyes around without the world appearing to whizz around, we have to keep track of our eye movements. The question is how we do this. Sherrington proposed that we monitor the movements of our eye muscles, and by comparing retinal image motion with *eye muscle movement* we can determine whether objects in the real world have moved. Helmholtz proposed a subtly different model of what was going on (which had the distinct advantage of being right). Helmholtz proposed that rather than comparing image motion on the retina with eye muscle movement, the comparison should be made with the *signal from the brain* that tells the eye muscle to move. So Helmholtz proposed that we take a copy of the signal to move our eyes (sometimes known as an efferent copy or collorary discharge) and compare this with any retinal image motion. Sherrington's theory is also known as the 'inflow' theory and Helmholtz's as the 'outflow' theory, but we keep forgetting which is which so we shall not mention this again.

Let us consider how the two models work (see Figure 6.2) and make some predictions.

1   Track a moving object. This provides no problem to either model. In each case there is no retinal motion signal, but there is a signal from the eye muscles (Sherrington) and there is a command sent to the eye muscles (Helmholtz), so in both case we should perceive the object as moving even though it is stationary on the retina. Score: Helmholtz 1 – Sherrington 1.

2   Stare at a bright light, or look into the camera when a flash is used. This will produce an afterimage that is 'burnt' onto your retina. If you now move your eyes this after-image will appear to move (even though it is stationary on your retina). No problem here either. There is no retinal movement of the after-image, but the eyes are told to move (Helmholtz) and do move (Sherrington), so the movement of the after-image is perceived. Helmholtz 2 – Sherrington 2.

3   Staring at the stationary world, give your eyeball a sharp poke. The world moves. Try it for yourself. A gentle push through the eyelid should suffice for this demonstration. Sharp sticks should be avoided. What you have done here is to move the eye and therefore you have stretched the eye muscle, but no efferent signal was sent by the brain to tell the muscle to move. According to Sherrington the eye-muscle movement is the important thing; it doesn't matter if it is moved by pushing with your finger, a pointed stick or an efferent signal. But it does matter to Helmholtz – only an efferent signal from the brain will do. So in this example the world should stay still for Sherrington and move for Helmholtz. And the Earth does move (perceptually at least). Helmholtz 3 – Sherrington 2.

4   If the Earth moved for you that time, try it with an after-image, preferably in the dark. Stare at a bright light for a while, or a camera flash, to get an after-image. It moves around when you move your eyes as expected (see 2 above). Now keep your eyes still

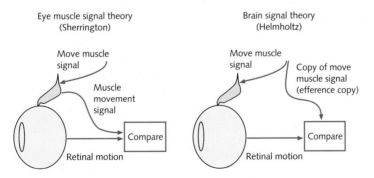

Fig. 6.2. In Sherrington's inflow theory the signals about eye movements come from the eye, whereas in Helmholtz's outflow theory they come from the brain.

and push the eyeball through the eyelid, with your eyelids closed (to make things dark). Does the afterimage move? According to Sherrington it should: there's no retinal movement, but there is eye-muscle movement, but according to Helmholtz it shouldn't: no retinal movement and no eye movement signal either. The after-image doesn't move. Helmholtz 4 – Sherrington 2.

5 Now for one you shouldn't try at home. What if we tell our eyes to move but we actually prevent the eyeball from moving? Helmholtz predicts that the stationary world will appear to move because the eye movement signal is not cancelled by the expected retinal movement. Sherrington predicts no movement because there will be no retinal movement and no eye-muscle movement. Good predictions, but how do we do the experiment? Well, there are two ways. Firstly, we can physically prevent the eyes from moving in their orbits by stuffing putty behind the eyes. Very nasty. Secondly, we can paralyse the eye muscles with a drug like curare. This sounds neater, but unfortunately curare paralyses much of the nervous system and, although your heart will keep beating, you can't breathe and you will suffocate. Nonetheless the experiment has been done both ways and the world does move, giving Helmholtz a well-deserved 5–2 victory which is a fairly typical result when Germany play England.

A motion detector

That was a lot of work just to figure out that the world seems to stay still when it doesn't move. But we have some important elements in our model (see Figure 6.2) that we should try to unpack. Consider the line labelled 'retinal motion'. How do we know if movement across the retina is up or down or left or right? How can we construct a 'movement detector'? And if we do construct one, will it behave like movement detectors in our visual system? Things could get complicated here, so let's start with a simple example.

If we want to tell the difference between a spot of light moving to the left and one moving to the right, what should we do? Imagine a spot of light moves from A to B (see Figure 6.3, top left). What might be useful is to have something that can detect the spot when it is at A, and one that detects the spot at B (two receptive fields would do the trick). We can then say that we require that both the receptor with a receptive field at A, and the one with a receptive field at B must fire within a certain time period – so if our spot moves from A to B within this time period we get firing and we have detected motion – hurrah! Unfortunately this detector would respond just as well to a spot of light moving left (B to A) as to the right (A to B). Clearly we must make our detector asymmetrical, and the easiest way to do this is by introducing a time delay (Figure 6.3, top right). The logic here is that if the spot moves from A to B it will excite receptor A before receptor B. If we put a time-delay on the output signal from A, then it will arrive at the comparison box, the

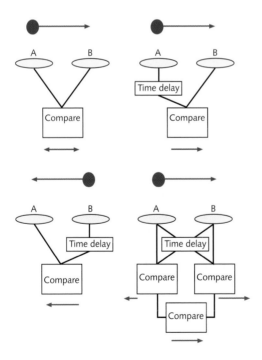

Fig. 6.3. How to build a motion detector. The key components in many motion models are two spatially separated detectors with a time delay between their responses. See text for further details.

detector, at the same time as the not-delayed signal from B, provided that the delay is as long as the time taken to travel from A to B. Movement from B to A will excite detector B first; some time later, when the spot has moved to A, detector A will fire. Its response will then get delayed and there is no chance of the activity from A and B reaching the detector at the same time. With such a scheme, we can ensure that movement from A to B will excite the detector but movement from B to A will not. Of course, this will only work if the speed of the spot is neither too fast nor too slow.

This simple model is often termed a delay-and-compare detector. This is not by any means the only way that we can make a directionally selective device, but the general principle of sampling from two different points in space with a time delay is at the heart of many more sophisticated models of motion.

Examples of such schemes exist not only in biological systems. Figure 6.4 shows an increasingly familiar object in many countries: the speed trap. Some of these things work by bouncing radar waves off moving vehicles, but although this may work, the trouble is that there is no documentary evidence of the alleged offence. It would be sufficient for the speeding driver to demonstrate that these things can be unreliable in order to be acquitted.

So the device in Figure 6.4 has an additional feature, which works rather like our motion detector above. The box contains a camera which is activated by an initial 'hey there's a speeding car' signal from the radar system. The camera takes two pictures a known time apart. Lines, a bit like a ruler, are painted on the road. The speed of the car is then simply worked out by the distance travelled in this known time period. If the car has moved more than some distance in the time between the pictures, then it is going too fast; and the photos exist to prove it. Of course, if you drive very fast, by the time the second picture is taken your car will be gone out of shot. However, we think you'd have to be going about 200 mph (320 km/h) to achieve this, so don't try it.

Let's elaborate our model with one further step. The top right of Figure 6.3 shows our simple left-to-right detector. Clearly it would be just as simple to make a right-to-left detector (Figure 6.3, lower left), and equally it is simple to combine both detectors so that only two sensors are used overall (Figure 6.3, lower right). Many models also then include a later stage that compares the output of left and right detectors in an antagonistic manner (such as subtracting one from the other). This means that anything that excites them both equally does not produce any signal after this subtraction.

Is there any evidence that such movement detectors exist in biological systems? The very fact that we can tell rightward movement from leftward movement tells us that somewhere in our heads we can do this, but it doesn't tell us where in the system such devices might be found. In primates it has been found that neither ganglion cells nor LGN cells can tell left from right, and that the first signs of direction selectivity arise in the primary visual cortex (area V1 – see Chapter 3). In area V5 (also known as MT; see below) it appears that nearly every cell has this property of directional selectivity (see Figure 6.5). However, in frogs, rabbits, and many other species direction-selective cells

Fig. 6.4. Speed traps. The upper part shows the speed camera. The lower parts show how it calculates speed by taking two pictures at slightly different times. The distance travelled can be calculated by the number of lines on the road the car has traversed between the taking of the pictures. Speed is calculated by the distance travelled divided by the time difference between taking the pictures.

> ### BOX 6.1   TV, film, and videotape
>
> In the UK and the rest of Europe television pictures are transmitted at a rate of 50 per second, but in each 1/50 of a second we only get half a picture, alternate lines of the image, so it takes 1/25 of a second to receive a full picture and we get 25 full pictures per second. In North America the transmission rate is 60 half pictures per second, so 30 full pictures per second are transmitted. In the cinema everywhere, 24 stationary images are presented every second. So what happens when films are shown on TV? In the UK it's an easy problem to solve; TV needs 25 pictures per second and the film has 24, so that's near enough. We simply steal the 25th frame from the next second of the film. This means that a film that lasts for 25 minutes in the cinema takes only 24 minutes to show on television, and nobody notices the difference. In the USA we can't get away with this trick; a 30 minute film would race through on TV in 24 minutes and someone might get suspicious. The solution is to repeat every 4th frame twice, so that the 30 minute film takes 30 minutes on TV.
>
> The human visual system is very sensitive to flicker and can detect something flickering at a rate of 24 times per second. So why don't films look very flickery? The answer is that film projectors have a shutter that opens twice, or even three times, for each individual film frame, so that although there are 24 pictures per second the flicker rate is much higher. The visual system is insensitive to very high rates of flicker, so flickering the movie more means we don't notice it. Incidentally, it was the sensitivity of the visual system to flicker that led to TV pictures being presented half a picture at a time, presenting the even-numbered lines on one frame and the odd-numbered frames on the next. This leads to less perceptible flicker than showing the whole image at half the rate.

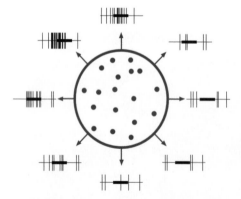

Fig. 6.5. Response of directionally selective cell, such as those found in area MT (V5) to different directions of motion of a pattern made of dots (random dot pattern). This cell fires the most when the motion is up and to the left.

can be found at a retinal level, and much of what we know about these detectors was actually first found in beetles and flies!

Indeed, thinking about beetles and flies may lead us to think about how important motion detection is to just about any animal. The task of detecting prey, or a predator, is made very much easier if the prey or predator moves. Watch a cat stalking a mouse or a baby bird to see an example of how the predator tries to move so slowly while getting into range that the prey cannot detect the motion – and then moves so fast when closing for the kill that the prey has no chance to respond, even though it can now see the motion.

The motion after-effect

Now if we have a detector that will respond to a certain direction of movement, there is no reason why we couldn't have a collection of motion detectors for all different directions. And indeed we do. So we now have a model of encoding the direction of motion that looks just like our model of how we encode the orientation of a line (see Chapters 3 and 4). In other words, we have a set of cells, or filters, each tuned to a different direction of motion and the one that is the most active signals the direction of motion of our object. Indeed, by staring at the same motion for some time we can produce direction-specific threshold elevation (i.e. it becomes harder to see an object moving in the same direction to which we just adapted, whereas one in another direction is just as easy to see as before adaptation) and a direction-of-motion after-effect, just as we produced tilt-specific threshold elevation and a tilt after-effect (Chapter 4).

However, these effects of adapting to motion differ from those of adapting to tilt in one fundamental and important aspect, and we have a chemist called Addams vacationing in the highlands of Scotland in the 1830s to thank for this observation (Figure 6.7; see Wade 1994). Addams wrote:

> During a recent tour through the Highlands of Scotland, I visited the celebrated Falls of Foyers on the border of Loch Ness, and there noticed the following phænomenon.
>
> Having steadfastly looked for a few seconds at a particular part of the cascade, admiring the confluence and decussation of the currents forming the liquid drapery of waters, and then

Fig. 6.6. An engraving of the Falls of Foyers near Loch Ness, Scotland. Observation of this waterfall produced one of the earliest reports of a motion after-effect and explains why it is sometimes known as the waterfall illusion. Not a single monster appeared that day, however.

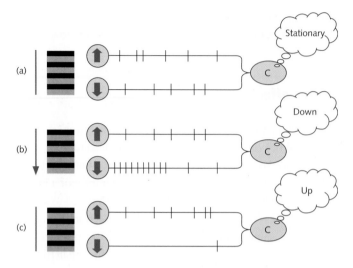

Fig. 6.7. An explanation of the motion after-effect (MAE). See text for details.

suddenly directed my eyes to the left, to observe the vertical face of the sombre age-worn rocks immediately contiguous to the water-fall, I saw the rocky surface as if in motion upwards, and with an apparent velocity equal to that of the descending water, which the moment before had pre-pared my eyes to behold this singular deception.

Ah, they don't write journal articles like that any more! Let's ignore the terrible composition of his second sentence, and note that this was the first paper devoted to what is now called the waterfall illusion, or more generally the movement after-effect (MAE). So, in slightly less flowery language: after you have been looking at something moving in one direction for a while, stationary things will appear to move in the opposite direction (the bit Addams wrote about the speed of the effect being equal to the speed of the water is completely wrong – but clearly he was rather excited, and we can forgive him this).

Why is the MAE so important for our understanding of motion perception? First, it's an extremely striking effect and so visual psychologists get terribly excited about it. Second, it is also an extremely simple and reliable effect; stare at something stationary, like a rock in the waterfall, which is surrounded by downward moving motion for a minute. Then look at a stationary pattern, and it will appear to move upwards. If you can't be bothered to find a waterfall, you can see the same effect in the cinema. The final credits after a movie often scroll up the screen. Sit there while they do so, staring at something that does not move (perhaps just above or below the screen). Listen to the music that plays over the credits, and ignore the people tripping over you as they try to leave your row of seats. At the end of the credits there's often a non-moving piece of text – this will appear to move downwards as a result of the MAE. Alternatively, transferring your gaze to something stationary after about a minute of adaptation should have the same effect. You can tell the vision scientists in cinemas, they all stay behind to adapt to motion. Of course, the film buffs stay too, in order to discover who the best boy or key grip was, but by actually reading the credits and moving their eyes to do so, they are depriving themselves of the maximum MAE. Finally, and best of all, there is a simple explanation for the MAE. All we have to do is to say that we determine whether an object is moving up or down (or is stationary) by comparing the activity in our 'up' and 'down' (or 'left' and 'right', etc.) detectors in some comparison mechanism (Figure 6.7).

Under normal conditions a stationary object would excite both the 'up' and 'down' detectors just a little, and about equally. So our device that compares the 'up' and 'down' detector responses would find no difference and this we take as stationary (Figure 6.7a). Now we present our waterfall (downward motion). This should make the 'down' detector fire a lot while the 'up' detector doesn't fire much at all. Our comparator should say 'down' and so we see downward motion (Figure 6.7b). Now prolonged stimulation of the 'down' detector means that it gets adapted and can't fire as much as it used to. Following this adaptation, the stationary pattern that would normally excite both 'up' and 'down' detectors equally will now excite the 'up' detector more than the fatigued 'down' detector. Of course this state (the 'up' firing more than the 'down') normally only occurs when there is upward motion – and so that is what is perceived (Figure 6.7c).

One more thing is interesting to consider about the MAE. When you see it, you see motion – but the objects in motion *never change position*. This seems paradoxical, but implies that the detectors of motion and detectors of position work independently.

Speed

In our discussion of motion so far we haven't mentioned the fact that motion doesn't just have direction, it also has speed. How might speed be coded in the visual system? One obvious suggestion is that the faster the speed, the faster the motion cell fires. This is a particularly seductive idea, and many have been seduced by it. Figure 6.8 shows the firing rate of a directionally selective ganglion cell in the rabbit retina (note that rabbits have directionally selective cells in the retina, whereas we do not encode direction until the cortex). In the absence of any moving stimulus the cell fires at some 'resting level', spontaneously generating nerve spikes at, on average, around 10 impulses per second. When a motion stimulus is shown that matches the preferred direction of the cell, the firing rate soars to over 60 impulses per second. But note what happens as the stimulus motion continues: the firing rate of the cell drops steadily (adapts) until a plateau is reached and it settles down to fire at around 25 impulses per second. Now, if firing rate encodes speed we would expect the rabbit to report that the moving stimulus started moving very fast and then it slowed right down. No one has asked a rabbit this question, but similar experiments on people produce exactly this result.

As we look at a moving pattern for a time it slows down quite dramatically, and in some cases can actually come to a complete stop (see Figure 6.9). Indeed, this illusion of 'slowness' is often experienced after driving quickly for a while – see Chapter 0. Notice,

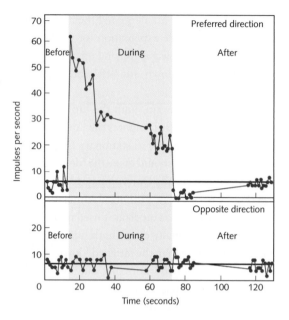

Fig. 6.8. Results from an experiment that recorded activity from a single ganglion cell in the retina of a rabbit. Stimulated by motion in its preferred direction the cell starts firing vigorously, but its response drops over time. When the motion stops, the cell's firing rate drops below its resting level. See text for details. Motion in the opposite direction has no effect on the cell's response (lower part).

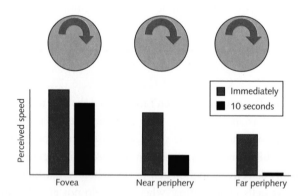

Fig. 6.9. Stopped visual motion. The speed of a rotating disc (or indeed any other moving pattern) is altered by both how close it is to the fixation point, and for how long we look at it. If we look at the disc on the left, then the ones to the right (falling in our peripheral retina) appear to be rotating more slowly (the effect get larger the further they are from the fixation). As we carry on observing this, the discs in the periphery get slower and even stop.

too, that the ganglion cell in Figure 6.9 also shows what happens to the cell when the motion stimulus comes to a halt: the firing rate drops, not back to its resting noise level of 10 or so impulses per second, but right down to zero for a few seconds – this is exactly what we hypothesized for the MAE, and we would predict that this particular bunny would be enjoying a MAE for a few seconds.

If you have read Chapter 4 then you might spot that there could be a problem with encoding speed by the firing rate of movement selective cells, namely that we already appear to code contrast by the cells' firing rate. How, then, do we tell the difference between a change in contrast and a change in speed? (Remember the principle of uni-variance we talked about in Chapter 5 – here is another example of encoding two dimensions of the stimulus with just the activity in one group of cells.) If we reduce the contrast of a moving pattern, would its perceived rate of movement drop? Strangely, the answer is that it does – at least to some extent. This effect may explain why so many people drive too fast in fog: foggy conditions reduce contrast, reduced contrast leads us to believe we are travelling slower than we really are, so we speed up until we feel we are going at an appropriate speed. Until we hit the truck in front of us.

Apparent motion

But we are getting a little side-tracked. Let's go back to our basic movement detector in Figure 6.3. It responds to a bar moving across it from left to right, but it would work equally well if we flashed a stationary object at A and then another stationary object at B a little later – we don't actually need to have the object moving in between. Does this work in the real world? Fortunately it does, otherwise we would have no television or cinema, both of which create an illusion of motion by very rapidly presenting a series of stationary images – what we term apparent motion (Figure 6.10).

Obviously, to generate apparent motion from a series of stationary images requires us to present the images at an appropriate speed – if the images are presented too slowly then no motion is seen, if they are presented too quickly then they appear simultaneous. If you think about it, the interval between movie frames needs to be of the same order as the delay in the detectors used to sample the motion, as shown in Figure 6.3.

You may think that the visual system does something like this: there was a spot of light there, and now it's here – so it must have moved. Indeed, if you occasionally glance at the clock during a boring lecture you can tell that the minute hand has moved even if you can't actually see the motion. So how can we make sure that people do really see the motion and don't just infer motion from the fact that things have changed position? One neat trick is to give them so many things to try and keep track of that it is impossible to do

Present dots on
three movie frames

See one moving dot

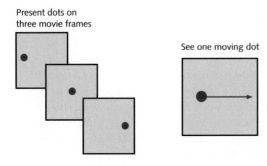

Fig. 6.10. Apparent motion. In these displays stationary images are presented in rapid succession. We interpret this as smooth motion. Many visual media (TV, films, cartoons, etc.) reply on this phenomenon to present us with apparently moving images.

> ### BOX 6.2   Apparent motion and the wagon wheel effect
>
> One problem that TV and film have is when very rapid motion needs to be shown, the frame rate can prove too slow to represent the movement. A classic case of this is the **wagon wheel effect** in which the stagecoach wheels appear to turn backwards on the screen. The reason for this is simple. The left side of the Figure 6.2.1 shows superimposed frames from a 'movie' of a turning wagon wheel.
>
>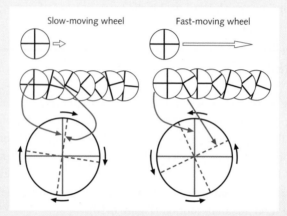
>
> **Fig. 6.2.1.** Explanation of wagon wheel illusion. It's easy to understand why the illusion should occur on TV, in movies, and under fluorescent lights, but can we also get the wagon wheel effect in sunlight? See text for details.
>
> Note that the spokes of the wheel turn a little between the two movie frames. In the first section the movement is small (the motion is slow) and so each spoke at time 1 gets matched to the same spoke at time 2 and so the motion is correctly recovered. However, for fast motion (the right side of the figure) the spokes move a long way between the movie frames. So much so that now the nearest spoke in frame 2 to each spoke in frame 1 is no longer itself but the one behind. The visual system therefore matches to this nearest spoke and produces the wrong direction of motion – and hence the wagon wheels appear to move in the opposite direction to the real motion. At faster speeds you may be able to work out what will happen. If the speed is such that the wheel moves exactly the distance from one spoke to the next between the movie frames, then the wheel appears stationary. At still faster speeds the spokes would once again move in the right direction, but too slowly. Indeed, as the speed gets faster and faster the wheel should keep appearing to change direction.
>
> Many people have told us that they have seen the wagon wheel effect in real life, most commonly when looking at car wheels (there just aren't too many wagons out there these days) under fluorescent light. What happens here is that the street light, which is actually flickering on and off so rapidly you don't notice it, is presenting essentially a series of near-stationary pictures for you to see, just like a movie. You might think that you should never see the wagon wheel effect in continuous lighting, but there is some evidence that it can occur. One explanation is that the visual system divides up its input into discrete 'moments' and these are a bit like frames of a film. Whether this 'temporal parsing' really can explain the effect remains controversial.

Fig. 6.11. Frames from a random dot kinematogram. From frame to frame a small section of dots is moved. When the frames are presented like this, the shape and movement of the area are impossible to see. However, if they are displayed in rapid succession the moving area is easy to see.

this. Random dot patterns (see Figure 6.11) do just this by having thousands of dots that are randomly placed. We now cunningly move just a small block of them on each of our movie frames – as has been done in Figure 6.11. I'm sure you find it very difficult, perhaps impossible, to see what area has moved – the randomness of the pattern is just too difficult to keep track of. However, when these frames are presented together in an apparent motion sequence (we have a big word for this – a **random dot kinematogram**) the area and its motion immediately pops out and is easily seen. Not surprisingly, many of the experiments that have examined our motion perceptions (and those of other animals) have taken advantage of such random dot kinematograms to ensure we are isolating the motion system by not allowing the subject to use the 'there then, here now' strategy.

Motion blindness and area MT (V5)

At the start of this chapter we briefly mentioned the strange case of a woman who cannot see motion. A small lesion has selectively knocked out the part of the brain that processes this aspect of our vision so that her world is apparently frozen into a series of still pictures, perhaps somewhat analogous to your own perceptions when dancing under stroboscopic lighting. Such patients (who are said to be **motion-blind** or **akinetopsic**), not surprisingly,

---

BOX
6.3   **Spooky movement**

We can exploit just how our visual system detects and signals movement to produce some illusory motion from stationary figures. Try rocking backwards and forwards while viewing Figure 6.3.1. You should see the two rings of elements appear to rotate in opposite directions (this is known as the **Pinna illusion** after its inventor). This illusion arises because our motion detectors only look at a very small part of the image (like looking through a small aperture) and signal the motion at that orientation. Thus they can only tell us about motion at this particular orientation.

Fig. 6.3.1. The Pinna illusion. If you rock your head backwards and forwards you should see the rings rotate. This compelling illusion can be understood in terms of the motion mechanisms we have described in this chapter.

This is illustrated in Figure 6.3.2 – here we see that with only this small aperture to look through we cannot tell the difference between the diamond moving upwards or to the right, as the two movements produce exactly the same signal within this small aperture. This is known as the **aperture problem**. Clearly, we can normally tell the difference between the two movements, so we must be able to combine lots of apertures to get it right, but that's another story we don't need for now.

Now examine the individual elements that make up the Pinna illusion (Figure 6.3.3 shows you some large ones to help). Notice that they are subtly shaded and tilted – this is deliberate, and vital to getting the illusion. If we blur these figures (or for those of you who remember Chapter 4, if we remove the high spatial frequencies) we see that they contain a blurry edge across their diagonal (Figure 6.3.3 has blurred them for you). Now let's see what happens when we move our heads towards the illusion. If these elements were on the far right of the figure they would move to the right as our head went forwards. However, the aperture problem means that cells can only signal movement either up and to the right for element 1 and down and to the right for element 2. In other words, the aperture problem distorts the signal about the true movements of these elements, and of course the motion of all the other elements is also being distorted in a similar way.

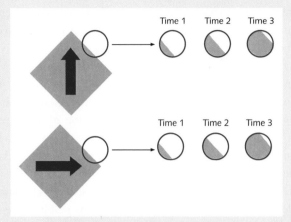

Fig. 6.3.2. The aperture problem. See text for details.

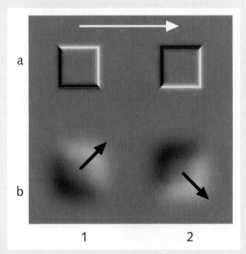

Fig. 6.3.3. Close-up of the individual elements of the Pinna illusion and a blurred version of them.

This distortion should produce a mixture of expansion and rotation, yet we only see the rotation – why? Well, this is the same reason that we tend not to see any expansion at all when we move our heads towards a normal object. The brain calculates the movement of our head and subtracts this from the signal, so that things normally appear stationary when we move. However, when this subtraction is done on this particular image the distortion of the motion caused by the aperture problem leaves us with a residual rotary motion, and this is what we see when we move our head back and forth. Having the inner and outer rings shaded in opposite ways means they move in opposite directions, and this also helps to make the illusion stronger.

fear crossing the road as they have a limited ability to calculate when a car might arrive. One patient described this act by saying '*I have a look down the road and note where the cars are. I then wait a while and then look again. If none have changed position then it is safe to cross*'. She also added '*. . . but I prefer not to cross roads*'.

The area affected in this woman is thought to be the human equivalent of an area well studied in the brain of the monkey – area MT (also termed V5 – so you can think of it as MTV5) – see Figure 6.12 for the location of MT. This area receives most of its input via the magnocellular layers of the LGN (having then passed through area V1 – see Chapters 1 and 3) and this gives us our first hint that area MT is important in processing the dynamic aspects of vision. More importantly, nearly every cell in this area responds well to a moving image, and is fussy about the exact direction of the movement. MT also appears to have a 'column' structure just like area V1, but now all the cells have the same preferred direction of motion (rather than preferred orientation). All these facts provide us with strong hints that this area is interested in motion in the world.

We should therefore expect that if this area were deliberately damaged an animal would not be able to see motion. This has been tested by making a very small lesion in area MT of a monkey. The lesion damaged a small part of the visual field but left most of the monkey's visual field intact. The animal's motion perception was then tested in both the damaged and undamaged parts of its field by requiring it to make a decision about which direction a pattern moved in (up or down). The visual stimulus used in the task was fiendishly clever and is illustrated on the right-hand side of Figure 6.13. Imagine a pattern of moving dots where all the dots move in a random direction. If we ask the monkey whether the dots are moving up or down, he can't say (obviously), but he can't indicate a direction by pressing a lever or making some eye movement either, because there is no

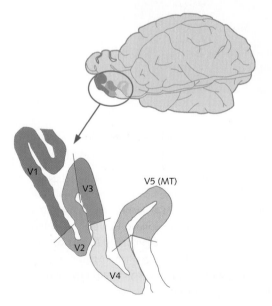

Fig. 6.12. Location of area V5 (MT) in the primate brain.

reason to choose up rather than down. Now let's make a few of the dots move upwards (or downwards) while the rest continue to move in random directions. Can the monkey spot the direction of these correlated dots? The answer is yes, provided enough of them move in the same direction. So by measuring what percentage of the total number of dots we must move in the coherent direction for the monkey to detect the direction reliably, we can establish a motion threshold. The results of this experiment are shown on the left of Figure 6.13. Notice that in the parts of the field that had not been damaged the monkey required as few as 5% of the elements to move in the target direction (a well-trained undergraduate normally needs 10%). However, if the pattern was presented in the damaged part of the field the monkey needed nearly 100% of the dots to move in this direction. Note that this wasn't because the monkey could not see this stimulus – other tests of the animal's vision showed that its ability to see stationary patterns, and its colour vision, were unimpaired – the animal simply seems just to lose its ability to see the motion. Results from our motion-blind patient are also plotted on this figure for the same task. Her vision resembles that of the damaged monkey, in that she needs nearly all the elements to move in the target direction before accurate judgements can be made.

If area MT is indeed the site at which motion perception is occurring, then it should be possible to influence which way a pattern appears to be moving by simply manipulating the response of cells in this area of the brain. The neuroscientist Bill Newsome and colleagues (Salzman *et al.* 1990) performed just such an experiment. First they identified a group of cells within area MT that all had the same preferred direction of motion (for the sake of example, let's say they preferred downward motion). They then placed a stimulating electrode near to these cells. Meanwhile the monkey was asked to make judgements about which direction it thought the stimulus was moving (up or down). When the

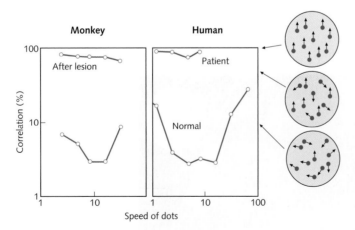

Fig. 6.13. Effects of lesions of area V5 (MT) on motion perception. The ability to see motion is measured by the percentage of dots that have to move in the correct direction (the others move in random directions) in order to see the motion. At optimal speeds both human and monkey need less that 5% of the dots to move in the correct direction in order to do this task. However, after specific lesions to MT in the monkey, or brain damage in the human thought to affect area MT, performance is very poor.

stimulus appeared, the experimenters could stimulate these cells so that they responded vigorously. They found that when they stimulated these cells the monkey was far more likely to report 'downward' motion. So by simply stimulating these direction-specific cells, we can fool the animal into 'seeing' motion that was not actually shown to it.

We are now able to image areas of the human brain thought to be involved in motion perception, thanks to modern brain imaging techniques – see Chapter 12 for details of these. By subtracting an image of brain activity when viewing a stationary image from an image of the activity when viewing a moving image, we can see just the activity that was caused by the motion. The area highlighted by this technique is thought to be the human equivalent of area MT or V5 (Figure 6.14).

Can we also see the illusory motion in a similar manner? One experiment seems to suggest that this is so. Subjects adapted to a set of rings that continually expanded, or adapted to a set of rings that expanded and then contracted every second or so. Both these patterns of movement excited the human area MT as expected. However, when this motion ceased, the first continuously expanding pattern caused a contracting MAE in a set of stationary rings, whereas the expanding and contract motion did not. Sure enough, the activity in area MT continued for longer (see Figure 6.15) in the first condition than in the second condition. The time course of this activity appears to mimic the time course of the after-effect motion.

Another interesting finding is that area MT is active when we see another kind of illusory motion. Figure 6.16 is a reproduction of the painting 'The Enigma' by Isia Leviant. Many people report seeing an illusory circular motion in the areas between the spokes. When viewing this figure it has been shown that area MT is activated. Although these demonstrations are impressive, we are still left with a fundamental question – does area MT become active because of the illusory motion, or do we see illusory motion because area MT is active?

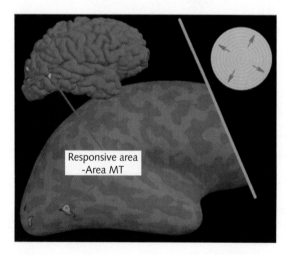

Responsive area
-Area MT

Fig. 6.14. Area MT in the human highlighted using fMRI technique.

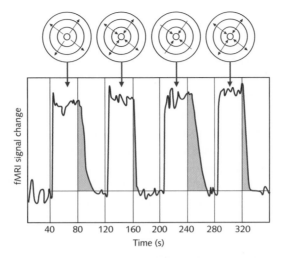

Fig. 6.15. Activity in area MT during and after presentation of motion. The diagram shows the activity during four different forms of stimulation (each lasting 40 s) and in the periods in between when the screen was blank. In all four stimulation periods there is about the same amount of activity in area MT. However, in the blank periods following this stimulation the activity dissipates (decreases) more slowly following either pure expansion or pure contraction, than with a mixture of the two. A motion after-effect is experienced only after the pure expansions and contractions. It is suggested that this extra activity in the blank periods after these motions is caused by the motion after-effect.

Fig. 6.16. 'The Enigma' by Isia Leviant (1984). Many people (but not all) report seeing illusory whirling motion in the rings.

How do we tell what moves and what stays still?

As we have seen in this chapter, we are often faced with scenes in which some things are stationary on the retina and other things are moving. But sometimes the stationary things are moving and the moving things are stationary – for example when we track a moving object (remember Figure 6.1) – so it is a real problem for the visual system to decide what's stationary and what's moving. Sometimes it gets it wrong. Have you ever looked up at the moon on a windy night when there are clouds scudding across the sky? What we see is the moon racing in the opposite direction. Or have you ever looked up at a tall building on a windy day with clouds moving across the sky and felt the building was falling down? These are examples of induced movement. We normally assume that backgrounds are stationary and that objects move against the background. But in these examples it is the backgrounds that are moving and we perceive them as stationary with the really stationary objects – the moon and the building – in motion. There is a simple way to demonstrate this induced movement at home. Turn the TV on when there is an exciting game of football on, one with lots of action. Put a big black dot on the centre of the screen and see what happens. As the camera follows the ball back and forth on the field, your black dot will appear to race in the opposite direction of the moving background. It's a compelling effect and one that will certainly fascinate any football fans who are trying to watch the game.

So we can usually calibrate our idea of what's stationary by our knowledge of the outside world – we know walls and buildings usually don't move. But what happens when we take away those stationary backgrounds? Again, this can easily be done at home. All you need is a totally dark room and a cigarette. Light the cigarette, an ordinary cigarette. Don't inhale. Place the cigarette upright on the far side of the room and look at the faint glowing tip. After a while the dim light will appear to move against the totally dark background. This is known as the autokinetic effect, and at one time was used by social psychologists to investigate something or other. In one classic study Rechtschaffen and Mednick (1955) told subjects that the autokinetic light would spell out words. One female subject, asked to say what words were written by the stationary light replied, 'When men are tired and depraved, they become mean and callous individuals. When men learn to master their souls, the world will be a more humane and tolerant place in which to live. Men should learn to control themselves.' How true.

Vection and stability

We are all familiar with the experience of sitting in a stationary train looking out of the window, or even reading a book, with another stationary train alongside us (especially since rail privatization in the UK). We then feel our train move off, the train alongside us slips away, but to our disappointment we discover a few seconds later that we are still in

BOX 6.4   Biological motion

Motion perception can tell us not only about the movement of objects in our world, but also just what these objects are. One of the most famous demonstrations of this is termed **biological motion**. In these displays a person is made to dress all in black and is viewed against a black background – so that their body is rendered invisible to us. Now a few spots of light can be attached to the person, so that as they move these lights move (Figure 6.4.1). Each frame of such a

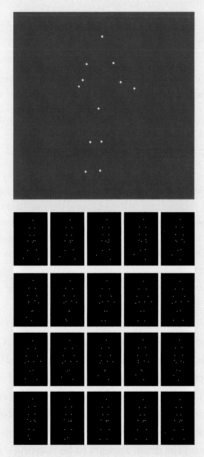

Fig. 6.4.1. Frames from a Johansson figure (biological motion). See text for details. Can you tell what is happening? When these frames from a biological motion movie are shown rapidly in sequence, we see a figure walking.

movie appears as a boring bunch of spots, but together in a movie the person's movements are brought to life and although we can only see the movement of a few dots the person's actions are easily recognizable. These spotty figures are known as **Johannson figures** after their inventor.

This technique shows us that a few moving lights on a person (and many other things – see below) are enough for us to gather lots of information. Here is a brief list of some of the things that's that have been found using Johannson figures:

- We can tell our friends and family from the way they walk.
- We can identify the gender of the person walking.
- We can tell the age of the person walking.
- It's possible to lip-read from Johansson lips.
- We can tell what animal it is, using Johansson animals (well, cats and dogs at least – no one has been brave enough to try Johansson tigers or great white sharks).
- Other animals can also do it – cats are good at identifying Johansson cats.
- Some cells in the primate brain (in the superior temporal sulcus, if you need to know) that appear to be selective for a person that is walking also fire just as well to Johansson figures.

So we are clearly very sensitive to these complex patterns of motion. It should be stressed that this is not something that we have to work out, the perception is automatic. So for instance, if we turn our Johansson figure upside down the perception of a person is lost and it now just looks like a bunch of moving spots.

Brain imaging studies have shown a unique pattern of activity for Johansson figures, suggesting that there are areas that respond only to this biological motion. To do this the scientists compared brain activity when the person was viewing a Johansson figure, compared to when they viewed the same movie but with the frames jumbled up. Note that in both cases exactly the same dots are shown but only in the first case do we get the sensation of a person walking.

the station – it was the other train that was moving, not ours. Clearly this is an example of induced movement. The inducing background is the small view out of the carriage window and we are sitting in the stationary part of the world that appears to move, so we feel ourselves moving. This feeling of self-motion is termed vection. A particular apparatus for inducing vection is shown in Figure 6.17. This optokinetic drum is basically a large cylinder that can be rotated around a person. If the drum begins to rotate, at first the person feels stationary and the drum appears to be rotating – which is fine because that's what's happening. However, after a few seconds the percept changes and the subject feels that they are rotating and the drum is stationary – which is weird, because that's not what's happening.

It takes a few seconds for this percept to happen, because normally when we move we get a signal from our vestibular organ (the balance organs in the ear) that lets us know that we are beginning to move. However, the vestibular organ only signals changes, so that once we reach a steady speed it no longer signals movement to us. Hence at first when the drum rotates we get no signal from our vestibular system (as we are not moving) and we

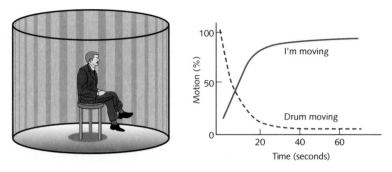

Fig. 6.17. An optokinetic drum, used in research on vection and motion sickness. When the drum first begins to move the person correctly believes the drum is moving and they are still, but after a few seconds they come to believe that they are moving and the drum is still.

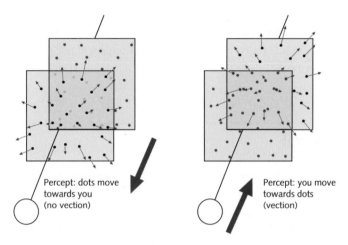

Fig. 6.18. An experiment to show that the 'background' causes the feelings of vection. The observer sees two sheets of transparent dots. In one case (left) the dots in the foreground move towards the observer – the observer sees dots moving towards them. In the other case (right) the dots in the background move towards the observer – the observer feels themselves moving forwards (vection).

therefore attribute the perceived motion to the drum. A few seconds later we would not expect a signal from our vestibular system – hence there is nothing to override our sensible assumption that walls do not move, therefore we must be moving. The key thing about vection is the expectation that if the background is moving this is probably because we are moving, and if it is stationary then we feel stationary. This idea can be illustrated by a simple experiment (see Figure 6.18).

Subjects viewed a screen full of dots that moved as if they were coming towards the subject (somewhat akin to the opening credits of the original *Star Trek*). The experimenters also presented a set of stationary dots that could either appear just in front of the moving ones, or just behind, and measured whether or not the stimulus induced vection. They found that if the stationary dots were behind the moving ones no vection was felt, but if the stationary ones were in front strong vection occurred. In this latter condition the subjects report that the stationary dots appear to move along with the subject, as if they were dirty marks on a windscreen. This result shows that when the stationary dots were the background (appeared behind) the subject feels no motion, but when the stationary dots are the foreground (appeared in front), and therefore the moving dots are the background, a feeling of vection does occur.

Such movements of the outside world are also important in maintaining our balance. If the world moves forwards this might be because we are swaying backwards and hence we correct for this by swaying more forwards. With this in mind some shameless psychologists who should remain nameless (Lee and Lishman, 1976) exploited the inability of young children to stand very easily. They placed the toddlers in a room in which they, the experimenters, could move the walls while keeping the floor stationary. When a toddler had managed to get to her feet they moved the walls slightly. This caused the toddler to fall. What is more, they could predict just which part of her anatomy she landed on. If the walls moved away from her, this made the toddler think she was swaying backwards, so she swayed forwards and landed on her nose. Similar logic will tell you how to make the toddler land on her bum.

Vection and vomit

Feelings of vection may have lots of uses and can be lots of fun – fairgrounds often used to have an attraction called the 'Haunted Swing', where the walls of a room could be swung back and forth, making the stationary observers feel that they were swinging – but they can also have bad side-effects. One of these is the feeling of motion sickness. Many people (particularly people from east Asia) who are placed in an optokinetic drum (Figure 6.17) quickly develop feelings of nausea and, if the experimenter is too slow in stopping the motion, vomit all over the apparatus. The exact reasons for these strange reactions (and the related ones of travel sickness and even space sickness) are not well understood. One hypothesis is that there is a mismatch between the senses, so, for example, vision tells you that you are moving but the vestibular system (or other senses) disagree. That may be so – but why attempt to solve the problem by emptying your stomach? It is suggested that this mismatch between the senses might be an indication that something was going wrong with them – perhaps due to being poisoned. Therefore any indication of a mismatch induces us to get rid of what may be poisoning us – we therefore vomit. Clearly, this is an unfortunate consequence for some people, and a possible handicap in a world where virtual reality simulators are likely to play an increasing role.

Conclusion

Motion perception is vitally important to most living organisms and hence nearly all have specialist equipment within their visual systems designed to calculate the directions and speeds both of things moving out in the world, and of their own movements within this world. Humans (and other primates) appear to have an area within the brain (known as area MT or area V5) that is dedicated to seeing motion (in fact there are several other areas as well, but we skipped that bit). These areas help us with the complicated task of working out just what is moving, and how it is moving, from the complex pattern of motions that hit our retina and need to take into account information about how our eyes, head, and body are also moving.

● READINGS AND REFERENCES

There is a whole book devoted to motion perception (Smith and Snowden, 1994), and since it is by one of us, we shall unashamedly recommend that you buy it. There is also a whole book devoted to the motion after-effect (Mather *et al.*, 1998), and as another of us has a chapter in it we recommend that too. It will provide even the most enthusiastic with more information on this topic than is healthy.

Papers on specific issues

The motion detector How to build a motion detector is covered by Borst and Egelhaaf (1989), which covers findings from many different species (including ourselves).

Apparent motion The study of apparent motion has a long history and has been studied both in humans (Braddick, 1980) and in animals (Mikami *et al.*, 1986; Newsome *et al.*, 1986).

Speed The effects of contrast on speed were first documented by Thompson (1982), and then pinched by Snowden *et al.* (1998). Recent work has begun to look at speed responses in the cells of various brain areas – the papers by Liu and Newsome (2003) and Perrone and Thiele (2001) are interesting.

The motion after-effect A delightful historical review of this famous effect is given by Wade (1994), which also points to many other readings. Descriptions of the MAE and area MT can be found in Tootell *et al.* (1995a).

Area MT (V5) For studies of lesions and single cells, Movshon and Newsome (1992) provide a very easy review. For studies of human MT, see Tootell *et al.* (1995b) and Culham *et al.* (2001). The 'Enigma' picture is studied by Zeki *et al.* (1993).

Vection and vomit The study looking at foreground and background can be found in Ohmi and Howard (1988), and the nauseating effects of motion are reviewed by Stern and Koch (1996). The evil fiends making toddlers fall over are Lee and Lishman (1975). That Asians are more susceptible to motion sickness can be pursued in Stern *et al.* (1996).

The wagon wheel effect Whether the effect can really be seen in continuous illumination remains an unresolved issue, but the review by Andrews and Purves (2005) weighs up the current knowledge.

Biological motion The classic work of Johansson is well documented in Johansson (1975). More recent work on similar issues can be found in Shiffrar (1994), and the inevitable fMRI hunt for the brain areas involved is in Grossman *et al.* (2000).

● POSSIBLE ESSAY TITLES, TUTORIALS, AND QUESTIONS OF INTEREST

1 How has the study of illusory motion helped us understand how we perceive motion?

2 Why doesn't the world appear to move each time I slowly move my eyes?

3 Is there a special place for processing motion in the human brain?

4 What is vection, and why does it arise?

References

Addams, R. (1834). An account of a peculiar optical phænomenon seen after having looked at a moving body. *London and Edinburgh Philosophical Magazine and Journal of Science* 5, 373–374.

Andrews, T. and Purves, D. (2005). The wagon-wheel illusion in continuous light. *Trends in Cognitive Sciences* 9, 261–263.

Borst, A. and Egelhaaf, M. (1989). Principles of visual motion detection. *Trends in Neurosciences* 12, 297–306.

Braddick, O. J. (1980). Low-level and high-level processes in apparent motion. *Philosophical Transactions of the Royal Society of London B* 290, 137–151.

Culham, J., He, S., Dukelow, S. and Verstraten, F. A. J. (2001). Visual motion and the human brain: what has neuroimaging told us? *Acta Psychologica* 107, 69–94.

Grossman, E.D., Donnelly, M., Price, R., Pickens, D., Morgan, V., Neighbor, G. and Blake, R. (2000). Brain areas involved in perception of biological motion. *Journal of Cognitive Neuroscience*, 12, 711–720.

Johansson, G. (1975). Visual motion perception. *Scientific American* **232**, January, 76–88.

Lee, D. N. and Lishman, R. (1975) Visual proprioceptive control of stance. *Journal of Human Movement Studies* 1, 87–95.

Liu, J. and Newsome, W. T. (2003). Functional organization of speed tuned neurons in visual area MT. *Journal of Neurophysiology* **89**, 246–256.

Mather, G., Verstraten, F., and Anstis, S. (1998). *The motion after-effect – a modern perspective*. Cambridge, MA: MIT Press.

Mikami, A., Newsome, W.T., and Wurtz, R. H. (1986). Motion selectivity in macaque visual cortex. II. Spatiotemporal range of directional interactions in MT and V1. *Journal of Neurophysiology* 55, 1328–1339.

Movshon, J. A. and Newsome, W. T. (1992). Neural foundations of visual motion perception. *Current Directions in Psychological Science* 1, 35–39.

Newsome, W. T., Mikami, A., and Wurtz, R. H. (1986). Motion selectivity in macaque visual cortex. III. Psychophysics and physiology of apparent motion. *Journal of Neurophysiology* 55, 1340–1351.

Ohmi, M. and Howard, I. P. (1988). Effect of stationary objects on illusory forward self-motion induced by a looming display. *Perception* **17**, 5–12.

Perrone, J. A. and Thiele, A. (2001). Speed skills: measuring the visual speed analyzing properties of primate MT neurons. *Nature Neuroscience* **4**, 526–532.

Pinna, B. and Brelstaff, G. J. (2000). A new visual illusion of relative motion. *Vision Research* **40**, 2091–2096.

Rechtschaffen, A. and Mednick, O. (1955). The autokinetic word technique. *Journal of Abnormal and Social Psychology* **51**, 346–348.

Salzman, C. D., Britten, K. H., and Newsome, W. T. (1990). Cortical microstimulation influences perceptual judgements of motion direction. *Nature* **346**, 174–177.

Shiffrar, M. (1994). When what meets where. *Current Directions in Psychological Science* 3, 96–100.

Smith, A. T. and Snowden, R. J. (1994). *Visual detection of motion*. New York: Academic Press.

Snowden, R. J., Stimpson, N., and Ruddle, R. A. (1998). Speed perception fogs up as visibility drops. *Nature* **392**, 450.

Stern, R. M. and Koch, K. L. (1996). Motion sickness and differential susceptibility. *Current Directions in Psychological Science* 5, 115–120.

Stern, R. M., Hu, S., Uijtdehaage, S. H., Muth, E. R., Xu, L. H., and Koch K. L. (1996). Asian hypersusceptibility to motion sickness. *Human Heredity* **46**, 7–14.

Thompson, P. (1982). Perceived rate of movement depends on contrast. *Vision Research* **22**, 377–380.

Tootell, R. B. H., Reppas, J. B., Dale, A .M., Look, R. B., Sereno, M. I., Malach, R., Brady, T. S., and Rosen, B. R. (1995a). Visual motion after-effect in human cortical area MT revealed by functional magnetic imaging. *Nature* **375**, 139–141.

Tootell, R. B. H., Reppas, J. B., Kwong, K., Malach, R., Born, R. T., Brady, T. S., Rosen, B. R., and Belliveau, J. W. (1995b). Functional analysis of human MT and related visual cortical areas using magnetic resonance imaging. *Journal of Neuroscience* **15**, 3215–3230.

Wade, N. J. (1994). A selective history of the study of visual motion after-effects. *Perception* **23**, 1111–1134.

Zeki, S., Watson, J. D. G., and Frackowiak, R. S. J. (1993). Going beyond the information given: the relation of illusory visual motion to brain activity. *Proceedings of the Royal Society of London B* **252**, 215–222.

CHAPTER 7

The third dimension

'Valley' by the artist/scientist Akiyoshi Kitaoka. The centre of the figure seems to be disappearing into the distance. The lines are actually straight! One of the cues we use to perceive depth is the changing size of the 'square' elements. Our brains interpret these changes not as changes in the shape itself, but as seeing the same shape from a different angle.

CHAPTER OVERVIEW

Vision has evolved so that we can interact with our world – picking up our pint of beer, steering our car along a winding road (not necessarily in that order!), or throwing a ball to land in just the intended spot. Each of these activities (and thousands more) requires that we have a good estimate of how far away the glass, the bend in the road, or the catcher, is located. However, when we consider the picture formed by our eye upon the retina, we see that this is no trivial task. The picture formed on the retina of each eye is flat (two-dimensional) yet the visual system must somehow interpret this flat image as one with depth (and the correct depth at that). In this chapter we see that there are many possible routes to achieving this depth information, ranging from the fact that we have two such images (because we have two eyes), to simple cues such as the pattern of shadows in the image. This information about depth in turn helps us decide about the shape and size of the objects around us.

Introduction

Figure 7.1 shows a picture of what you might see while walking through a forest. Light reflected from each tree makes an image on the retina, and its position on the retina tells us about its position in space – that is, how far to the left or right, up or down the tree is from our fixation point. However, the position on the retina does not tell us anything about how far away the tree is. If we are to avoid crashing into it, we need this information. Without this information we shall also be unable to make other judgements about the trees, such as how large they are – is tree x bigger than tree y, or is it merely closer to us? You may already be saying to yourself something like *'well, I can tell that tree x is closer because it blocks the view of tree y'*. In other words, you could use your knowledge about the world – such as occlusion or size – to give clues to the depth of things. We shall see in this chapter that this knowledge is indeed used in order to help us give depth to the scene. However, rather than needing to be thought about consciously, this knowledge is implemented automatically early in our visual systems so that we have no choice but to see the world in three dimensions (3-D). This is illustrated by Figure 7.2. It appears that the staircase continually goes up. Or down! Clearly this is impossible in the real three-dimensional world. The artist's 'trick' is simply that it is possible to draw such a thing in two dimensions – however, your brain insists in interpreting this image in three dimensions even though you know that the perceptual solution that arises from this is wrong.

Fig. 7.1. A forest. Can you tell how far away each tree is? How large is each tree?

Fig. 7.2. An impossible staircase. One of the wonderful drawings by Maurits Escher showing how 2-D images can represent impossible 3-D worlds.

Stereoscopic vision

Have you ever pondered about why most people have two eyes? Or indeed why nearly all animals have two (rather than one, or three, or more) eyes? Do we simply carry a 'spare'? And why are they positioned where they are?

Many animals have their two eyes positioned on the sides of their head (e.g. rabbits and chickens – Figure 7.3), and this seems a very useful design as it means they can see all around their bodies (Figure 7.4). On the other hand many other animals (such as cats, owls, and we primates) have eyes close together at the front of their heads and pointing in the same direction. Hence we cannot see round the back of our heads (despite what teachers writing on blackboards might claim). This appears to be a massive drawback compared to chickens and rabbits. So what is the reason for this positioning of our eyes?

Fig. 7.3. In many animals the two eyes are positioned on either side of the head; others have them both at the front. Generally predators have their eyes at the front and prey have them on the side of the head.

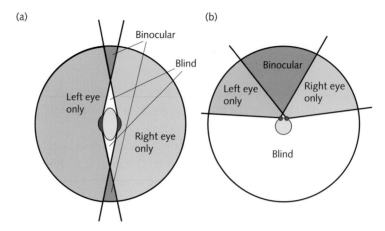

Fig. 7.4. Differences in view depending on whether the eyes are positioned at the side or the head (a) or at the front of the head (b).

What is the great advantage conferred by having our two eyes close together that outweighs being able to see all around ourselves?

As illustrated in Figure 7.4, the only advantage of placing the two eyes close together on the front of our faces is that a larger area is seen by both eyes. This area of binocularity must confer some advantage over just being able to see the world with one eye. In this binocular region the eyes share most of the same view of the world, but do so from slightly different positions because our eyes are about 6–6.5 cm apart. This means they do not receive exactly the same view of a scene. To illustrate this, hold a finger a few centimetres from your face directly in front of your nose and then place another finger at arm's length beyond the first finger, also directly in front of your nose. When you close your right eye you will see the far finger to the left of the near finger; when you close your left eye you will see absolutely nothing if you've still got your right eye closed, so make sure it's open. Now the far finger is to the right of the near one. This should be straightforward, but look at Figure 7.5 if you need more clarification.

Being scientists, we have invented special words to describe these situations. First, if we stare at (or fixate) a close object it will be imaged on the fovea of each eye. We regard the foveas (or *foveae* if you've been to a proper school) as being at the same points on the two eyes and therefore images falling on the foveas are said to have no retinal disparity. Closer objects and more distant objects are imaged on different parts of each retina and are said to have retinal disparity, with objects further away from us than the fixation point being said to have a positive disparity or uncrossed disparity. Closer objects are said to have a negative disparity or crossed disparity. If we could extract this information about retinal disparity we would have valuable information about depth relative to where we are looking – things with a negative disparity are closer and those with positive disparities are further away. What is more, the greater the disparity, the closer or further away the object must be.

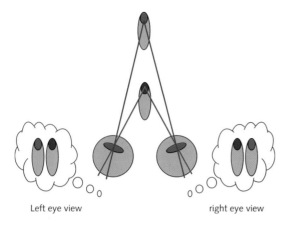

Left eye view   right eye view

Fig. 7.5. Illustration of how binocular disparity arises. See text for details.

Fig. 7.6. A Victorian stereogram. Two pictures of a scene taken from cameras about 6.5 cm apart.

Most of us can indeed use this information about retinal disparity to get a strong impression of depth and we term this **stereopsis**. To illustrate this we would like to produce a **stereogram**. Such stereograms consist of two pictures of the same scene but with the two cameras at slightly different positions (ideally they would be about 6.5 cm apart so as to mimic the positions of our own eyes). Note that although the pictures are very similar there are subtle differences due to the slightly different viewpoints (Figure 7.6). These differences *are* the binocular disparity.

Now we need a technique to ensure that our left eye views only the picture taken by the left camera, and the right eye views only the picture taken by the right camera. There are several ways this may be achieved.

Red/green anaglyphs

This technique is perhaps the most famous, and is very simple and very effective. This is how it works. We take a picture of the scene from the left eye position with a red filter on the camera, and one from the right eye position with a green filter on the camera (Figure 7.7a). The two pictures are now combined; note that bits of the scene that are in both images will add the red and green images to appear white, like the circle in our picture. Now we look at our composite image with red and green goggles – a red filter over the left eye and a green filter over the right (Figure 7.7b). Now this is the clever bit; through the red filter the red bits of the image will look red and the white bits will look red as well, but green things will look black and so can't be seen against the black background. So the left eye just sees the bits of the picture taken by the left-hand camera. And, of course, the right eye sees just the bits of the picture taken with the right-hand camera, and our brain then reconstructs the original 3-D scene. This technique was popular with movie makers in the 1950s (Figure 7.8), but it suffers from some serious drawbacks, the chief of which is that it really messes up the colour of the movie. If you go to a new IMAX cinema you might get to see 3-D films using a different sort of goggles that allows the colours to be preserved. These goggles have two grey filters and the trick is that they separate the two images by using the polarization of the light rather than red and green, but the logic of the method stays the same.

Stereoscopes

Another method is to use mirrors or lenses to present each image to each eye – you may well remember playing with your View-Master stereoscope as a child. Stereoscopes became popular in Victorian times until it was found that the ideal image to give good depth was one with soft sensuous contours, with firm rounded peaks and plunging cleavage (Figure 7.9). Whereupon they ceased to be beloved of dirty old men and became children's toys: they survived to bore us with pictures of Alpine landscapes and the Eiffel

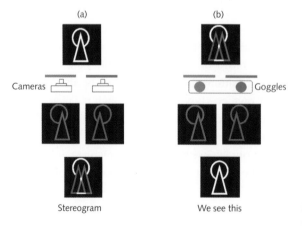

Fig. 7.7. How to produce a stereogram. See text for details.

Fig. 7.8. Cinema audience enjoying a 3-D movie.

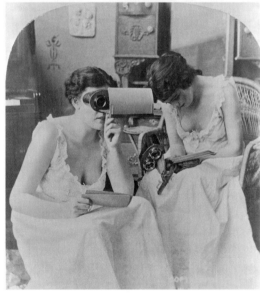

Fig. 7.9. Two young ladies enjoying a stereoscope.

Tower during the 1950s, and View-Master is now owned by Fisher-Price, with the current product range featuring mainly dinosaurs and Disney characters.

Nowadays many virtual reality headsets use the technique of presenting the two images on alternate frames of a movie. All the odd-numbered frames (1, 3, 5, . . .) are shown to the left eye only and the even-numbered frames to the right eye. To achieve this, electronic shutters over each eye open and close rapidly as each frame appears – and this is so quick that the flickering is not visible.

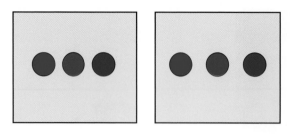

Fig. 7.10. A simple stereogram for free fusion.

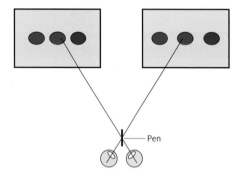

Fig. 7.11. How to free-fuse a stereogram.

Free fusion

Finally, the low-tech way is to cross your eyes (known as **cross-fusion** or free fusion). Figure 7.10 is a simple stereogram designed to help you achieve the 3-D percept. Hold the book at approximately arm's length. Now hold a pen (or a finger will do) so that the top of the pen is directly between the two images on the page. Now stare at the top of the pen and slowly bring the pen towards your nose – *keep focusing on the pen*. You will notice that the red and green dots will start to move and, when the pen is about halfway to your nose, it will appear that there are three pictures! When this happens, keep staring at the pen but try to relax your vision so that the image in the middle comes into focus. If this happens you should get a strong impression that the red dot is further away and the blue dot nearer. If this works then go back to Figure 7.6 and use the same technique to cross-fuse those two images. You will probably have seen Magic Eye pictures and perhaps have wondered how they work. Well, they are just using free-fusion in a very clever way, as we explain in Box 7.1.

When we look at the 'real' world we don't need these tricks since each eye gets different images anyway – that is the whole point of stereopsis. The tricks are needed to fuse 2-D *images* of the world or simpler scenes. Of course, this is what happens in many experiments since it's easier to control images than the real world!

OK, we now have our ways of getting the different images into each eye. What we see, however, is not the two flat (2-D) images we presented but one image that has depth (3-D). The brain has fused the two images together to form one, using the differences (which we termed retinal disparity) to calculate the depth of each part of the image.

Magic Eye pictures or autostereograms

There is a clever way to engage stereopsis that uses only one image. You have doubtless seen **Magic Eye** pictures, which you stare at for some time and gradually notice that a pattern in depth emerges as if by magic.

Unfortunately, there's no magic. Such patterns, known by serious people as **autostereogram**s, were described first by Christopher Tyler, and are a neat way of ensuring that slightly different images get routed to each of our two eyes. Figures 7.1.1 and 7.1.2 show two examples. The first is a complex example, of the sort commonly referred to as Magic Eye.

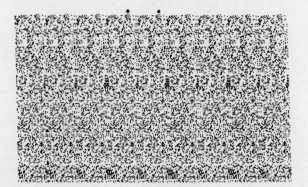

Fig. 7.1.1. One of the original autostereograms devised by Christopher Tyler in 1979. Cross your eyes slightly so that the two solid fixation dots above the figure appear as three dots in a line. Focus on the centre dot until the rest of the display if perceived as a chequer board in depth.

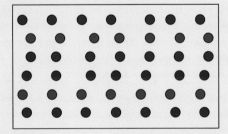

Fig. 7.1.2. Simplified autostereogram.

The second is a simplified version – but it works in exactly the same way. In this simplified version it is easy to see that the pattern repeats itself over and over again in a series of stripes, somewhat like wallpaper (indeed, early versions of this phenomenon were known as the **wallpaper illusion**). However, notice that the stripes do not repeat perfectly – some of the elements are displaced in their position within the stripe.

The key to understanding how this trick works is to realize that, normally, the two eyes converge so that the fovea of each eye is pointing at the same point in space, some point on the surface of the autostereogram, as in Figure 7.1.3. However, if we do this (as a Magic Eye novice might), the stereo effect cannot work *because each eye is seeing the same image*, and the retinal disparity is therefore zero, all elements will appear at the same depth and the flat image will look like, well, a flat image.

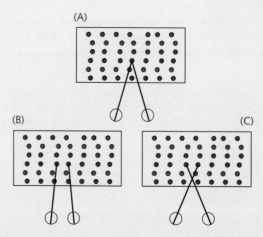

Fig. 7.1.3. How autostereograms work. The critical thing about them is that you must fuse different objects from the picture so that they appear to be a single object in depth.

Now, imagine that you learn to change the way your eyes converge so that the two eyes are no longer looking at the same spots, but that one eye looks at one spot while the other eye looks at a different spot. This can be done in two ways. The first, favoured by the authors, is to hold the picture very close to your face so that the eyes cannot converge enough to fuse the disparate images, so you get double vision. Now as you move the picture slowly away from your eyes there should come a time when one eye is converging on one spot and the other on the adjacent spot, as in Figure 7.1.3B. We now have different spots being seen by each eye and because of the small shifts in the position of the dots in each stripe we have retinal disparity . . . . And we know how the brain interprets retinal disparity. Hey presto – we see depth.

We can also use the method of looking at our pen top placed in front of the autostereogram – see Figure 7.1.3C – to get our eyes looking at the different stripes. This reverses the depth relationships compared to the first method, and so the Magic Eye picture may appear strange as they are generally designed to be viewed by the first method.

There is, however, a down-side to this illusion. As mentioned earlier, other repeating patterns such as wallpaper can cause illusions of depth. One such culprit is the tiling often found above the urinal in pubs – just take our word for this, girls. Do not be tempted to rest your head on the tiles while using the urinal. The combination of poor vergence control induced by alcohol and the wallpaper illusion can lead you to think the tiles are closer (or further away) than they actually are – with disastrous consequences.

The correspondence problem and random dot stereograms

Now that we have observed this effect, let us think a little as to just what our brain has done to give us this wonderful impression of depth. We have tried to say that each part of the scene will have a retinal disparity, and the sign and magnitude of this disparity will give us this depth. All well and good – all our brain then has to do is to find the corresponding parts of the image in the left and right eyes' view and calculate this disparity. We could call the first part of this operation the **correspondence problem** – which part of the

---

BOX 7.2 **Binocular rivalry and diplopia**

When the two eyes see slightly different images, the brain can fuse these images into one, and turn the differences between the two eyes' images into information about the depth of objects. But what would happen if the brain cannot fuse the two images into one because they are so different, such as those illustrated in Figure 7.2.1A?

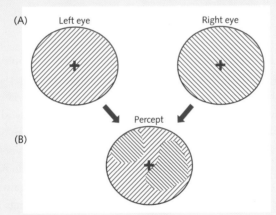

Fig. 7.2.1. Binocular rivalry. If the eyes receive very different pictures of the world, they alternate between seeing bits of each picture.

Such very different images often give rise to the phenomenon of **binocular rivalry**. Under these conditions the observer sees bits of both images but not in the same part of the field, and what they see changes over time. To illustrate this Figure 7.2.1B shows what happens if we show right-tilting green lines to the left eye and left-tilting purple lines to the right eye. We get a percept of parts of the green lines and parts of the purple lines. This percept changes over the course of a few seconds, with other parts of the pictures entering your conscious vision. At some points in time the whole of one picture might dominate, while at other times the other picture might be visible. How long one dominates depends upon various factors, but very dull pictures with few contours tend to be dominated by ones with many contours, especially moving contours. In cases of abnormal vision where one eye is much weaker than the other the strong eye always seems to win this battle – this is called **binocular suppression**.

In other cases we seem to see both images at the same time (Figure 7.2.2) – this is known as **diplopia** or **double vision**.

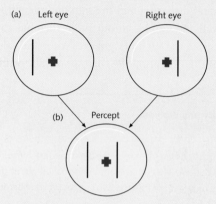

(a)   Left eye   Right eye

(b)   Percept

Fig. 7.2.2. Illustration of diplopia – seeing double.

image in the left eye matches which part in the right eye? For example, in Figure 7.6 we could find a gravestone in the left image and the same gravestone in the right image and then calculate the disparity in the two images and hence the depth. This is fine if there is only one gravestone in the scene, but what if there were two nearly identical graves (as there are on the far left of the pictures)? How would the visual system decide which cross in the left eye goes with which cross in the right eye? What if there were not two possible matches but many, possibly thousands? An example in real life would be to look down at pebbles or, even worse, sand on a beach – now for each pebble or grain of sand identified in one eye there are many thousands or even millions of similar things in the other eye – how can a match be achieved?

This problem was highlighted and exploited by the use of **random dot stereograms** introduced by the Hungarian scientist Bela Julesz in the 1960s (an example is given in Figure 7.12). One half of the stereogram consists of many thousands of identical dots randomly arranged. To produce the other half the same dots are copied, but a small section of them is moved horizontally and the resulting gap is filled in with more dots. This small section will now have a different retinal disparity from the other dots, and will therefore appear to have a different depth (Figure 7.13). Confused? Imagine you are looking at a sheeting of paper covered with random dots and you now place a small square of paper covered with similar random dots somewhat closer to you. Can you see the smaller square of dots? Yes, of course you can, and you can see them at the correct depth too. But think what each eye is seeing

Fig. 7.12. A random dot stereogram. See text for details.

Fig. 7.13. The same random dot stereogram as in Figure 7.12, but with the area of shifted dots highlighted. See text for details.

Fig. 7.14. Appearance of a random dot stereogram.

individually; the left eye will see some random dots on a background random of dots and so will the right eye. So each eye sees nothing but random dots, but the brain picks up the disparity in the patterns of the random dots and creates for us an image of two squares hovering in front of the background (Figure 7.14).

You might argue – and you would be right to do so – that in our example above we will see the edges of our floating squares of dots and, what's more, the dots will be slightly larger on the forward squares. But in the computer-generated random dot stereograms of Bela Julesz these problems don't arise, and we can still see the 3-D image.

In our stereogram in Figure 7.12 we first created a pattern of random dots (this is the left image), and then made a copy (this is the right image). In this copy we selected two areas (each 8 × 8 dots big) and moved all the dots in one of the sections by 1 dot to the right, and all the dots in the other section by 2 dots to the right (in Figure 7.13 we have coloured the moved dots so as to make it obvious how they have moved). When you look at either of these images (the ones that are all the same colour) it is not easy to spot the difference between the patterns – they look equally boring. However, try and fuse them together to get the depth (remember the pencil trick). What you should see now is these two square areas floating above the background, and the one that was shifted the most (and therefore has the larger retinal disparity) should appear to float above the other (Figure 7.14).

What is crucial to remember from this demonstration is that in the view from each eye alone there are no such squares! They are only present when the images from the two eyes are combined by our brain. Note that if you rotate your head these shifts are no longer in the horizontal plane with respect to your eyes, and so the squares disappear. This principle of introducing small differences between the two eyes in order to simulate (and stimulate) depth can produce any arbitrary pattern (see Figure 7.15).

Random dot stereograms are not just fun – indeed, some of you will think that they are not *even* fun – they tell us something very important about what it is that is matched from one eye to the other. In Figure 7.6 we suggested that we might find the gravestone in one image and match it to the same gravestone in the other image. This would be equivalent to

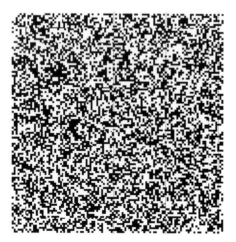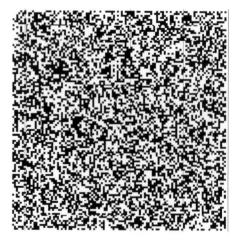

Fig. 7.15. Complex random dot stereogram. Can you see the 3-D object hidden in the stereogram? The stereo image can take quite a long time to emerge, especially when you're not used to looking a random dot stereograms. But be patient, it'll be worth the wait.

saying that in Figure 7.12 let's find one of the large squares in one eye and match it to one of the large squares in the other eye. However, there are no squares in the left eye or in the right eye alone! This demonstration shows that whatever is matched between the two eyes, it is not a highly complicated form such as an gravestone or a particular shape, but must be some rather low-level aspect of the image such as individual dots or clusters of dots. To put it another way, and this is the important bit, so concentrate: when we look at a regular stereoscopic scene (like the stereogram in Figure 7.6) it would make sense that what we do is first find the edges, then calculate the disparities between the edges in the two images, and finally covert these disparities into depths. This sensible scheme is completely contradicted by Julesz's random dot stereograms. They show that it is possible for the extraction of disparity to come before the extraction of contour, because there is no contour in the random dot stereogram until we've sorted out the disparity.

So how do we extract the disparity information? If it is done at the level of the individual dots this poses a huge correspondence problem: pick a blue dot in the left image and try to match it to one in the right image – this clearly won't work, because it could match any one of thousands of blue dots. Yet your brain appears to do this automatically and swiftly. Well, you might say, I managed to solve it by looking at a group of blue dots in one eye and matching them to an identical group of blue dots in the other eye. This is probably a very good strategy, but how big is the group of dots that is matched? Is it 2 dots, 4 dots, 16 dots, or more?

Many schemes have been suggested to help perform this matching operation, and some have been remarkably successful. This area remains of great interest not only to people working on biological vision, but also to those trying to produce artificial visual systems needed for guiding robots and other machines.

Physiological mechanisms and disparity

In the above discussion we have tried to highlight the notion of retinal disparity as a major cue to depth. We should therefore expect to find cells within the brain that are sensitive to retinal disparity. Clearly, to find such cells we need to look in a place where information from the two eyes comes together. Moving back from the retina, the first place where information from both eyes comes together is in the striate cortex (area V1) and it has indeed been shown that many of these cells are sensitive to the retinal disparity of the images in the two eyes.

Figure 7.16 shows the firing rates of four cells as a function of the depth of the test area (where depth is being defined by retinal disparity). We can see that the cell illustrated in the top section responded vigorously to small disparities (particularly slightly negative ones) but not to large disparities – such cells have been termed **tuned excitatory**. Other cells fire only to large disparities and these are termed **tuned inhibitory**. Some cells fired most when the test stimulus was further away from the point of fixation (i.e. had positive or uncrossed disparity) and this type of response was termed a **far** cell. Again there are

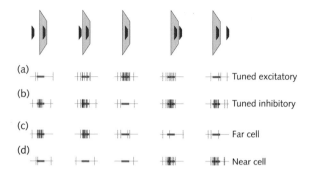

Fig. 7.16. Response of cells to different binocular disparities: (a) a cell that fires most to small binocular disparities (tuned excitatory); (b) a cell that fires least to small binocular disparities (tuned inhibitory); (c) a cell that fires most to positive binocular disparities (far cell); (d) a cell that fires most to negative binocular disparities (near cell). Such cells have been found in areas V1 and V2 in primates.

similar cells responding to negative disparities termed **near** cells. Studies have shown that many cells of areas V1 and V2 are able to respond to random dot stereograms in the same disparity-tuned manner. Thus these cells must have some manner of solving the difficult correspondence problems set by these stereograms.

Stereo-blindness

Some readers will by now be scratching their heads and wondering what we have been talking about. Around 5% of the population are unable to make out the figures such as those embedded in Figures 7.12 and 7.15, and are therefore said to be **stereo-blind**. (Of course, perhaps more than 5% of you may have no idea what we have been trying to say, although you have fine stereo vision, simply because you are hard of understanding. We offer our sympathies to both groups.) The condition of stereo-blindness seems to arise from visual problems in early life – most typically these individuals might have had a squint (sometimes called a strabismus or lazy eye) when young. This means the two eyes are not properly aligned, which is crucial if similar images are to fall on corresponding points in the two eyes. Without similar images in the two eyes the brain fails to learn how to put the images together during these crucial early years, and so never learns how to use the retinal disparity to calculate and see this 3-D information. In Chapter 8 we shall explore early vision and its development in more detail, including the development of stereo vision.

It may have been surprising to learn that 5% of people do not share the ability to see the depth through stereopsis. Indeed, the greatest surprise is felt by the individuals who are stereo-blind, as most of them are unaware of their 'problem'. After all, they do not appear different, and they can pick up beer glasses and drive cars just like the rest of us. Likewise, if those of us who do have stereopsis shut one eye the world does not normally shrink into a flat 2-D picture. Clearly, then, we must have other ways to get information about depth.

Motion parallax

Stereoscopic vision, as we have just seen, relies on getting two slightly different views of the world because our eyes are in slightly different positions. We could also get slightly different views by moving one eye to different positions. Let us try our two-finger demonstration again. Shut one eye and again hold two fingers out in front of you, one behind the other. Now move your head from side to side while keeping your fingers still. You should notice that the finger near you seems to move more than the finger further away (and that the background moves very little). Likewise, as you stare out from the window of a train the nearby tracks appear to whizz by, but the hills in the distance appear almost stationary. The geometry of these situations resembles that illustrated in Figure 7.6 for the stereo case, and is illustrated in Figure 7.17. Put simply, as we move around in the world, objects that are close to us move a lot on our retina, and objects that are far away move very little. So if we calculate the motion of these points in the image we could again use this to assign depth to each of the points (of course this assumes that the motion of the objects is caused by the movement of the viewer and not of the objects themselves). The way in which objects at different depths appear to move as we move is called **motion parallax**, and can be a very powerful depth cue.

A vivid demonstration of this was provided by Rogers and Graham (1979). They made a pattern of random dots on a screen. When stationary, these dots looked flat (as indeed they were). However, and this is the clever bit, Rogers and Graham yoked the movement of these dots to the movements of an observer so that if she moved her head, say, to the left, the dots would move in the manner expected if they were attached to a piece of corrugated iron (i.e. separate rows moved at different speeds – see Figure 7.18). Instead of seeing dots at the same depth moving at different speeds (which was actually what she was seeing) the observer interpreted the movements of the dots as arising from a stationary object that had depth (like a piece of corrugated iron covered in spots) with the movement being due to motion parallax rather than real movement. So what she actually

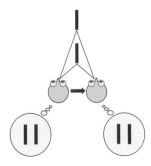

Fig. 7.17. Motion parallax. As the head or eyes move, things closer to us move more across our retina than things far away from us.

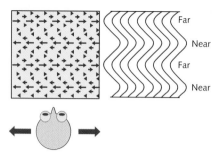

Fig. 7.18. Perception of depth from motion parallax. See text for details.

views is a set of moving dots on a flat screen; what she perceives is a set of stationary dots on a screen with depth.

Motion parallax is such a salient cue to depth that it is not surprising that it is widely used throughout the animal kingdom. We are sure that you will have observed a cat ready to pounce upon some unfortunate prey (or perhaps an unfortunate ball of wool). The cat typically moves its head from side to side or bobs up and down, trying to extract more exact depth information in order to ensure that its pounce will be accurate. Professional golfers can also be spotted in similar behaviour before a crucial putt.

Pictorial cues

Have a look at Figure 7.19. In this scene we cannot make use of stereopsis – the flat page has no depth – and we cannot make use of motion parallax either. But we can see depth in this picture.

The cues that give us this information from simple 2-D stationary pictures are therefore termed the **pictorial** cues. Each of them relies on certain assumptions about how the world is organized. As we describe these various cues in the sections below, have a look back at Figure 7.19 and work out to what extent each cue is present in the image.

Occlusion or interposition

In the real world, if one object is directly in front of another it will occlude some part of it. In Figure 7.19 you will find it easy to identify objects in the foreground because they block out the stuff behind them which is further away. Now look at Figure 7.20, which shows a figure known as the Necker cube. This is an ambiguous figure in that it can be seen in two forms with the front surface down to the right (B) or up and to the left (C). You should find that cube A spontaneously flips from one percept to the other. This is because it is not clear which parts of the cube are in front and which parts are behind. However, if we add in some information about occlusion, as has been done in cubes B and C, then we can remove the ambiguity. The parts that are occluding the others are seen as the front of the object.

Fig. 7.19. Can you spot the depth cues that make this picture appear to have depth?

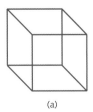 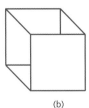 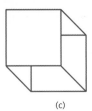

(a) (b) (c)

Fig. 7.20. Necker cubes. The cube on the left is ambiguous, but those to the right have had their ambiguity reduced greatly by the introduction of occlusion.

Before we leave the Necker cube, note that we said that it was an ambiguous figure because it can be seen in one of two ways. This, of course, is nonsense. There are many combinations of lines that could produce this image on the retina, but the strange thing is that we so easily fail to see the Necker cube for what it really is, a flat hexagonal shape with some lines on it. This illustrates how determined our visual system is to interpret 2-D images as representing 3-D objects.

Size cues

As an object gets further away from us, its image on our retina becomes smaller (Figure 7.21).

Thus if we look at railway lines disappearing into the distance, the width of the track in retinal terms gets thinner and thinner as it recedes into the distance (Figure 7.22). This cue is often termed linear perspective, and is taught to all young artists, but it can be thought of as an example of a size cue. If we know the real or relative size of something, then we can get an impression of its distance from us by how large its image is. Hence as we look along a row of parked cars we assume that those that look small are not toy cars, but normal cars that just happen to be far away from us. When we are viewing a scene that contains elements that are fairly similar in size such as a field of corn, the markings on a road, or the pebbles on a beach, we can get a vivid impression of depth, since these elements decrease in size as they recede into the distance (Figure 7.23). Sometimes this is

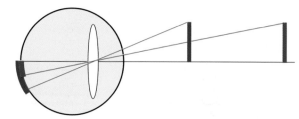

Fig. 7.21. Image size and distance. When objects double their distance from us, their image size on the retina is halved.

Fig. 7.22. Termini railway station, Rome. An example of linear perspective.

Fig. 7.23. Pebbles on a beach – an example of a texture gradient.

called 'texture perspective' or **texture gradients**. It is not necessary to know the 'real' size of the objects. Scientists studying depth perception use textures with arbitrary shapes and sizes (a bit like crazy paving – Figure 7.24) known as Voronoi patterns. These provide strong depth cues, despite the viewer not knowing what the real size of each element might be. The fact that, on average, they get smaller gives us the impression of a surface sloping away from us.

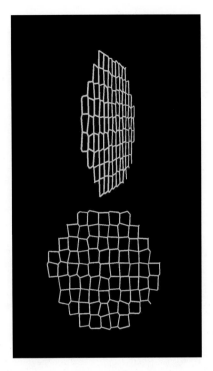

Fig. 7.24. Voronoi textures give a strong impression of depth.

Shading and shadows

A vivid impression of depth can be imparted to pictures by the appropriate use of shadows and shading. The brain (perhaps quite sensibly) seems to assume that light comes from above and can therefore decode shading and shadows to infer depth relationships. Look at the circles in Figure 7.25a. Those that are light at the top and dark at the bottom appear to stick out, whereas those that are light at the bottom and dark at the top appear to be indented into the page. Try turning the book upside down. You should find that those that used to stick in are now the indented ones, and vice versa. Try turning the book on its side. Now it's hard to be consistent about which are in and which are out – individual ones can appear to flick backwards and forwards. Now try another trick. Turn yourself upside down while viewing the figure! Which are seen as in and which out? You should find that the figures that stick out are the ones that have the light bit towards the top of your visual field (even though these light bits are now at the bottom with respect to the real world). It appears that this trick of 'light bit to the top' is implemented in your brain, with the assumption that you view things from an upright position. This is probably a very sensible assumption for most animals but not for students of vision science (or some practitioners of yoga)! Actually, the picture with bumps and dents is a bit boring, but look at Figure 7.25b; it really is hard to believe that these two images are identical, so turn the book upside down to convince yourself.

(a)

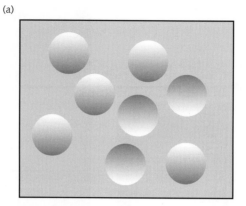

(b)

Fig. 7.25. (a) Shaded circles give the impression of depth. What happens if you turn the figure on its side, or upside down (or turn yourself upside down)? (b) Two identical pictures of a wood carving. Notice that we automatically assume that light is coming from above in these pictures.

Shadows, as we saw in Chapter 3, can also exert a great influence over how we interpret an image. Look at Figure 7.26. Where the shadows are directly under the balls we see the balls as lying on the floor, but where the shadows are separated from the balls we get a completely different interpretation of the depth in the picture.

Aerial perspective

Light gets scattered as it travels through the air; the further something is away from us, the more hazy it will appear. Figure 7.27 shows a picture taken in fairly misty conditions, and one can see that objects further away from the camera are indeed somewhat more hazy.

Fig. 7.26. Altering the position of the shadows alters the perceived position of the balls.

Fig. 7.27. Aerial perspective. Elements of the picture that are far away appear more hazy than those that are near.

The effects are also present in our original Figure 7.19. Aerial perspective normally only works over the large distances needed for changes in light scatter to produce significant haziness. However, under misty and foggy conditions this cue can affect our judgements of depth over smaller distances. Unfortunately it tends to make us think that things are further away than they are (under foggy conditions there is more scatter, and hence the impression of greater distance). Hence this particular cue may lead many drivers to drive too close to the car in front, or to misjudge the distance to a bend in the road, and may therefore be responsible for many accidents. Sometimes unusual aerial perspective makes us think that some objects are closer than they really are. This can happen at high altitude in mountains, or in deserts, where the air contains little of the moisture or pollutants that scatter light and make distant objects hazy. It would also happen most spectacularly if you ever travelled to the Moon, where there is no atmosphere.

The problem in such cases is that distant mountains look non-hazy and therefore close; in reality they may be much further away than you think.

The general point both here and elsewhere in this book is that if you find yourself in an unusual visual environments (fog, desert, the Moon), you become prone to making errors of visual judgement, because the visual mechanisms involved in making these judgements have been trained on 'normal' scenes.

Size constancy, depth perception, and illusions

Earlier we noted (Figure 7.1) that if a tree has a particular retinal size, this could be because you are looking at a small tree nearby or a large tree far away (or indeed an infinite range of trees and distances). This is true for any retinal image – any size of retinal image could be due to many combinations of size and distance. So as your friend walks towards you, how do you know whether she is approaching you rather than just swelling up like a balloon? The answer seems to be 'size constancy' – we have a built-in assumption that objects stay the same size and the most likely reason for an object's size to get bigger on your retina is that the object is now closer to you.

So how do we to get at the real size of an object? It appears that the brain has a fairly simple rule based on geometry. In the physical world the size of the image gets smaller in proportion to the distance from the observer, remember Figure 7.21; hence, the brain seems to employ the rule that *for a given retinal image size, perceived size is proportional*

to perceived distance – this relationship is termed Emmert's law after its inventor. Emmert's law can be easily demonstrated by burning a hole in your retina! There are several way to achieve this – the safest is to view Figure 7.28 under a very bright light and stare, with your eyes as still as possible, for a few seconds at the centre of the figure. A second way is to look directly into a flash from a camera's flash gun. (Looking directly at the Sun is *definitely not* recommended – this really will produce long-term damage to your retina. Sir Isaac Newton almost certainly burnt a permanent hole in his retina by so doing; he reported black disk-shaped after-images months after looking at the Sun.)

Bright lights temporarily bleach the photoreceptors and therefore provide a retinal image of constant size in the form of an after-image. Once you have got a good strong after-image, look at something close such as your hand in front of your face – the after-image appears quite small. Now look at a wall some distance away – the same after-image looks large (Figure 7.29)! This is because the constant size of the retinal image is being automatically scaled by the perceived distance of the after-image. If it is thought to be further away, then it must be a larger object.

Emmert's law may be responsible for a whole host of illusions of size. Remember that Emmert's law tells us that our perceived size of something is dependent on how far we believe the thing is away from us. Thus if we can fool the viewer into misjudging the distance of something we should also fool them about the size of the object (see

Fig. 7.28. After-image generator – see text for instructions.

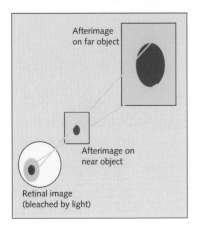

Fig. 7.29. The after-image appears larger as you focus on things that are further away.

Fig. 7.30. Size-constancy illusion. Identical globes appear to differ in size because of the depth indicated by the texture pattern on which they are superimposed. The images are best viewed monocularly through an aperture.

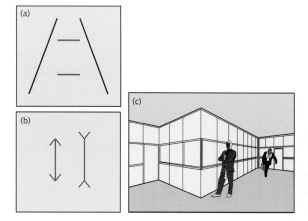

Fig. 7.31. Size illusions caused by misjudged depth: (a) the Ponzo illusion; (b), (c) the Muller–Lyer illusion. If you think a depth interpretation of the Muller–Lyer illusion seems a bit far fetched, look at the cartoon on p. 225.

Figure 7.30). A classic example of this is the Ponzo illusion (we mentioned it in Chapter 4, if you're wondering where you've heard the name before) where two lines simulate (by linear perspective) something akin to a road receding into the distance (Figure 7.31a).

Thus the top horizontal bar is perceived as further away than the lower one. Given that they have the same retinal image size (as they are the same size on the paper), this must mean that the top line is larger than the bottom one in the real world! With a bit of imagination a similar explanation can be given to the version of the Müller–Lyer illusion illustrated in Figure 7.31b,c. The general term used for this explanation of these illusions is misapplied constancy scaling – we scale the retinal size because we are fooled by the depth cues in the image. Indeed, given the wealth of cues to depth we have described above, you should be able to invent your own size illusions.

In these examples we had objects that were really at the same distance but we attempted to fool your visual system into thinking they were at slightly different depths. We can of

BOX 7.3   **Misapplied constancy scaling – does it really work?**

Although misapplied constancy scaling appears to explain the Ponzo and Muller–Lyer illusions (see main text), there are many situations where it seems to fail. For instance, we can produce versions of the Muller–Lyer illusion that replace the 'wings' with circles and therefore appear to have no depth (see Figure 7.3.1a), and yet the illusion still appears.

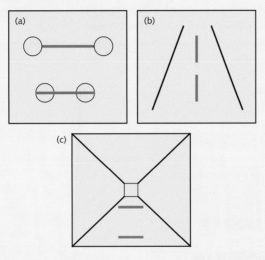

Fig. 7.3.1. Illusions that look very similar to the Ponzo and Muller–Lyer illusions but do not fit the misapplied constancy scaling theory.

Likewise, it has been claimed that if the test figures in the Ponzo illusion are vertical (see Figure 7.3.1b) the illusion is lost, despite the depth information being identical to when the test figures were horizontal. Finally, the bottom section of Figure 7.3.1c produces another version of the Ponzo illusion. In this case the figure is actually ambiguous and the central square can be seen as either receding into the figure (as if we're looking into a tunnel) or advancing out of the figure (think of flying over the pyramids). This in turn should govern which of the pink test lines is seen as closer to us, and therefore the perceived size of the lines according to the misapplied constancy scaling hypothesis. However, as the ambiguous figure flips from one interpretation to the other there is no sign of the illusion reversing. It is clear that there is far more to these (and other illusions) than just misapplied scaling – can you think what else might cause these illusions?

course reverse this logic and try to make you think that two things at the same distance when they are not. A classic example of this is the **Ames room** (Figure 7.32). The room appears to be inhabited by a giant and a dwarf. The room is actually highly distorted and the 'dwarf' is actually standing further away than the 'giant', so that the retinal image of her is smaller than that of the giant. However, the room is constructed so that there are no cues to this difference in depth and thus you naturally believe this to be a normally shaped room with the people at the same distance from you. Hence your visual system concludes that the people are of greatly different size. This logic also explains the table-top illusion you may remember from Chapter 0 (Figure 7.33). The table tops actually have exactly the same (2-D) shape – you can check this for yourself by cutting out a piece of paper to match the shape. However, despite this demonstration that the table tops are exactly the same, it is still hard to believe! Our 3-D interpretation of the scene tells us there is a short fat table and a long thin table, and this automatic perceptual interpretation of a world in 3-D cannot be overcome.

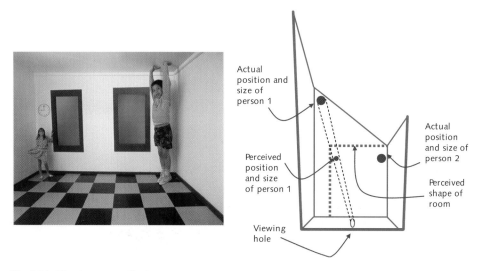

Actual position and size of person 1

Actual position and size of person 2

Perceived position and size of person 1

Perceived shape of room

Viewing hole

Fig. 7.32. The Ames room illusion.

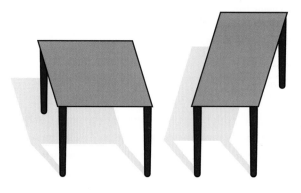

Fig. 7.33. The tables illusion. These two tabletops are identical in shape. The determination of our visual systems to interpret 2-D figures as 3-D objects leads to them appearing very different.

Combining cues to depth

In this chapter we have described lots of cues (but by no means all) that help us see the world in depth. However, what happens when the cues don't agree? For instance, when you look at a picture in a book or on a TV screen the stereo cues and the motion cues say that there is no depth, yet many pictorial cues say that there is depth (Figure 7.4.1). Are some cues more important than others?

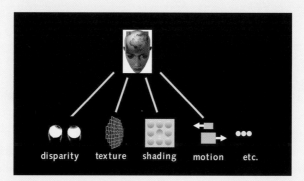

disparity   texture   shading   motion   etc.

Fig. 7.4.1. Most of the time there are many simultaneous cues to depth – how do we combine them?

One way to investigate this is to put the cues in competition. So we could have a surface where the texture cues say that it is sloping one way, while the stereo cues say it is sloping the other way (see Figure 7.4.2). Which cue would win? The answer seems to be that we use both cues to form something in between what the two (or more?) depth cues are saying. Which one carries more weight (i.e. is the perceived slope closer to that specified by the stereo information or the texture information) depends on which is the most 'reliable' signal. So under circumstances where the texture gradient gives good information about depth and the stereo information is poor, then texture will win, and vice versa. In fact this way of combining information by using the reliability as a weighting factor also seems to work for other situations, such as when an object's location is being specified by both sound and vision.

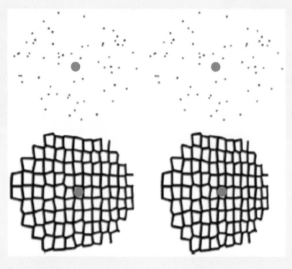

Fig. 7.4.2. Competing cues.

Conclusions

The brain uses a wealth of information to transform the 2-D retinal image into a 3-D percept. The use of the disparity of images between the two eyes can give us stereoscopic information, while the differential motion as we move our eyes yields motion parallax. These are supplemented by a wealth of information about how the world is constructed – light comes from above and casts shadows, objects far from us give a smaller retinal image and appear hazy, and so on. These cues automatically generate perceptions of distance that in turn feed into how large we believe the object is.

● READINGS AND REFERENCES

The classic in this field is the book by Bela Julesz (1971), which contains many random dot stereograms (and other stereograms) for your entertainment. A more up-to-date look into this world of stereo and related subjects is covered in great detail by Howard and Rogers (1995).

Papers on specific issues

Binocular vision and stereopsis

- *Human vision*. As mentioned above, the books of Julesz (1971) and Howards and Rogers (1995) contain all you need. For more recent findings you might want to look at Nerl *et al.* (1999).

- *Models of stereopsis*. Though the topic is covered only briefly in this chapter, there is a great literature on trying to produce models of how stereopsis works. Some are based on what we think humans (and other animals) are doing. Two classics of this approach are Marr and Poggio (1976) and Pollard *et al.* (1985).

- *Response of cells*. Early work and a superb introduction to the field can be found in Pettigrew (1972), which also gives a history of the subject of binocular vision. The work describing various types of cells in area V1 and beyond can be found in Poggio (1979). More recent work in this field can be found in Cumming and Parker (1997), and good reviews of that area are Cumming and DeAngelis (2001) and DeAngelis (2000).

Binocular rivalry and double vision A great paper to get started is that of Blake *et al.* (1980), which examines what exactly is being used to gain access to 'vision' when the two eyes receive different images. A recent review by Blake and Logothetis (2002), including what happens at the level of cells in the visual cortex, is well worth a read.

Shape from shading A most entertaining review of some of this work can be found in Ramachandran (1988). Kersten *et al.* (1996) shows how shadows are of great importance in understanding depth and movement. Though it is not covered in this chapter, you might be wondering how individual cells respond to such cues as shading and shadows. Look no further than Lee *et al.* (2002).

Motion parallax The classic paper in this field is that of Rogers and Graham (1979).

Illusions to do with depth The debate as to whether many illusions can be explained by depth constancy still rages. Its origins can be found in Gregory (1968). For a review of some classic demonstrations (including the Ames room), Ittelson and Kilpatrick (1951) is still the place to look.

Combining cues to depth The work described here is not the easiest read, but comes from Hillis *et al.* (2004). For something a bit more palatable try Nawrot and Blake (1989).

● POSSIBLE ESSAY TITLES, TUTORIALS, AND QUESTIONS OF INTEREST

1 Why do we have two eyes?

2 Describe a computational method for solving the correspondence problem of stereopsis.

3 What visual illusions can be explained by misapplied constancy scaling?

4 What are the pictorial cues to depth? What assumptions must be embedded in our visual systems for the cues to have their effects?

5 How do we combine the different cues to depth?

References

Blake, R. and Logothetis, N. K. (2002). Visual competition. *Nature Reviews – Neuroscience* **3**, 13–23.

Blake, R., Westendorf, D. H., and Overton, R. (1980). What is suppressed during binocular rivalry? *Perception* **9**, 223–231.

Cumming, B. C. and Parker, A. J. (1997). Responses of primary visual cortical neurons to binocular disparity without depth perception. *Nature* **389**, 280–283.

Cumming, B. G. and DeAngelis, G. C. (2001). The physiology of stereopsis. *Annual Review of Neuroscience* **24**, 203–238.

DeAngelis, G. (2000). Seeing in three dimensions: the neurophysiology of stereopsis. *Trends in Cognitive Sciences* **4**, 80–90.

Gregory, R. L. (1968). Visual illusions. *Scientific American* **219**, November, 66–76.

Hillis, J. M., Watt, S. J., Landy, M. S., and Banks, M. S. (2004). Slant from texture and disparity cues: optimal cue combination. *Journal of Vision* **4**, 967–992.

Howard, I. P. and Rogers, B. J. (1995). *Binocular vision and stereopsis*. New York: Oxford University Press.

Ittelson, W. H. and Kilpatrick, F. P. (1951). Experiments in perception. *Scientific American* **185**, August, 50–55.

Julesz, B. (1971). *Foundations of cyclopean vision*. Chicago: University of Chicago Press.

Kersten, D., Knill, D. C., Mamassian, P., and Bülthoff, I. (1996). Illusory motion from shadows. *Nature* **379**, 31.

Knill, D. C. (1998). Surface orientation from texture: ideal observers, generic observers and the information content of texture cues. *Vision Research* **38**(11), 1655–1682.

Lee, T. S., Yang, C. F., Romero, R. D., and Mumford, D. (2002). Neural activity in early visual cortex reflects behavioural experience and higher-order perceptual saliency. *Nature Neuroscience* **5**, 589–597.

Marr, D. and Poggio, T. (1976). Cooperative computation of stereo disparity. *Science* **194**, 283–287.

Nawrot, M. and Blake, R. (1989). Neural integration of information specifying structure from stereopsis and motion. *Science* **244**, 716–718.

Nerl, P., Parker, A. J., and Blakemore, C. (1999). Probing the human stereoscopic system with reverse correlation. *Nature* **401**, 695–698.

O'Brien, J. and Johnston, A. (2000). When texture takes precedence over motion in depth perception. *Perception* **29**(4), 437–452.

Pettigrew, J. D. (1972). The neurophysiology of binocular vision. *Scientific American* **227**, August, 84–95.

Poggio, G. F. (1979). Mechanisms of stereopsis in monkey visual cortex. *Trends in Neurosciences* **2**, 199–201.

Pollard, S. B., Mayhew, J. E. W., and Frisby, J. P. (1985). PMF – a stereo correspondence algorithm using a disparity gradient limit. *Perception* **14**, 449–470.

Ramachandran, V. S. (1988). Perceiving shape from shading. *Scientific American* **259**(2), 76–83.

Rogers, B. J. and Graham, M. (1979). Motion parallax as an independent cue for depth perception. *Perception* **8**, 125–134.

CHAPTER 8

The development of vision

A child wearing red/green glasses so that his stereo vision can be assessed (see Chapter 7). Finding out how well a child sees in early life is of great importance, because normal adult levels of seeing are never achieved if the visual input is poor during these early years.

CHAPTER OVERVIEW

William James, a famous American psychologist and a much better writer than his brother Henry, famously described the baby's world as a 'booming, buzzing confusion'. Certainly it is a bit blurry. So what exactly can a baby see? Can it tell its mother from other people? Can it tell the colours, movements, and shapes that we see as adults? And how can we find out what a baby sees? We shall find that the answers to these questions are of great importance. Vision develops over the first few years of life, but its continuing improvement is not automatic and requires good input – if this is disrupted, then vision may fail to develop to the normal adult level.

Introduction

Over the course of the first few weeks, months, and even years of life the visual system appears to slowly change and mature until adult levels of vision are achieved. Figure 8.1 illustrates what children of various ages might see when viewing the same figure. The image has been processed so as to mimic the information we believe is available to the child, based on measurements of what children can detect. The blurry pictures in Figure 8.1 are based on measurements of babies' and children's contrast sensitivity (see Chapter 4 and Box 8.1) and suggest that adult levels of acuity are not reached until we become teenagers. From this figure we can see that the young child's vision lacks the detail of an adult's and its visual world is an impoverished version of our own. Of course it tells us nothing about the way in which babies see colour, motion, or depth, and probably gives a misleading picture of acuity too – just because we can't resolve fine detail it doesn't mean things 'look' blurry. After all, we can't see fine detail in our own adult peripheral vision, but the world doesn't appear blurry to us. Let's look to see how well the baby copes with these problems. But first we must consider how we can find out about a baby's

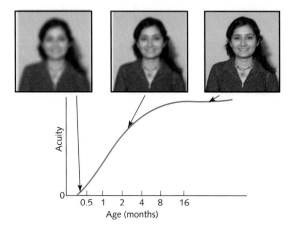

Fig. 8.1. Estimated acuity of young children. The insets give some idea of the 'blurriness' of the child's vision at various ages.

vision – the techniques we normally rely on, such as asking people what they see or getting them to press buttons depending on what they see, are useless.

Measuring a baby's vision

One technique for finding out what babies can see is called **preferential looking**. Here the baby is typically shown a card or TV screen (see Figure 8.2 and 8.3) on which a pattern appears. The pattern could appear on the left or right of where the baby is looking. (To get the baby looking at the correct spot to begin with normally involves flashing ducks or frogs or various toys to capture the interest.) An observer then monitors where the baby chooses to look – notice that this person is hidden behind the card so does not influence where the baby looks, and also doesn't know where the pattern on the card is. Normally babies find the pattern more interesting than the blank part of the card, and will look at the pattern. If they can do this reliably, this must mean that they can tell the difference between the blank card and the pattern – in other words, they must be able to see the

Fig. 8.2. Preferential looking card. The experimenter, hidden by the card, judges whether the child is looking to the left or right.

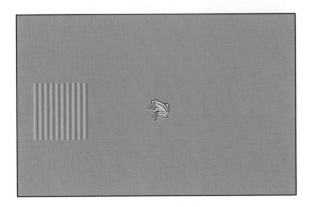

Fig. 8.3. An example of a preferential looking card.

pattern. By varying the width of the stripes on the card we can discover just how thin we can make the lines before the baby can no longer see them, and we have a measure of acuity. Likewise if we were to vary the contrast of the stripes we could get a measure of the smallest contrast that they can perceive – their contrast sensitivity (see Chapter 4).

The above technique relies on the baby preferring to look at the stripy patterns. Unfortunately, at around the age of 1 year, babies appear to lose their fascination with stripy patterns (most undergraduates seem to have the same problem) and can become very uncooperative in performing this rather laborious task. This has led to the development of optotype cards such as those in the Cardiff Acuity Test. An optotype figure is made out of a special line, constructed by having a white line surrounded by two black lines (see Figure 8.4). The amounts of black and white are carefully balanced so that when added together they cancel out to the same grey as the background. If you do not have the acuity to resolve the white and black parts of the line, they blur together and the pattern dissolves into the background and is no longer visible (trying walking slowly away while looking at Figure 8.4 and see how the pattern disappears). Using such lines we can now draw more interesting pictures, things like ducks, trains, and dinosaurs (hey, they're only 1–2 years old!) and get them to look at the card in search of the picture. By varying the width of the lines, and seeing which patterns the children can find, we once again have a good measure of their visual acuity. Such cards can also be used on other groups who

Fig. 8.4. An optotype, as used in the Cardiff Acuity Test.

might have difficulties with instructions, such as children with Down's syndrome. Margaret Woodhouse, the inventor of the Cardiff test, once encountered a particularly troublesome toddler who refused to be tested under any circumstance. So the tester simply presented the cards to the troublesome toddler's sister, and pretended to do the test on her. Of course the troublesome toddler couldn't help but look at the cards himself, and so the tester observed whereabouts on the card the toddler looked. A good measure of the toddler's acuity was thus obtained without him even knowing it!

A third technique to probe infant vision relies on two facts about babies – they get bored very easily and they like to suck things (again, a bit like undergraduates). If made to look at a pattern for a while a baby will get bored, and gets on with the more important job of thumb sucking. If the pattern is changed then the thumb sucking stops as attention is diverted to the new pattern. Thus, by measuring how much a baby sucks, we can tell how much they see!

The three techniques described above all rely on some behavioural response of the infant. There are, however, ways of measuring the responses within the brain of the infants. Visually evoked potentials (VEPs – see Chapter 12) can be recorded by placing electrodes on the child's skull and trying to record some of the electrical activity arising from the cells that are active beneath the skull. If we present a pattern to a baby, we expect some electrical activity to occur in the brain areas that process visual information. By recording this activity we can see if there is indeed a visual signal reaching this (or nearby) parts of the brain. However, these signals are very weak (they have to pass through the skull, for one thing) and there is also some background activity even when there is no visual signal. These problems are overcome by presenting the visual pattern many times (typically 100 times) to the child. The assumption is that the *signal* produced by the pattern is the same every time

but the random activity of the brain, the *noise*, is not correlated with the pattern and will be averaged out. Hence we hope these averaged trials will reveal if there is any activity near our electrode. Such a technique measures whether the child's brain can pick up a signal from a blank field. The technique can be altered to see if the brain can distinguish between two patterns (such as ones that change in colour if we wish to examine colour perception). We now simply alternate the pattern being presented between the two colours and see if a signal is produced each time the pattern changes.

Finally, we can drill a hole in the scalp of the infant and place electrodes directly into the brain – only kidding!

Spatial vision

We have already seen that a baby's vision is rather blurred (Figure 8.1) compared to our adult vision. To quantify this we can use our measure of visual acuity (the smallest thing that they can make out) – the more blurred their vision then the larger the thing has to be in order to be seen. Figure 8.5 illustrates how acuity changes over the first 32 months of life; you can see that the changes are quite dramatic. But this is not the only difference between a baby's vision and our own. Not surprisingly, the contrast sensitivity function (Chapter 4) of babies has been measured in order to evaluate fully what they see. Figure 8.6 shows contrast sensitivity functions at various ages. We can see that as well as not being able to see the fine detail in the image, babies can't see medium or low spatial frequencies too well either. In fact it takes quite a long time for vision to develop to the levels we enjoy as young adults: for humans, adult levels are not reached until around 8 years of age, although this time is much less in other animals – for example in the monkey (the subject of a lot of research) the equivalent time is just over 1 year. During this time vision gets better and better, but do all aspects of vision get better at the same rate?

Let's look at two tasks and examine how they develop over the course of a baby's life. The first we already know a lot about – visual acuity, measuring the finest pattern a baby can tell from a blank screen (Figure 8.7, upper part). The second task we haven't told you

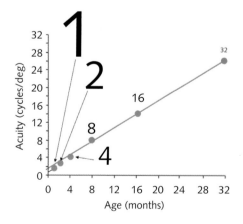

Fig. 8.5. Acuity as a function of age. The numbers in the graph are approximately the acuity limit at the age given (from a normal reading distance).

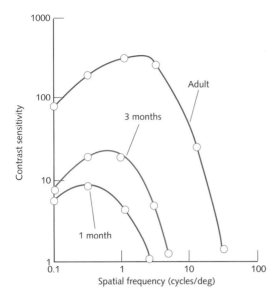

Fig. 8.6. Contrast sensitivity as a function of age.

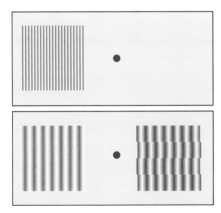

Fig. 8.7. Testing visual acuity and Vernier acuity. See text for details.

about before. It's called **Vernier acuity**, and is the smallest displacement of a line that can be detected. So for example in Figure 8.7 (lower part) you can see that the lines themselves are easily visible, but the baby has to judge which set of lines has the displacement in them. Note that this small shift in the rather fat lines is the measure of Vernier acuity, not the thickness of the lines themselves. To make this stimulus even more interesting for babies we can also move the displacements up and down and use our preferential looking technique to see if they can spot it.

Results from such experiments are shown in Figure 8.8. What is interesting is that newborn babies are very poor at the task of Vernier acuity, so that their threshold for seeing these displacements is far worse than their ability to see lines at all (grating acuity). However, this ability gets better rapidly – far faster than their ability to see the lines – so that by around 16 weeks of age the two abilities are the same. As a baby gets even older,

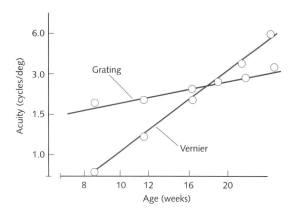

Fig. 8.8. Grating and Vernier acuity as function of age.

its Vernier acuity still increases more rapidly than its grating acuity, so that this ability becomes far better than grating acuity – in adults our Vernier acuity can be 10 times better than our grating acuity, allowing us to detect very small changes in the alignment of things.

So it is clear from this that not all things develop at the same rate – here we see our Vernier acuity increasing more rapidly than our grating acuity. The question we need to ask is, why do things change at different rates? The answer lies in the different maturation rates of different parts of the brain. Grating acuity is highly dependent upon the optics of the eye (if your vision gets blurry your grating acuity goes down), and on the cells within the retina. However, Vernier acuity seems to be much more dependent upon the cells of the visual cortex (in particular those in area V1). So what these different rates of development tell us is that different parts of our brain are developing at different rates. As a rule of thumb, the earlier parts of the visual system (e.g. the retina) appear to be more developed at birth, whereas the later parts (e.g. the visual cortex) are less developed and therefore change more over the first stages of life. As we shall discover, these latter areas are more prone to damage if things go wrong in early life.

Feature detection

In Chapter 3 we described how the primary visual cortex contains cells that are designed to detect the orientation of specific features. So, are we born with this ability, and if not when and how does it come about? After all, this function of orientation selectivity must be cortical, as it was in the cortex that we found orientation-selective cells in the first place.

Braddick *et al.* (1986) used the technique of VEPs to examine this. They produced a pattern that altered orientation every so often, say twice a second (a frequency of 2 Hz), and recorded the activity over the visual cortex to see if there was any signal with this frequency. However, would such a signal really be due to the changes in orientation? The stimulus they used was like the one on the left of Figure 8.9. We can see that when the pattern changes orientation some of the white bits turn black, and some of the black bits turn white. So our signal at 2 Hz might be due to these local changes in brightness, rather than to changes in orientation. To get round this problem they cleverly changed the phase of the stripes – the precise position of where the black stripes and the white stripes are – six times per second (6 Hz); note the subtle difference in the right-hand side of Figure 8.9. So now any signal that remains at 2 Hz must be coming from the changes in orientation.

Braddick *et al.* found that the changes in position produced a signal at the earliest age tested, showing that activity was reaching the cortex. However, there was no activity that corresponded to the changes in orientation, suggesting that orientation selectivity was not present at birth. By testing children of different ages, or by testing the same children at different ages, they found that activity corresponding to the orientation changes normally emerges at around 6 weeks of age and gets stronger over the following weeks.

Both preferential looking and habituation have also been used to investigate orientation sensitivity in newborn infants. Unfortunately, the conclusions seemed to conflict with the findings of the VEP study. The studies showed pictures of gratings at one orientation (let's say vertical) to the newborn child for a while and then gave it the choice of two gratings to look at, one at the same orientation and one at a novel orientation. The newborn tended to look at the novel grating rather than the boring old one. But of course, the new pattern is only new and exciting when you can tell the difference! So the newborn must have been able to tell the two orientations apart – it must have orientation-tuned cells. It must also get fed up of looking at gratings (this may be happening to you too by now).

So why the difference between the studies? It appears that the dynamic nature (i.e. quickly changing from one orientation to another) of the stimulus used in the VEP studies

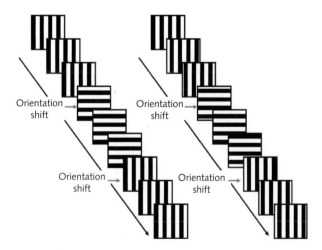

Fig. 8.9. The Braddick *et al.* experiment. See text for details.

was crucial. When the habituation experiments were repeated using flickering stimuli, the baby was no longer able to distinguish between the orientations. It appears, therefore, that some tuning orientation must be present right from birth, but that this matures as the baby develops and not till some time later that can it be demonstrated for dynamic stimuli. Which leads us to ask how well the child can process dynamic stimuli.

Motion perception

Similar techniques can be used to assess the child's ability to detect motion. We could move a stimulus backwards and forwards at a certain rate and see if we can record VEP activity time-locked to the change in direction. Alternatively, we could use a preferential looking technique. In the test illustrated in Figure 8.10 a screen full of dots is moved up and down the screen, but one section moves out of phase with all the other dots – when the majority are moving upwards, they are moving downwards (the thin black lines and the red arrows weren't there in the real experiment). If the baby can spot the difference, it might have an urge to look at this odd-man-out section of the pattern. Again the results of such studies show that motion perception develops over quite a long period of time, with the first signs of being able to spot this motion occurring around 12 weeks. Responses first emerge for 'medium' speeds of movement, with responses to slower and faster speeds emerging later. This may explain why the dynamic stimuli used in the orientation studies failed to find orientation tuning.

If you can remember Chapter 6 you'll know that motion stimuli can come in various forms. One study seems to suggest that some aspects of motion, namely looming stimuli, may be understood from a very early age. Here's the experiment. The experimenters swung what appeared to be a large concrete slab towards a young child. They measured the alarm induced in the child by this predicament. Surprisingly (or not, depending on where you're sitting) the young children seemed capable of distinguishing concrete slabs that would hit them and those that would miss! Perhaps then this most useful of

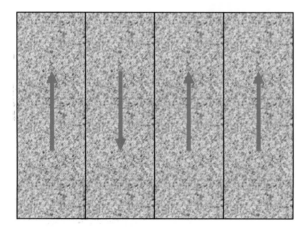

Fig. 8.10. Probing infant motion perception with an odd-man-out experiment. See text for details.

reflexes – to recognize an impending collision – is something we're born with and no further learning is required. Progress in this area would seem to be hampered by a lack of volunteers.

Colour

Babies can certainly see in colour, but whether those colours look the same as they do to adults is a difficult question. They can certainly discriminate red from green very early in life and, although their discrimination of blue may be poor at 1 month, it improves dramatically by 2 months.

Depth perception and stereopsis

How can we tell if a newborn infant can perceive depth? The obvious answer is to follow Michael Jackson's example and dangle it over a balcony several floors up and observe if the baby appears at all distressed. Although he probably didn't know it, Michael Jackson was repeating a famous experiment carried out by Eleanor Gibson in 1960. The set-up for the experiment is known as the 'visual cliff' (Figure 8.11). Essentially, the infant can be placed on a sheet of glass either suspended over a void or placed directly on a patterned surface. The youngest infants tested were only 6 months old and yet all showed an aversion to the depth.

The visual cliff may show that infants are sensitive to depth, but that does not necessarily mean that they have stereopsis – remember from Chapter 7 that there are plenty of cues to depth other than stereoscopic disparity. However, preferential looking has been

Fig. 8.11. The visual cliff. Eleanor Gibson's classic experiment showed that even very young babies avoided the cliff.

used to probe the sensitivity of infants to stereo cues. A random dot stereogram (see Chapter 7) can be constructed in which an area protrudes in depth. If the baby looks towards this protrusion then we have some indication that the baby is sensitive to the stereo disparity, as no other depth cues are present. Using this technique it appears that the ability to see these stereo-defined forms is absent at birth but develops rapidly at around 4–6 months of age.

Development of face perception

All these experiments show how vision gets better over the first few months and years of life. So you may be surprised to know that some abilities of young children are actually better than yours (assuming that you are over 10 months old!). Have a look at the pictures of the two humans and the two monkeys in Figure 8.12.

At first glance the two humans are probably easily distinguishable, whereas you might think that the two monkeys are actually two pictures of the same monkey. Closer inspection will reveal that they are indeed two different monkeys. Your inability to distinguish between the monkeys may not be too surprising. After all you are human, and as we shall see in Chapter 10, you are therefore an expert in distinguishing between human faces. However, it appears that 6-month-old babies can tell the two monkeys apart whereas by 10 months they can no longer do this. How can this be shown? The scientists used the habituation and preferential looking technique described earlier in the chapter. They first showed a picture of one of these individuals (either human or monkey) for a while (to produce habituation) and then showed pairs of pictures as in Figure 8.12. The 6-month-old babies looked at the face that was novel (i.e. the one they hadn't just seen) more than the old one. Clearly they could tell the difference! Such experiments support

Fig. 8.12. Adults find it easy to see that the two human faces are different, but find the discrimination of the monkey faces hard. Infants can tell the monkeys apart better than adults can.

the notion of perceptual narrowing. We may start life with the ability to distinguish between many categories (not just in vision – similar things happen to our language abilities) but those that we are not exposed to are lost, so that we are left with only the ones that are important to us. Hence we maintain our ability to distinguish between humans, but not between monkeys. This predicts that if a human child were to be raised by monkeys he or she would find it easy to distinguish individual monkeys but lose the ability to distinguish between humans. We are currently trying to find Tarzan in order to perform this test. Of course this process should also work across human groupings, and may explain why we tend to think that people from other races all look the same (see Chapter 10).

Summary

This brief survey of some of the visual capabilities of children and babies seems to show a general finding that obeys the first two parts of Movshon's law (*'Things start out badly, then they get better; then, after a long time, they get worse again.'*). The baby comes into the world with some rudimentary ability to process various aspects of the visual world, but there then follows a prolonged period over which these various aspects of vision improve. Thus 'nature' provides us with a start, but leaves room for 'nurture' to shape the final outcome. Figure 8.13 attempts to summarize a large body of findings showing when the various aspects first appear and over what period they improve. It should be noted that some visual functions progress rapidly to their final adult-like levels, whereas others (e.g. contour integration – Figure 8.14) take many years to reach this state.

We have seen that vision improves during our early childhood, but this does not tell us *why* it improves. Is this merely the unfolding of a preprogrammed set of events, or is the improvement of vision a response to what's out there in the world? The simplest approach to answer this question has been to change the visual environment in some manner and see if this changes the ability to see at a later date. Clearly we cannot deliberately impoverish the vision of a baby human and so our understanding has come from two sources – selective rearing experiments in animals, and studying the effects of naturally occurring problems in humans.

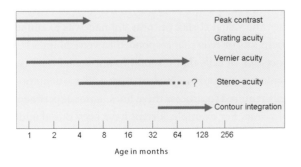

Fig. 8.13. An indication of the development of various visual functions in young children. The start of the bar indicates the first appearance of this property and the end of the bar indicates that there is no further development.

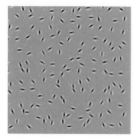 

Fig. 8.14. Contour integration. Can you join the small elements together to form a contour? Young children are very poor at this task.

Selective rearing experiments

If we want to know if the visual environment affects the way in which our visual system develops, then we need to raise animals in weird visual environments and examine the effects. What happens if we simply do not allow one of the two eyes to see during early life? Such experiments were performed on kittens by closing one of the eyes from birth for a period of time and then allowing both eyes to see together. The result is that the animal sees perfectly normally with the eye that was always open, but is practically blind when looking through the eye that was temporarily shut. If the cells in the visual cortex of normal animals are examined we normally get cells driven by either eye or by both eyes together (see Figure 8.15). Similar recordings in our experimental animal show that all the cells that are active are driven by the normal eye alone, with none dedicated to the once-shut eye or even a mixture of both eyes. This finding is very important: it tells us that unless we have vision in the eye things do not develop properly – things do not get better over time, they actually get worse. So how good does the input have to be in order to develop good vision?

This question has been answered by experiments that have performed 'environmental surgery' – here something is cut out from the visual image that the animal sees, rather than from its brain. For example, Blakemore and Cooper (1969) raised kittens in a world that only contained vertical lines (Figure 8.16). When adult, the vision of these cats was tested by presenting them with lines of various orientations. The animals had no problem when the test lines were vertical, but appeared blind to any lines that were horizontal (similar experiments also revealed that a kitten raised in a world of only horizontal lines would later fail to detect vertical lines). When the visual cortex of these animals was examined the experimenters found that there were lots of cells that responded to vertical lines best (see Chapter 3) but there was a distinct lack of cells that respond to horizontal ones (see Figure 8.17). We can conclude that unless we get to see lines of a particular orientation, then the brain will not develop the cells required to process these lines. Later experiments have examined many other aspects of vision. For example, kittens have been raised under strobe lighting. As you have no doubt experienced when dancing in a club, the strobe lighting interferes with our ability to see movement (the dancers appear as a series of still

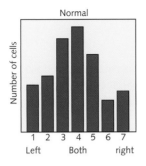 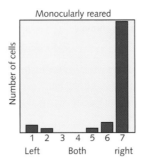

Fig. 8.15. Ocular dominance in normal cats and in cats who had one eye shut (left eye) in early life.

Fig. 8.16. A kitten being raised in a world that only contained vertical stripes. Note the ruff around the cat's head to prevent it seeing its own body.

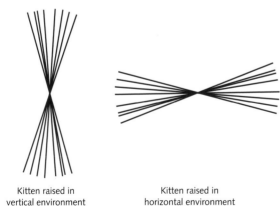

Kitten raised in vertical environment

Kitten raised in horizontal environment

Fig. 8.17. Example of distribution of orientation-tuned cells in cats that had been raised as kittens in a world of vertical (left) and horizontal (right) stripes. Each line represents the preferred orientation of a cell.

BOX 8.1 **Development of vision in other animals**

The key messages of this chapter are that the visual system is plastic during the critical period and that active vision is important in coordinating vision and touch even in adults. These findings would lead you to suppose that vision is more learned than innate, more nurture than nature. However, as with most things in life, the story isn't this simple.

In 1925 a zoologist called Robert Matthey cut through the optic nerve of an adult newt. Matthey was excited because he noticed that over time the optic nerve regenerated and the newt appeared to recover normal vision. At this point Matthey got a bit carried away and transplanted an eye from one newt to another – and the eye connected to the correct part of the second newt's brain, so the brain of one newt was seeing with the eye from a second newt! How could this happen? How could the severed optic nerves from the transplanted eye grow into right parts of a stranger's brain? It seems that there were two possibilities. It could be that the optic nerves were pro-grammed by heredity to connect with certain bits of the brain, or it could be that the nerves learned where to go. This puzzle was answered by an experiment that was fiendishly clever, and possibly fiendish and clever.

Roger Sperry took Matthey's ideas one step further; first he took an eye of newt and, having cut the eye muscles, twisted the eye upside-down without damaging the optic nerve. What would this do to the newt's vision? Sperry reasoned that if the newt *learned* how to see then it should adapt to its upside-down world, just like humans appear to do if they wear inverting prisms. But Sperry's newts never learned. If a piece of food was placed above them they dug for it in the gravel of their cage. If food was placed behind them they sprang forward. Even 2 years later they had not learned, but when their eyes were surgically rotated back to their correct orientation the newts behaved completely normally. Next Sperry rotated a newt's eye but he also severed the optic nerve. After about a month the animal started to regain vision in the eye – the nerve had regrown to the brain, just like in Matthey's newts. If the regeneration was guided by learning, the eye should now be able to see a proper right-way-up world; if guided by some predetermined process, the newt should respond as if things were upside-down. And sure enough, it behaved as if things were upside-down. In the newt (and we now know in the frog and salamander too), nature rather than nurture is the key.

Experiments in chicks lead us to the same conclusion. Eckhard Hess raised chicks with prisms over their eyes. These prisms shifted the visual world a little bit to the left or to the right. When the chicks pecked at scattered pieces of grain, they missed their target by a few millimetres. Did they learn to correct their pecking the way we would if we wore such lenses? No, they didn't, and Hess even reported that two of his chicks died of starvation even though grain was scattered all around them. Clearly kittens and humans have something that chickens and newts don't. It's called a brain (well, a cortex to be more exact).

---

snapshots). Hence when these kittens were tested (now under normal lighting), they were unable to tell which way a simple bar pattern was moving. Again the conclusion is that unless we get the information required the brain's ability to process this aspect of the visual world is lost – it's a case of *'use it or lose it'*.

These experiments all show that if the young animal is deprived of some aspect of vision for a period of time, its ability to sense this aspect of the world is lost. However, if the same experiment is performed on adult animals their vision does not change. By careful experiments that have manipulated just when the period of deprivation takes place (and its duration), it has been found that there is a critical period when such deprivation has the strongest effect (actually there may be many such critical periods, as the various aspects of our vision develop at different rates, but we won't worry about that here). During the critical period it appears that vision is developing and needs good input; after the critical duration has taken place deprivation no longer influences the visual system. In the cat the critical period is relatively short – perhaps a few months – and in monkeys it is longer – maybe a year or more.

Can we reverse the deleterious effects of deprivation? Experiments have been performed whereby an animal is deprived of vision in one eye as described above, but then the situation is reversed – the once-open eye is now shut and the once-shut one is now open. If this reverse occurs within the critical period, it appears that what would have been the bad eye now recovers. This is an important finding, as it demonstrates that deprivation doesn't just lead to parts of the visual cortex degenerating. Monocular deprivation or raising kittens in vertical stripes does not reduce the number of active cells in the visual cortex; what happens is that the receptive field properties of the cells alter in response to the environment.

The conclusions and implications seem clear. During our early life vision is developing, but requires a good input if it is to achieve normal adult levels. If there is a visual problem during this critical period vision will not develop properly, but if we can detect this problem and put it right, then the visual system will develop normally once again and recovery may take place. We therefore need to be able to spot visual problems in young children and take appropriate steps to help them develop normally.

Problems of vision

There are many possible visual problems that can occur in young children – for example astigmatism, refractive error, or a strabismus (squint or lazy eye). Each of these affects the vision in one eye (or sometimes both eyes) and, if it occurs during the critical period, will mean that vision cannot develop correctly. Let's take the problem of strabismus as an example.

In strabismus the two eyes fail to align. As a result they look at different points in space, and hence receive different images. This means the two eyes receive very different views of the world, and binocularly driven cells cannot develop normally. Usually the child favours one eye (otherwise they will suffer from double vision), and the other one drifts away from the point of interest and therefore fails to get a sharp image focused upon its retina. If this is happening during the child's critical period it will mean that the visual cortex will not develop cells that can process sharp images from the lazy eye, because

BOX 8.2   **Eye movements in infancy**

Have you ever noticed that babies are very good when it comes to a staring contest? This may be because the mechanisms that control the movements of our eyes, and of our attention, have also to develop over the first months of life. Measurements of these movements have shown that babies of approximately 6 months of age have been found to have much longer dwell times (the period when the eyes are looking at one particular point) between the rapid movements from place to place known as saccades (see Chapter 11). These dwell times are approximately 2 s, compared to only 0.75 s by the age of 13 years. At this earlier age the fixations are also always on to a contour and never into a blank area of the scene.

Babies' saccadic eye movements are also strange. As an adult, when we want to move our eyes to a particular target we do so with one fast movement of the eyes (the saccade), which gets us roughly where we need to be. Young babies, on the other hand, make a series of smaller movements, each of which covers only a small part of the distance (see Figure 8.2.1), until the eye gets to its target. Particularly sneaky scientists have tried removing the target while our hapless child is doing this, and found that the baby continues to make such movements going well past the target's original location. You may think the baby uses small movements because it cannot make larger ones. This is not so. If the child moves its eyes to a target 10° away it might do so using two eye movements of 5° each. To move its eyes to a target 20° away the baby might make two movements of 10° each.

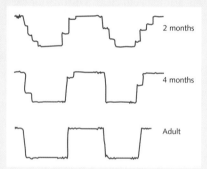

Fig. 8.2.1. Eye trace records. The participants were looking between two objects that were 44° apart. The upper trace is for a 2-month-old baby. Note that to get from target to target the baby makes a series of smaller movements, whereas the adult (lower trace) only makes one larger movement.

It has been suggested that this change in the pattern of eye movements may be due to the different rates of maturation of two pathways that help us (as adults) control our eye movements. One of these pathways passes through an area in the front of our brains known as the frontal eye fields (FEF – see also Chapter 9). This area is thought to control volitional (voluntary) movements of the eye, whereas a separate pathway from the striate cortex to the superior colliculus controls the saccades that are more driven by the environment. It is thought that this latter system is controlling movements in the 6-week-old child, while the FEF system, which develops later, is available at around 12 weeks and hence the change in the nature of the eye movements.

sharp images are not formed on the lazy retina. Of course, we could put right the mis-alignment of the eyes (this is a routine operation involving adjustment of the muscles that control the eyes) but if this operation is delayed until after the critical period is over the cells in the brain that are needed for processing sharp images are lost, and even though the eyes are now in alignment, this eye will not see as well as it should do. When this happens we call this condition amblyopia (meaning 'blunted vision') and the sufferer an amblyope. Strictly speaking, we have described strabismic amblyopia, in deference to the original problem that caused the blunted vision.

One might ask if we have this sequence of events the right way round – might not a problem in the visual cells cause this eye to be weak and therefore not to be used? This has been tested in monkeys by deliberately causing a strabismus or by deliberately making the image blurry, and examining the consequences. Sure enough, the animal does develop amblyopia and examination of its visual cortex shows a lack of cells that respond to the fine details of an image. This is also reflected in the action of individual cells. Interestingly the cells in the early part of the visual system, those in the retina and in the lateral geniculate nucleus (LGN), appear quite normal. However, those in the visual cortex do not. There are far fewer cells that can detect high spatial frequencies (fine detail) and the cells appear to need more contrast in the image in order to respond (in other words, they are less sensitive). Hence it is clear that this poor input in early life leads to poorer cells in the visual cortex and to poorer vision for the adult. So is there anything we can do about this?

Putting things right

In the last section we examined how an early visual problem can lead to later problems, but we have also seen that an eye deprived of vision can be corrected if appropriate action is taken. This gives us a way of helping children if the problem can be found early enough in life before the critical period is over. The major therapy for children with strabismus has been to place a patch on the good eye (Figure 8.18). This forces the child to use its poor eye, so this eye will therefore receive a much better input and its development will be far better than if no such action were taken. For the therapy to be effective the child does not have to wear the patch continuously; normally a 2 hour session a day is sufficient to effect a change. In humans it appears that such therapy can have some effect up to the age of around 6 years (though clearly the earlier this can be done the better the prognosis). However, patching means that the two eyes are never working together and so other visual functions, such as our ability to see depth through stereopsis (see Chapter 7) will fail to develop even if such therapy takes place.

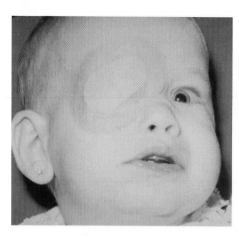

Fig. 8.18. Patching as a treatment for lazy eye. The good eye is patched, making the lazy eye work harder – this really does seem to help in restoring the balance between the two eyes.

Active versus passive vision

The above experiments have all pointed to the need for a good quality visual input in early life if we are to develop good adult vision. However, is this enough? Other experiments have suggested that, in itself, it is not. In order for vision to develop properly the image must be good *and* the recipient must interact with the world. The classical demonstration of this is known as the 'kitten carousel'. In this experiment two kittens that previously had had no visual experiences were placed in an special environment. One of the animals was free to explore for 3 hours a day but wore a collar while doing so. The other animal was placed in a special gondola that was yoked to the collar of the first animal (see Figure 8.19). By this arrangement both animals received much the same visual input, but one of them also was active and receiving visual feedback based on its movements. At a later date both animals were tested for their visual abilities, in particular their depth perception. It was found that the animal that had received only passive visual information was very poor at these tasks, whereas the one that had had active vision performed like a normal cat.

Can similar effects be found in humans? Well, obviously we can't mess up the visual experience of babies deliberately, but we can see if adults can adapt to a change in their visual world. Early experiments in this area altered vision quite dramatically and then watched to see if the unfortunate person was able to cope with this altered perception. Stratton (1897) and Kohler (1962) had participants wear a set of goggles that completely inverted the visual image. Not surprisingly, the users found this extremely disconcerting and had trouble performing the simplest of tasks. When they moved their arm up they saw it moving down; no longer was there the familiar correspondence between their visual sense and their proprioception – our feeling of where our body bits are. Nevertheless, over a period of days the goggle-wearers adapted to their new world and were able to perform complex tasks. Stratton himself even successfully rode a motorcycle through his home

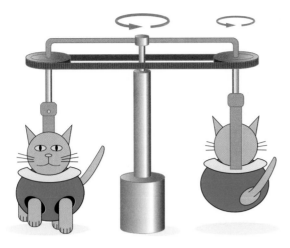

Fig. 8.19. The kitten carousel, as used by Held and Hein (1963).

BOX 8.3   **Spatial vision and amblyopia**

In the main text we have described how our vision develops over a critical period early in life and how we need good quality input to the brain in order to reach our maximum performance. Under conditions where the visual input is impaired, due to the eye being misaligned (squint or lazy eye) or being blurry due to poor focus, things do not develop in a normal way. We also found out that not all visual functions develop at the same rate – we found that Vernier acuity changes far more rapidly than grating acuity (see Figure 8.8).

One way to think about what poor visual input does to the development of vision is to see it as slowing down the changes. When the critical period ends, the visual system has not reached its mature stage. Hence we can conceptualize the visual system of the adult who had problems with vision in early life (remember we termed such a person an amblyope) as somewhat equivalent to that of a child. Further the worse the visual input in childhood, the slower the development, and the more 'childlike' the visual system of the amblyope will be. How can we show this? One way has been to use the different rates of development of different visual functions. If the visual system of the amblyope is really like that of the child, we should expect that Vernier acuity should be far more affected than grating acuity, and indeed there should be some severe amblyopes whose grating acuity is actually better than their Vernier acuity. This has been found for many humans, and also for those monkeys that were deliberately raised with a squint or with a visual blur.

---

town of Innsbruck while wearing the inverting optics. Is this adaptation the result of learning a clever way to compensate for their now-distorted visual input, or had the subjects actually recalibrated the way in which vision interacted with proprioception? A simple test gives us the answer. What do we expect to happen when such a subject takes off his inverting goggles? If he were merely trying to compensate for the presence of the goggles, then presumably he could abandon this strategy when the goggles are removed and return to normal. However, if real recalibration has taken place we might expect the world, which the subject now reports as appearing the right way up, to become inverted again! The results suggest that this latter is exactly what happens: the subject once again is very poor at even simple eye – hand coordination in a world that now seems inverted again. These effects may be relatively fleeting, as the experiences of a lifetime of correlation between vision and touch win out.

There is a certain irony to these experiments that investigate whether we can adapt to an inverted visual world – because we do just that everyday without realizing it. Our retinal images are actually upside down and the visual system doesn't bother to turn them the right way up. Therefore we have been walking on the ceiling all these years without any difficulty, sucked up there by gravity.

So if we can compensate to some extent for changes in our visual input, are we like the kittens in the carousel? Again remember that the kittens were naive and in their critical period, and we're looking at adult humans. We are not concerned with the development of a normal visual cortex – both the active and the passive kittens will achieve that, because they have normal visual experience. The issue here is whether there is normal correlation between vision and action. Would Stratton have adapted to his inverting goggles if he had been stuck in a basket? The answer appears to be no. Held and Bossom (1961) placed prisms on subjects that shifted their vision sideways by (say) 10°, and looked for evidence that they could adapt to this change (Figure 8.20). To index the effect of the prisms, the subjects were asked to point quickly to a target. Not surprisingly, all of the subjects pointed incorrectly to begin with. Then they all went on a tour of the campus (yes, the subjects were students of course) for an hour or so. They went in pairs, with one subject in a wheelchair and one pushing the wheelchair. By this arrangement the person in the wheelchair received only passive stimulation while the pusher received active stimulation – just like the kitten carousel. When they returned to the pointing test the person who had been pushing now pointed more accurately (i.e. they had adapted to the

Fig. 8.20. Students carrying out an experiment with distorting prism glasses. You can see that they are having a little difficulty in coordinating their vision with their actions!

prisms) but the pushee made errors just as before. However, when the prisms were removed the pusher was now poor at the pointing task while the pushee was good. These results mirror those of the kittens – with active vision we can learn to compensate for changes in our input, with only passive vision we cannot.

Vision in old age

Finally, no chapter on the development of vision would be complete without at least a mention of old people. We know little about this topic but fortunately Burton *et al.* (1993) and Spear (1993) do.

● READINGS AND REFERENCES

The book by Daw (1995) gives excellent coverage of most aspects of visual development. Likewise Atkinson (2000) provides a very comprehensive account of the area. The classic early work of Fanz, Gibson, and others is well told in Fanz (1961) and Gibson and Walk (1960). A fascinating account of early work in the area is available in Teller and Movshon (1986). For a more specialized view of babies' pattern of eye movements and what they like to look at, see Haith (1980).

Papers on specific issues

What can a baby see? Atkinson and Braddick (1998) covers this area well. For some clever experiments, see Shimojo *et al.* (1984).

Selective rearing experiments and amblyopia Some of the classics are Hubel and Wiesel (1970) and Blakemore and Cooper (1970). For some more recent work using more 'natural' occurring problems that lead to amblyopia, see Kiorpes and Movshon (1996) and Kiorpes *et al*. (1998).

Development of vision The experiments illustrating form perception and the behavioural techniques used to explore baby vision were by Braddick *et al*. (1986) and Slater *et al*. (1988). An up-to-date review is provided by Atkinson (2000).

Face perception The early work of Fanz (1961) is of interest and its more recent extensions can be found in Morton and Johnson (1991) . The interesting idea that babies may be able to see some facial differences that adults can't is illustrated by the study of Pascalis *et al*. (2002).

Active versus passive vision The classic prism experiments can be found in Held (1965), and for some more up-to-date experiments you might start with Kitazawa *et al*. (1995).

Eye movements in infancy The original reports of strange saccadic eye movements can be found in Aslin and Salapatek (1975), and some insights into what babies look at can be found in Bronson (1994).

Vision in old age Our lack of information on this topic can be remedied by reading Burton *et al*. (1993) or Spear (1993).

● POSSIBLE ESSAY TITLES, TUTORIALS, AND QUESTIONS OF INTEREST

1 How can you measure what a baby is seeing? Why is it important to know this?

2 How does vision change over the course of our lifetime?

3 What have experiments involving 'environmental surgery' told us about how our visual systems develop?

4 What happens if your visual world is suddenly changed, for example, if someone placed image-inverting glasses over your eyes?

5 What's gone wrong in the visual system of the amblyope?

References

Aslin, R. N. and Salapatek, P. (1975). Saccadic localization of visual targets by the very young human infant. *Perception and Psychophysics* 17, 293–392.

Atkinson, J. (2000). *The developing visual brain*. Oxford: Oxford University Press.

Atkinson, J. and Braddick, O. (1998). Research methods in infant vision. In: J. G. Robson and R. H. S. Carpenter (ed.), *Vision research: a practical approach*. Oxford: Oxford University Press.

Blakemore, C. and Cooper, G. F. (1970). Development of the brain depends on the visual environment. *Nature* 228, 477–478.

Braddick, O. J., Wattam-Bell, J., and Atkinson, J. (1986). Orientation-specific cortical responses develop in early infancy. *Nature* 320, 617–619.

Bronson, G. W. (1994). Infant's transitions towards adult-like scanning. *Child Development* **65**, 1243–1261.

Burton, K. B., Owsley, C., and Sloane, M. E. (1993). Aging and neural spatial contrast sensitivity: photopic vision. *Vision Research* **33**, 939–946.

Daw, N. (1995). *Visual development*. New York: Plenum Press.

Fanz, R. (1961). The origin of form perception. *Scientific American* **204**, May, 66–72.

Gibson, E. J. and Walk, R. D. (1960). The 'visual cliff'. *Scientific American* **202**, April, 64–71.

Haith, M. M. (1980). *Rules that babies look by: the organization of newborn visual activity*. Potomac, MD: Laurence Erlbaum Associates.

Held, R. (1965). Plasticity in sensory-motor systems. *Scientific American* **213**, November, 84–94.

Held, R. and Bossom, J. (1961). Neonatal deprivation and adult rearrangement: complementary techniques for analyzing plastic sensory-motor coordination. *Journal of Comparative Physiological Psychology* **54**, 33–37.

Held, R. and Hein, A. (1963). Movement-produced stimulation in the development of visually guided behavior. *Journal of Comparative and Physiological Psychology* **56**, 872–876.

Hubel, D. H. and Wiesel, T. N. (1970). The period of susceptibility to the physiological effects of unilateral eye closure in kittens. *Journal of Physiology (London)* **206**, 419–436.

Kiorpes, L. and Bassin, S.A. (2003). Development of contour integration in macaque monkeys. *Visual Neuroscience* **20**, 567–575.

Kiorpes, L. and Movshon, J. A. (1996). Amblyopia: a developmental disorder of the central visual pathways. *Cold Spring Harbor Symposia on Quantitative Biology* **61**, 39–48.

Kiorpes, L., Kiper, D. C., O'Keefe, L. P., Cavanaugh, J. R., and Movshon, J. A. (1998). Neuronal correlates of amblyopia in the visual cortex of macaque monkeys with experimental strabismus and anisometropia. *Journal of Neuroscience* **18**, 6411–6424.

Kitazawa, S., Kohno, T., and Uka, T. (1995). Effects of delayed visual information on the rate and amount of prism adaptation in the human. *Journal of Neuroscience* **15**, 7644–7652.

Kohler, I. (1962). Experiments with goggles. *Scientific American* **206**(5), 62–72.

Morton, J. and Johnson, M. H. (1991). CONSPEC and CONLERN: a two-process theory of infant face recognition. *Psychological Review* **98**, 164–181.

Pascalis, O., de Haan, M., and Nelson, C. A. (2002). Is face processing species-specific during the first year of life? *Science* **296**, 1321–1323.

Shimojo, S., Birch, E. E., Gwiazda, J. and Held, R. (1984). Development of vernier acuity in infants. *Vision Research* **24**, 721–728.

Slater, A., Morison, V., and Somers, M. (1988). Orientation discrimination and cortical function in the human newborn. *Perception* **17**, 597–602.

Spear, P. D. (1993). Neural bases of visual deficits during aging. *Vision Research*, **33**, 2589–2609.

Stratton, G. M. (1897). Vision without the inversion of the retinal image. *Psychological Review* **4**, 341–360, 463–481.

Teller, D. and Movshon, J. A. (1986). Visual development. *Vision Research* **26**, 1483–1596.

CHAPTER 9

Attention and neglect

Schematic depiction of hemispatial neglect as induced by repetitive transcranial magnetic stimulation (TMS) – see Chapter 12. In neurological neglect, patients suffer from impaired attentional resources on one side of space.

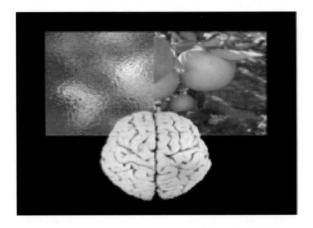

A flash of lightning by night, the report of a firearm, the sudden prick of a knife, or a violent internal pain, all these for the moment so occupy our notice that everything else becomes feeble or is banished.

Bradley (1886)

Introduction

The quote above tries to summarize our subjective feelings about events in our world. It appears to us that all events do not have equal priority or status in our mind. Thus when we concentrate on reading (as we hope you are now) you may not notice other sounds that are occurring – such as the ticking of a clock, the hum of a fan, or even the music from a radio. Stop reading for a moment, and you might then notice the sounds and sights that you were unaware of while reading. Thus it is generally believed that 'attention' alters our perception in some way – it filters out information that is not needed and frees our resources for the task in hand. However, being more precise about this 'filtering' has proved more difficult than one might suppose. What is filtered out? How is it filtered? Where does the filtering take place? And just what are these 'resources' that are freed by attention?

Many of you will have had the strange sensation of hearing a clock *stop* ticking! While the ticking was going on you were unaware of it, yet its sudden absence is then most striking (and you seem to become aware of the last few ticks!). Clearly some part of our brain must have been processing the ticks, otherwise you could not have noticed their absence. So if they were being processed, how come you didn't notice them before?

Figure 9.1 shows some purple and blue figures that overlap. Look briefly at the two figures and make a judgement as to whether the two blue figures are exactly the same (the purple figures are there to make it harder). OK – now turn to Figure 9.2 (it's deliberately on the next page). People find this task very difficult. It appears that even though you must have looked directly at these purple figures while trying to make the judgement about the blue ones, your attention was not on them and so they received very little processing and therefore couldn't be recalled later.

Fig. 9.1. Carefully examine the shape of the blue figures – are they exactly the same?

Fig. 9.2. Which of these purple figures were you looking at in Figure 9.1?

This simple demonstration tells us that our vision is an active process. Just because the eyes are pointing at an object doesn't mean that the person will see it (we discuss the relationship between attention and eye movements later, in Chapter 11). It seems to be necessary that we put some sort of 'effort' into processing the object. Likewise we must also remember that our vision changes markedly from the central foveal region to the periphery. Normally when we move attention from one place to another we also move our eyes so that objects of interest are focused on the fovea. This form of 'overt' attention will be covered in greater detail in Chapter 11, but it is also clear that we can move our 'mind's eye' without necessarily moving our real eye. This is what we shall discuss in this chapter.

Fundamental questions arise from this:

- What are the differences between our vision with attention and vision when our attention is elsewhere?

- How do we decide what we should be paying attention to?

Moving attention

How can we study attention? One of the most popular approaches has been the cueing paradigm. It goes like this. A particular part of our visual field is cued, and performance to targets in this part of the field is compared with another part that was not cued. The technique is illustrated in Figure 9.3a. In each trial a fixation mark is provided and the subject is instructed to always look at this mark. To the left and right of the fixation mark are two boxes in which a target might appear. One of these boxes might then flash, to signify that it is the box most likely to contain the target. The target then follows after some (normally brief) time interval and the subject must detect this target. Occasionally the experimenter can be sneaky and present the target in the other box – these are known as invalid trials (and the first type are called valid trials) (Figure 9.3b). Thus we can compare performance at the cued location with performance at the uncued location. Some experiments also include neutral trials consisting of either no cue or cueing both boxes. We can look at the benefits (by comparing valid with neutral trials) and the costs (by comparing invalid with neutral trials) of attention. It is most important to note that this technique looks at covert movements of attention – i.e. the eyes remain still and it is only the mind's eye that we hope to manipulate.

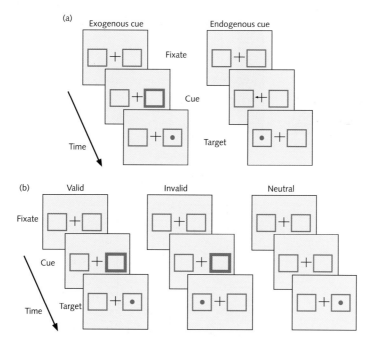

Fig. 9.3. Illustration of covert cueing paradigms. (a) Flashing the box the stimulus is going to appear in automatically captures our attention and is an exogenous cue. A more subtle arrow pointing at the location of the upcoming target allows you to direct your attention to see the target; this is an endogenous cue. (b) Cues can be valid (the target appears in the cued location) or invalid (the target appears in the other location – sneaky). See text for details.

Typical results from such experiments are illustrated in Figure 9.4. The graph plots reaction time to detect the target (or say something about it, such as its colour) for the three types of trial. Note that such experiments typically get this pattern of results with both benefits of attention at the valid location and costs at the invalid location.

Figure 9.3a illustrates a typical cueing trial for two different types of cue. On the left of the figure the cue is one of the boxes flashing, on the right the same box is cued by pointing an arrow at it. These different types of cue seem to mirror our intuition as to how we attend to something. Sometimes we can decide consciously that we are going to attend to something, whereas on other occasions something happens that just grabs our attention. So, for example, if an attractive male (or female – whatever floats your boat) were suddenly to walk into the room, this might automatically grab your attention (a bit like the flashing of the box, only more fun). However, you could know that this person was about to enter the room and so you could deliberately try to keep your attention on this location (a bit like paying attention to the box with the arrow pointing at it). Of course you want to conceal your interest in this person (gawping is *so* uncool) so your eyes remain fixed on your beer glass – your attention is moved covertly to the person of interest. These two different types of attention have been termed exogenous (the one that grabs

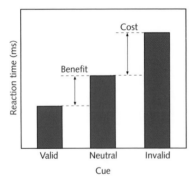

Fig. 9.4. Typical results from a covert cueing paradigm.

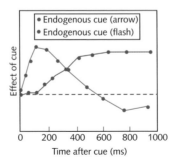

Fig. 9.5. Typical results from exogenous and endogenous cueing experiments. Note that the exogenous cue (the box flashing) grabs attention quickly (strong effect only 100 ms after flash), but its effects disappear by around 500 ms and can actually hinder performance at longer times after the flash (known as 'inhibition of return'). The effects of the endogenous cue are not seen for a few hundred milliseconds as the cue is processed and its meaning extracted. However, the cue's effect can be more long lasting.

your attention) and endogenous (the one that you wilfully direct yourself). They can also be thought of as 'bottom-up' or 'top-down' respectively. The two systems appear to do similar things, but in slightly different ways. The exogenous system is fast but transient (i.e. disappears after a short while) and fairly automatic (i.e. such flashes are hard to ignore), whereas the endogenous system is much slower but sustained and requires the conscious effort of the subject (see Figure 9.5). So, for example, if the subject is given a distracting task to do while performing such experiments (such as trying to count backwards in threes) the exogenous cues still produce their benefits and costs while the endogenous cues no longer produce these effects.

So, to return to our 'reading a book' analogy, we see that endogenous attention is first used to engage our attention on the words in the book (you have to be motivated to do this in the first place!) but attention can then be pulled away by the exogenous events occurring elsewhere (such as your friend entering the room). These exogenous events could even be the offset of something – such as the clock failing to tick.

Spot the difference – change blindness

It's likely that you've played the simple 'spot the difference' type of game illustrated in Figure 9.6. The game consists trying to find the differences between pictures that are identical save for a few deliberate changes. This task is surprisingly difficult to begin with,

Fig. 9.6. Spot the difference I. How many differences can you spot between these pictures?

> ### BOX 9.1
>
> ## Moving attention
>
> Where in the brain does 'attention' reside ? Corbetta *et al.* (1993) have used positron emission tomography (PET) measurements to try to highlight the areas that are active when we are shifting attention. PET works by injecting small amounts of radioactive glucose into a person's bloodstream and then seeing where it goes within the brain by detecting the radiation. The glucose is needed by neurons that are active and hence we can see what areas of the brain are involved in a particular task (see Chapter 12 for more details of this technique). To highlight the 'attention' area(s) of the brain the subjects had to perform a task where they detected targets that would occur one after the other in a known sequence. On most trials (80%) the target appeared at a predictable location (for example, in the next box to the right of the last target), but occasionally the target would appear in a different location. Hence this task should require a lot of endogenous attention as the subject deliberately moves their attention from one location to the next. To look at exogenous attention the subject merely viewed the stimuli as they were flashed up at the peripheral locations – just like the cues used in the Posner cueing paradigm. Of course such tasks also involve key presses (and therefore motor activity) and target detection as well as attention, so Corbetta *et al.* had to devise control conditions where the same activity took place, but no shifts of attention were needed. They could now compare the activity in the brain when the control tasks were being performed with those that also required shifts of attention. They hoped that the difference in brain activity would highlight the areas involved in shifting attention. They found that an area in the parietal lobe was activated for both the attention tasks, suggesting that this region is involved in shifting our attention from one place to another (see Figure 9.1.1). This fits with the data from patients who have damage to this area. One of the classic symptoms of damage to the parietal lobe is that of the neglect of objects that occur on the contralateral side to the damage (see main text). During the endogenous task, but not during the exogenous one, another area in the superior
>
>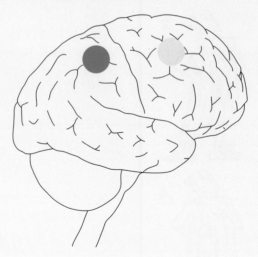
>
> **Fig. 9.1.1.** Brain areas active when people are moving their attention. Two areas become active, one in the posterior parietal lobe (green) and one in the superior frontal cortex (pink). Damage to these areas (particularly the parietal lobe) can cause the phenomenon of 'neglect' where half the word is ignored (see p. 277).

frontal cortex was also very active. It is suggested that this area might be crucial with the intentions and planning of the observer.

The brain has also been imaged while observers performed visual search tasks. Corbetta *et al.* (1995) had observers searching for targets that were defined by colour or by motion (single feature searches), or by a conjunction of colour and motion. The task was to press one button if a target was present and another button if it was absent. In a control condition the observers were presented with exactly the same stimuli but now they had merely to press alternate keys on successive trials, regardless of the visual display. They found that the conjunction search activated the same area in the parietal lobe as they had found previously for the cueing experiments. This makes sense, as the observers have to actively move their attention from item to item to find the target. However, the single feature searches did not activate this area. This may be because the subject didn't require attention for this task – just as feature integration theory predicts. However, it could be that attention was drawn to the target location automatically (as in an exogenous cue). As this attention shift is automatic it should also occur even when the subject was merely viewing the stimulus without actively searching. Hence there would be no difference between the control condition and the experimental condition. Further investigation is needed to decide between these possibilities.

but once you have spotted a change it seems ridiculously easy and therefore hard to understand why originally you took so long. The two pictures in Figure 9.7 are taken from an experiment that did not present the images side by side as we have here, but one after the other in an ever-repeating movie. This makes the task trivial – the subject spots the change straight away. However, if a very brief time interval (just 0.1 s) is put between the frames, the task is now very difficult once again – until, of course, you find the right spot and then it again appears trivially easy and you wonder why you didn't spot this straight away.

It seems possible to explain these results in terms of the attentional systems we have already discussed. When the images are presented in quick succession the differences in the image cause a temporal transient (a sudden change in a part of the image) that draws attention exogenously to this area and the difference is spotted. However, when the pictures are side by side there is no exogenous signal and so attention does not go automatically to the relevant area. We must use our endogenous attention to laboriously check each part of the image in turn. In the case where there is a small time gap between the frames it appears that all of the 'new' frame can be thought of as a transient and hence attention is drawn to all of the image rather than the bit that has been deliberately changed. Once again, therefore, we have to deliberately use our endogenous attention to find the changed area.

Some types of objects (important ones) attract our attention and we are likely to spot changes to them – you probably noticed that the girl had changed position in Figure 9.7. However, other parts of the image seem to be less interesting and attention is rarely deployed on these – hence we may have been able to move the mountain without your noticing!

Fig. 9.7. Spot the difference II. Frames such as these are presented either in rapid succession or with a small delay (0.1 s) between the frames. In the first case the change is spotted immediately, but in the second case subjects often take many seconds to find the change.

No mudsplashes   With mudsplashes

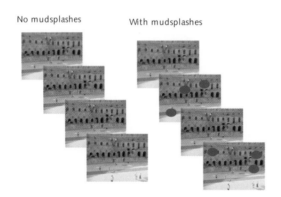

Fig. 9.8. Mud splash experiment. As in other 'change blindness' experiments the two pictures are seen one after the other over and over until the person spots the change. Without the mud splashes this task is easy, but with them it becomes very difficult.

These ideas are supported by a number of other observations. One is that other irrelevant temporal transients also render the crucial change hard to spot. Let's go back to the situation where one image follows the other immediately and our exogenous system alerts us to the difference in the two pictures. Now, at the moment we switch from one picture to the other we introduce some 'mud splashes', randomly placed splodges on the picture (Figure 9.8). These mud splashes also cause changes in the image, and therefore your attention is drawn towards them (this is the exogenous system again). While your attention is busy with these irrelevant changes, the crucial changes are missed. The theory also suggests that 'natural' interruptions to vision will also make us miss important events such as when we blink or when our eyes flick from position to position (more on this in Chapter 11).

Notice that this theory suggests that we have remarkably little knowledge of what we are currently seeing, except for where our attention is at any one moment! This feels intuitively wrong – we certainly 'feel' that we know a great deal about most of what we are looking at, such as the colours of the things around us. Look at the cross in Figure 9.9. You probably get the feeling that you can see the colour of all the purple and green circles at the same time. OK – do this and then quickly switch your gaze to Figure 9.10, where

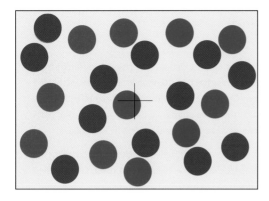

Fig. 9.9. Look at the cross – you may get the feeling that you are aware of the colours of each of the circles. In a moment we want you to move your gaze to Figure 9.10 which has chosen one of the circles you are now seeing.

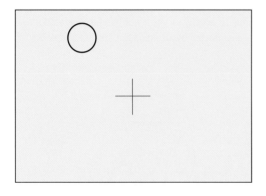

Fig. 9.10. What was the colour of the circle at this position in Figure 9.9?

just one of the circles remains. What colour was that circle in Figure 9.9? You probably have no idea. It seems that until attention arrives at the object its colour is not known, despite the subjective feelings we have that we do know this. Thus this impression of a world of solid objects that we believe we perceive may be rather false. Instead we seem to only know about a tiny bit of the world at any time, but we can move this little bit around to sample any bit of the world we want to. However, this leaves us with a problem. How do we know to move our attention to important parts of the image if we are not processing anything but a tiny bit? Clearly we must do some processing of the rest of the image – so the question reverts to what is the difference between the tiny attended bit of our vision and large unattended rest of our vision? One idea is that the unattended image is just a set of 'features' – lines, colours, motion, etc. – that has yet to be glued together into objects – we shall return to this topic later in the chapter in the form of feature integration theory.

Another question which arises here is as follows: if, in spite of thinking that we have a full mental description of the world around us, we have an extremely impoverished representation of the objects in that world, how come we don't make dreadful mistakes all the time? The answer is that the world itself is pretty stable – things tend not to appear or disappear when we blink our eyes. If they do, they usually make a noise or move rapidly – and we have sensory systems precisely to detect such sudden change and to move

Where does attention have its effects?

In the main text we have told you that your vision of an attended area or object is different from that in an unattended area. Where in the brain does this effect of attention kick in? Presumably the photoreceptors (hope you remember them from Chapter 1) are immune to these effects, but it would seem likely that cells that respond to such things as emotional expressions or body parts (Chapter 10) might well be altered. Two techniques have been used to look at this issue.

- **Visually evoked potentials** (VEPs – see Chapter 12) record the activity in the brain following the presentation of a stimulus. We could then compare these potentials when a person is attending to the stimulus compared to when they are not (see Figure 9.2.1). Several studies have found that the early (in time) components of this response, those occurring less that 0.1 s after the stimulus, are not affected, but the later ones are. In particular the C1 component (which occurs after just 80 ms), which is thought to occur due to activity in V1, is not altered by attention. Hence the conclusion is that extrastriate areas are affected by attention but area V1 and earlier are not.

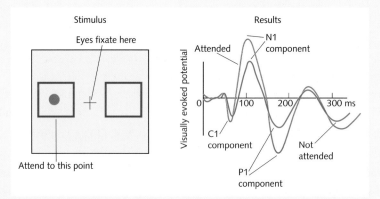

Fig. 9.2.1. Stimulus and results from experiment to investigate how the visually evoked potential (VEP) is altered by attention to the stimulus. VEP when attending is in purple, not attending in green. Note that the early component (C1) thought to arise in area V1 is unaffected, whereas the later components (N1 and P1), thought to arise in extrastriate cortex, are larger for the attended stimulus.

- **Functional magnetic resonance imaging** (fMRI – see Chapter 12), has also been used to investigate this issue. Studies agree that the extrastriate areas are indeed altered by attention to the stimulus. However, the findings in area V1 are less clear cut. Figure 9.2.2 illustrates an experiment in which the activity to a grating stimulus was monitored when the subject was attending to it, or not attending to it. It was found that the activity to the attended grating was greater than the unattended one. Clearly, then, activity in area V1 can be altered by attention.

How can the results from the two techniques (VEPs vs fMRI) be reconciled? One possibility is a consequence of the time course over which the two techniques work. VEPs measure the activity occurring immediately after the stimulus occurs, whereas fMRI measures activity over several seconds. Perhaps when the activity first arrives in area V1 there is no effect of attention, but later, as signals which are fed back from the extrastriate areas arrive into area V1, the activity changes. Hence the two techniques show different results. Further experiments are needed to test this idea.

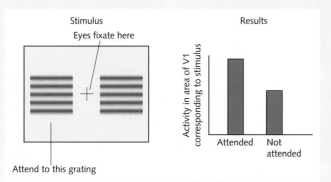

Fig. 9.2.2. Stimulus and results from experiment to investigate attention on activity in human area V1.

our attention to it. So, if we lived in a world which was much less stable (for example, if we were a gnat flying in a swarm of gnats) and our perception worked this way, we *would* mess up precisely in the way in which we don't mess up in a stable world. Magicians exploit this inability of ours to notice what is going on by distracting us while doing something else at the same time. It would be interesting to find out if they are therefore less likely to be fooled by these change blindness demonstrations.

Objects and space

Results from these experiments on seeing changes have tempted many researchers to think about attention as a 'spotlight' that can be shifted from position to position – indeed, this analogy has been most valuable when considering people who might have problems with their attention such as occurs in brain damage or schizophrenia. The spotlight analogy has been tested and refined in many ways, in order to answer many questions such as: How fast does it move? Does it really pass through all locations on its travels or does it jump from place to place? Can its size be varied like a zoom lens? Can we have more than one spotlight?

However, more recently it has been suggested that, as the real world is not a blank screen but rather is full of objects, it might be more sensible to attend to objects rather than parts of space. Again this can be illustrated using a cueing paradigm. Figure 9.11 illustrates two overlapping triangles. We could now cue one of these objects (let us say the green one) and see if people are faster at spotting targets (which one of the circles is

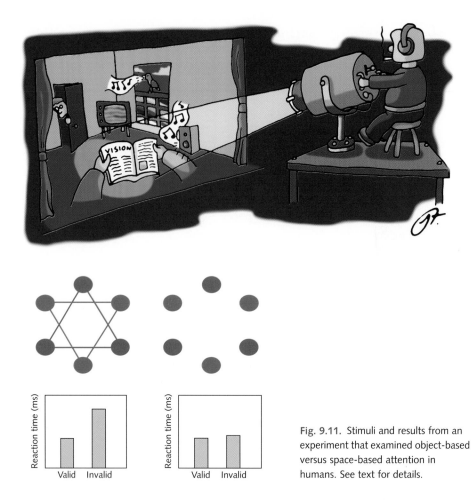

Fig. 9.11. Stimuli and results from an experiment that examined object-based versus space-based attention in humans. See text for details.

flashing) that occur on the green triangle rather than on the red triangle. The subject doesn't know which of the three circles on the green triangle is going to flash, so is forced to spread attention over the whole green object. The question of interest is whether subjects can confine their attention to the green triangle alone. If our attention is purely space-based it would seem that we would also have to pay attention to the red triangle as well, because the two overlap in space. The results (using both exogenous and endogenous cueing methods) show that we are better at spotting targets on the cued object – hence it seems that at least some aspects of our attention are object based and not space based. As a final check of this idea the experiment can be repeated with the lines taken away so only the circles remain. The image no longer looks like two objects. We now find that when subjects are cued to attend to the green circles they are no faster for these circles than for the red ones.

A second method for illustrating object-based attention has used a paradigm where attention has to be divided. An example is given in Figure 9.12 where two objects

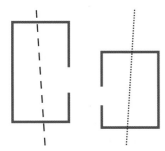

Fig. 9.12. Example of stimuli used in divided attention experiments. See text for details.

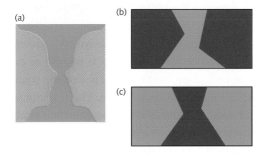

Fig. 9.13. (a) Rubin's vase (1915). The figure can be seen either as two faces, or as a vase. (b), (c) Simplified versions of Rubin's vase used in experiments on attention and neglect. In these figures the observer must decide which angle is higher, the one on the left or the one on the right.

(a box and a line) are presented superimposed upon one another. Figures similar to this were flashed briefly to a subject who then had to answer two questions from a possible four:

1 Is the box large or small?

2 Is the gap in the box on the left or right?

3 Is the line tilted to the left or right?

4 Is the line dashed or dotted?

Note that questions 1 and 2 refer to the box, and questions 3 and 4 to the line. It was found that subjects performed well if both the questions came from the same object, but poorly if they came from different objects. It appears that you can make several judgements about one object, but not about several objects.

Of course, there is still the problem of deciding what an object is in the first place (we shall see below that some theories need attention to form objects in the first place). For example, when we look at the left part of Figure 9.13 do you see two faces or one vase? People appear to alternate – sometimes it can appear as a vase, sometimes as two faces. By concentration and effort you should be able to flip from one 'interpretation' to the other. This type of stimulus has been simplified in the diagrams on the right-hand side of this figure. Scientists have used figures like these to further examine this issue of space versus objects. When given one of these figures (let us say the top one) subjects were asked to judge if the angle on the left was larger or smaller than the angle on the right. Note that this figure could be seen in one of two ways – either as a blue figure on a red background, or as two red figures on a blue background. The experimenters tried to manipulate what the subject saw by telling them to attend to either the blue areas (and therefore an interpretation of one object in the upper figure and two objects in the lower figure) or red area (and therefore an interpretation of two objects in the upper figure and one object in the lower figure). Note that the two things to be judged (the points of the triangles) would therefore belong to the same object or to two different objects respectively. Sure enough, those who saw the stimulus as two objects were less accurate than those who interpreted it as one object.

A remarkable demonstration of our inattentiveness to things we appear to be looking at was provided many years before the experiments we have just described. Subjects watched two films superimposed on the same screen at the same time. One film showed two pairs of hands playing a clapping game, and the other film showed a group of people passing a basketball around. It was found that subjects could easily follow the basketball game (assessed by having them press a button each time the ball was passed) or easily follow the clapping game (press a button for each clap), but they were poor when trying to do both tasks at the same time, even when the film was slowed down. This is reminiscent of the subjects described above who could make two judgements about the line or about the box, but not one about the line and one about the box (Figure 9.12). Now for the interesting bit. In a second experiment subjects monitored the clapping game. While they were doing this some odd things happened to the players in the basketball game. The ball disappeared, characters were replaced by players of the opposite sex, in later experiments some characters even brought on umbrellas or were dressed as gorillas. In perhaps the most celebrated experiment the scientists got carried away and had the gorilla stop in the middle of the game, thump his chest, and walk off again (Figure 9.14). These bizarre events were hardly ever noticed by the subjects!

Such a demonstration shows us that merely having our eyes pointing in the right direction is not enough to ensure that we will process or appreciate the information. This can lead to some very worrying situations in the real world. Recently, many aircraft have begun to use 'head-up' displays (Figure 9.15). In such displays some of the information

Fig. 9.14. Gorillas in our midst. A still frame from the Simons and Chabris movie. Many subjects failed to see the gorilla at all while their attention was captured by a demanding task. See text for details.

Fig. 9.15. Head-up display from the C-130J Hercules Tactical Transport Aircraft.

needed by pilots is placed in their line of sight so that it is superimposed on the view from outside the cockpit. The idea is that this will save the pilot having to look down as they can now 'see' both the instruments and the outside world at the same time. This situation is very reminiscent of the superimposed films, where subjects failed to notice the presence of gorillas playing basketball while attending to the other scene. Experiments have compared head-up with conventional, 'head-down' displays. Subjects had to land a plane (simulations were used, you will be glad to hear) under cloudy conditions. They were instructed to say when they first saw the runway and to abort the landing if there were any problems. Subjects were indeed better at spotting the runway with the head-up display; however, they were much slower at spotting unexpected events (such as another plane coming on to the runway that they were about to land on!). Some of the subjects tested were real airline pilots; when they realized that they had not seen a plane on the runway, they were shocked and worried about their professional competence. It is probably the case that however 'good' you might be at some task you are prone to make errors of this kind unless you lead a life where such stuff happens all the time. Since pilots do *not* usually see new planes on the runway while looking at head-up instruments, they cannot possibly be immune from this kind of error, however competent they may be.

Visual search

Look briefly at the top left part of Figure 9.16. Chances are that you were drawn to the odd black item and it seems to 'pop out' at you. Formal experiments using displays similar to this show that a person's ability to detect such a black target does not depend upon how many white 'distractors' there are – 1 white item or 1000 makes no difference. The lower part of Figure 9.16 plots 'typical' results from just such an experiment – no matter how many items there are, or whether the target is present or absent, you are just as fast with many distractors as with few distractors. Results such as these have tempted

BOX 9.3 **Attention to stimulus features**

The discussion in the main text has concentrated on attending to a particular point in space or to particular objects. However, we could also attend to particular features. So, for example, could we attend to a particular colour in the image, or to the motion in the stimulus?

Figure 9.3.1 shows the stimulus used in an experiment designed to test whether we can attend to elements defined by a particular colour. The subjects were informed that the target (a flashing of one of the lines) would occur only on, let's say, a green line. They found that subjects were better at identifying the orientation of the target element if it was on a line with the attended colour, but that just detecting the flash was not changed by attention. Hence the answer seems to be that we

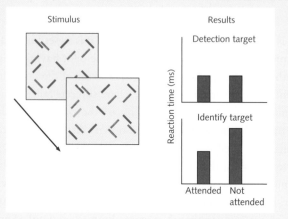

Fig. 9.3.1. Stimulus and results from experiment to investigate attention to colour.

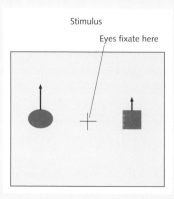

Fig. 9.3.2. Stimulus and tasks used by Corbetta *et al.* (1990) to investigate effects of attention on activity caused by the stimuli. Task 1: Shape. Which target is an ellipse? Task 2: Colour. Which target is green? Task 3: Motion. Which target is moving faster?

can indeed selectively attend to the elements with a particular colour, but whether this makes a difference depends upon the task. This may well be related to the idea that early activity (needed to detect the flash) is not affected by attention, but later activity (needed to identity the shape of the target) is (see Box 9.2).

Another technique monitors brain activity (using PET or fMRI) but changes the task a person must do. For example (Figure 9.3.2) we could show the subjects two stimuli separated in time, and get them to make judgments about the motion, colour, or shape of the targets. The beauty of this technique is that the stimulus during each of these judgements is identical – it is only the task, and therefore the subject's attention, that varies. Using this technique it has indeed been found that brain areas such as MT (see Chapter 6) are more active when a person is making judgements about motion. Indeed this technique was one of the first used to show that the human brain does indeed contain areas that are specialized for different aspect of the stimulus such as motion, colour, and shape.

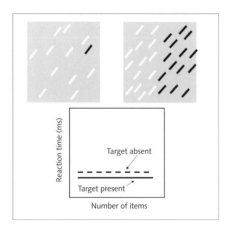

Fig. 9.16. Visual search paradigm I. Searching for a single feature like colour or orientation is easy. See text for details.

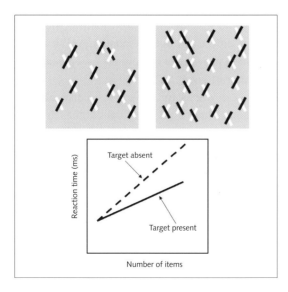

Fig. 9.17. Visual search paradigm II. Searching for a conjunction of colour and orientation is hard. See text for details.

researchers to say that such a search can be performed in parallel right across the visual field and is not subject to the constraints of attention. Indeed, a popular term to describe elements that produce this type of result has been preattentive search or parallel search. Differences in line orientation, colour, movement, size, and depth have all been shown to be processed in this manner (at least for large differences in these dimensions). It is also worth noting that these same differences seem to provide for instantaneous segmentation of figure from ground – see the right upper part of Figure 9.16.

Now look briefly at the top of Figure 9.17 – can you see the odd item? Chances are that you had to struggle for some time to spot the one whose black line slopes to the left while its white line slopes to the right. It does not seem to stand out in the manner of the target in Figure 9.16. Note that this search is made up of two 'easy searches' – considering all the lines with left slope, only one is black (as in Figure 9.16), and considering all the lines with right slope, only one is white. Yet when these searches are combined into a conjunction search it becomes very difficult – it feels as if we have to check consciously and laboriously each item one by one to see if it has the correct combination of elements. When experiments are performed that vary the number of distractor items we now see that reaction time to spot the target increases as the number of distractors increases (Figure 9.17, lower part). Often we see that the slope of this function is steeper when the target is absent than when it is present – normally it is twice as steep for the absent trials. Results such as these have tempted researchers to say that this type of search cannot be performed in parallel right across the visual field but requires a serial search that requires focal attention to be applied to each element (or small group of elements) in turn. Hence the more elements, the longer it takes. The difference in slopes for present and absent trials is also easily explicable. For absent trials the subject will not know that the target is absent until all the elements have been searched. On the other hand, when the target is present, it could be either the first item searched or the last item, or indeed any in between – therefore on average it will be found after about half have been searched. Of course, once it has been found there is no need to search any more items. So, on average, the subject only has to search half as many elements for the present trials compared to the absent trials – hence the slope is half as steep.

From visual search experiments we seem to have identified two mechanisms – first, a preattentive process extracts simple features from the scene (such as colours and oriented line segments). A second process – focal attention – then appears to perform further processing on these items. This attentional process, at least at first glance, has similarities to the 'spotlight' of attention invoked in order to explain results from the cueing paradigm.

Feature integration theory

Treisman and her colleagues (see Treisman, 1986) made these ideas more explicit in their feature integration theory. They suggest that 'features' are extracted by a preattentive (something that occurs before attention) system of modules with each module designed to extract some particular feature. Thus there are separate modules for different features such as orientation, colour, stereo, depth, and so on. Within each module are a number of feature maps – thus the colour module might have maps for purple, blue, and green. If a target makes a unique sensory feature in such a map (i.e. the only green thing) then it can be detected simply by the presence of activity in a separate map for that feature. For these features to be combined, something must glue them together. According to the feature integration theory, this is the job of focal attention. Focal attention selects a particular location within a master map of locations, and all features that have this location are automatically retrieved (Figure 9.18).

Feature integration theory has certain attractions. First, it seems to gel nicely with some notions of physiological processes which claim that different areas of the brain handle different bits of information – such as an area for motion (MT – see Chapter 6) or an area for colour (V4 – see Chapter 5) as well as the known physiological properties of cells in

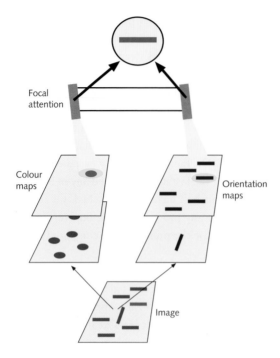

Focal
attention

Colour
maps

Orientation
maps

Image

Fig. 9.18. Feature integration theory.
The image is broken down into its
constituent dimensions such as colour
and orientation (there would also be
maps for motion, depth, etc.). Within
each dimension there would be feature
maps; for example, for colour there
might be maps for green, purple, and
blue. In order to combine information
from the feature maps, focal attention is
required.

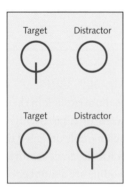

Target   Distractor

Target   Distractor

Fig. 9.19. Circles and lollipops – do you think it
would be harder to spot a circle in a field of
lollipops, or a lollipop in a field of circles?

the primary visual cortex such as orientation selectivity. Second, it has had some striking
successes that other theories struggle with. Consider the two stimuli depicted in Figure
9.19. One is a circle, the other a circle with a line in it (a lollipop). In visual search
experiments, do you think it would be easy to search for the lollipop in a field of circles?
Or would it be easier to search for the circle in a field of lollipops? Try these searches for
yourself – examples are given in Figure 9.20. You probably found the first search very
easy and the second difficult – at least that is the result reported by most observers (see
bottom part of Figure 9.20). The result is quite easily explained by feature integration
theory. The two features (the line and the circle) are split into separate maps. So in the first

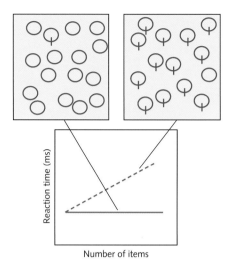

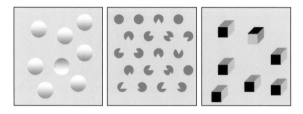

Fig. 9.20. Typical results when searching for circles and lollipops. See text for details.

Fig. 9.21. Some 'higher-level' features also produce searches that do not increase in difficulty with number of elements.

search there is a map with lots of circles and a map that contains just the one line. As this line feature is unique, it pops out. In the latter case there will be a map with lots of circles and one with lots of lines. The only way to know if there is a line for each circle is to combine them. This requires focal attention to glue each line and circle together to see if they match (until it finds a circle without a corresponding line – the target) and hence performance gets slower with increasing number of items.

Feature integration theory has had many successes, but it is not without its problems. First, the list of 'features' has steadily grown and many of them no longer appear to be the low-level visual tokens once envisaged. Figure 9.21 gives some examples of these, such as items defined by shading, shadow, and even illusory contours (see Chapter 4). Second, some conjunction searches can be done in parallel. For example, if one of the features is stereoscopic depth, it appears that a person can selectively search all the elements at one depth and spot the odd one out (see Figure 9.22). Similar reports have also occurred for motion conjunctions. It may be that these types of cue are able to segment the scene into surfaces and that our search mechanisms then selectively search each surface in parallel but only one surface at a time. This should remind us of our earlier debate between space-based and object-based theories of attention. There, we suggested that attention was at work on a scene that had already been segmented into objects (or

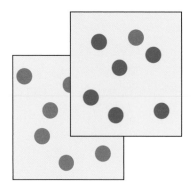

Fig. 9.22. A conjunction search (for a combination of depth and colour) that does not get slower with increasing number of elements.

surfaces) rather than merely a mass of undifferentiated features. Clearly, a synthesis of the ideas arising from cueing experiments and those arising from search experiments is needed – after all, both purport to be analysing attentional processes!

Guided search

Given the limitations of feature integration theory, it is not surprising that alternative theories have arisen. We shall not try to cover them all, but merely give a flavour of what they have in common. In guided search theories elements in the image are once more analysed according to features such as their colour, motion, and so on. However, this information is then used to form a salience map that is independent of what caused that salience. Hence an element could be salient because it is the only green element, or because it is the only vertical line, and so on. Salience is decided to some extent by 'bottom-up' factors. Therefore a red target in a bunch of orange distractors would be less salient that the same red target in a bunch of green distractors. However, salience can also be influenced by 'top-down' factors. For example, if we know that the target is red then this information can be used to give a greater weight to all red items that contribute to the salience map. Items are chosen from this salience map for inspection in a sensible order – hence we search the most salient item first and then the next most salient one, and so on. If, of course, the first item searched (the most salient according to this theory) is indeed the target, then the search ends. We can now explain parallel search (e.g. a purple circle target and green circle distractors) as being merely an instance where the target is highly salient and hence the first thing inspected. In serial search situations the target is not highly salient, and hence may not be the first thing searched. However, it has been shown that some knowledge of the colour of the target can help. Let us compare the two situations in Figure 9.23. In both cases you have to search for an >-shaped element that is purple. It is clear that this knowledge can be used to limit the search to elements that share the target's colour and hence search is must faster. Indeed, in the extreme case where the only element that is purple is the target then search may appear 'parallel' as this is the only salient item.

Fig. 9.23. Search for a target is enhanced by being able to discount some distractor elements. If we know we're searching for a red shape then we can completely discount all the green distractors.

Neglect

Some patients behave in a manner that suggests their mechanisms of attention have been severely affected. The most famous of these is a condition known as unilateral visual neglect. Lesions in various sites in the brain can lead a person to behave as if information in the world on the side opposite to this lesion does not exist. The site of damage most often associated with this condition is the right parietal cortex (Figure 9.24). Lesions here can lead to the patient dressing only the right side of their body, shaving or applying make-up only to one side of their face, and eating food only from the right side of the plate (turning the plate through 180° allows them to finish the meal) – they also often deny that they have any problems. Some typical clinical tasks and results are shown in Figure 9.25. When asked to copy a picture of a clock, the patient leaves out the numbers on the left. Often they know that there should be 12 numbers, so they include them all – but all on the right of the clock. When asked to cross out all the marks on a page, the patient crosses out those on the right and then happily reports that all the marks have been crossed out. Fortunately, extreme neglect is rare and tends to fade with time. Often the patient is left with a less extreme form of neglect known as extinction. Here, when a single object is presented on the left there appears to be little problem. However, if two things are presented, one on the left and one on the right, the patient reports only the one on the right.

If neglect is a problem of attention then we can ask similar questions of the neglect condition as we did of normal attentional processes – such as whether the neglect is of space or of objects. Figure 9.25B shows the response of one particular patient when asked to cross out the elements of the two figures. She did not neglect the left figure but rather neglected the left side of both figures, suggesting an object-based representation. However, such clinical tests are hard to interpret conclusively. For instance, in this example of crossing out the elements from two figures the patient might have fixated the centre of each figure in turn – hence for each figure the neglect could still have been space based. Presumably the copying of drawings involves many such fixations and so again, although the results are striking, they are hard to interpret (see Figure 9.26).

More rigorous tests of space-based versus object-based neglect have also been performed. Suppose we present a neglect patient with figures like those illustrated in

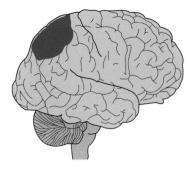

Fig. 9.24. Brain areas implicated in the control of attention and where damage can cause neglect and extinction.

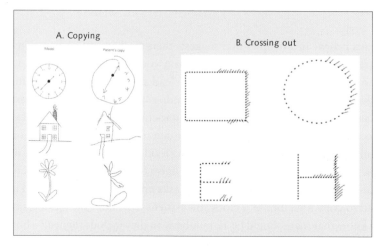

A. Copying   B. Crossing out

Fig. 9.25. Common tests for the presence of visual neglect.

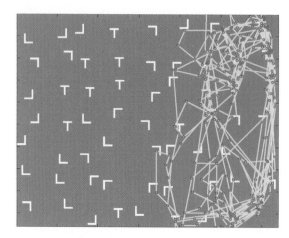

Fig. 9.26. Eye movement records made by a patient with unilateral visual neglect. Note that all the activity is on the right of the picture. The issue of eye movements and attention is considered further in Chapter 11.

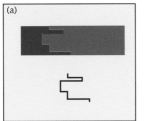 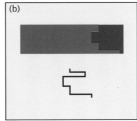

Fig. 9.27. Tests for space-based versus object-based theory of neglect. The jagged edge of the figure has to be matched to the line below. In (a) the purple area's jagged line is to the left of space, but on the right side of the (purple) object. In (b) the jagged edge is on the right side of space, but on the left side of the purple object. See text for results.

Figure 9.27. The patient fixates a central fixation mark and the figures are presented so briefly that eye movements cannot take place. In such figures the small bright area in purple is normally seen as an object and the other area (in green) as background. Note, therefore, that in Figure 9.27a the wiggly edge is on the right of the purple object but to the left of the fixation point (space), whereas in Figure 9.27b the wiggly edge is on the left of the object but to the right of the fixation point. Hence if our patient's neglect is space based, performance will be poor for the stimuli on the left of the figure, but if his neglect is object based, performance will be poor for stimuli depicted on the right of the figure. The result was that the patient was around 80% correct (which was as good as normal people for this very hard task) for the targets that appeared on the left of space but the right of the object (like Figure 9.27a), but only 50% correct when the line was on the right of space but the left of the figure (like Figure 9.27b). Remember that if you shut your eyes and guessed you should still get 50% correct by chance! The result clearly shows that this particular deficit can be described as object based.

For the patient to show this pattern of results he would have to have the same figure–ground allocation as normals do – in this case assigning the bright purple thing as the figure. Scientists therefore looked to see if this patient also had any processing of the left side of the figure (even though it is neglected). They utilized a phenomenon illustrated in Figure 9.28. When this is viewed, subjects automatically assign either the purple or white areas to be the figure and the other the ground. Try looking near the top of the picture – which is figure? Now try the bottom. You should find that you gave a different answer, depending on whether you looked at the top or bottom. The reason is apparent on much closer inspection of this figure. You will see that in the top half the white elements are symmetric – that is, the two sides of a white column are mirror reflections of one another. In the lower half of the figure, the black elements are symmetric. Symmetry is one of the cues that helps us decide which parts of a picture are figure and which parts are ground. Many objects are reasonably symmetric – such as faces, humans, most animals, trees, cars – at least, compared to the general background – and the brain takes advantage of this cue. But to do so it must, of course, be able to analyse both sides of the figure and then do some comparisons. So would our patient who neglects

Fig. 9.28. Are the banisters white or purple? See text for details.

the left side of figures be influenced by symmetry? The patient was shown such figures and simply asked to say which colour they saw as figure (the colour of the figure was of course varied from trial to trial). He behaved just as a normal person does, and chose the symmetric area to be the figure on nearly all occasions. Clearly, then, some part of the patient's brain must process information about the left side of column even if he never becomes aware of the existence of this side of the figure. (Note that if such a patient is given a single column and asked whether it is symmetric, he performs at only a chance level.)

So just how much information do such patients extract from their neglected area? John Marshall and Peter Halligan looked to see whether the semantic information or the 'meaning' of information on the left of a picture would influence patients – even though they could not report what the information was. They presented a patient with a picture of a house that had flames coming from the left-hand side. The subject reported that this was a perfectly normal house and did not comment upon its perilous state (note that when presented with one with flames on the right the subject quickly pointed this out to the experimenters). The subject was then presented with two houses – one with the flames on the left and one without – and asked if the pictures were the same or different. The subject reported them as the same. The experimenters then asked *'which house would you prefer to live in?'*. Not surprisingly, the patient thought this was a silly question (*'because they are the same'*) yet when she was forced to choose she reliably chose the one without the flames. The patient eventually did spot the flames after over 20 such tests (including other pictures with the flames on the right to try to prime her into seeing the one on the left) and declared *'oh my God, this one's on fire!'* So it appears that even though the patient was not consciously aware of the information about the fire, that information was able to guide her behaviour to some extent – she had the sense to choose to live in a house that was not on fire.

The results we have just discussed are from individual case studies and are meant to highlight certain issues rather than give an account of how all neglect patients behave. Many patients show patterns of results different from those emphasized here. It is clear that neglect can arise from lesions in many parts of the brain including the frontal eye fields, thalamus, basal ganglia, and cingulate cortex (better read a book on neuroanatomy if you want to know where these bits are), as well as the parietal lobes mentioned earlier. It would appear that attention is better thought of as a distributed network rather than something residing in some specific part of the brain. Lesions are no respecters of the labelling that scientists have given to brain areas; each lesion is different in size and position to any other lesion. Often neglect patients show many such lesions. The attentional disorder will therefore be different in each patient, and it is therefore hardly surprising that the behaviour of each patient will be somewhat different. A major task for the years ahead will be to get a clearer understanding of the relationships between these

● READINGS AND REFERENCES

Visual attention is only part of a much broader consideration of attention. The book by Styles (1997) gives an easy introduction to this larger field. The book by Posner and Raichle (1997) is also very informative and again places the findings of visual attention in a broader context. It also gives a lot more information on brain areas involved in attention.

Papers on specific issues

Cueing paradigm There are literally thousands of studies that have used this paradigm. A couple of our favourites ask what really are the costs and benefits of attention (Jonides and Mack 1984) and whether colour cues can also drive attention (Snowden, 2002). You might also want to consider whether auditory cues can also shift visual attention (and vice versa) – see Spence and Driver (1997).

Attention to space, objects and features The experiments mentioned were by Duncan (1984) and by Brawn and Snowden (2000). Related issues in Box 9.2 about whether we can attend to specific features within an image were taken from Brawn and Snowden (1999). The use of PET techniques and attention to stimulus dimensions was from Corbetta *et al.* (1990).

Brain activity and attention We have given very little information in this chapter about where in the brain attention is governed. This can be rectified by reading Corbetta and Shulman (2002). The studies mentioned in Box 9.2 on how what brain areas are involved in moving attention are by Corbetta *et al.* (1993, 1995).

There is also a nice review of what happens at the level of individual cells, VEPs, etc. during attention (Kanwisher and Wojciulik, 2000). The studies cited in Boxes 9.2 and 9.3 were Clark and Hillyard (1996) for VEPs, Gandi *et al.* (1999) for activity in area V1, and Corbetta *et al.* (1990) for attention to visual features (e.g. colour).

Change blindness/spot the difference The classic experiments using superimposed films are to be found in Neisser and Becklen (1975), with some modern amendments in Simons and Chabris (1999). The change blindness experiments are well explained by Rensink *et al.* (1997) and the mudsplashes by O'Regan *et al.* (1999).

Visual search The field was dominated for a long time by the work of Treisman and colleagues, and the work is well summarized in Treisman (1986). More recently the distinction between serial and parallel searches has been shown to be too simplistic, and models of feature integration have been usurped by guided search-type models – a review of these can be found in Wolfe and Horowitz (2004).

Neglect Some of the experiments mentioned in the chapter are by Marshall and Halligan (1988), Marshall and Halligan (1995) and Driver *et al.* (1993). For reviews of this work see Driver and Mattingley (1998). For more basic information on neglect and extinction see Rafal (1994).

● POSSIBLE ESSAY TITLES, TUTORIALS, AND QUESTIONS OF INTEREST

1 Discuss the similarities and differences between the exogenous and endogenous control of visual attention.

2 In the visual search paradigm it has been found that some searches do not get any slower as more elements are added, whereas others get much slower. Why are there these differences?

3 Is visual attention and/or visual neglect best conceptualized as being space based or object based?

4 Under what circumstances do people fail to spot large changes in the visual scene? What are the practical consequences of this finding?

5 How does the brain's activity alter when we attend versus not attend to a stimulus?

areas and their implications for the behaviours of both normal people and those with attentional difficulties.

References

Bradley, F. H. (1886). I. – Is there any special activity of attention? *Mind* XI(43), 305–323.

Brawn, P. T. and Snowden, R. J. (1999). Can one pay attention to a particular colour ? *Perception and Psychophysics* **61**, 860–873.

Brawn, P. T. and Snowden, R. J. (2000). Attention to overlapping objects: detection vs. discrimination of luminance changes. *Journal of Experimental Psychology: Human Perception and Performance* **26**, 342–358.

Clark, V. P. and Hillyard, S. A. (1996). Spatial selective attention affects early extrastriate but not striate components of the visual evoked potential. *Journal of Cognitive Neuroscience* **8**, 387–402.

Corbetta, M., Miezin, F. M., Dobmeyer, S., Shulman, G. L., and Petersen, S. E. (1990). Attention modulation of neural processing of shape, color, and velocity in humans. *Science* **248**, 1556–1559.

Corbetta, M., Miezin, F. M., Shulman, G. L., and Petersen, S. E. (1993). A PET study of visuospatial attention. *Journal of Neuroscience* **13**, 1202–1226.

Corbetta, M. and Shulman, G. L. (2002). Control of goal-directed and stimulus-driven attention in the brain. *Nature Reviews – Neuroscience* **3**, 201–215.

Corbetta, M., Shulman, G. L., Miezin, F. M., and Petersen, S. E. (1995). Superior parietal cortex activation during spatial attention shifts and visual feature conjunction. *Science* **270**, 802–805.

Driver, J. and Mattingley, J. B. (1998). Parietal neglect and visual awareness. *Nature Neuroscience* **1**, 17–22.

Driver, J., Baylis, G. C., and Rafal, R. (1992). Preserved figure-ground segmentation and symmetry perception in a patient with neglect. *Nature* **360**, 73–75.

Duncan, J. (1984). Selective attention and the organization of visual information. *Journal of Experimental Psychology: General* **113**, 501–517.

Gandi, S. P., Heeger, D. J., and Boynton, G. M. (1999). Spatial attention affects brain activity in human primary cortex. *Proceedings of the National Academy of Sciences of the USA* **96**, 3314–3319.

Husain, M., Manna, S., Hodgson, T., Wojciulik, E., Driver, J., and Kennard, C. (2001). Impaired spatial working memory across saccades contributes to abnormal search in parietal neglect. *Brain* **124**, 941–952.

Jonides, J. and Mack, R. (1984). On the cost and benefit of cost and benefit. *Psychological Bulletin* **96**, 29–44.

Kanwisher, N. and Wojciulik, E. (2000). Visual attention: insights from brain imaging. *Nature Reviews – Neuroscience* **1**, 91–100.

Marshall, J. C. and Halligan, P. W. (1988). Blindsight and insight in visuo-spatial neglect. *Nature* **336**, 766–777.

Marshall, J. C. and Halligan, P. W. (1995). Seeing the forest but only half the trees. *Nature* **373**, 521–523.

Neisser, U. and Becklen, R. (1975). Selective looking: attending to visually specified events. *Cognitive Psychology* **7**, 480–494.

O'Regan, J. K., Rensink, R. A., and Clark, J. J. (1999). Blindness to scene changes caused by mudsplashes. *Nature* **398**, 34.

Posner, M. I. and Raichle, M. E. (1997). *Images of mind*. New York: Scientific American Press.

Rafal, R. D. (1994). Neglect. *Current Opinion in Neurobiology* **4**, 231–236.

Rafal, R. (2001). Virtual neurology. *Nature Neuroscience* **4**, 862–864.

Rensink, R. A., O'Regan, K., and Clark, J. J. (1997). To see or not to see: the need for attention to perceive changes in scenes. *Psychological Science* **8**, 368–373.

Rubin, E. (1915). *Visuell Wahrgenommene Figuren*. Copenhagen: Gyldenalske Boghandel.

Shepard, R. N. (1990) *Mind sights*. San Francisco: W. H. Freeman.

Simons, D. J. and Chabris, C. F. (1999). Gorillas in our midst: sustained inattentional blindness for dynamic events *Perception* **28**, 1059–1106.

Snowden, R. J. (2002). Visual attention to color: parvocellular guidance of attentional resources? *Psychological Science* **30**(13), 180–184.

Spence, C. J. and Driver, J. (1997). Audiovisual links in exogenous covert spatial orienting. *Perception and Psychophysics* **59**, 1–22.

Styles, E. A. (1997). *The psychology of attention*. Hove, UK: Psychology Press.

Treisman, A. (1986). Features and objects in visual processing. *Scientific American* **255**, November, 106–115.

Wolfe, J. M. and Horowitz, T. S. (2004). What attributes guide the deployment of visual attention and how do they do it? *Nature Reviews – Neuroscience* **5**(6), 495–501.

CHAPTER 10

The perception of faces

'Old Age, Adolescence, Infancy (The Three Ages)', by Salvador Dali (1940). Dali often used the technique known as double imagery, where objects and figures are grouped so as to make other images. Our brains can't help but interpret these objects as three faces of different ages.

CHAPTER OVERVIEW

It is perhaps a truism that the perception of faces is an important part of our everyday activities. We need to recognize our family and friends, as well as our enemies, so that we can recollect information about them and behave appropriately. We (well, women mainly) are also equipped with the ability to read people's faces so that we can recognize their moods, and even discern their thoughts through the subtle changes in their facial expression that signal emotions. We (well, men mainly) also make value judgements about the beauty of faces, or lack or it, and may use this subjective opinion as a guide to decide with whom to spend most of our lives! Thus as humans we (well, women mainly) spend inordinate amounts of time grooming, plucking, painting, and decorating this part of our anatomy (Figure 10.1). In this chapter we shall look at the notion that we have evolved a special ability for the visual processing of faces, and we shall consider the distress and problems that occur when these abilities are taken away from us.

The face as a special stimulus

Given that we see hundreds of faces every day, and their importance to us, perhaps it is no surprise that we seem able to extract faces from the most minimal of information. Figure 10.2 presents a group of circles, each of which contains two small circles and a

Fig. 10.1. Examples from around the world of how people decorate their faces.

Fig. 10.2. Simple cartoon faces – can you spot the sad one?

Fig. 10.3. We see faces everywhere. We see faces in the fire, we see the 'man in the moon'. Here we cannot but see a face in this cloud.

crooked line. We're confident that you actually see this as a crowd of faces and will report that nearly everybody in this crowd is happy, save for one individual who is not enjoying himself. So even looking at such an impoverished version of a face seems enough for us to interpret it as a face and to read into it an emotional content. Indeed, people seem to see faces almost everywhere, in mountain ranges, in the moon, misshapen vegetables, clouds, and so on (see Figure 10.3).

Our ability to recognize such a simple facial configuration appears very early in life. In a series of famous experiments Fanz (see also Chapter 8) presented cartoon faces (see Figure 10.4) to babies at a range of ages. To test their ability to recognize the 'face' configuration, Fanz gave the babies a choice of two things to look at (remember preferential looking in Chapter 8). One was the face in its correct configuration; the other was a scrambled version that contained all of the same features but now arranged haphazardly. Babies as young as 2–3 months spent more time looking at the correctly arranged face than the scrambled one. This must mean that they could tell the difference, and preferred the correct facial configuration (one fears that a young Picasso might have ruined this experiment). In Fanz's original study the pictures were stationary, but more recently there

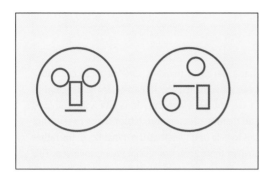

Fig. 10.4. Cartoon faces and scrambled faces as used by Fanz.

have been studies in which the pictures were waved from side to side in front of newborn infants. The hapless child's first experience of life was to have pictures of cartoon faces, and scrambled cartoon faces, waved in front of her eyes. The waving is the crucial difference. Apparently the newly arrived baby (some tested successfully within an hour of their birth!) spent more time looking at the picture of the moving face than they did any of the control stimuli (such as the scrambled face).

This response to the moving face stimuli actually appears to deteriorate when the child is around 1–2 months old and it has been suggested that this very early preference for moving face-like stimuli has developed to ensure that the baby learns about a vital piece of information for its survival – namely the ability to recognize its mother and other caregivers. Indeed there is evidence that babies as young as 2 days old spend more time tracking a picture of their own mother than pictures of other plausible mothers. So this automatic orienting to the earliest faces the baby sees may be a form of imprinting in humans, similar to that seen in young chicks that automatically follow the first large moving thing they are exposed to – in all probability their own mother. One hopes that the babies who took part in these experiments have now stopped following cardboard cartoon faces and have grown to love their mothers.

Unfortunately as we grow older our fascination for looking at normal faces rather than scrambled faces diminishes – so can we demonstrate differences in the perception of normal and scrambled faces in adults? This has been done simply by presenting either a face or a scrambled face very briefly and measuring an observer's ability to say whereabouts the stimulus occurred. Observers did indeed need less time to detect the stimuli when they were in a face-like configuration than when the same faces were presented in a scrambled configuration. It seems, therefore, that even as adults we maintain our special skills at detecting faces.

Just how good are we at recognizing faces?

Our ability to recognize faces seems special and is illustrated in the following story. Several years ago some dons (professors) at Cambridge University used to enjoy skinny-dipping in the river Cam that flows past the colleges. On one such occasion a boat

BOX
10.1
Direction of eye gaze

Faces offer a wealth of information about what a person is thinking. One of these clues to a person's thoughts can be obtained from their eye movements, and in particular the direction of their gaze. In the famous eyes of Figure 10.1.1 we can tell where the Mona Lisa is looking (and therefore where her attention is likely to be), and there is a temptation to turn round to see what she has seen over our shoulder. We use such clues to help us understand the dynamics of the rather complex social interactions that can take place when there are a number of people involved. This may seem to be a conscious process – Bob can see that Tom is looking at Pete (though he seems occasionally to be glancing at Jane – I wonder why?) and therefore he knows that what Pete is saying is meant for Tom's ears, but Tom is slightly bored by this and is easily distracted by Jane, etc. Indeed, such an ability to understand gaze direction has been used as a measure of a theory of mind – our ability to understand what another person knows, is seeing, and is thinking. Those who appear to have problems in social interactions, such as autistic children, have also been shown to have deficits in their abilities to use direction-of-gaze signals.

Fig. 10.1.1. The eyes of Leonardo da Vinci's Mona Lisa.

However, there may be some situations in which these cues could act in an automatic fashion without our intention or conscious decision to be aware of this. For instance, if Tom's gaze suddenly jumps to one side this might be because there is something of interest he has spotted (the entry of Sharon into the room?) and it might therefore also be of interest to Bob. In our evolutionary past this might have been the sudden appearance of a predator (ah, *that* Sharon), so a mechanism that automatically shifts Bob's attention to this location might be life-saving.

This idea of an automatic shift of attention has been tested. The paradigm is similar to the pre-cueing paradigm introduced in Chapter 9. A cue is presented (in this case a picture of a face with the eyes staring in one direction – see Figure 10.1.2) followed by a target. The direction of gaze is actually unrelated to the target's position (if the eyes point left the target could appear on either the right or left with equal chance), so there is no conscious reason for the subject to shift their attention. Nevertheless for about 200–600 ms after the presentation of the cue the subject is faster at detecting targets that occur on the same side as the gaze direction. At longer time intervals (greater than 1 s) this advantage disappears. If we were deliberately moving our attention, this advantage should not disappear. So this simple experiment shows that we do automatically move our attention in response to the gaze direction of someone else. Not surprisingly, if we scramble the face or invert it, this effect is reduced.

Fig. 10.1.2. Paradigm used for testing for attentional shifts due to changes in gaze direction.

containing several young women came down the river towards where the dons were frolicking. The dons quickly swam to the bank and grabbed their towels. Most of the dons wrapped their towels round their private parts but one wrapped the towel around his head. On being questioned as to why he did this he replied ' *well, I don't know how you are recognized around Cambridge, but . . .*'

The above discussion would seem to imply that we are exceptionally good at perceiving faces – but are we really any better at recognizing faces than say, dogs or chairs or, indeed, private parts? One way to test this would be to present a person with a large number of different pictures, each presented just briefly. Then in a test stage present them with another set of pictures, some of which they had seen before and some of which were novel. The subject is then required to say whether each picture seen is one they previously saw or whether it is new. Various studies of this sort have been carried out, and our ability to recognize face pictures we have seen before has been compared to our ability to recognize dogs, aeroplanes, or arbitrary shapes such as ink blots. All the studies agree that performance for face stimuli is far better than for other stimuli, confirming our notion that faces are special.

The research seems to say that our ability to recognize faces is accurate and reliable. However, this does not seem to square with research on eyewitness testimony. Unfortunately (for both the innocently accused and the victims of the crime) eyewitnesses are notoriously bad at fingering the villain, which has led to much research aimed at explaining the discrepancy between the laboratory studies described above and our fallibility in real life. No single reason has emerged as the answer, but many factors have been identified that reduce our ability to recognize a face. For example, quite minor changes in hairstyle, or even clothing, cause large changes in our ability to recognize people, and we are better if we are asked to recognize them in the same setting as the original encounter. Perhaps unsurprisingly, we are better if we have longer to study the face at first encounter rather than the brief glimpse that may characterize a real crime scene. All these factors add up to make eyewitness identification far less reliable than one might hope.

Given what we have just said, it might seem strange that *America's Most Wanted*, *Crimewatch UK*, and other programmes of this ilk often present us with a face and say '*have you seen this man?*'. Your chances of recognizing this person if you were to meet them the next day are actually very small – all the factors we noted above are against us when the TV programme is the first encounter and the meeting is the 'test'. However, if the person is already known to you, so that the TV programme becomes the test phase, then the brief presentation matters less and recognition is good.

Feature configurations

Our normal, remarkable sensitivity to extract information about how a person is feeling is demonstrated in Figure 10.5 – known as the Thatcher illusion – which we mentioned briefly in Chapter 0. The faces are meant to be upside-down, it's not a printing error; Oxford University Press does not make printing errors. Here the two faces differ in that one is a 'normal' picture, but in the other the mouth and eyes have been inverted. The two faces appear highly similar, given that such a dramatic manipulation has taken place – in fact few people notice the change at all if the picture is presented briefly without telling the observer what is amiss. Now turn the book upside down (so that you view the picture the correct way up) and a very different percept occurs – one face takes on a grotesque appearance. This demonstration shows us that our remarkable ability to understand expressions is absent when we see the face under conditions that we are not used to – in other words, we're only good at decoding facial expressions when the faces are seen in their usual configuration (the right way up). The Thatcher illusion illustrates some important principles in face processing. Faces are made up of various features – the eyes, the nose, the mouth, and so on – but it seems that we don't recognize faces simply as a collection of these features. Rather we recognize faces **holistically** – it is the whole face that is encoded,

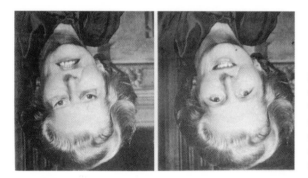

Fig. 10.5. The Thatcher illusion. Facial expressions are hard to recognize when they are not in their usual orientation. Here we see that the grotesque features of the 'thatcherized' face are not detected until the face in rotated into its more normal orientation.

Fig. 10.6. Pete, Tom, and Bob – learn their faces, you will be tested soon.

including information about the relative position of the various features. This is a difficult concept to grasp, and some of the research on face perception may make it clearer.

In one experiment participants were required to learn the names of faces that were constructed from a kit of various features. Later they were presented with individual features and had to identify which face each one came from (Figure 10.6). Now here's the clever bit: subjects did better if the feature to be identified was presented in the context of its owner's face. So the experiment goes a bit like this: the subject learns to recognize Bob, Tom, and Pete. Now they are presented with a nose in isolation and have to identify whether it is the nose of Tom, Pete, or Bob. Participants found this difficult (try it for yourself in Figure 10.7A). Now try to identify whose nose (Tom, Pete, or Bob) is presented in Figure 10.7B. You may find this much easier, even though the task is the same. Having the rest of the face clearly helps you identify the nose. So we say that the feature (the nose) is helped by the configuration (the rest of the face) that it's in. Hence we can talk of configural or holistic cues and contrast them with recognition by featural cues, that is just the individual features – eyes, nose, or mouth – on their own.

To show that this effect is special to faces, the experiment was repeated with pictures of houses and no such holistic advantage was found. Furthermore, it can be shown that faces show no advantage when they are upside-down or when the features of the face are scrambled. Upside-down faces are extremely hard to recognize, as can be seen from Figure 10.8 which shows that many 'celebrities' become completely unrecognizable when dangled by their feet.

Fig. 10.7. A. A nose in isolation. Does it belong to Pete, Tom, or Bob? B. A nose in context. Does it belong to Pete, Tom, or Bob? People find task B easier.

Fig. 10.8. Some famous faces upside down – can you recognize them?

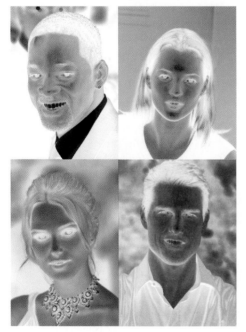

Fig. 10.9. Some famous faces in negative – can you recognize them?

Another manipulation that robs us of our usual skill in recognizing faces is to present them as negative images (see Figure 10.9). All the edges of the stimuli will be preserved (and we know from cartoons that faces can be recognized easily when presented just as line drawings), and hence all the features are still in the same place, yet this contrast inversion has a marked influence on our recognition. (Figure 10.10 shows the faces as we are accustomed to seeing them.)

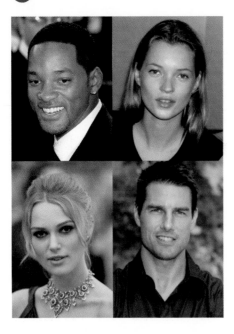

Fig. 10.10. The same famous faces as in Figure 10.9 in normal view.

Fig. 10.11. The chimaera.

  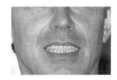

Fig. 10.12. Chimeric faces are ones in which the top half of one face is attached to the bottom half of another. It is harder to recognize the components of the chimeric face than the two half faces presented separately. Top half: David Cameron, leader of British Conservative Party. Lower half: Tony Blair, British Prime Minister.

Further evidence against the idea that faces are just a collection of independent features comes from an elegant study by Andrew Young and colleagues in which they generated what they called chimeric faces. As you will know, the chimaera was a fabulous beast that hung about the Lycian coast of what is today southern Turkey. It had the head of something, the body of something else, and probably the tail of yet something else (Figure 10.11). After all that, Young *et al.*'s chimeric faces were a bit sad – just the top half of one famous face stuck on to the bottom half of another. Their subjects were able to recognize the top halves of the faces better when presented alone than when they were presented with an inappropriate bottom half; Figure 10.12 illustrates the effect. The two half-faces together make a plausible whole face, one that we have never seen before, but one that can benefit from holistic processing. The effect disappears when the two halves are not closely aligned, with one half offset horizontally from the other. Now we have two halves without one interfering with the other, and recognition improves. This brings us back to the Thatcher illusion. In an upright face we can effortlessly discriminate the expression, but when it is presented upside-down we are deprived of those special abilities that make faces so special; the face becomes just a bunch of features, and we fail to perceive the small differences that contribute to an enormous difference in expression.

Recognizing individuals

This special ability to process information about faces allows us to discriminate between our friends and enemies even though they all (probably) have faces made up of fairly similarly placed eyes, noses, and mouths. Although it seems so easy to us to make these discriminations, we should not underestimate just how challenging the task actually is. We are, after all, faced (sic) with the problem that nearly everybody looks pretty much alike.

It is clear that our ability to differentiate faces is to some extent learnt. How many of us when travelling in a land far from our home have had the impression that 'everyone tends to look the same'? Of course, visitors from this distant land visiting our country might well be having exactly the same feelings that everybody in our homeland tends to look the same! This subjective impression has been backed up by laboratory data. For example, our ability to identify black or white faces has been investigated. About half the participants were white and half were black. As suggested above, the white people were better at identifying the white faces than the black faces, but the black participants were better at identifying the black faces than the white faces, and by about an equal amount.

It appears, then, that we are best at recognizing individuals who belong to similar groups to ourselves (Figure 10.13). This is probably because we are far more exposed to this group and have therefore 'learnt' how to differentiate this group of faces (for more on the development of face recognition, see Chapter 8).

Fig. 10.13. Groups of faces from different racial groups. Most people think that their own racial group has the most variation.

This clearly predicts that if we are exposed enough to faces from other racial groups then we should become better at distinguishing them. Indeed, such an argument can be applied to other domains of perception. To one of the authors, in his ignorance, most red wines taste pretty much the same and he could not tell you what grape, region, or year that any one belonged to. However, after rather too much practice some individuals (e.g. the other two authors) are able to make such identifications amongst many thousands of (cheap) wines. Likewise, judges at a dog show or an Olympic diving event, or even birdwatchers, have all trained their vision to spot differences to which the rest of us are, effectively, blind. Interestingly, if our dog expert has to recognize dogs from pictures that are turned upside-down (or pictures of dogs turned upside-down) their special abilities are lost, just as our ability to process faces is lost when the picture is inverted. We can therefore think of ourselves as specialists in spotting the differences in the faces of the people that we usually encounter. When travelling in a foreign land you might also want to bear in mind another finding lest you find yourself in an embarrassing situation – we are far worse at telling males from females in other-race faces!

Caricatures

We are all familiar with the idea of caricatures as used by cartoonists. A drawing of Mick Jagger (Figure 10.14) portrays him with even more grossly enlarged lips than the man himself. Prince Charles is portrayed with grotesquely protruding ears, and President Bush with a brow even more Neanderthal than the reality. By accentuating the differences between people's faces, the cartoonists are in fact mimicking the way our brains appear to encode the faces of individuals. In exaggerating these differences, the cartoonists make the face *more* recognizable that the actual face of the person! For example, Rhodes *et al.* (1987) produced caricatures by specifying a number of points on

Fig. 10.14. Caricatures take a person's most prominent features and exaggerates them further.

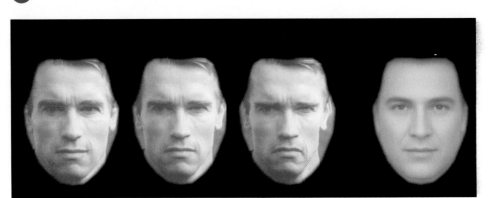

Fig. 10.15. Which is the real 'Arnie'? The real picture of Arnold Schwarzenneger is the one in the middle of the three Arnies. The one on the far left is an anticaricature whilst the one on the right is a caricature. This caricature is made be comparing the real face of Arnie with an 'average' face (far right) and then exaggerating the differences between them. The anticaricature is made by reducing these differences. Interestly many people think the caricature looks more like Arnie that the real Arnie!

a face and comparing these points with those on a 'mean' (= average) face made up from an average of many faces – wherever a face differed from the mean face, that difference was exaggerated to make a caricature (Figure 10.15). They found that such caricatures of famous people were identified faster and were even rated as being better likenesses than exact line drawings!

Expressions

As well as our ability to recognize a particular set of marks as a face, we also have remarkable abilities to decode the exact configuration to give us information about mood and thoughts through their expressions. For example, in Figure 10.1 we saw that that most of the faces were 'happy', and that the individual who was 'sad' was easy to spot.

Our facial expressions allow us to communicate our current emotions to others effectively, and in many cases this occurs even if we do not want it to. The expressions also appear to have a great degree of universality. By this we mean that the facial expression that signals 'sadness' or 'happiness' appears to be pretty much the same all across the world (see Figure 10.16). Our ability to recognize (as well as produce) emotions also appears universal. Infants as young as 12 days old can recognize and respond to some facial expressions, and by the age of just 1 year will use the expressions on others' faces to try to guide how they should behave in various situations.

Clearly, when we put on a 'happy' face we are not able to produce exactly the same face each time. There will be subtle changes in the arrangement of muscles and skin. Likewise, we are able to recognize a happy face, whether it is pulled by our friends or by a person we have never met (Figure 10.17). To do this we must be able to categorize the face as happy and ignore all the irrelevant information. This ability to categorize information as all the same (e.g. 'happy' or 'sad'), despite the many differences in the stimuli, is very useful; however, it comes at a cost. It is actually harder to tell apart stimuli that belong to the same category than those that belong to different categories. An example might help you here. Let us imagine (even better, look at Figure 10.18) that we are trying to distinguish between wavelengths of light (remember Chapter 5 on colour?). You will notice that the colour spectrum shows wavelengths that change at a constant rate from the short-wavelength blue end to the long-wavelength red end. However, we don't see the colours changing at a constant rate; there seem to be boundaries where the colour changes rapidly from, say, blue to green or from green to yellow. So if we compare two patches of colour that differ by about 20 nm, as we do in Figure 10.18, sometimes we

Fig. 10.16. Happy faces are the same the world over.

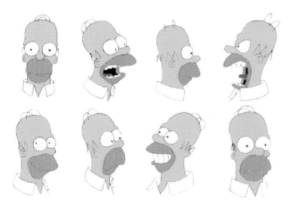

Fig. 10.17. Even cartoon faces can easily represent the expression that our cartoon character is feeling.

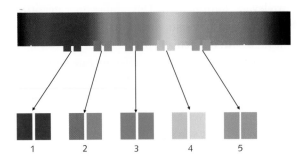

Fig. 10.18. Categorical perception. Each of the pairs of colour blocks (1–5) is separated in wavelength by approximately the same amount. However, most people find pairs 2 and 4 most different. Note that these pairs fall near the boundaries of our perceptual categories.

can tell them apart easily (when the two patches fall on either side of one of the category boundaries) and sometimes both patches look very similar – they both look blue, or red. This pattern of behaviour of poor discrimination within the category and good discrimination across the boundaries is the hallmark of what we term categorical perception.

So now let's do the same experiment but using faces instead of coloured patches. To do this we start with a picture of someone with a 'happy' face and the same person with a 'sad' face. We can then morph the pictures (make a mixture of the two pictures – you'll have to read the original papers if you want to know how this is done) to make intermediate pictures that contain, say 50% happy and 50% sad (or 80% happy and 20% sad, and so on). Examples are shown in Figure 10.19. Here three pairs of faces are shown that differ slightly (but all by the same amount) in their happy/sad ratio. Which pair appears the most different? Most people report that pair B appears the most different. In the real experiment people first categorized the various blends of pictures as either happy or sad. Those with lots of 'happy' in were nearly always categorized as happy, and likewise pictures made with lots of the 'sad' pictures were labelled as sad. For the pictures that were nearly 50:50 in their ratio of happy to sad, people sometimes labelled then as happy and sometimes as sad. No surprises so far then. Crucially, when they had to distinguish between pairs of pictures (as you just did in Figure 10.19) performance was best for these pictures near the 50:50 ratio – at the boundary between the categories of sad and happy (see Figure 10.20). Hence we can say that our perception of happy versus sad faces is indeed categorical. This methodology also shows many other categories of our expressions including fear, anger, disgust, and surprise.

We can also use these morphed faces to evaluate just how facial expression and facial identity are encoded in the brain. The left side of Figure 10.21 shows someone with an 'angry' face, while the right side shows them with a 'happy' face. The face in the middle is a morphed version that most people think is neither happy nor angry. Now we can use our method of adaptation (see Chapter 4 if you've no idea what this is) to investigate how our perceptions can be altered. If you look at the angry face on the left for about 60s, and then quickly look at the picture in the middle, you should find that this person now appears happy! Likewise if you stare at

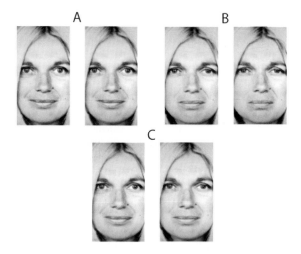

Fig. 10.19. Which pair of faces appears most different?

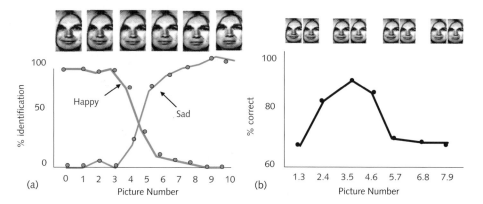

Fig. 10.20. Results from an experiment on the categorical perception of faces. Starting with a happy face (0) and a sad face (10), intermediate faces were 'morphed'. (a) Subjects classified the faces as being either happy or sad. Note that faces 4–6 are ambiguous and were sometimes were put in the happy category and sometimes in the sad category. (b) Percentage of correct responses when having to discriminate between pairs. Note that performance is better for the pairs that are near the category boundary than for those clearly within a category.

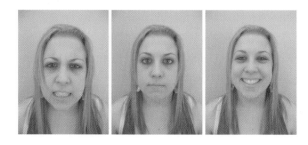

Fig. 10.21. An angry face (left), a happy face (right) and a mixture of the two (middle) Adaptation (see text) to the angry face makes the middle face appear happy.

Fig. 10.22. Will adapting to a happy face make any neutral face look angry? And will adapting to an angry face make any face look happy? Try it for yourself.

the happy picture on the right for 60 s, then the middle picture appears angry. These after-effects may arise as cells encoding these expressions (see below) are deactivated by the presentation of their favourite stimulus (e.g. a 'happy' cell reduces its firing after firing for a long time due to the presence of a happy face), hence when the neutral face is presented its 'happiness' is underestimated and it appears more angry. Just like the tilt after-effect we described in Chapter 4.

OK – so such after-effects are useful in telling us we must have something (presumably cells in our brain) that encode such features as 'happy', 'angry', or whatever, but we can use this technique to further explore just what is going on. For example, in Figure 10.22 we have replaced the original happy and angry faces with those from another individual. Using such a technique we could ask if the coding of the identity of the face and the expression of the face are completely independent, or whether you only get the after-effect when the expressions belong to the same person. Try it for yourself – what do you think? The answer appears to be 'something in between', in that an after-effect does occur but it is not as strong as when the same individual is used for both test and adaptation stimuli. Similar experiments have shown that the after-effect is pretty much independent of the viewpoint (i.e. if you adapt to a side view you still get a strong effect when testing on a front view), just like some of the face cells described below. Finally, we showed earlier that a negative image of a face (Figure 10.9) does not appear very 'face-like' – adaptation to such a negative stimulus does not produce this after-effect, confirming that it isn't just the local edges of the shape of the face that produce such an effect – it is the recognition of the emotion behind the face that is crucial.

Physiology of face recognition

Identity

For some years now it has been known that certain individual cells in the monkey's temporal cortex appear to be sensitive to 'faces' – you may remember a discussion of these cells in Chapter 3. Some face cells respond to any old face, whereas others seem to respond to specific faces and – here's the clever bit – they respond to that face regardless of its expression. These cells can be regarded as 'identity' cells (see Figure 10.24). Indeed, similar

Fig. 10.23. Adaptation techniques can also be used to probe our ability to detect the identity of someone. Stan Laurel (right), Oliver Hardy (left), and a Laurel and Hardy hybrid in the middle. Adaptation to Laurel makes the hybrid look like Hardy, and vice versa.

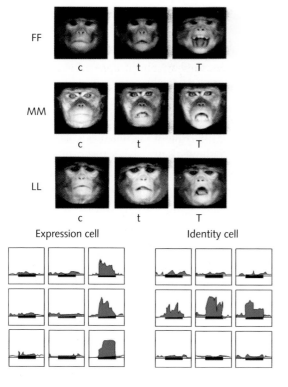

Fig. 10.24. Illustration of the stimuli of Hasselmo *et al.* (1989). The stimuli consist of three different monkeys producing three expressions. The results of the experiment show that 'expression cells' (bottom left) respond to a specific expression, irrespective of which monkey produced it, whereas 'identity cells' (bottom right) respond to one animal irrespective of what expression it has.

cells have been found in other species of animals so, for example, sheep quite sensibly appear to have cells that respond only when another sheep comes into view – more strangely, the very same sheep appear to have cells that recognize human faces! Perhaps this is an example of the type of learning we described in the section 'Recognizing individuals'. If a sheep wants to get to the front of the queue when feeding time comes around, then it makes sense to devote some resources (in the shape of special cells) to the job of recognizing the man who brings the food. And that is exactly what the sheep does – after all, sheep aren't (completely) stupid... However, despite many studies that have detailed the existence of such cells in other areas of the monkey's cortex, and in several species of animals, it is still far from clear how these cells might actually produce this remarkable selectivity. The cells in the areas known to provide an input to these 'face' areas, such as area V4 (see Chapter 3), seem to respond to quite simple stimuli such as lines or simple patterns, so how we can produce a cell that is just sensitive to faces is still a great mystery.

If a sheep can have face-sensitive cells then it seems not unreasonable to ask whether humans might also have face cells in the same part of the temporal cortex. The advent of brain imaging techniques has allowed this notion to be tested. Indeed, some studies have gone beyond merely finding the parts of the brain involved in face recognition and have used this technique to ask the question we posed earlier – are faces special, or just an example of a complex object?

Kanwisher and her colleagues (1997) have recorded brain activity (fMRI, see Chapter 12) while a subject viewed pictures of faces and of other non-face objects. Of course both faces and non-faces will produce activity in the retina, the lateral geniculate nucleus (LGN), and the early parts of the visual cortex, so if we want to find out if faces produce activity in some special part of the brain we must subtract the activity in the visual system produced by the non-face stimuli from the activity produced by the face stimuli. This is just what they did. They found that an area in the inferior occipitotemporal region in the right fusiform gyrus, which Kanwisher helpfully called the fusiform face area (FFA), so we know where it is and what it does, was active only when the subject was looking at faces. Figure 10.25 shows Kanwisher's fusiform face area (FFA) in red as well as a subsidary face area, the occipital face area (OCA). In the picture it's the red bit near the ear. Further experiments have exploited the manipulation that Fanz used many years ago (see page 287). Comparison of activity caused by faces and scrambled faces again reveals this particular area as face specific.

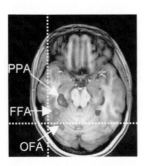

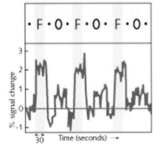

Fig. 10.25. The red areas, fusiform face area (FFA) and occipital face area (OFA) light up when processing faces. Parahippocampal Place Area (PPA) respond best to pictures of places and other complex objects.

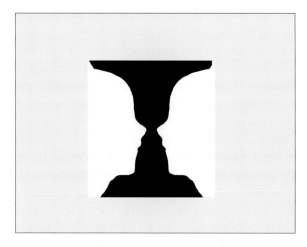

Fig. 10.26. Rubin's vase. The figure alternates between being seen as a vase or as two faces.

Another line of evidence for the importance of the FFA in face detection comes from ambiguous figures such as Rubin's vase (see Figure 10.26). Such a picture can be seen either as faces or as a vase and you might remember it from Chapter 9. If we compare activity in the brain during times when we see the figure as faces against the activity when it is seen as a vase then the FFA is more active. This result is important in that the actual stimulus is identical in both conditions! It is only the person's perception that has changed. It would be interesting to know whether it is the person's perception that causes the changes in the activity in this area, or whether it is the change in activity in this area that causes the person's perception to change.

However, the existence of this face area is controversial. Recent research has questioned whether this part of the brain is active when we do *any* task that requires a high level of visual expertise. And, because we are all experts in face recognition, it lights up when we see faces. There is evidence that the same area lights up in keen birdwatchers when they are shown pictures of birds to identify, and in sad people when shown different types of car to identify.

Expressions

In the preceding section we suggested a distinction between recognizing the identity of a person, and recognizing the emotions that flicker across the face. Perhaps, then, you will not be surprised to hear that different parts of the brain seem to be involved in recognizing identity and emotion. We have already heard about cells in area IT and about the human FFA. Cells involved in the processing of information about emotion have been found in the superior temporal sulcus (STS), well away from those appearing to be involved in processing identity. These same STS cells also are responsive to the direction of eye-gaze (see Box 10.1). Look back at Figure 10.24. We have seen that identity cells (in area IT) respond to a particular face regardless of expression, but this figure also shows that there are expression cells (in area STS) that respond to a particular expression, regardless of whose face the expression is on.

As well as certain emotional pictures activating areas within our cortex, it has often been noted that a subcortical area called the amygdala is also activated, in particular if the picture depicts a 'fearful' expression. Quite remarkably, this activation of the amygdala occurs even if the person is not able to consciously perceive the face because it is presented very briefly or outside the focus of attention. It has therefore been suggested that there might be a fast track for important information (e.g. about possible threats) that bypasses much of the normal visual cortex in order to get the information to the amygdala as quickly as possible (for more on these pathways, see Chapter 11). In line with this idea it has been found that it is only the low-spatial-frequency information that activates the amygdala – images that contain only high spatial frequency information do not cause this activation (see Figure 10.27). This low spatial frequency information is thought to be carried by the magnocellular pathways whereas the high spatial frequency information is carried by the parvocellular pathways (see Chapter 1).

So it may well be that the story of how we see faces is rather complicated. Recognizing an individual may be different from merely seeing a face, and recognizing emotions may need different structures again. However, the techniques of brain imaging seem to offer us an opportunity to understand not only where these abilities reside within our brains, but also what the relationship between them might be. Further, the idea that a specific part of our brain may be needed for a task, such as recognizing a person, suggests that if that part of the brain is damaged we should lose this ability. It is to this remarkable condition that we now turn.

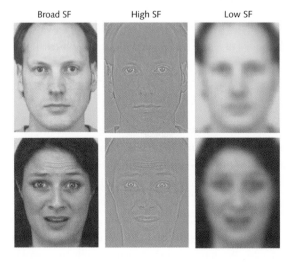

Fig. 10.27. Examples of stimuli used by Vuilleumier et al. (2003). Left side shows normal pictures of faces, middle section a version with only high spatial frequencies, and right side a version with only low spatial frequencies.

Prosopagnosia

We take our ability to recognize our friends and family for granted – what could be more natural than recognition of your siblings, partner, or parents? It therefore seems amazing that for some individuals this ability is lost. Such patients, known as prosopagnosics, can often appear to have quite normal visual functions. They can read books and eye charts, they can ride a bicycle, play the piano, and do nearly all the things that people with 'normal' vision can do. Nearly but not all, because prosopagnosics will fail to identify

---

BOX 10.2 **Beauty and the eye of the beholder**

What makes one face attractive and another, well, unattractive? Is beauty the same all over the world? The answers to such questions have been sought in recent years using techniques that vary facial features systematically by computer graphics and get people to rate the attractiveness of the various manipulated faces. The answer to the first question appears to be rather dull – we find 'average' faces the most attractive. This is illustrated in Figure 10.2.1 and appears to hold true for both male and females. Why might an average face be the most attractive? In the process of generating an average face by adding together more and more individual faces, all minor blemishes and deformities are lost and the final face acquires a peachy perfect complexion. It is possible that we find such an image attractive because the face is a sign of health and reproductive fitness – hence this would be a good potential mate. This type of averaging to produce an attractive face seems also to work for all the different racial groups that have been tested so far, so it seems that at least this principle is the same the world over.

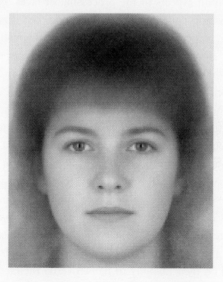

Fig. 10.2.1. 'Averaged' faces from various racial groups. By averaging many faces we can construct one that appears to be particularly attractive.

However, this is far from the whole story, which is comforting news for those of you with spotty complexions and a host of minor deformities. If a set of real faces is rated for attractiveness by a large number of people there is some agreement – but far from total agreement – about who is the fairest of them all. As the saying goes 'beauty is in the eye of the beholder' and if you are plug ugly, take heart – there may well be someone out there who will find you beautiful. Probably your mother.

This averaging business has been possible for quite some while. In Victorian times, Galton decided to make a composite of all faces of violent offenders so that he could show the 'average evil face'. To his embarrassment, the average evil face was rather attractive.

pictures of famous people, will fail to greet old friends, and even fail to recognize their spouse. Much research has established that prosopagnosics can 'see' perfectly well, in that they perform quite like other people in tests of visual acuity, contrast sensitivity, and the other things you have learned about. So what has gone wrong? Perhaps they have simply lost the memory for these people? It appears not. The same prosopagnosic patient who fails to recognize his wife when looking at her face may well recognize her from a variety of other cues, such as the colour of her shoes, the sound of her voice, or even something in the way she walks. Obviously the patient still remembers the person (they can even describe how she looks!) but the presentation of the face does not provide a route for location of the person's identity.

The study of such brain-damaged individuals has provided a wealth of data about how information concerning faces may be organized in the normal brain. In line with the studies of cells and brain imaging presented above, it has become clear that there isn't just one area that deals with all aspects of the processing of faces, but that there are many areas that may, or may not, contribute depending on what the person is trying to do (understand an emotion, recognize a friend, spot a potential boy/girlfriend). Some cases of brain damage appear to impair the person so they can no longer recognize famous faces, but can still recognize what emotion is on the same face that they cannot recognize, while another patient could tell you the name of the face but not the expression upon it. Even more puzzling is a wonderful report that a prosopagnosic farmer could not recognize members of his family but still recognized each of his cows, so just because he couldn't recognize his wife and children didn't mean that he couldn't tell Daisy from Ermintrude! This suggests that prosopagnosia can be specific for just human faces. As well as these intriguing cases of what we might call pure prosopagnosia, there are also cases of patients who have a wider range of problems; as well as failing to recognize faces they will fail at some of the other tasks requiring visual expertise that we mentioned in the last section, such as recognizing different makes of cars.

Another dissociation of function that has been described in some prosopagnosic patients is a distinction between (a) their inability to name overtly the face presented to them and (b) measures of their covert behaviour, which suggest that they can differentiate familiar

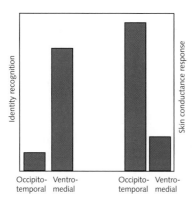

Fig. 10.28. Results from an experiment by Tranel and colleagues. See text for details.

faces from unfamiliar ones. For example, Tranel and colleagues measured the skin conductance response (as the skin sweats its electrical resistance changes and this is picked up by electrodes) as faces were presented to prosopagnosic patients who had damage in their occipitotemporal region (Tranel and Damasio 1985). They used two different types of faces in the experiment, 'familiar' faces that the patients knew before the brain damage occurred and 'unfamiliar' faces that the patients had encountered only after the brain damage (for instance the doctors and psychologists who were testing them). Although the patients were very poor at naming any of these faces when asked to do so, the familiar faces produced responses in the patient's skin that unfamiliar faces did not – they produce a covert response without any overt response. In other words, they could not say which faces they had seen before, but their skin responded differently to familiar and unfamiliar faces.

Thus there must be some dissociation in the brain regions that produce the 'feeling of familiarity' and those that allow us to specify the facts about the face (such as the name of the person). If this is so, then surely we should be able to find the opposite pattern of results – brain damage that allows us to say who a person is, but fails to spark this feeling of familiarity. In the same study Tranel tested patients who had damage much further forward in their brain (in the ventromedial frontal lobe) and this group showed just such a pattern of results (see Figure 10.28); they were able to identify nearly all the faces presented to them but their skin conductance did not change when presented with the faces familiar to them before their brain damage.

Delusions

The distinction described above, about recollecting the name/identity of a person and having a feeling of familiarity, seems to explain a feeling you may find all too common if you are like us. Have you ever found yourself talking to someone whom you know that you know (you have a feeling of familiarity), who clearly knows you, but yet you are unable to recall who the person actually is?

In this case the feeling of familiarity is present but you cannot recall the information about identity. Could the opposite happen – could you get the information about the person (it's your sister, say) but no spark of recognition? If so, what would this feel like? It has been suggested that exactly this type of problem is occurring in delusional mis-identification syndromes – rare psychiatric disorders that involve changes in the recognition of people (and sometimes objects or pets too). One of the most extensively studied of these is Capgras syndrome. In this disorder the patient believes that someone (perhaps one of their children or spouse) has been replaced by an impostor or a double. Perhaps not surprisingly, such patients have often been diagnosed as schizophrenic, or just plain mad, but Ellis and Lewis (2001) suggest that such cases could be thought of as the 'mirror image' of prosopagnosia. The patient recognizes the person, but may fail to get the feeling of familiarity that should accompany this person (see Figure 10.29). Hence they do not believe it is this person, and attempt some rationalization for this state of affairs (they must have been replaced by a double, or a robot, or an impostor impersonating this person – known as Fregoli syndrome). Capgras patients are well aware that what they are claiming is unbelievable, and that people might think them insane for making such claims, nevertheless they continue in their belief that this has indeed happened. In line with this idea that the emotional valence of the faces has been impaired in Capgras patients, it has

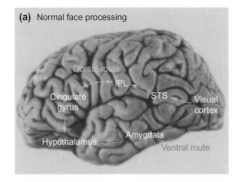

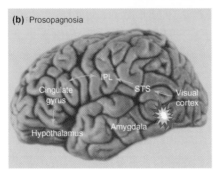
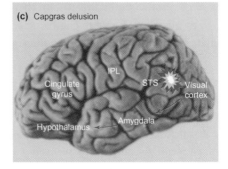

Fig. 10.29. Lesions of the brain that are thought to produce prosopagnosia and Capgras syndrome (a) normal face processing; (b) prosopagnosia; (c) Capgras syndrome.

been demonstrated that they do not show the usual skin conductance response to familiar faces (but can show perfectly normal skin conductance responses to auditory stimuli such as loud bangs).

BOX 10.3   **Searching for faces**

Another way to examine if faces are 'special' is to see if our ability to find a face is different from finding other objects. To examine this we can use the visual search paradigm (see Chapter 9) where our target is hidden in a large number of distractor stimuli.

Fig. 10.3.1. Can you find the human face hidden in these pictures?
In Figure 10.3.1, see how long it takes you to find the picture of the human face? Probably took a second or so. Now try to find the animal face in Figure 10.3.2? You probably took a few more seconds to find this one. Finding other 'categories' of objects (such as houses or cars) takes even longer.

Proper experiments show that finding the face in situations such as Figure 10.3.1 takes approximately the same amount of time if there are just a few distractors or if there are lots and lots of them. On the other hand, finding the animal face takes longer as the number of distractors increases (likewise searching for cars, or even car keys, as I'm sure you will know). Thus the faces

Fig. 10.3.2. Can you find the animal face hidden in these pictures?

Fig. 10.3.3. Can you find the scrambled human face hidden in these pictures?

are special in the sense that they can be spotted in a manner that is different to other objects. Of course you might argue that it might be something trivial that the person spots, such as the colour of the face (despite faces coming in many colours). A good way to check for this is to use the same pictures as before but shuffle each picture (see Figure 10.3.3) so that qualities like its brightness or colour are preserved, but the 'faceness' is destroyed. We're sure you will find it difficult to spot the scrambled face in Figure 10.3.3.

Conclusions

We clearly have a specialized system for encoding aspects of faces, their identity, expression, etc., that is essential for our survival as social beings. The system appears to be sensitive only to the 'normal' configuration of the face and is disrupted if the face is scrambled, or presented upside down. Within our brains there appear to be cells specialized for detecting these various signals with many areas involved that may encode differing aspects of the face. Thus brain damage can produce selective losses to our face recognition systems that can result in apparently bizarre behaviours.

● READINGS AND REFERENCES

There are some recent books devoted purely to the perception of faces. Particularly readable, and beautifully illustrated, is Bruce and Young's *In the eye of the beholder* (2005), and for a similar treatment you may want to look at Liggett (1974). More detailed coverage of these issues can be found in Young (1999).

Papers on specific issues

Configural cues The Thatcher illusion was first presented in Thompson (1980) and the various other experiments mentioned are from Tanaka and Farah (1993), Rhodes *et al.* (1987), and Young *et al.* (1987). You may also be interested in looking at the effects of the loss of configural cues on the activity in the brain in George *et al.* (1999).

Expressions The classic work in this area is that of Paul Ekman (Ekman 1992). The work described on categorical perception is that of Calder *et al.* (1996).

Face cells A good review of the early work in this field can be found in Desimone (1991), and the work showing different areas for identification was done by Hasselmo *et al.* (1989). The problem of how such cells attain their selectivity is not discussed in the text and is still highly controversial, but progress is being made and Riesenhuber and Poggio (1999) is well worth reading. You should also note the similarity of 'face cells' to the 'grandmother cells' discussed in Chapter 3.

Brain areas of humans involved in face perception This is a very fast-moving field. The paper first identifying the area (and discussed in the text) is Kanwisher *et al.* (1997), and the experiment utilizing Rubin's vase was by Andrews *et al.* (2002). More up-to-date work can be found in Grill-Spector *et al.* (2004). The paper looking at the fast track of fearful stimuli to the amygdala is by Vuilleumier *et al.* (2003).

Prosopagnosia and delusional misidentification A nice review of this area can be found in Ellis and Lewis, (2001), which covers a lot of normal face recognition as well.

Attractiveness and beauty A good start to this interesting area is Perrett *et al.* (1994).

● POSSIBLE ESSAY TITLES, TUTORIALS, AND QUESTIONS OF INTEREST

1 Are the images of faces processed differently from those of other stimuli?

2 What has the use of functional brain imaging told us about the processing of the images of faces?

3 Is 'beauty in the eye of the beholder', or are there regularities in what people find beautiful?

References

Andrews, T. J., Schluppeck, D., Homfray, D., Matthews, P., and Blakemore, C. (2002). Activity in the fusiform gyrus predicts conscious perception of Rubin's Vase – Face illusion. *NeuroImage* **17**, 890–901.

Bruce, V. and Young, A. (2005). *In the eye of the beholder.* New York: Oxford University Press.

Calder, A. J., Young, A. W., Perrett, D. I., Etcoff, N. L., and Rowland, D. (1996). Categorical perception of morphed facial expressions. *Visual Cognition* **3**, 81–117.

Desimone, R. (1991). Face-selective cells in the temporal cortex of monkeys. *Journal of Cognitive Neuroscience* **3**(1), 1–8.

Ekman, P. (1992). Facial expressions of emotion: an old controversy and new findings. *Philosophical Transactions of the Royal Society of London Series B, Biological Sciences* **335**, 63–69.

Ellis, H. D. and Lewis, M. B. (2001). Capgras delusion: a window of face recognition. *Trends in Cognitive Sciences* **5**, 149–156.

Ecobank, M. P., Schluppeck, D., and Andrews, T. J. (2005). FMR – adaptation reveals a distributed representation of inanimate objects and places in human visual cortex. *Neuroimage* **28**, 268–279.

George, N., Dolan, R. J., Fink, G. R., Baylis, G. C., Russell, C. and Driver, J. (1999). Contrast polarity and face recognition in the human fusiform gyrus. *Nature Neuroscience* **2**(6), 574–580.

Grill-Spector, K., Knouf, N., and Kanwisher, N. (2004). The fusiform face area subserves face perception, not generic within-category identification. *Nature Neuroscience* 7, 555–562.

Hasselmo, M. E., Rolls, E. T., and Baylis, G. C. (1989). The role of expression and identity in the face-selective responses of neurons in the temporal visual cortex of the monkey. *Behavioural Brain Research* 32, 203–218.

Hershler, O. and Hochstein, S. (2005). At first sight: a high-level pop-out effect for faces. *Vision Research* 45(13), 1707–1724.

Kanwisher, N., McDermott, J., and Chun, M. M. (1997). The fusiform face area: a module in human extrastriate cortex specialized for face perception. *Journal of Neuroscience* 17, 4302–4311.

Liggett, J. (1974). *The human face*. London: Constable.

Perrett, D. I., May, K. A., and Yoshikawa, S. (1994). Facial shape and judgments of female attractiveness. *Nature* 368(6468), 239–242.

Rhodes, G., Brennan, S., and Carey, S. (1987). Identification and ratings of caricatures: implications for mental representations of faces. *Cognitive Psychology* 19, 473–497.

Riesenhuber, M. and Poggio, T. (1999). Hierarchical models of object recognition in cortex. *Nature Neuroscience* 2, 1019–1025.

Tanaka, J. W. and Farah, M. J. (1993). Parts and wholes in face recognition. *Quarterly Journal of Experimental Psychology* 46A, 225–245.

Thompson, P. (1980). Margaret Thatcher: a new illusion. *Perception* 9, 383–384.

Vuilleumier, P., Armony, J. L., Driver, J., and Dolan, R. J. (2003). Distinct spatial frequency sensitivities for processing faces and emotional expressions. *Nature Neuroscience* 6, 624–631.

Tranel, D. and Damasio, A. R. (1985). Knowledge without awareness: an autonomic index of facial recognition by prosopagnosics. *Science* 228, 145–1454.

Tranel, D., Damasio, H. and Damasio, A. (1995). Double dissociation between overt and covert face recognition. *Journal of Cognitive Neuroscience* 7, 425–432.

Young, A. (1999) *Faces*. Oxford: Oxford University Press.

Young, A. W., Hellawell, D. H., and Hay, D. C. (1987). Configurational information in face perception. *Perception* 16, 747–759.

CHAPTER 11

Vision and action

Although our perceptual system sees a visual illusion, is our visual action system fooled? This experiment suggests not. Two identical disks that appear to be different sizes in the Ebbinghaus illusion produce identical and appropriate grasping actions when the subject attempts to pick them up.

CHAPTER OVERVIEW

Our visual system was not designed just to provide us with pretty pictures of the world. Rather, we have to understand these images and use them to guide our behaviour if we want to catch our prey, or work out whom we'd like to date, or avoid getting run over by a bus. We use our vision to actively explore and manipulate the world around us. Over the past few years there has been a lot of interest in studying this 'active' vision. This approach sees vision as a means of planning and controlling behaviour, and to study it without considering this behaviour is like looking at a sports car and its engine without ever going for a ride. So, in this chapter we will turn on the engine and see what it drives like. First, let's remind ourselves about the motor and the transmission system.

'What' and 'where' streams in vision

Up until now we have suggested that information in the visual system progresses from the eye to the lateral geniculate nucleus (LGN) down the axons of the ganglion cells (Chapter 2). From there we learnt that the information leaves the LGN and arrives at the cortex and is processed in an area known as area V1, the primary visual cortex (Chapter 4). In turn this information leaves area V1 and is then processed in a large number of areas collectively known as the extrastriate cortex. In order to get an understanding of this complex situation, many scientists and students use the simplifying notion that each of these extrastriate areas can be placed into one of two streams – the 'what' stream and the 'where' stream.

The 'what' stream travels ventrally to the inferotemporal cortex, and is interested in seeing objects and discriminating between them. The 'where' stream travels dorsally (remember the dorsal fin on a shark is the one that sticks up out of the water) up into the posterior parietal cortex. The 'where' system is involved in locating objects in the world and in interacting with them.

What would happen if one or other of these pathways got damaged? A monkey with a lesion in the inferotemporal cortex cannot learn simple visual discriminations. Figure 11.1 shows an experiment carried out by Mishkin and his colleagues. Food is placed under one of the objects in front of the monkey. It chooses an object and, if it chooses correctly, it gets the food. The two objects are moved randomly from trial to trial, and the monkey continues to guess where the food is. A normal monkey will learn very rapidly that the food is always under (say) the cylinder shape, but a monkey with damage to the inferotemporal cortex does not learn this simple discrimination. However, the monkey is by no means blind – just hungry by now. It can reach the objects, but can't use the simple shape information to learn the task.

Object discrimination does not present a problem for a monkey with a posterior parietal lesion. To show a deficit here we need a different task, shown in Figure 11.2. The

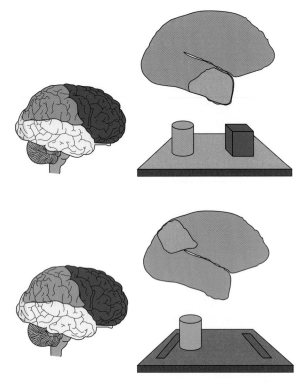

Fig. 11.1. Lesions in the monkey inferotemporal cortex (shaded grey area) in experiments by Ungerleider and Mishkin (1982) cause the monkey to become unable to make object discrimination decisions. This gave rise to the ventral stream, which is damaged here, becoming known as the 'what' pathway.

Fig. 11.2. Lesions in the monkey posterior parietal cortex (shaded grey area) cause the money to become unable to make decisions based on position information in the scene. This gave rise to the dorsal stream, which is damaged here, becoming known as the 'where' pathway.

monkey must again choose between two food wells. One contains food, the other doesn't. Now the task is to choose the well close to the cylinder. The cylinder moves position randomly between trials, to be close to one or other of the wells. This is a task that the parietally lesioned animal can't learn, even though it is simple for the monkey with the inferotemporal lesion. So this monkey (which presumably is just as hungry as its mate) does not seem able to use information about the location of things.

So there you have it: there are two 'streams' of processing; one tells us what shape or other properties things have, and the other tells us where they are or how to interact with them (Figure 11.3). Perhaps 'active' vision is not that hard, really.

Blindsight

Sorry. Things are a bit more complicated than this, as we shall now discover. What would you expect to happen to the vision of a man who has had his left primary visual cortex removed? Well, clearly we would destroy all the information arriving via the left LGN, and we know that the left LGN processes information from the right visual field. We would therefore expect our patient to have severe problems in seeing things in this area. In fact we would expect him to have a right field hemianopia, which just means he is blind on the right-hand side of his visual field (Figure 11.4). People who have sustained such

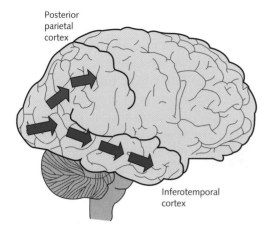

Fig. 11.3. Information from the retina passes through the LGN and on to the primary visual cortex, V1. Beyond V1 the visual pathway divides into two streams, the ventral stream into the inferotemporal cortex tells us 'what' things are and the dorsal stream into the posterior parietal cortex tells us 'where' things are.

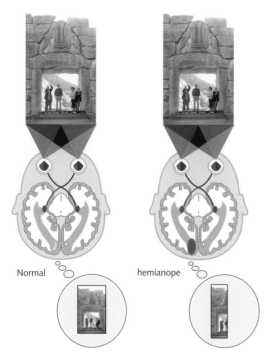

Fig. 11.4. Right field hemianopia. Someone with damage to the left side of the area V1 will report seeing only stimuli that occur to the left of the point of fixation.

damage do indeed report not being able to see anything on the right side of their visual field (and those with damage to the right side report being blind to the left visual field). However, some patients who have parts of V1 missing and who believe themselves, not unreasonably, to be blind in some parts of the visual world, can actually tell us about objects placed in their blind field. This extraordinary phenomenon has become known as 'blindsight' and has been the subject of intense research.

One piece of evidence that patients diagnosed as being 'cortically blind' can process visual stimuli is that, when a light is shone in their blind field, although they say they can't see it, nonetheless their pupils constrict (get smaller) appropriately. This does not happen in a truly blind patient (someone who has had their optic nerve severed, for example). More impressive demonstrations have shown that cortically blind patients can move their eyes towards lights they cannot 'see', and they can even point towards lights they cannot 'see'. These abilities may not seem particularly earth-shattering, but gradually we are discovering that more and more information can be accessed from patients' blind fields. It has become clear that some patients are able to report the colour of lights presented in their blind fields – 'I can't see the light, but it's green!' – and they can often tell which direction objects are moving in, even though they cannot see them. Of course there is a limit to what blindsight patients can tell us about things in their blind field, but if V1 is not passing visual information to higher visual areas, how is the information getting there?

The experiments just described were performed on humans with brain damage that we think had affected their area V1. However, brain damage in humans occurs for accidental reasons and therefore doesn't just neatly affect area V1 while sparing other areas. Nor does it take out all of area V1. This makes the interpretation of blindsight somewhat difficult – could there be some bits of V1 that are unaffected by the lesion, providing little islands of vision that could explain blindsight? To make accurate lesions that just affect area V1 we need to do this deliberately and therefore we have to use an animal. When this was first done in a monkey the results seemed most puzzling. The animal, of course, could not tell us that it didn't see things (or did see things, for that matter) but its behaviour suggested that it was hardly impaired at all. It could move around and find food with about as much ease as before the lesion. Either the damage to V1 hadn't rendered the animal blind (in which case much research which has used these animals as a model of our own visual systems has a serious problem) or blindsight might be more profound than we had realized. To answer this puzzle, the following experiment was performed. A monkey with V1 removed from one hemisphere performed two separate tasks. In one set of trials a target was presented in one of two locations and the animal had to indicate in which location the target appeared. The animal performed almost as well when the target locations were in its blind field as when they were in its normal field. This suggests that the animal could see pretty well in its blind field. In a second set of trials, the monkey just had to indicate whether a target was present or absent at a specific location on the screen. When this task was presented in the normal visual field the animal correctly indicated its presence or absence. However, when the task was presented in the blind field the animal nearly always indicated that no target was present. So, given the choice, the animal indicates that it sees no target in its blind field, but if forced to choose where it didn't see this target, it gets it right! This does indeed resemble our patients with damage to area V1, and collective sighs of relief must have come from many a researcher.

The model that we have presented so far suggests that the bifurcation (that's a clever way of saying splitting into two) of the visual pathway into the ventral ('what') and dorsal ('where') streams occurs after the primary visual cortex and that all the information about the visual world that gets to the visual cortex comes from the retina, via the LGN. However, the blindsight experiments we have just described show that this cannot be the whole story. If your V1 is destroyed and all information that reaches both the ventral and dorsal streams comes through V1, then you should be really, really blind. The bit of the story we haven't told you yet is that though the route from the retina to the cortex via the LGN and V1 (the geniculostriate pathway) is the main visual pathway, there is another way for information to get from the retina to the cortex.

The superior colliculus route

Not all the ganglion cell axons lead to the LGN; some head off to another region called the superior colliculus (Figure 11.5). From there the information is passed to the pulvinar, and from the pulvinar to the posterior parietal cortex. It has been known for many years that cells along this route, particularly those in the superior colliculus, are important in the control of eye movements. Putting this information together with what we know about the ventral and dorsal streams from V1, we now have a more complete view of our visual pathways (Figure 11.6).

This new story suggests that although people with blindsight have no functioning ventral stream to the inferotemporal cortex because of damage to V1, they still have a route to the posterior parietal cortex via the superior colliculus and pulvinar (Figure 11.7). Any ability they show to describe visual stimuli in their blind field must come via this route. This is actually a very simplified account, and the story we are telling is probably, as usual, wrong, but please don't worry too much about that.

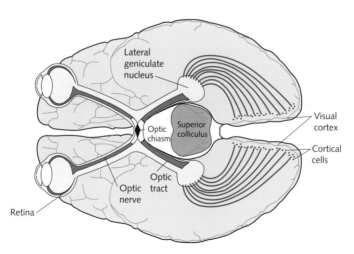

Fig. 11.5. Location of the superior colliculus.

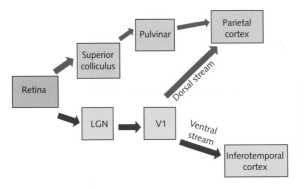

Fig. 11.6. The dorsal stream also receives input from a pathway that does not lead through the lateral geniculate nucleus (LGN) and primary visual cortex (V1). Instead, there is a route through the superior colliculus and pulvinar that leads to the posterior parietal cortex.

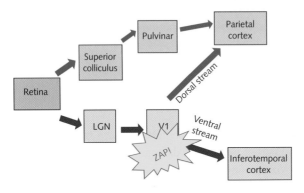

Fig. 11.7. In blindsight the primary visual cortex (V1) is damaged, so information cannot reach the ventral pathway at all, but the dorsal pathway can be stimulated via information through the superior colliculus and pulvinar.

As we have just said (see also Chapter 12), one complication is that people with neurological damage tend not to have conveniently localized lesions. A physiologist may be able to destroy V1 more or less cleanly, but a patient with a tumour is unlikely to have it affecting just V1. Consequently if a patient with blindsight can correctly identify (and some can) the colour of flashes of light in his blind field, we don't know whether this really suggests that the subcortical superior colliculus/pulvinar pathway can code colour information, or whether some pathway from the LGN bypasses V1, or whether some small region of V1 has been spared. However, it does appear to be consistently the case that patients in whom V1 is destroyed and who, thus, have no connection from V1 to the inferotemporal cortex, have no conscious vision (see Box 11.1). Meanwhile let's turn our attention to the possibility of damaging the posterior parietal cortex in humans without damage to V1. That is, can we see what disability befalls the patient who has only the ventral, inferotemporal pathway with no posterior parietal pathway?

BOX
11.1

Consciousness not explained

One of the most baffling questions that anyone interested in perception can ask (with the possible exception of why people like country music) is: Why are we conscious of some things and unconscious of others? As neuroscience and the new techniques for imaging what's going on in the brain get ever more sophisticated, this question is arousing more and more interest. To some it is the last great question for neuroscience to answer. Perhaps the champion of this quest was the late Francis Crick, a man who was instrumental in uncovering the double helix structure of DNA and who spent his later years devoted to the study of the visual system. In deliberately provocative papers Crick (and his co-worker Christof Koch) challenged our rather conservative views on consciousness. In one of their most famous papers they pose the issue thus:

'We can state bluntly the major question that neuroscience must first answer: It is probable that at any moment some active neuronal processes in your head correlate with consciousness, while others do not; *what is the difference between them?*' (Crick and Koch 1998).

So Crick and Koch first decided not to be sidetracked by questions such as What is consciousness? Is my dog conscious? Are plants conscious? Could a digital computer be conscious? It's not that these aren't good questions, it's just that, as Crick and Koch say, 'valuable time can be wasted arguing about them without coming to any conclusion'.

What Crick and Koch were after are the 'neural correlates of consciousness' and started their quest by looking at V1. Now we have seen that without V1 a patient exhibits blindsight, so does this mean that consciousness resides in V1? Not at all. You can poke your eyes out and you'll be unaware of any visual stimuli, but that doesn't mean consciousness resides in the eyes. No, blindsight suggests that we are not conscious of the visual pathways to the posterior parietal cortex – the 'how' or 'action' pathway. Indeed there is good evidence that we do not have conscious access to activity in V1. Consider the phenomenon of **utrocular perception**. This is a fancy way of describing an intriguing effect; if we were to sit you in a totally dark room and then flash a small light into just one of your eyes you would be unable to say which eye had received the light. 'So?' – we hear you cry, but think about it. The light excites cones in one eye but not the other, it excites ganglion cells in one eye and not the other, it excites monocular layers in the LGN and monocularly driven cells in V1, and yet we clearly do not have conscious access to any of this information. Crick and Koch note that beyond V1 all cells have equal inputs from the two eyes and so such cells will be unable to tell which eye the light entered. That we are not conscious of what goes on in the retina is perhaps no surprise, but the claim that V1 plays no part in conscious experience is more controversial. Given that there are possibly millions of cells there that can tell the difference between a light to the left eye and one to the right eye, maybe there's something in it. So is there other evidence for this proposal?

One popular line of enquiry has been to examine binocular rivalry, a phenomenon we talked about briefly in Chapter 7. Suppose we present a grating moving upwards to one eye and a grating moving downwards to the other, what do we see? The answer is that sometimes we see upwards motion and sometimes downwards motion. That is, our conscious awareness changes, even though the stimulus doesn't. So, in our quest for the neural correlates of consciousness we want to find cells in the brain whose firing reflects our percept, waxing and waning as the perceived nature of the stimulus changes. We'll come to an experiment that does just that in a moment but first an ingenious experiment that uses our old friend the motion after-effect (see Chapter 6).

Let's adapt to upwards motion in the left eye and downwards motion in the right eye. Now testing the left eye only produces a downwards after-effect and testing the right eye produces an upwards after-effect. So we suspect that cells in V1 must be involved as these effects are monocular and V1 is the only place in the brain with monocular and directionally selective cells. Now the clever bit, an experiment by Lehmkuhle and Fox (1975). During the adaptation period they measured which of the two gratings the subject actually experienced at any time. On average you'd expect the subject to 'see' the up grating for half the time and the down grating for half the time. Now by measuring how long the after-effect lasts, and remember that the longer the adaptation period, the longer the after-effect, Lehmkuhle and Fox discovered that the after-effect duration was appropriate for the length of time the motion was on the retina, rather than the time it was experienced. This suggests again that V1 is not the neural correlate of consciousness, because adaptation there occurs regardless of whether we perceive the motion or not.

A different story emerges when we look in area MT. Logothetis and Schall (1989) recorded from cells in MT of monkeys looking at a grating moving up in one eye and down in the other. The monkey was trained to indicate in which direction it saw the motion and, sure enough, its perception alternated between up and down, just as a human's would. Now, although the response of many of the cells recorded from remained constant throughout, reflecting a response to the stimulus on the retina, some cells' responses reflected what the animal reported it was seeing. That is, a cell that preferred upwards motion would response vigorously when the animal reported it was seeing upwards motion and poorly when it reported downwards motion. Remember that the physical stimulus never changes, only the animal's percept.

So does this mean that cells in MT are conscious? Not quite; there are always back-projections from higher levels in the cortex that might be responsible. And just because a cell behaves in a way required to be a 'neural correlate of consciousness' does not make that cell conscious itself. Crick and Koch's view, based on much evidence that we don't have space to discuss here, is that the frontal lobes of the brain have a large role to play in consciousness. Imagine that the front of the brain is looking at the sensory input, most of which comes into the back of the brain. And the front bit is where consciousness resides.

To say that locating consciousness is a controversial pastime would be an understatement. Many would regard such an enterprise as conceptually bonkers, and they may be right. Perhaps the way to bring this matter to a close is to remind you of the late Stuart Sutherland's entry on the subject in the *International Dictionary of Psychology*:

'Consciousness is a fascinating but elusive phenomenon; it is impossible to specify what it is, what it does or why it has evolved. Nothing worth reading has been written on it'.

Bálint–Holmes syndrome or optic ataxia

In 1909 Bálint reported finding a patient with damage to the posterior parietal cortex. This patient had difficulty in reaching out to grasp objects. A decade later, Holmes examined patients with gunshot wounds to the head (1918 was a pretty good time to do this, as there was a distressingly ready supply of such cases). Holmes reported that patients with this damage seemed unable to determine the orientation of objects in space. We now use the term Bálint–Holmes syndrome to describe these problems (Figure 11.8).

As in the case of the blindsight patients, we must remember that humans are unlikely to have precise and clear damage to just one area of the brain and less likely to have such damage in both hemispheres equally. So Bálint's patient was probably a bit different from Holmes's patients, but the general idea is the same. Nowadays these patients would be described as suffering from optic ataxia, but it doesn't really matter what we call it – the interesting thing is to examine what these patients can and cannot do. As you might expect, some of them have abnormal eye movements – remember the superior colliculus is involved in eye movements and feeds into the posterior parietal cortex – but the important thing is that they can actually see pretty well, and they are conscious of their pretty good vision. They can describe the orientation of lines, and they can judge distance as well. Their problems arise when they reach out to objects in the world. In a classic study, Perenin and Vighetto (1988) showed that a patient with optic ataxia could accurately report the orientation of a slit in a target but was unable to post a letter through the slit (see Figure 11.9).

The parts of the brain that the patient needs to consciously see the target are intact, but the parts needed to perform the act of orienting the hand appropriately to interact with the world are damaged. Optic ataxia patients also have difficulty in reaching to pick up objects. Just think for a moment what you do when you pick up an egg between thumb and forefinger. As you reach towards the egg you open the gap between thumb and forefinger slightly further than necessary and then, as you approach the egg, the fingers

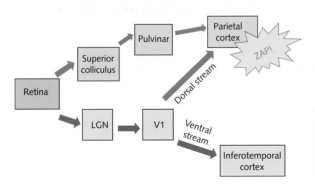

Fig. 11.8. Damage to the parietal lobe (the dorsal pathway) leaves only the ventral route intact and may be responsible for Bálint–Holmes syndrome (optic ataxia).

Fig. 11.9. Reaching behaviour in an optic ataxia patient with a tumour in her right parietal cortex. When reaching towards the slot in her unaffected right visual field (left), she behaves normally, orienting her hand to the orientation of the slot, but when the slot is in her right visual field (right), she cannot orient her hand properly to pass through the slot.

close around it. Note that you will grasp the egg either at top and bottom (along its length) or across its equator. These 'grasp lines' ensure the egg does not slip from your grip. Optic ataxia patients have a real problem here (Figure 11.10).

So, imagine you have a letter you need to post; would you rather entrust it to a person with blindsight or one with optic ataxia? Well, the blindsight patient might not be able to see the post-box but will probably post the letter OK; the optic ataxia patient will be able to see the post-box, no problem, but will have trouble picking the letter up; and then he

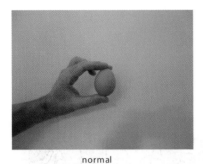

normal   Ataxia patient

Fig. 11.10. On the left, the normal way of holding an egg – note that the fingers grasp the egg across one of its two main dimensions. On the right, the way that a patient with optic ataxia may hold the same egg. The chances of a mess are much greater here.

won't get the letter in the slot. The solution is to send them both together; might be a strange conversation on the way, though:

Blind Sight (BS): 'OK, we have to post this letter I have in my hand. I know that we need a post-box but I can't see anything at all . . . although I have a strange feeling that there is something on my right. Is it a post-box?'

Optic Ataxia (OA): 'There is a large dog somewhere close, no post-box; which way is right?'

BS: 'Over there. Hey, I feel that we may be getting close to something else. What is it?'

OA: 'Ah . . . we are close to a post-box, it's red and has a horizontal slot, but I don't know how to get the letter in.'

BS: 'I can't see the slot at all, but – wow! – I have just managed to post the letter through it! Thirsty work, this . . . I could murder a pint.'

OA: 'Which way's the pub???'

(And so on. Holding hands probably isn't safe enough – they should be handcuffed to each other. Imagine the disaster if they got separated in a crowded place!)

So we have suggested that perception (knowing that you can see something) and action (being able to use the visual information to guide your behaviour) may be dissociated, and that the ventral and dorsal streams may have something to do with this. This theory therefore sees the roles of these two streams as a 'what' (perception) and a 'how' (action) system, somewhat akin to, but somewhat different from, the 'what' and 'where' distinction we made earlier in the chapter. 'How' is more general than 'where', in the sense that in order to know 'how' we need to know 'where' plus a whole bunch of other stuff like 'which way', and 'what if I slip', and so on. The scientists who proposed this theory (Goodale and Milner) developed their theory based on the finding that people with damage to the dorsal stream could see things fine – they clearly have visual awareness or visual consciousness – but they can't act on this information.

Visual form agnosia

Remember that people with blindsight, caused by damage to V1, retain their 'action' posterior parietal vision via the superior colliculus pathway. However, they do not report visual awareness, so we might reasonably assume that the posterior parietal cortex doesn't do consciousness. And this in turn might make us assume that it is the infero-temporal pathway and the ventral stream that give us visual awareness. We discuss this notion in Box 11.3, but suffice it to say now that this type of thinking is extremely dangerous and should be avoided at all costs. Meanwhile, consider what consequence we would expect if we had damage to our inferotemporal cortex, leaving V1 and the dorsal stream intact (Figure 11.11). Would this person be just like a blindsight patient? The answer, because there are unfortunate people with this type of damage, appears to be 'not quite'. The most celebrated patient, a woman called DF in the literature, suffered brain damage as a result of carbon monoxide poisoning from a faulty gas water-heater (remember to get these things checked out, unless you'd like to be a subject in lots of these kinds of experiments – or dead, which is probably worse). The upper part of Figure 11.12 shows the results from a task in which DF (and a normal control) turned a handle to make a line match the orientation of a slot. To make it easy for us to understand the results, the orientation of the slot is presented as vertical (even though in the real experiment its orientation was varied randomly from trial to trial). The various lines show the ori-entation DF chose to match that of the slot. Clearly the orientations are random – she was

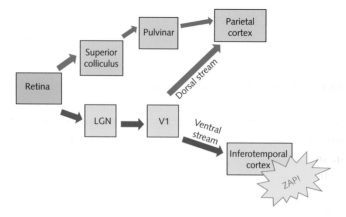

Fig. 11.11. Damage to the inferotemporal lobe (the ventral pathway) leaves only the dorsal route intact and may be responsible for visual form agnosia.

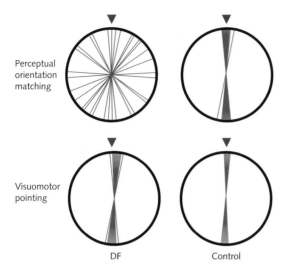

Perceptual orientation matching

Visuomotor pointing

DF   Control

Fig. 11.12. Two tasks from the investigation of patient DF. The top row shows results of DF (left) and a normal control subject (right) when they were asked to report the perceived orientation of a slot. DF's results are random, whereas the control subject does fine. The bottom row shows results when both subjects had to post a letter through a slot. DF now performs as well as the control.

very poor at this task. In the second task, the bottom row in Figure 11.12, DF was asked simply to post a letter through the same slots. Once again the actual rotation of the slot was varied from trial to trial but it is always plotted as vertical. Now DF performs this task as well as you or I. So patient DF's performance is the reverse of those patients with optic ataxia. Patients with optic ataxia can see the orientation of the slot OK but can't post the letter through it. Patient DF can't tell the orientation of the slot but then posts the letter just fine!

So how does DF differ from a blindsight patient? Critically she has visual awareness; she doesn't deny the existence of objects in her visual world, but she does have immense difficulty in knowing what they are. So her condition is a bit like blindsight without the 'blind' bit. DF's condition is called visual form agnosia and studies on her vision have been immensely important in shaping our thinking about the contribution of the ventral and dorsal streams to perception.

Dissociation of perception and action

Are there occasions when we can demonstrate in normal subjects the working of these two visual streams of processing? The answer is obviously yes, or we wouldn't have mentioned it. In an ingenious experiment scientists used a visual illusion called the Titchener or Ebbinghaus circles illusion that fools us about apparent size (we have met this illusion before, in Chapter 4). The central circle looks bigger when surrounded by small circles than when surrounded by big circles – a kind of simultaneous size contrast illusion (Figure 11.13, which is suspiciously like Figure 4.14).

Subjects now have to reach out and grasp the central circle, as in Figure 11.14. Will their grasp be appropriate for the real size of the circle or for the distorted perceived size of the circle? Intriguingly, according to Agliotti and his colleagues, our grasp is not fooled by the illusion even though our conscious perception is. In other words, though we see the central circle in the right half of the figure as smaller than that in the left, our fingers perform as if we see them as the same size.

The scientists who produced these results suggest that our perception may be fooled by the illusion but our actions are not. In turn this suggests that the ventral pathway ('what') is subject to such illusions, but that the dorsal pathway ('how') is immune to them. This experiment is so clever, and the result so neat, that it all seems a little too good to be true. And so it might prove to be in the future. Already some research suggests that this elegant story might not be quite as clear as we had hoped, and might have more to do with whether there are two figures present (as in our diagram) or whether we present them one at a time. But in visual perception we're used to that by now.

Why might it be easier to show ventral–dorsal dissociation in patients with lesions rather than in the intact brain? Suppose that there are really these two separate pathways. To what extent are they cross-connected? Neuroanatomy textbooks will tell you that

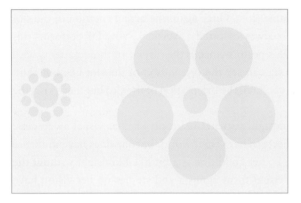

Fig. 11.13. The Ebbinghaus or Titchener circles illusion. The two central circles are actually the same size, but the one on the left looks bigger than the one on the right.

Fig. 11.14. Normal subjects are asked to grasp at the central circle in a Titchener circles illusion display, and the separation of the fingers is measured. Does it reflect the perceived or actual size of the circle?

each neuron is connected to about 1000 other neurons. There are 10^{10} neurons in the brain – that's ten thousand million, a staggeringly large number. But that means that there are ten million million connections (10^{13}) – a number that is mind-bogglingly large. So – imagine you are sitting on a given neuron. How many synapses would you have to travel through in order to get to *any* other neuron? This is a bit like those questions about how long it takes to fill a bath with water from a tap. So let's do it. One neuron allows you to go to 1000 other neurons. From each one of those you can get to a further 1000 (let's ignore backward connections for now). So now you can be in any of 1 000 000 neurons. From each of those you could get to 1 000 000 000 (that's via only three synapses). And from one of those you could reach 10^{12} neurons in total, which is 100 times more than we have. So, assuming random wiring, you can get from anywhere to anywhere in no more than four jumps. But of course the wiring is not totally random, at least not in most people. Certain connections are bound to be more popular than others. What about the perception and action pathways? Do we expect there to be cross-connections? Why ever not? They both carry important visual information that needs to be known about in tandem. So we could expect massive potential connectivity in the intact brain between these pathways. Thus, finding strong *dissociations* between them in the intact brain is really asking a bit much. Perhaps this is why attempts to find such independence are difficult. In brain-damaged patients, of course, the story is different. One of the pathways is dead, so the interconnections are dead as well, since they have nowhere to go at one end. Thus, we can more easily see the actions of one pathway in people or animals with brain damage. But we need a note of caution – studying the action of a damaged brain may therefore not be like studying the action of an intact brain, because of the lack of important cross-connections that might operate in the intact but not the damaged system. That is an inescapable danger of the neuropsychological approach to neuroscience.

Eye movements

The role of how and why the eye moves has not received as much interest from vision researchers as it should. However, things are changing, and how, why, and when we move our eyes is becoming a major topic of interest. After all, when we want to look at something, what do we do? Yes – we look directly at it. Remember (Chapter 3) that vision is not uniform across the scene. Instead, the very centre of our vision is the only place that can see in great detail, and hence if we want to find out about the detail of something, we need to point the fovea at it. This requires an eye movement.

Suppose you decide to look at the clock on the wall. You will look away from the page and move your fovea to point at the clock. Such an eye movement is called a saccade and is rapid, taking perhaps only 30–40 ms to turn the eye through many degrees of angle (see Box 11.2).

This kind of saccade is voluntary – you decided to look at the clock and then you did it. This is very similar to the endogenous shifting of attention that we talked about in

> **BOX 11.2** **Eye movements**
>
> **Saccadic eye movements** occur several times per second as we scan the world. They have certain characteristics in that they are stereotyped and ballistic. **Stereotyped** means that each time we make a saccade of a particular size, the eyes follow the same pattern of movement (see Figure 11.2.1). The eye initially accelerates, reaches its maximum velocity, and then rapidly slows down as it reaches its target. Hence the maximum speed of the eye depends on how far it has to move, and speeds can reach over 100°/s. The movements are **ballistic** in that they are planned ahead of time and once initiated cannot be altered. Hence if we are sneaky and move the target item during the time of the saccade, then the saccade is doomed to miss the target as it cannot alter its preselected path once it has started.
>
>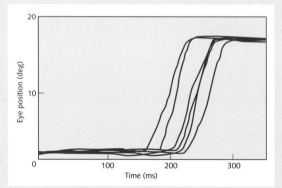
>
> **Fig. 11.2.1.** A series of human saccadic eye movements to a target that moves 15° to the left. Note that all the movements are very rapid (many hundreds of degrees per second) and they are all roughly the same. However, they all have a quite long (nearly 200 ms) latency (i.e. the length of time from when the target moved to when the eye starts moving), and this is somewhat variable from trial to trial.
>
> There are other kinds of eye movement too. When something moves across your field of view you can track it. This involves an eye movement that has the same speed as the thing that's moving, such as a speeding car. Such an eye movement is known as a **pursuit eye movement**, or sometimes just **smooth pursuit**, and is discussed a little in Chapter 5 where we discussed motion perception. There are other eye movements caused by the movement of large areas of the visual field (such as when you are looking out from a train window). Here the eye rotates automatically in order to maintain fixation on a particular area.
>
> Finally, the eyes jitter about all the time, with movements known as **tremors** or **drifts** (see Figure 11.2.2). This introduces small but significant changes to the stimulation of individual cones and stops them adapting to an unchanging light signal. If we prevent someone from moving their head (often done by getting them to bite on a bar) and then we remove all their eye tremor with drugs which paralyse the eye muscles, the hapless subject's vision fades to grey – and they no

longer see anything. This demonstrates that changes in light flux are needed to keep the cones working.

Fig. 11.2.2. Demonstration to show you that your eye is never still. First, look at the orange dot at the centre of the image intently for around 20 seconds. Then transfer your gaze to the other orange dot. You should see an after-image of the grid, and no matter how hard you try to keep your eye still on the orange dot you will see that this image dances around. Returning your gaze to the other orange dot will repeat the cycle.

Chapter 9. Is shifting gaze really the same thing as shifting attention? Well, not quite. If you try hard you can attend to some place where you are not looking, but it often seems a bit perverse and unnatural to do this. It is probably more true to say that one cannot make a saccade without making a shift of attention. So, let's just suppose for now that there is an intimate connection between attention and eye movements, and it's partly this that makes recording eye movements so interesting.

What about exogenous attentional shifts? Remember that these occur when something in the scene (like a light flashing on suddenly) tells your visual system to go and look there. This produces saccades as well. So, when inspecting a scene, your direction of gaze jumps around all over the place, sometimes driven by your voluntary decisions, and sometimes by stuff 'out there' that demands attention.

In fact we move our eyes an amazing number of times. In normal viewing we make about 3–4 saccades each second. So that's around 200 000 each day! If you make it to the ripe old age of 80 you might expect to have made over 6 billion of them. Figure 11.15 shows the pattern of eye movements made while viewing a picture. You need to note several things. First, the eyes do not slowly move over the picture but instead the eyes fixate one point (being pretty still for a while – this is termed a fixation), and then jump to another position (the saccade) for another fixation, and so on. These periods of fixation can vary but are typically in the order of 200–300 ms, while the saccade takes about

 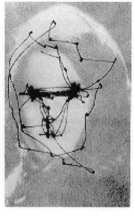

Fig. 11.15. Patterns of eye movements when viewing a picture. When an observer is viewing the face on the left their eye movements, shown on the right, jump from one interesting point on the face to another.

30 ms. Hence, we get 3–4 per second as mentioned above. Second, the position of the successive fixations is not particularly orderly – we don't start at the top left of the picture and then move a few centimetres to the right, and so on. At the same time it is clear that the position of the fixations is not random – there are some points in the picture that get fixated and others that do not. It seems as if the person deliberately fixates the points that are of most interest (e.g. the eyes). Indeed, some parts of the image get several fixations at nearly the same point. Of course the phrase '*of most interest*' depends on your goals. Given a picture of a person some people may take most interest in the eyes, others may choose to move their gaze to different parts. Hence it seems likely that the pattern of fixations and saccades will be heavily dependent upon what the person doing the seeing is trying to achieve. And this is the point of 'active vision' – we are not merely passive cameras recording what happens to come into our view, we are creatures who have goals, and therefore these goals affect how and what information we try to gather.

Saccadic suppression

Fortunately we are largely unaware of all these eye movements – remember they are controlled largely by our dorsal 'action' pathway and, as we have already seen earlier in this chapter, we are blissfully ignorant of what it is doing most of the time.

If we are constantly moving our eyes about then surely, even if the world appears to stay still while it moves across our retina (remember Helmholtz and Sherrington in Chapter 4), it should still look blurry, just as a photograph will look blurry if you move the camera as you take the picture. But it doesn't, and the reason is that we suppress our vision during the saccades. Our failure to see anything during eye movements can be easily demonstrated. Get a friend to stand facing you and ask them to stare into your eyes. This may be the only time such a thing happens for some of you. When they move their gaze from one of your eyes to the other, you will have no trouble seeing their eye

BOX
11.3

Eye movements and attention

In Chapter 9 we learnt that just because our eyes are directed at a particular point in space it doesn't mean that we are necessarily attending to this point. Nevertheless, it seems logical that there must be some relationship between the point of attention and the point at which we are looking. In fact it appears that attention always seems to move ahead of the eyes. Let us consider a cueing paradigm that we discussed in Chapter 9 (Figure 9.2.1). Remember that in this paradigm the person looks at the central cross, a cue appears (such as the flashing of one of the boxes) and then a target. We assume that the flashing cue attracts attention and this is what then causes the target to be processed better if it occurs at this cued location. Of course the flashing cue also makes us want to move our eyes to this location – and we have to resist this in order to do the task properly. Hence the cue attracts both attention and the priming of an eye movement.

Some ingenious experiments have shown that priming an eye movement also attracts attention. Several brain areas are involved in our saccadic eye movements, including the frontal eye fields (FEF) and the superior colliculus (SC). In these areas there are maps of the world just as there are in other visual areas such as V1. However, some of these maps are motor maps; that is, if you electrically stimulate just a small part of the map, the animal will move its eyes to this location. Now this happens if the current that you stimulate with is strong enough. If it is too weak the eye movement does not happen – this is given the grand title of **subthreshold microstimulation**. In these particular experiments the scientists first established by normal microstimulation where about their electrode was within these eye movement areas. They then placed targets at these locations. They found that the animal saw the targets more easily when they also gave a pulse of subthreshold microstimulation just before the target appeared, even though this pulse did not produce an eye movement. In other words, merely priming activity that is normally associated with the intention to move the eye to a location is enough to lower thresholds for seeing a target in exactly the same way attentional cueing does. Hence it appears that there is a very close link between movements of attention and movements of the eye.

movements. Now replace your friend with a mirror. Look into your own eyes and move your gaze from one eye to the other. Do you see your own eyes move? No, you don't. One second you're fixating one eye, the next moment you can see yourself fixating the other, but you never see your eyes move!

Eye movements in real tasks

Reading

One task where eye movements have been studied quite extensively is reading. You might think that this is highly artificial – after all, when reading this page you just need to know that English writing is read by looking ever more rightwards along the line, then jumping down a line, back to the left-hand end of the line, and carrying on. It's a simple, effective strategy that is usually rapidly acquired by kids when they learn to read. But this illustrates a very important point – the points of fixation we choose are not random (see above) and hence we learn the best places to look when doing a task. This is true for many tasks such as driving a car, and hitting or catching a cricket ball (or baseball if you must). Indeed, studies have shown that professional athletes in these sports have specific fixation strategies they use to help them solve these very difficult tasks, and that these differ from us mere amateurs trying to do the same. Reading is just an example of such learning in which we hope university students can be thought of as 'professionals'. However, this simple picture of moving in jumps along the line and then down a line is actually far too simplistic. As we shall see, real reading is more complicated and has produced many interesting results about how we choose where to look, and what we take in during each fixation.

A typical pattern of fixations and eye movements for reading a sentence is given in Figure 11.16. There are various things to note. First, the eyes tend to move forward in the text by around eight character spaces. You may think this will probably depend upon the size of the text – as the text is made bigger this figure would reduce – but surprisingly it doesn't. Our oculomotor system (the fancy term for the system that controls the eye movements) easily readjusts to the size of the text to keep this constant over nearly all viewing conditions. Second, not all movements are forward. We occasionally make small jumps back in the text even when reading 'easy' sentences – these are known as refixations. Of course we also occasionally make much larger jumps back over several lines when we have to read difficult passages. Third, the places of fixation are not random. We rarely fixate the spaces between words, instead we tend to fixate somewhere between the beginning and the middle of a word.

What can we understand from this? Well, it is clear that if the movements are not random then we must know something about the text ahead of us, otherwise those fixations could easily fall in the spaces or at the end of words. So the question of interest becomes, What information is taken in during each fixation? To answer this question a number of ingenious methods have been devised. They all rely on our ability (or at least a computer's ability) to change the text depending on where the person is looking – hence they are known as **gaze-contingent paradigms**. In Figure 11.17 we illustrate three such paradigms. In the **moving window paradigm** all the information outside a particular window is replaced by nonsense information (in this case xxxs) so that the person can only use the information within the moving window. By manipulating the size of this window we can get a good indication of the area over which a person is actually taking in useful information about the rest of the text. In the **moving mask paradigm** the opposite occurs, and wherever the person is looking the text is replaced by xxxs. In the **boundary paradigm** we can change a word that is ahead of the current word being read and see to what extent this change alters how easily the text is read. Together these techniques have helped us learn a great deal about what is taken in on each fixation and where we decide to move our eyes.

The results of using the moving window and moving mask type paradigms have revealed that the area over which we take in information (termed the **perceptual span**) is

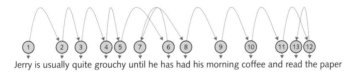

Jerry is usually quite grouchy until he has had his morning coffee and read the paper

Fig. 11.16. Pattern of fixations when reading a sentence.

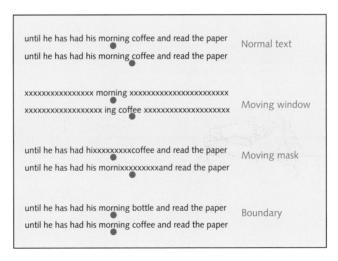

Fig. 11.17. Gaze-contingent paradigms. In each part the first sentence represents the image presented duration a particular fixation (the pink dot marks the place being fixated) and the second line represents the image presented during the next fixation. Three paradigms are shown: moving window, moving mask and boundary, along with a normal reading control.

surprisingly small. If the masked area is about seven characters long, reading becomes almost impossible. Under the converse conditions the moving window paradigm has shown that this area is asymmetric. Modifications to letters 4 characters to the left of fixation have little effect, whereas modifications of over 10 characters to the right may still cause some detriment to reading. Not surprisingly, this asymmetry for reading English is reversed for languages that are read in the opposite direction (e.g. Hebrew).

As mentioned above, our fixations tend to alight on the front half of words, so we must be able to 'see' the words up ahead in order to do this. But what information do we really extract? Using the boundary paradigm (the one where the word just ahead of the current fixation is changed) we can manipulate the nature of this 'next word' to see what aspects of it are seen. In one experiment the scientists made several manipulations of the word that was there before the word that was then to be read. As an example, let's say the person eventually had to read the word 'tune'. We could have a non-word that is physically similar (e.g. 'turc'), a word that is similar in meaning (e.g. 'song') and one that was not similar at all (e.g. 'door') (Figure 11.18). Compared to conditions in which the word was always 'tune', a word that was not similar at all produced much slower reading, showing that we must indeed extract some information about this word. Perhaps more surprisingly, the word that was similar in meaning (termed semantically similar) was just as bad as the completely different word, whereas the word with similar physical appearance (termed orthographically similar) produced better reading performance.

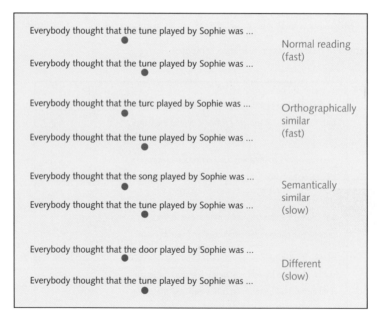

Fig. 11.18. Conditions used to explore what information is abstracted from the text just in front of the point of current fixation (pink dot). Four conditions are shown: normal reading, orthographically similar, semantically similar, and different. The words underneath each condition tell us the relative speeds of reading in each condition.

From this experiment we could conclude that we only seem to process the next word at very shallow level – we are able to extract some information about the shapes of the letters that are there, but not about the meaning of the words. A very nice example of our lack of extraction of meaning of the next word also comes from a similar experiment that took advantage of bilingual people (and why not?). The subjects had to read English text but sometimes the 'next word' was in Spanish (fortunately these people were bilingual in English and Spanish). They reasoned that if the meaning was being extracted from the next word, this meaning would be available even if the word was in Spanish. However, this did not happen, supporting the view that only physical information, not meaning, is extracted just ahead of where we are fixating.

Visual search

In Chapter 9, we saw how the technique of visual search has been used to study the way in which visual attention is deployed when looking for a target among distractors. In these paradigms you may remember that the subject has to search for a target amongst a set of distractor items. Try searching for the L in Figures 11.19 and 11.20. You probably had to move your eyes around the picture to find the L in both of these examples. This will

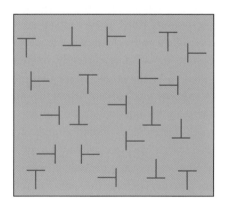

Fig. 11.19. Visual search paradigm – can you find the L?

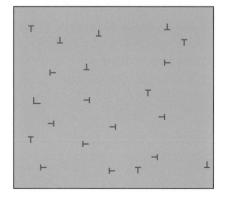

Fig. 11.20. Another visual search paradigm – can you find the L here?

have certainly been so in the latter one, as the actual elements were made small so that unless the fovea (the central part of your vision – see Chapter 1) was near the target, then it would have been impossible to distinguish the L from any of the Ts. Hence although it is possible to do some visual searches without eye movements, in most situations we naturally use our eyes when searching.

Recent experiments have begun to explore eye movements during such tasks. Perhaps not surprisingly, there is a close correspondence between the amount of time we take to find a particular target and the number of saccade-fixations that we make. This pleasing correspondence between time taken and number of fixations made may allow us to further understand how the search has taken place. Using the eye-movement records we could infer what the subject's strategy was by examining where they chose to fixate. From such data it seems that for parallel search (see Chapter 9) only a single saccade is made – straight to the target element. This is interpreted as the subject being able to extract information from all the elements in the display and that the target element is very salient, hence we can move our eyes straight to it. However, for serial searches many saccades and fixations can occur. It appears that our pattern of fixations is not random and is governed by two rules. First, we tend to fixate on things that look a bit like the target (the similarity rule). Thus if we know that the target is a red square we might tend to fixate on the red things, while not fixating on the green things. Second, we tend to fixate on things fairly close to where we have just previously fixated (the proximity rule). These findings seem best interpreted as searching for things that are most likely to be the target. Hence we must be extracting information about the items that we are not currently fixating (e.g. their colour) so that our next move is more likely to be the target. Given that our perceptual span (see above) is small, we are unlikely to know much about targets that are far from the current point of fixation, and hence these are the ones which we can select from possible inspection (hence the proximity rule). These ideas should sound very familiar in that they are similar to the ideas of 'guided search' we discussed in Chapter 9. Perhaps this is not surprising, as the task is the same (find the target) – the only difference lies in whether we allow eye movements to be used or whether we force the subject to rely only on covert movements of attention.

Some findings are more surprising. For example, it appears that we have little memory for where we have recently moved our eyes. We often return to areas that have previously been searched. In other words, we do not carry a lot of information from one saccade to the next. This is consistent with experiments on change blindness that we talked about in Chapter 9. Remember these showed that we could make large changes in the image and these would not be spotted if vision was interrupted in some way. Saccades are one such instance of vision being interrupted.

Doing 'real world' tasks

So what is the strategy for moving our eyes when doing something in the real world such as driving a car, or trying to catch a ball? Work in this area has led to some notable

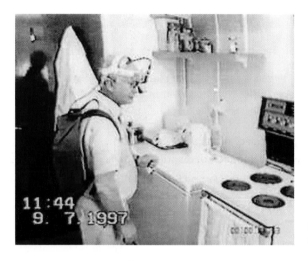

Fig. 11.21. Recording eye movements while making a cup of tea.

international differences – British scientist have studied making a cup of tea and playing cricket, whereas Americans have studied the problems involved in making a peanut butter and jelly sandwich and catching flyballs (whatever they may be).

Suppose we ask a subject to make a cup of tea in an unfamiliar kitchen and we monitor his eye movements while he performs this task (see Figure 11.21 for a picture of a scientist making a cup of tea – who said scientists are geeks?). At random times, we switch off the lights and ask the subject to recall where he had just been looking. His ability to give an accurate report is found to be restricted to what he had just been looking at just before the last saccade, and no more. It seems that we act out a dynamic, strategic 'dance' with our eyes and visual attention, without much awareness of what we are doing, except for the immediate goal in the strategy (e.g. 'find the teabag'). Our consciousness knows about the goal, and our success in getting to it, but knows very little about how we achieve that goal.

So what about tasks that require lots of skill, such as reading music, or hitting a cricket ball, or driving a Formula One racing car? It turns out that the eye-movement strategy we adopt depends on our level of skill in doing the task. For example, when we are about to hit a baseball or cricket ball with a bat, we do not follow the ball as is commonly thought. Instead, we arrange for our eyes to fixate at a point *ahead* of the actual position of the ball during its flight towards us. The extent to which the fixation is ahead of the ball position is dependent on the level of skill of the player. Similarly, in driving a racing car, a professional racing driver fixates further ahead when approaching curves in the track. The same is true for reading sheet music. The story that emerges from all of this work is that the location of fixation of the eyes is arranged to go to places that are about to be visited by us, or with which we will come into contact, or which we will execute some hand gesture from. Visual fixation is predictive of what we are about to do – and we are gloriously unaware of most of this, except in the vaguest of ways.

Conclusion

In this chapter we have seen that vision is not merely a simple recording of the world. Instead, our behaviours and goals actually change how and what we see. Vision is a series of snapshots of the world as our eyes scan the world in front of us. To understand vision we need therefore not only to understand the processes that take place during each snapshot, but also the processes by which we chose our successive snapshots. The integration of this active view of vision is likely to be a major area of future research.

● **READINGS AND REFERENCES**

There are two books that have been highly influential in this area: Milner and Goodale (1995) and Findlay and Gilchrist (2003). For more specifics on eye movements, see Carpenter (1988).

Papers on specific issues

'What' versus 'where' The experiments described looking at the effects of brain lesions in the ventral and dorsal streams are described in Mishkin *et al.* (1983).

Blindsight The experiments described stem from Cowey and Stoerig (1995), and a discussion of blindsight and its controversial history can be found in Cowey (2004).

Optic ataxia The classic studies of Perenin *et al.* are described in Perenin and Vighetto (1988); for a recent rethink that links to the notions of action and perception, see Rizzolatti and Matelli (2003).

Perception versus action The notion that we might have separate visual representations is still very controversial. The original hypothesis is well laid out in Goodale and Milner (1992) and Milner and Goodale (1995). The experiment using the Titchener circles can be found in Aglioti *et al.* (1995).

Eye movements The importance of eye movements is well documented by Martinez-Conde *et al.* (2004). A good review of saccadic eye movements and in particular their generation is provided by Carpenter (2000). For the relationship between eye movements and attention, the subthreshold microstimulation experiments mentioned were by Moore and Fallah (2001) and Müller *et al.* (2005).

Eye movements and real world tasks The experiments on reading are presented in an easily digestible form by Starr and Rayner (2001). Those interested in sports should try Land and McLeod (2000); those interested in driving, Land and Lee (1994); and those who prefer a cup of tea, Land *et al.* (1999).

Visual consciousness Crick and Koch (1995) is a good starting point, but you might prefer their *Scientific American* article (Crick and Koch 1992). Much of the monkey psychophysics is described by Logothetis (1998). For an erudite yet entertaining view, try Chapters 12–16 of Morgan (2003).

● POSSIBLE ESSAY TITLES, TUTORIALS, AND QUESTIONS OF INTEREST

1 'How', 'where', 'what', or 'when'? What is the best way to describe the streams of processing within the extrastriate cortex?

2 What is blindsight? What does the person see, and why don't they tell us this?

3 Can some illusions fool the eye but not the hand?

4 What is the difference between 'passive vision' and the 'active vision' approach to understanding visual perception?

5 Describe the pattern of eye movements during a real world task. Why do we get this pattern of eye movement?

6 What is the point of consciousness?

References

Aglioti, S., DeSouza, J. F. X., and Goodale, M. A. (1995). Size-contrast illusions deceive the eye but not the hand. *Current Biology* 5, 679–685.

Carpenter, R. H. S. (1988). *Movements of the eyes*. London: Pion.

Carpenter, R. H. S. (2000). The neural control of looking. *Current Biology* 10, 291–293.

Cowey, A. (2004). The 30th Sir Frederick Bartlett lecture: Fact, artefact, and myth about blindsight. *Quarterly Journal of Experimental Psychology Section A – Human Experimental Psychology* 57, 577–609.

Cowey, A. and Stoerig, P. (1995). Blindsight in monkeys. *Nature* 373, 247–249.

Crick, F. and Koch, C. (1992). The problem of consciousness. *Scientific American* 267, September, 152–159.

Crick, F. and Koch, C. (1995). Are we aware of neural activity in primary visual cortex? *Nature* 375, 121–123.

Crick, F. C. and Koch, C. (1998). Consciousness and neuroscience. *Cerebral Cortex* 8, 97–107.

Findlay, J. M. and Gilchrist, I. D. (2003). *Active vision: the psychology of looking and seeing*. Oxford: Oxford University Press.

Goodale, M. A. and Milner, A. D. (1992). Separate visual pathways for perception and action. *Trends in Neurosciences* 15, 20–25.

Land, M., Mennie, N., and Rusted, J. (1999). The roles of vision and eye movements in the control of activities of daily living. *Perception* 28, 1311–1328.

Land, M. F. and Lee, D. N. (1994). Where we look when we steer. *Nature* **369**, 742–744.

Land, M. F. and McLeod, P. (2000). From eye movements to actions: how batsmen hit the ball. *Nature Neuroscience* **3**, 1340–1345.

Lehmkuhle, S. and Fox, R. (1975). Effect of binocular rivalry suppression on the motion aftereffect. *Vision Research* **15**, 855–859.

Logothetis, N. (1998). Single units and conscious vision. *Philosophical Transactions of the Royal Society of London, Series B* **353**, 1801–1818.

Logothetis, N. D. and Schall, J. D. (1989). Neuronal correlates of subjective visual perception. *Science* **245**, 761–763.

Martinez-Conde, S., Macknik, S. L., and Hubel, D. H. (2004). The role of fixational eye movements in visual perception. *Nature Reviews – Neuroscience* **5**, 229–240.

Milner, A. D. and Goodale, M. A. (1995). *The visual brain in action*. Oxford: Oxford University Press.

Mishkin, M., Ungerleider, L. G., and Macko, K. (1983). Object vision and spatial vision: two cortical pathways. *Trends in Neurosciences* **6**, 414–417.

Moore, T. and Fallah, M. (2001). Control of eye movements and visual attention. *Proceedings of the National Academy of Sciences of the USA* **98**, 1273–1276.

Morgan, M. (2003). *The space between our ears*. London: Weidenfeld & Nicolson.

Müller, J. R., Philiastides, M. G., and Newsome, W. T. (2005). Microstimulation of the superior colliculus focuses attention without moving the eyes. *Proceedings of the National Academy of Sciences of the USA* **102**, 524–529.

Perenin, M.-T. and Vighetto, A. (1988). Optic ataxia: a specific disruption in visuomotor mechanisms. I. Different aspects of the deficit in reaching for objects. *Brain* **111**, 643–674.

Rizzolatti, G. and Matelli, M. (2003). Two different streams form the dorsal visual system: anatomy and functions. *Experimental Brain Research* **153**, 146–157.

Starr, M. S. and Rayner, K. (2001). Eye movements during reading: some current controversies. *Trends in Cognitive Sciences* **5**, 156–163.

Sutherland, S. (1989). *The international dictionary of psychology*. New York: Continuum.

Ungerleider, L. G. and Mishkin, M. (1982). Two cortical visual systems. In: D. J. Ingle, M. A. Goodale, and R. J. W. Mansfield (ed.). *Analysis of visual behavior*. Cambridge, MA: MIT Press, pp. 549–586.

CHAPTER 12

How we know it might be so...

fMRI reconstructions of the brains of three animals – macaque monkey, chimpanzee, and human. Many of the most important findings in vision research have come from the study of non-human animals. Recently the visual system of the macaque has been the most commonly used, because of its supposed similarities to our own. From this image the huge difference in brain size can be appreciated, and with this may come differences in our visual systems. Hence modern techniques of human brain imaging are beginning to take the place of reliance on animal work. However, there are many things that we still cannot do in the human, so appreciation of the similarities and differences between the brains is of great importance.

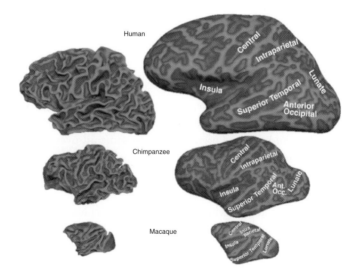

CHAPTER OVERVIEW

The study of the visual system has a long history and contains contributions from such notables as Aristotle, Newton, Descartes, and even your authors. However, it doesn't mean they got it right! Aristotle, for example, thought that the eye emitted a ray that struck objects and allowed us to see them. Descartes had the ingenious idea of cutting a hole in the back of the eye of a bull to see what it sees, and was surprised that the image he could see was upside down. In more recent times a combination of ingenuity and technology has led to many new ways of exploring how we see. Over the past century we have learnt how to record from just one of the many millions of neurons that make up the visual system, but clearly this is a technique that cannot be used to investigate human vision directly. However, other techniques have been developed that reveal the activity of small parts of our own human brains. Using these techniques, we hope to learn how the brain does this amazing trick of vision. But the answers we get from the brain are only going to be useful if the questions we ask are good ones. Hence vision scientists also have to think carefully about the input (what the person is looking at or trying to do) as well as the output (reports of what they see, actions based on what they see, activity in the brain, and so on). In this chapter we cover some (but not all) of the main techniques that have told us what we know about the visual system.

Anatomical techniques

Staining techniques

You can learn a lot about vision by looking closely at dead brains. Fresh brain tissue is yellowish white and appears pretty much the same all over. Some differences are just noticeable; for instance, some areas near the surface appear grey and other bits appear whiter. With great insight the grey stuff was called 'grey matter' and the white stuff was called 'white matter'. We now know that the grey matter is grey because cell bodies are grey and the white matter is white because that's the colour of the fatty axons. However, what's really needed is a way to see the cells themselves – a technique that would make these cells visible. Staining does this. There are many stains (with exotic names like cresyl violet and lucifer yellow) used by neuroanatomists to study the brain. First, the brain that is to be studied is removed and sliced into very thin slices using a glorified bacon-slicer known as a microtome. Dipping them in appropriate solutions then stains the slices. The cells take up the stain (or in some cases the fatty tissue takes up the stain), allowing us to see what has been stained as different from the other bits. Figure 12.1 shows the primary visual cortex stained in two ways. The Nissl stain on the left shows the cell bodies, revealing the different layers of V1, and the stain on the right shows that cytochrome oxidase is concentrated in layers 4B and 4C.

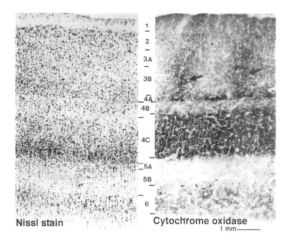

Fig. 12.1. Examples of visual cortex (area V1) that have been treated with different stains. In the left picture Nissl stain was used, which colours only the cell bodies. In this picture we can see the changes in density of the cell bodies as we move through the sections. In the right-hand picture a similar section has been stained for cytochrome oxidase activity, which is an indication of the amount of activity taking place within the section. Note the very dark band in layer 4C. You might also be able to make out two large 'blobs' in layers 2 and 3 (the large red arrows are there to help). Cells within these blobs appear to have some different properties, such as colour sensitivity, compared to other cells nearby.

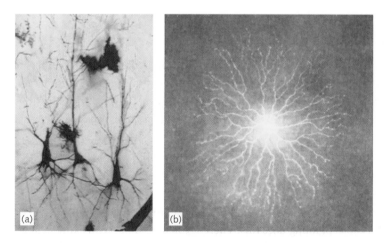

Fig. 12.2. Two individual cells that have been stained: (a) A cell from human visual cortex – a large pyramidal cell from layer III of area V1. (b) An aptly named starburst amacrine cell from the retina.

We might want to stain just a few cells. To do this a pipette (a very thin, long, hollow, glass tube) is pushed through the cell wall and a dye is injected into the cell itself. The dye then moves around the cell and can reveal all the processes of the cell. Some beautiful examples of such stained cells are shown in Figure 12.2.

As well as being able to see the cells within the visual system, we would also like to have some idea of the connections between the cells in the brain. There are three main ways to do this. Firstly, we can make a small lesion in the cortex; this will damage some axons and these will degenerate. Now by a stroke of luck if you stain the cortex with silver you find this is taken up more in the damaged fibres than elsewhere. So now we can tell where the damaged axons lead to. The second cunning method is to inject radioactive amino acid into the cortex. The radioactivity is transported down the axons and reveals where the cortical cells connect to. Thirdly, finally and perhaps most cunningly of all, you can inject the enzyme deliciously named horseradish peroxidase (HRP) into an area where you know there are some axon terminals. The HRP travels *back* along the axons and ends up in the cell bodies. These methods allow us to discover which areas connect with other areas, but we can also determine which layers within the areas do what. From such work very intricate maps of how the brain areas are connected have been established.

Recording techniques

Recording activity in the brain has been one of the mainstays of vision researchers and brain scientists in general. This section takes us through the major techniques and what actually is being recorded.

Single cell recording

Neurons communicate with each other by sending action potentials along their axons (Figure 12.3), which in turn trigger a chemical signal message that communicates with other cells. These action potentials can be thought of as very brief bursts of electrical activity, so if we could get a sensor that can detect such small bursts of electricity we could record the action potentials of a cell.

To do this the scientist uses a microelectrode – a tiny electrode. To make this a very fine wire is coated in something electrically resistant such as glass, but the very tip of the electrode is left without any insulation (i.e. without the glass) so that it can detect electrical changes. This tip is very, very small indeed: Figure 12.4 illustrates a highly magnified image of a microelectrode next to some neurons. You can see that its tip is smaller than a single cell! If the tip of this electrode is then placed near cells (we'll come back to this rather tricky part in a moment), it will be able to detect the minute electrical activity that occurs each time any of these nearby neurons produces an action potential. These very small electrical signals are then amplified and can be displayed on a computer monitor or TV screen (see Figure 12.5).

How do we know we are recording from just one cell? The electrode actually picks up activity from lots of nearby cells, so we need to isolate somehow the responses that come from just one of them. To do this we take advantage of the fact that each cell produces a characteristic signal that is the same each time the cell fires an action potential. For

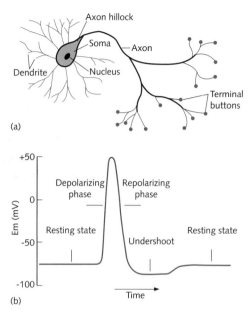

(a)

(b)

Fig. 12.3. (a) A typical nerve cell. Information from other cells arrives through the dendrites to the cell body or soma. These inputs are added (some are positive and some can be negative) causing fluctuations in voltage (electrical charge) at the site of the axon hillock. If this level reaches a crucial threshold an action potential is initiated that travels all the way along the axon to the synaptic terminals, which in turn transmit messages to the dendrites of other nerve cells. (b) The action potential. Normally the membrane (the skin) of the cell has a charge of around −70 mV, known as its resting state. Changes in the voltage of nearby membranes can cause a shift in this level, which cause a chain reaction whereby the membrane allows certain ions to cross the membrane and the membrane depolarizes. When the potential reaches +30 mV another set of processes kicks in that causes the potential to eventually return to the resting level. This large change in membrane potential causes the membrane nearby to change too, and hence the same reaction takes place a little further along the axon. This carries on and on, moving the action potential along the axon to its end.

instance, the blue cell in Figure 12.6 produces first a positive electrical response followed by a negative one, whereas the purple one produces a small negative followed by a positive each time it fires. This difference arises because the cells are all at different positions and angles from the electrode. So we can count the response of just a single cell by counting the firing rate of just one of these characteristic signals (in reality this is quite difficult, as the cells can fire at up to 500 times per second – hence we get a computer to do this for us). Typically this is done while particular images are presented to the eyes of the animal. For example, an experiment might count how many times per second the cell fires in response to the presentation of various different stimuli in order to see what this cell is signalling. The example given in Figure 12.7 comes from the classic work of Hartline (see for example Hartline *et al.* 1956), who was recording from the cells within the retina of the horseshoe crab (*Limulus* – Figure 12.7a) and showed that these cells show lateral

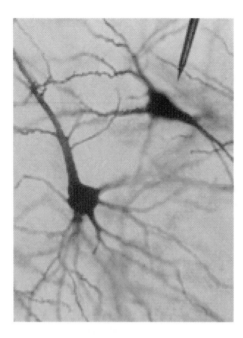

Fig. 12.4. Cells in area V1 with a microelectrode superimposed.

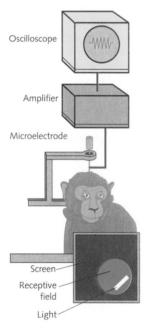

Oscilloscope

Amplifier

Microelectrode

Screen

Receptive field

Light

Fig. 12.5. Basic equipment needed to record from single cells within a brain.

inhibition (see Chapter 2). The eye of *Limulus* (Figure 12.7b) contains many 'mini-eyes' known as ommatidia. Hartline found that if he shone light on just one of these ommatidia it responded with a steady stream of action potentials. However, if he also stimulated other nearby ommatidia at the same time then the response of the first ommatidium fell. He termed this finding lateral inhibition, and we now know that cells in the retina of

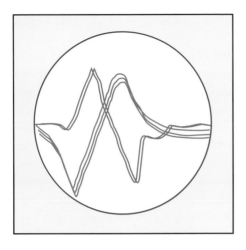

Fig. 12.6. Simulation of action potentials on an oscilloscope. Each cell has quite a different 'signature' of peaks and troughs, which is highly similar each time an action potential is elicited.

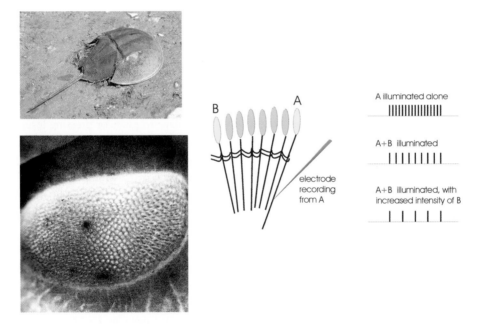

Fig. 12.7. The photographs show a horseshoe crab and one of its eyes. The diagram shows recording from a single ommatidium A. When light falls only on A a strong response is observed, but if light also falls on the surrounding ommatidia, the response is smaller. The more light that falls on the surround, the more the inhibition of A's response. This is known as 'lateral inhibition'.

mammals such as cats and monkeys also do similar things. Since this time single cell recording has been applied to many species, and many of the most important findings in vision research have come using this technique. For instance, we have learnt that cells in V1 only respond to lines of a certain orientation (see Chapter 3), that cells in MT only respond if the image moves in a certain way (see Chapter 6), and that within later regions of our brain lurk cells that only respond when a face is the object at which we are looking (Chapter 10).

In the above explanation we skipped over the important details of how you get an electrode near to a group of cells. This really depends on where these cells are. Perhaps not surprisingly, the first cells of the mammalian visual system that were recorded from using this technique were those in the retina. This makes sense as it starts at the beginning (a very good place to start) and also because it's easier to get our rather flimsy electrodes through the squidgy eyeball without too much damage to the target area or to the electrode. However, the visual cortex is another matter. To get there requires getting through the bone of the skull, and we must use the invasive technique of cutting a hole in the skull in order to pass the electrode into the brain. This of course requires anaesthetic in order to produce such a hole. For ethical reasons such experiments have only rarely been performed on humans (and only when the surgeons were opening up the skull for other medical reasons), and so nearly all our data about cortical neurons have come from non-human animals, primarily cats and monkeys.

For many years these experiments were performed on animals that were under anaesthetic, because of the surgical procedures needed to insert the electrodes into the brain. This has two major drawbacks. First, the anaesthetic is known to reduce the firing rate of nerve cells. Thus the cells are not really behaving as they would in the alert animal, though as far we know, their tuning properties, such as spatial frequency and orientation selectivity, are unchanged. Second, the anaesthetized animal is unable to perform any behaviour (such as moving its eyes from place to place or pressing levers). Although this may not be that important for cells in the early part of the visual system, it is vital for later cells that might be involved in moving the eyes, helping the animal pay attention, or deciding on whether another person is smiling or frowning at them. So if we need an alert, behaving animal for our experiment we have to do things differently. First we carry out some surgery under a general anaesthetic, implanting a tube through the skull of the animal. When the animal has recovered the tube can be opened and an electrode lowered through the tube into the brain. Fortunately the brain does not contain any receptors for feeling or pain, so the animal is completely unaware that this is occurring. After the recording session the electrode can be removed and the tube carefully sealed. This procedure can be repeated many times, so a large number of cells can be recorded from the one animal, which again is good news as far fewer animals need to be used.

The above description refers to the technique of extracellular recording, which means that the electrode sits outside the cell and records the action potentials that are being generated. However, it is possible (though very difficult) to pass the tip of the electrode into the body of the cell itself and record inside the cell (intracellular recording). Here the cell's overall electrical state can be measured, not just the action potentials that it emits, and so we can understand the input to the cell and how this input can be transformed into its output (the action potentials).

Visually evoked potentials

To record visually evoked potentials (VEPs), the electrodes are not lowered down into the brain but are merely taped or glued on to the surface of the skull. Once again the electrical activity that the electrode can detect is amplified and can be stored by a computer (see Figure 12.8). The electrical activity that is recorded is once again caused by the action potentials of the cells firing in the brain, but there is now no way to isolate that activity of one cell and so what we record is the activity of lots (perhaps many thousands) of cells. You might think that we could at least say that the activity must be from the cells that are just underneath the electrode, but not even this level of precision is possible because of the complicated way in which our brains are folded into our heads.

Another problem faced by this technique is that the tiny signals from the cells being excited by our stimulus are very small compared to all the other background activity in the brain. We call this random background activity noise, even though you can't hear it. So to detect our signal among all this noise, we need a technique that will somehow isolate the signal. We can do this by taking advantage of the fact that each time we present a stimulus it should produce the same signal, whereas the noise should be random (different) each time we present the stimulus. Thus by adding together the activity from lots of separate presentations of the stimulus we should get more and more signal and the random noise should cancel itself out to nothing (see Figure 12.9).

Although the VEP technique has the disadvantage of not knowing exactly where we are recording from, it still is very good at preserving the timing aspects (i.e. exactly how long

Fig. 12.8. VEPs can be recorded at any age.

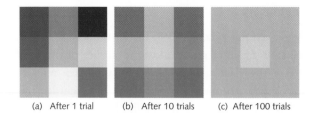

(a)   After 1 trial   (b)   After 10 trials   (c)   After 100 trials

Fig. 12.9. Signal averaging: (a) On each trial a block of 9 squares is presented. Each square is given a random luminance (noise) but then a small signal is added to the luminance of the middle square. On any single trial this added signal is hard to see, because of the random luminance of all the other squares. However, as we average together lots of trials this extra luminance begins to become visible as the random fluctuations of luminance in the other squares cancel out. By 10 trials the middle square is noticeably brighter (b), and by the time 100 trials are averaged the signal is obvious (c). The same technique of averaging is used to detect the small signal in the brain arising from activity related to the presentation of a visual stimulus.

after the presentation of the stimulus the activity occurs) of the signals, and has the major advantage of being non-invasive (not having to get inside the skull). Hence this technique has been widely used with subjects where we cannot get inside the skull (humans) and especially where traditional psychophysics is difficult (babies).

Magnetoencephalography (MEG)

This is a new technique that allows us to measure the electrical activity inside the brain. In many ways it is similar to VEPs, but the machines cost lots more money and the technique is altogether sexier (Figure 12.10). Here's how it works. Electrical activity in the brain will set up magnetic fields that, although tiny, are potentially measurable outside the head. As these fields are much smaller than the earth's magnetic field you need a special room shielded to exclude any extraneous magnetic field, then you need superconducting coils that have to be kept unbelievably cold, close to absolute zero. This requires large quantities of liquid helium. Now, by measuring the magnetic fields outside the head we can infer, by way of sophisticated software that only a few scaly creatures understand, the site of the electrical activity inside the head. This technique has several advantages; it means we can buy a very expensive toy, and it is completely non-invasive. This means it can be used with absolute safety even on babies, and it can be used on the same individual over and over again. One drawback is that, as with more conventional VEP measurement, the location of activity in the brain is not as precise as we would like. However, it does tell you about activity that is happening right now. Unlike the next technique we shall tell you about.

Functional magnetic resonance imaging (fMRI)

You may not know this, but your head contains billions upon billions of little magnets (approximately 1000 billion billion billion if you must know) in the form of hydrogen atoms (remember that your brain is mainly made of water, which may be why you find

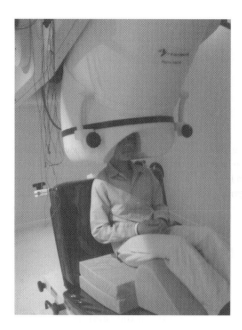

Fig. 12.10. A subject ready to participate in a MEG experiment. The large container is full of liquid helium which cools the superconducting coils that detect the brain activity.

university so difficult). If we place a small magnet near a large one the small magnet will align itself with the magnetic field of the large one (think of a compass needle aligning to the earth's magnetic field). We can do the same to your brain by placing you in a very large magnet so that all your hydrogen atoms align with the field. Now if the little magnets are all put out of alignment by a brief radio signal, they give off a small amount of energy as they return to their aligned position. Your brain, indeed all your body, is made up chiefly of fat and water. And we say that without ever having met you, so rest assured it's true of everyone and not just fat people. The watery bits, and this includes blood, have lots of hydrogen atoms and the fatty bits have fewer hydrogen atoms. So when our hydrogen atoms are forced to give off a bit of energy, we can detect which parts of the brain (or any other part of your body) contain lots of water. This whole operation can be done in something called a magnetic resonance imaging machine, or MRI for short. Figure 12.11 shows a picture of such a machine and, like the MEG machine, it is reassuringly expensive. Now look at the picture it creates of someone's brain (Figure 12.12). Note that features within the brain are visible because some bits of the brain contain more water (like the cortex, which is made up of the nerve cells) than other bits (the fatty white matter underlying the cortex).

Why does a picture of the water help? Well, such MRI pictures let us see if there are bits missing, or we can measure how large various bits are, or we can see abnormalities like tumours. However, they do not tell us much about function. To do that we need to add the 'function' to our magnetic resonance image, and predictably this is known as **functional MRI** (fMRI).

When nerve cells become active they use up some of their energy and therefore need to replace it. A cell's energy comes from oxygen carried by the blood, so a few seconds after

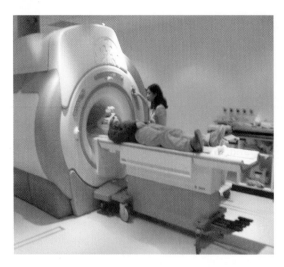

Fig. 12.11. A magnetic resonance imager (MRI). The same machine is used for fMRI.

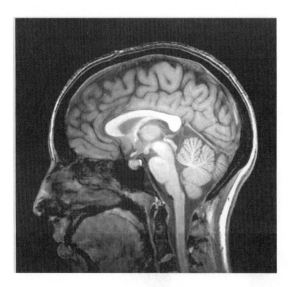

Fig. 12.12. An MRI scan of a vertical slice though the human head.

firing there is an increase in oxygen-rich blood flowing to this part of the brain (know as the haemodynamic response). Oxygenated blood has different magnetic properties from deoxygenated blood, and this change shows up on our MRI scan and can be tracked over time. Hence areas that are very active when we present a stimulus should need lots more fresh blood than areas that are not active, and by comparing the brain at times when the stimulus is presented against times when it is not we can get an idea of where the blood is, and therefore where the cells are active.

To illustrate, let's see how the technique has been used to map out the visual areas of the brain (see Chapter 3). Typically, stimuli such as those shown in Figure 12.13 are used. On the left a wedge of chequerboard continually flickers, so provides a strong visual signal. As it flickers it also slowly moves around the clock, so that at one point in time the wedge will be stimulating the upper visual field, then a few seconds later the right visual field, then the lower field, and so on. As we believe the brain contains many orderly maps of the visual scene, this means that within each of these maps different parts of the map will be active at different times as the stimulus moves around the clock. By recording when each part of the brain is active we can therefore get a picture of these maps (providing our visual area is activated by this stimulus and does indeed contain such a map). A stimulus that changes eccentricity over time (i.e. stimulates the fovea and then the periphery – see Figure 12.13, right section) also helps us to construct these maps.

Human brains are so large that they have to be scrunched up in order to fit into our heads, and this folding differs slightly for each person. In order to help us understand the maps produced by the fMRI (Figure 12.14), clever computer techniques can be used to virtually 'blow up' the brain in order to get rid of the folds (imagine taking a bicycle pump and pumping up the brain till all the folds come out), or 'flatten' the brain (Figure 12.15).

fMRI is telling us a great deal about how the human brain works, including how it sees. However, it also has some problems that are worth noting. First, areas can be active not only because the area is being excited, but also because it is sending a large inhibitory

Fig. 12.13. Simplified versions of stimuli used to map areas of visual cortex. In the left panel the stimulus is a checkerboard pattern that reverses in contrast (i.e. the white areas turn black, and the black areas white) several times per second and slowly moves around the clock so that it excites the upper visual field, then the left visual field etc. in turn. In the right panel the stimulus starts in the periphery of the visual field and moves slowly towards the centre. In reality, some of the stimuli can be more complex. For example, sometimes the size of the checks varies with eccentricity (because we know that small checks are invisible in our peripheral field).

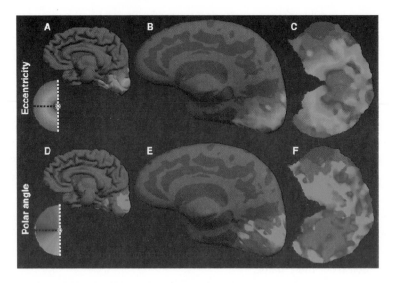

Fig. 12.14. Maps of activity in the human brain according to the location of the stimulus in the visual field. The colour-coded semicircles on the left show stimuli of different eccentricity in different colours (e.g. blue marks central vision and red far peripheral vision). A. The areas activated by these stimuli can be seen in the unfolded brain (hence the areas inside the folds cannot be seen). B. The brain has been 'blown-up' so that all of the cortical surface is visible – the light grey areas were visible in A and the darker grey areas were previously hidden in the folds (sulci). C. The areas with activity are presented in a 'flattened' format. D, E, and F show similar maps for stimuli that vary in polar angle.

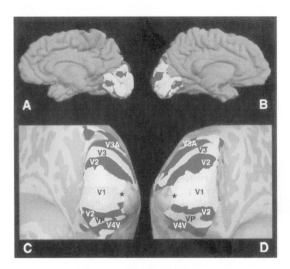

Fig. 12.15. From the activation maps illustrated in Figure 12.14, visual areas can be mapped.

signal (both need equal amounts of energy). The blood signal occurs some 4–6 seconds after the nerve cells' response, and so is rather sluggish. This would not be a problem if all of the brain had exactly the same delay (we could just take a few seconds off all the responses), but this delay seems to change across individuals, different brain regions, and even the nature of the task being performed. This means that the temporal resolution of fMRI isn't very good. Its spatial resolution (i.e. how far apart two points have to be in the brain to be told apart in the fMRI image) is only around 0.5 mm (the width of a grain of rice). This may seem quite precise, but it is not a good enough resolution to record from, say, an orientation column in area V1.

Optical imaging

fMRI uses changes in blood flow to get an image of the brain. However, it is also possible to see these changes in blood flow rather more directly. If the brain is exposed we can just take pictures of it and compare its appearance during periods of visual stimulation with periods when there is no visual stimulation. Of course the changes are very, very small, so you need an excellent camera, a steady hand, and lots of averaging over many images. Again, a computer can be used to do all this. The results of such experiments are shown in Figure 12.16. The individual ocular dominance columns and orientation columns of area V1 can be seen (see Chapter 3). Or course there are many limitations to this technique. The most obvious is that you need to have the cortex exposed, which means removing the skull – a highly invasive technique. Further, as only small parts of the brain are exposed at the surface (much of the cortex is hidden in the folds of the brain) only this part can be recorded from. Structures deep within the brain, such as the lateral geniculate nucleus, cannot be imaged by this technique.

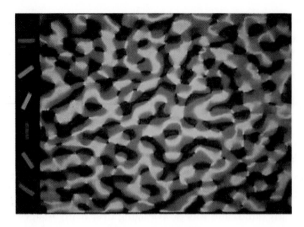

Fig. 12.16. Maps of activation of visual cortex by stimuli of different orientations, using optical imaging.

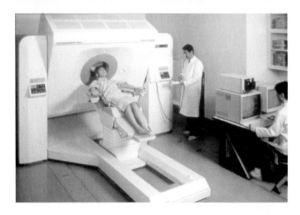

Fig. 12.17. A patient in a PET scanner.

Positron emission tomography (PET)

Like fMRI and optical imaging, PET also relies on blood flow in order to highlight activity within the brain. In this technique the person first ingests or is injected with radioactive glucose or a similar substance that will be carried via the blood to the brain. Of course the most active parts of the brain should preferentially take up this radioactive substance and therefore give off the most radioactivity. To measure the radioactivity we need to have radiation detectors positioned around the person's head (Figure 12.17). Again we can compare the activity of the brain when the person is looking at a particular stimulus or when looking at a control stimulus. As an example, we could compare activity in the brain when someone is looking at a coloured picture and compare it with when they are looking at the same picture but in black and white. The difference in activity might tell us about the processing of information about colour in the human brain.

You may be alarmed at the idea of putting radioactivity into humans in order to further the cause of vision science. The radioactivity used typically has a half-life of around 2 minutes (that is, every 2 minutes it will be giving off only half the radioactivity it did 2 minutes before), so after around 10 minutes there is only around 3% of the activity just after administration. Indeed, it is claimed that a person in a typical PET experiment receives only around 10% of the allowable yearly dose for a worker running an X-ray machine in a hospital, or a worker in a nuclear power station such as Three Mile Island, Chernobyl, or Sellafield. So I'm sure we all feel safe now.

Microstimulation

In this technique we attempt to make a cell, or group of cells, fire by artificial means. This can be done either by sending a tiny electrical signal via a microelectrode (see single cell recording) to stimulate the cell, or by squirting on small amounts of a chemical that excites (or indeed inhibits) the cell. We can then use other techniques to see what happens when we do this. For example, we could be recording from a cell in one brain area while we stimulate in another area.

A more ambitious use of microstimulation is to look at changes in behaviour (which we assume are due to changes in perception) while microstimulation takes place. The experiment we are going to describe is a bit complicated, so pay close attention. The first step is to train a monkey to tell the difference between a pattern of dots moving upwards and one of dots moving down. It indicates the direction of the dots by moving its eyes to one marker for up and another for down. Now we make the task harder; not all the dots move up or down, most of them wander around at random with just a fraction of them moving in a coherent direction. As we increase the fraction of the dots that move (say) upwards, the probability of the monkey responding 'up' increases. So far so good. Now suppose we choose an ambiguous pattern that the monkey only sees as going up on a small fraction of trials. Just as we present the stimulus, we stimulate a group of cells in area V5 (MT) that we know to be sensitive to upwards motion. Now we observe the monkey making far more 'up' responses than before. Using this technique we can even present the monkey with a pattern that it would normally report as going 'down' but, by stimulating 'up' cells in V5, make the animal respond 'up'.

Lesioning

If we want to know what a particular part of the brain is doing, an obvious technique would be to destroy it and see what happens to our perception. This can be done in several ways. First, we can use surgery and carefully extract the target area from the brain (while the animal is under appropriate anaesthesia, of course). We can then compare the animal's vision measured before the surgery with its vision after recovery from the surgery. Of course there may be effects of the surgery that are not due to removal of parts of the brain but rather due to non-specific effects such as having to have anaesthetic, so often we have to have a control animal that goes through the same surgery apart from the removal of part of the brain (animals in such a control are often known as 'shams'). Lesioning techniques have many problems. First, we require several animals, as individual differences in performance mean that we need large enough groups to see what effect the lesion had. As scientists strive to use as few animals as possible, this is undesirable. Second, the surgeon's knife not only removes the nerve cells within the area we are interested in, it also removes much of the white matter. This white matter can contain axons (remember that these are the long connections that link cells) from many other visual areas. Hence our lesion in one part of the brain can actually have an effect on areas a great distance away. Finally, the boundaries of most brain areas are invisible to the surgeon's eye and require special techniques such as staining in order to make them visible (see page 346). Hence it's almost impossible to remove all of one area without damaging nearby areas.

A more precise lesioning technique is to use special neurotoxins that destroy only a very small part of the brain. In such a technique an area of the brain is first identified by either anatomical or recording techniques so that the location of the lesion can be precise. Then a tiny drop of the neurotoxin is delivered through a very fine tube. This neurotoxin only destroys nerve cells, and spares other brain processes such as the axons in the white matter. In areas where there is a precise and orderly map of the visual world this small lesion will only cause damage to one small part of the visual field and hence the other parts of the field can be used as a control (no need for sham controls) to assess the effect of the lesion. The experiments of Schiller and colleagues described in Chapter 2 are an example of this technique. Neurotoxins continue to be developed that enable even more sophisticated lesions. For example, it is possible to get a neurotoxin that only attacks certain types of cell (such as those that use acetylcholine as their means of signalling) and hence we can see not only what each area might be doing, but also what roles different types of cell within the area might be playing within this overall picture.

Even these more sophisticated versions of the lesioning technique have some limitations. Imagine using the lesioning technique to understand the working of a car. We randomly remove some part and then see what happens. Let us say we remove brake pads. We would then turn on the engine and find that nothing is wrong, and may conclude that the brake pads serve no useful function in the car. Only if we perform the correct test (needing to stop quickly) will we understand the function of this part. Likewise, it is only if we set the correct task that we will understand what the lesion has done. Of course, we don't know what the correct test is until we understand the function of the area. Catch 22!

OK – let's go back to your car and remove another bit. We now turn on the engine and find that the car makes a loud whining noise. What can you conclude? You might be tempted to conclude that you must have removed the 'whine suppression mechanism' from the car, and sure enough when you replace this part the whining stops. Of course this would be wrong – the whine probably occurs because the system is now faulty, rather than being a normal system working well but producing a noise. So we are now studying a faulty system rather than discovering how the intact system works. There is also strong evidence that the brain changes in response to damage. For example, often an animal that has lost visual function for a day or so after a lesion no longer appears damaged several days later. Indeed, the changes can be huge. In particularly amazing experiments ferrets had their optic nerves re-routed so that they terminated in an area that would normally be

auditory cortex. Nevertheless these animals were not blind, but learned to 'see' using the part of the brain normally reserved solely for their sense of hearing. In humans it is also well known that parts of our brain that in the 'normal' system have one function can be recruited into other functions in the case of damage (such as blindness).

Temporary lesions

There are also techniques that can be used to stop activity in a part of the brain on a temporary basis. One is to cool the part of the brain so that all metabolic activity stops. This can be done by placing special cooling plates on to the surface of the brain (or occasionally inserted into the brain) and then cooling until all activity stops. Typically this can be done for minutes or hours, and then the brain is allowed to return to its normal temperature. This sort of technique is used to see how the input from one brain area (the cooled one) affect cells in another brain area. This technique is clearly highly invasive, and can only be used in animals.

Another very temporary lesion (lasting only a fraction of a second) can be induced by **transcranial magnetic stimulation (TMS)**. Here a powerful electromagnet is placed close to the head above the brain area of interest (Figure 12.18). The electromagnet is then switched on for a very brief pulse. The strong magnetic field disrupts the normal activity of the cells nearby, so that they cannot signal or process in the way that they usually do. The technique is claimed to be harmless and can be used many times on humans (though data on long-term effects are not available). The technique has the unique ability to disrupt a visual process with great temporal precision (though poor spatial resolution) and, though in its infancy, may prove a most valuable addition to the researcher's arsenal.

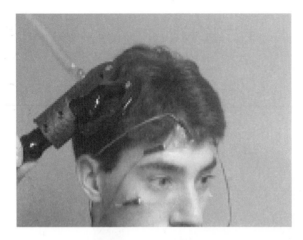

Fig. 12.18. Transcranial magnetic stimulation. The 8-shaped coil produces a magnetic pulse that causes inactivation of a small area of cortex beneath the coil for a very brief period.

Neuropsychology

In the previous section we discussed ways in which a lesion could be made deliberately by various techniques. However, nature offers us many cases of people who have damage to their brain from a large variety of reasons. Many present with focal lesions (ones that are reasonably well located to a single site or a small number of sites), perhaps from a bullet entering the brain, or a stroke (cerebrovascular accident), or a road traffic accident. Other lesions are more diffuse, such as those caused by carbon monoxide poisoning or from excessive use of drugs or alcohol. Of course in reality these are only loose divisions. A car crash can cause focal lesions if something penetrates the skull, but can cause also much diffuse damage as the brain is thrown violently around within the skull causing bruising as well as cell damage. Further, the damage may not be due to a single incident. For instance, the 'punch-drunk' boxer's brain damage may result from thousands of small lesions.

As well as all of the problems we have already outlined for lesion studies, human neuropsychological studies also must struggle with the fact that lesions do not respect the brain's functional neuroanatomy. Lesions will rarely be confined to just one visual area, and will often cover many visual areas. Even within an affected area some bits of this area will be damaged and other bits left intact. Also, it must be appreciated that no two patients will ever be damaged in quite the same way. All car crashes, strokes, and gunshot wounds are different, so all produce different lesions. Therefore many neuropsychologists prefer to work on individuals, trying to find out what tasks they can and can't do. So if we find a patient who can see colour but not motion, and another patient who can see motion and not colour, this double dissociation of function tells us that there must be some separation of function between colour and motion in the brain. Note that if we only had one patient, say one who could see motion and not colour, this would not prove that colour and motion were separate as it could be that the colour task is more difficult than the motion one and the lesion only affects difficult tasks.

Psychophysics

So far all these clever techniques have told us when cells are firing, when brains are active, and so on, but what we really need to know is what a person sees. After all, we noted in Chapter 11 that many parts of the visual system can be active, but the person may deny seeing anything. So if we really want to understand how this brain activity is related to vision, we need techniques to try and understand vision itself.

The most obvious thing we can do is to ask a subject when she can see something. If you aren't reading this chapter just to find out how the book ends, you may have read Chapter 4. In that chapter we discussed a great deal of psychophysics, even though we didn't frighten you at the time by calling it this. One technique we looked at was adaptation, a method of probing the human visual system that is so useful that it has been dubbed 'the psychologist's microelectrode'. We won't discuss adaptation any further here, but we will look at something else we encountered in Chapter 4. Do you remember the contrast sensitivity function? This measured when we could just detect a sine-wave grating. How would we actually do such an experiment? The obvious approach would be to get the subject to twiddle a knob that increases and decreases the contrast of some grating until it is only just visible. This value is then the contrast detection threshold. This method of adjustment, as it's called, is a very quick technique for getting the threshold, but it is frowned upon by purists who regard it as being very dirty as well as quick. One problem is that some people might decide they need to be able to see the pattern really clearly before they are happy with their setting, and others will say they can see the pattern on the flimsiest evidence. A better method is to use a forced-choice procedure. Now we present two patterns, either side by side or one after the other. One pattern is completely blank and the other is the target pattern (e.g. a grating). The subject must say which side (or time

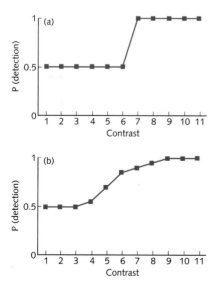

Fig. 12.19. Psychometric functions. See text for details.

BOX 12.1   Subthreshold summation and masking

Psychophysicists have a range of techniques they can use to infer the mechanisms at work within our visual system. In several chapters you find that we discuss experiments that use adaptation, where the presentation of one stimulus produces brief changes within the visual system that we can measure. Here are two other well-used techniques.

Subthreshold summation

Imagine that in order to detect a particular light we need 100 units of energy. What would happen if we were to present two such lights, each of 50 units? Well, we know that one light of 50 units is not visible – it is subthreshold (below the threshold of seeing). But if we could somehow put the lights together (summate them) to make one of 100 units, we might be able to see this. To illustrate the point, let's say we present two brief lights in the same place but one after the other. If we do this fast enough then this should be the same as presenting one light, and hence we should be able to see the light even though the two flashes if presented by themselves would be invisible. However, if the lights were presented several seconds apart it seems unlikely that they could summate. By systematically varying the time between the lights we can therefore measure the time interval over which two stimuli can interact. Figure 12.1.1 shows some results from such an experiment done under bright conditions (when the cones are active – purple) and done under dim conditions (when the rods are active – blue). From this we see that under bright conditions we only summate light over a brief (< 50 ms) interval, and we can also get some cancellation (where we actually need each of our lights to be greater than 100 units) at intervals of around 100 ms. Under dim conditions much greater temporal summation takes place (over 100 ms) to help us see in such conditions. There is also now no cancellation phase. This illustrates how things interact over time, but we can use the same logic to see how things interact over space, orientation, wavelength, or direction of motion.

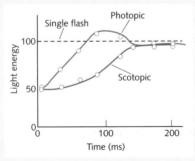

Fig. 12.1.1. Amount of light needed to detect the presence of two brief flashes of light separated in time. A single flash needs around 100 units in order to be detected (see dashed line). At very short intervals each light needs only be around 50 units in order to be detected, suggesting perfect summation. Purple curve is for bright (photopic) conditions and blue is for dark (scotopic) conditions.

Masking

In the masking paradigm we look to see if one pattern can alter our ability to detect the presence of another pattern. At the top of Figure 12.1.2 (marked A) you should be able to see a rather faint vertical grating. In sections B – E we have placed a second, higher-contrast grating over the top of this faint vertical grating. To our eyes the vertical grating is no longer visible in B and C, but is still detectable in D and E. This loss of visibility is what we call masking, and in this example clearly shows that in order for one grating to strongly mask the presence of the other they must have similar orientations. Again, similar logic can be used to explore interactions between any patterns.

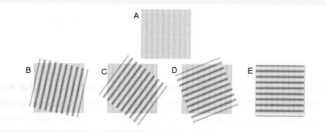

Fig. 12.1.2. Masking. The grating you can see in A can be masked by gratings of similar orientation, so it becomes impossible to see the vertical grating in B and (probably) C, but it is quite easy to see in D and E, when the mask orientations are very different from the vertical target grating. See text for details.

interval) contains the grating. If the pattern is too faint to be seen (its contrast is too low) then the subject won't be able to see it so she will have to guess which pattern is the grating, and she will get it right 50% of the time. So you would expect the results of such an experiment to look like Figure 12.19a; at low contrasts the subject can't see the grating so she has to guess which of the two patterns is the grating (the probability of detection is 0.5 or 50%) and when the contrast gets to some level she can see the grating clearly (the probability of detection is now 1.0 or 100% if you prefer). The point at which the subject starts to see the pattern is called the detection threshold. Easy peasy; except the graph never really looks like this. It always looks like Figure 12.19b; as the contrast increases the probability of the subject saying 'yes, I can see it' *gradually* increases. This graph is known as a psychometric function, and its characteristic shape emerges whenever we measure thresholds. We might measure absolute thresholds – how much contrast we need to see a

BOX 12.2   **Detection, discrimination, and matching**

In order to measure how good someone is at a task, we have to find out if they can do the task when it is really hard. So if we wanted to see how good someone is at detecting a grating pattern we can use a two-option, forced-choice task (see main text) and have them decide whether a grating is present either on the left side or on the right side of a screen (Figure 12.2.1 A). However, this would only tell us how good they are at this contrast. In reality we have to present gratings of various contrasts to produce a psychometric function (see Figure 12.22) and from this we can see what contrast would be needed to produce a correct response on, say, 75% of presentations. We call this the detection threshold – the ability to detect the mere presence of the stimulus.

If we look at Figure 12.22 we can see that we have to measure the visibility of gratings of 11 different contrasts. Let's say that in order to get reliable measures at each contrast we need at least 40 trials. This means we need 440 trials just to measure this one detection threshold! This also assumes that the points we chose would actually span the threshold – if this person's threshold had actually been at contrast 15, all this effort would have gone to waste. Not surprisingly, psycho-physicists have invented a couple of shortcuts to reduce these problems. One popular technique is to use a staircase method. Here we start by presenting a stimulus we believe will be easily visible. If the subject correctly detects this target, then on the next trial we make it harder to see by reducing the contrast. If they get this one correct then we reduce it again for the next trial, and so on. There should then come a point when the contrast gets so low that they get it wrong. When this happens we then increase the contrast for the next trial. By going up and down like this we should oscillate about the point at which the person can just see the target – and hence by averaging the last few trials we have our threshold in much fewer trials (Figure 12.2.2).

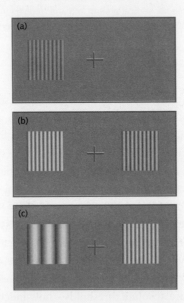

Fig. 12.2.1. (a) What a typical trial on a detection experiment might look like. A low-contrast grating is presented, and the subject has to determine if it occurs on the left- or right-hand side. (b) What a typical trial on a discrimination experiment might look like. Gratings are presented on both sides, with one of them having a little more contrast than the other. The subject has to decide which side contains the higher contrast. (c) What a typical trial on a matching experiment might look like. Different gratings are presented on both sides, with one of them having a little more contrast than the other. The subject has to decide which side contains the higher contrast.

Sometimes we are not interested in whether or not we can detect a pattern, but in whether we can tell two patterns apart. For instance in Figure 12.2.1B we have two gratings that differ in contrast by just a small amount – which we call δC (delta C). By varying δC we can measure such discrimination thresholds in just the same way as we did for detection thresholds.

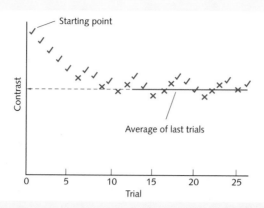

Fig. 12.2.2. The contrasts presented when using a staircase technique. Correct answers (ticks) cause the contrast on the next trial to be lowered, whereas incorrect answers (crosses) produce an increase in contrast for the next trial. The last few trials can be averaged, to produce a threshold.

Finally, we might not want to make patterns look identical, but might just want to match one property of the stimuli. So we might have gratings of very different spatial frequencies but we want to match the contrasts of those gratings (Figure 12.2.1 c). Again we can vary the contrast of one of the gratings from trial to trial and find the point at which they perceive contrast as being higher on 50% of occasions – this is the matching point.

grating, or the luminance we need to detect a light, or the amount we must displace an object for us to detect motion. We might be measuring difference thresholds – how much brighter one light must be from another to see the difference, or how much longer one line is from a standard to see the difference. But in every case we will find we can plot the result in the form of a psychometric function, and that might see a bit odd. After all, the psychometric function suggests that there is always a stimulus that we can detect or discriminate on 75% of occasions. That is, we can present a constant stimulus but the subject only gets the answer right three-quarters of the time. Why?

Let's just think what the visual system is being asked to do in an experiment where we want to measure the detection threshold for a spot of light. In Figure 12.20a we can see what might happen. A really dim spot of light is present on the receptive field centre of an ON-centre ganglion cell. It's too dim, so the cell doesn't respond and no signal travels up the visual pathway to the brain. The light is clearly below the threshold. Now we make the light brighter and the cell fires and, hey presto, we should be able to see the spot of light. Give the spot more luminance and it should look really bright. If this were the way things were then we should get the psychometric function we drew in Figure 12.19a – now you see it, now you don't. But if you cast your mind back to Chapter 2 you might remember that ganglion cells have what we called a baseline level of activity, and this means they fire at random even in the dark. Sometimes they might fire 10 times in

(a)

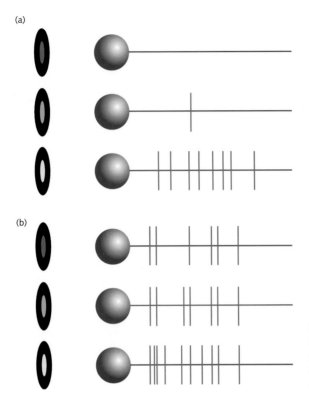

(b)

Fig. 12.20. (a) Firing of a cell with no baseline activity as the contrast of a stimulus increases. (b) Firing of a cell with baseline activity as the contrast of a stimulus increases.

a second in the dark, sometimes only once or twice, sometimes 16 times. So we must now redraw Figure 12.20a with this background activity added in and, as you can see in Figure 12.20b, it all becomes a bit of a mess! It is no longer possible to tell whether the firing rate of the cell contains a signal or whether it's all just noise.

Let's consider this problem in a little more detail. We have said the cells fire in the dark, and that this firing is fairly random so that sometimes it fires a lot and sometimes a little. So we could now plot this amount of firing, and we get a graph like Figure 12.21a. This shows that the average rate of firing of this particular cell is 10 impulses per second, with higher and lower rates being less common. This graph is just like one you might draw of the heights or the IQs of your friends or any other measure that is randomly ('normally', as the statisticians say) distributed around some mean value. Now we can call this the noise distribution of the cell's firing. It's what happens when there is no signal.

Now let's look what happens when we shine a very dim light on our cell's receptive field, so that the light produces just one extra nerve impulse. This situation is shown in Figure 12.21b (purple curve). Now the mean rate of firing is 11 impulses per second – 10 noise plus 1 signal. But if we now have to decide whether the cell has 'seen' a spot of light we are in real trouble. After all, if the cell fires 11 times per second it could be that the noise level was 11 or it could be a noise level of 10 plus 1 for the signal. We just don't know. But remember we are in a forced-choice experiment – we aren't allowed to say 'I

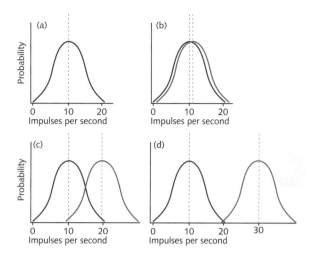

Fig. 12.21. (a) When no stimulus is present the amount of activity at any time varies around a baseline – here set at 10 impulses per second. (b) A weak stimulus causes a small increase in activity over the baseline activity (purple curve), and (c) a stronger stimulus causes a greater amount of activity. However, only very strong activation can cause the activity produced by the signal on every single trial to be stronger than that produced without any stimulation (d).

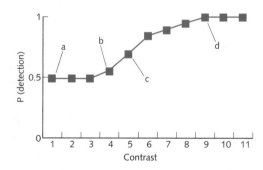

Fig. 12.22. The psychometric function for detecting a low-contrast stimulus. In a two-alternative forced experiment we have a 50% chance of guessing the correct interval, even if the contrast is so low it does not produce any signal (marked a). As contrast increases (b and c) the probability of detection rises, but it is only when the signal strength is large compared to the noise signal (d) that we come close to detecting the stimulus 100% of the time.

don't know'. So how can we make a decision? Well, remember that in a forced-choice experiment there are two intervals. In one there is no signal (just noise), and in the other is the signal (hence in the brain's activity there is signal plus noise). So a sensible strategy would be to pick the interval with the higher activity and say that is the one with the signal. Of course we will be wrong sometimes, because the noise in one interval could be larger that the noise plus the signal in the other. So with a signal strength that produces 1

Signal detection theory

BOX
12.3

In our rather dull description of the problems of determining whether a certain level of firing in a noisy ganglion cell indicates the presence of a light you will have realized, if you're smart, that there are four possible outcomes in any trial in the experiment:

1 On a trial with a light presented we say there is a light. We call this a **hit**.

2 On a trial with a light presented we say there is no light. We call this a **miss**.

3 On a trial without a light we say that there is a light. This is a **false alarm**.

4 On a trial without a light we say that there is no light. This is called a **correct rejection**.

Looking at detection thresholds this way is a bit strange and is called **signal detection theory**. It's a bit complicated for this book, but it really is relevant to everyday life. Imagine you're in a noisy, dimly lit bar. It's Saturday night, nearly time to go home, and you're alone. You glance across the crowded room and there you espy the most gorgeous creature and he or she winks at you . . . What do you do? Of course you sidle across the floor and say 'Hello gorgeous, do you want to come back to my place for a coffee?'. The gorgeous creature replies 'I thought you'd never ask, let's go.' This, in signal detection theory, is a hit. But it is not always so. Suppose the gorgeous creature was not winking but trying to remove some dust from its eye. The response then might be something like 'Go with you? Not while there are dogs in the street.' So cruel! – and a classic example of a false alarm. You thought the wink was a signal, but it was just noise. You should be able to work out the other two possibilities; you see the wink, decide that the gorgeous creature couldn't possibly be winking at you and you slink off home alone. And you were wrong! Gorgeous was winking – a miss. The fourth option is that you see the wink, decide that no one loves you, and you're absolutely right, they don't. Said creature was merely flicking something from its eye, a correct rejection in signal detection theory.

Let's get back to the ganglion cell we encountered in Figure 12.21 for a moment. We can represent all four outcomes (hit, false alarm, miss, and correct rejection) in our experiment on a graph (Figure 12.3.1). Let's suppose that we decide that any rate of firing of the ganglion cell greater than 15 impulses per second is a light, and less than 15 impulses per second is 'no light'. This means we set our **criterion** at 15 impulses per second. The criterion is shown on the graph by the vertical dotted line. Now we can see that the area under the signal curve which is to the right of our criterion represents 'hits', that is, we say there is a signal (the light) and there is. The area under the noise distribution to the right of the criterion represents 'false alarms', that is, we say there is a signal, but there isn't. You should be able to find the areas to the left of the criterion that represent 'misses' and 'correct rejections'.

If you've followed this so far then you're in a position to learn one of the most important lessons from this book. If you want to score more 'hits' in life, and we all do – remember our story of the bar on Saturday night – then you can do so in two ways. You can increase your sensitivity, that is the distance between the noise and signal distributions, or you can shift your criterion to the left. This latter course of action will increase your number of hits but it will also increase your false alarm rate. You may well find your prince (or princess) this way, but you'll just have to kiss a lot more frogs in the process.

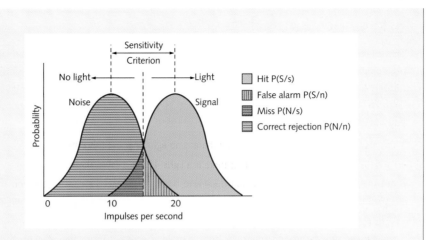

Fig. 12.3.1. Overlapping signal and noise distributions produce areas on the graph that can be identified as hits, false alarms, misses, and correct rejections. Moving the criterion to the left will increase the hit rate but it will also increase the false alarm rate. Only an increase in sensitivity, which moves the two distributions apart, can provide an increase in hits without an increase in false alarms.

extra nerve impulse we should get a few more responses right than just chance, but not many more. This level of performance is marked 'b' on Figure 12.22. Of course, if the signal gets much bigger then things get easier. Look at Figure 12.21c: now we have the light producing 10 impulses per second, taking the mean firing rate up to 20 impulses per second. We've now got a better idea if there's a light out there – any firing rate over 15 impulses per second and we've got a better than evens chance that we're not just dealing with noise (but not totally sure!). But if the cell fires 16 times per second, it could be we have a noise level of 16 impulses per second or it could be a noise level of 6 impulses plus the signal of 10 impulses. So in this instance we are more likely to get the answer right if we chose the interval with the biggest activity, but still performance is not perfect. Only when the two curves (the noise curve and the signal-plus-noise curve) have no overlap whatsoever can we be sure of getting it correct on every trial ('d' in Figure 12.22). We extend these ideas just a little further in Box 12.3.

Anyway, that's why our psychometric functions are the shape they are. If you find this the most interesting part of the whole book, then you're ready to move on to more grown-up books on vision and we wish you well in your adventures. If you find this really dull and boring, then look on the bright side – it's the end of the book.

● READINGS AND REFERENCES

There are few books detailing methods in visual science, but good information about physiological techniques can be found in most physiology textbooks, for example Carlson (2004). A very thorough guide to psychophysical techniques, with many findings, is given by Graham (1989). For some more specific information on how things are done in a laboratory, you might want to see Carpenter and Robson (1999).

Papers on specific issues

Brain imaging techniques To chart how these have developed over the years you might start with Tootell *et al.* (1996). Also the papers by Hadjikhani *et al.* (1998) and Tootell *et al.* (1998) give interesting insights into the application of these techniques.

Neuropsychology Given the advent of human brain imaging, is there any point in studying brain damaged individuals? Some people think so (Rorden and Karnath, 2004). TMS lesions are discussed in Walsh and Cowey (2000).

Lesioning in animals The work of Schiller *et al.* (1990) is a fine example of this technique, and is discussed in Chapter 1.

Microstimulation A classic example of this is Salzman *et al.* (1990).

Psychophysics There is no single paper that will tell you about psychophysics, but reading Graham and Nachmias (1971) will give you a clear indication of a psychophysicist in action.

● POSSIBLE ESSAY TITLES, TUTORIALS, AND QUESTIONS OF INTEREST

1 What can be learnt from lesions to the animal and the human brain?

2 Using the studies of Newsome *et al.* (1989) and Salzman *et al.* (1990), discuss the relationship between activity of a single neuron and perception.

3 Describe how visual areas of the human brain can be mapped by means of fMRI.

4 Has human brain imaging told us anything that we didn't already know?

References

Blasdel, G. G. (1992). Differential imaging of ocular dominance and orientation selectivity in monkey striate cortex. *Journal of Neuroscience* **12**, 3115–3138.

Carlson, N. R. (2004). *Physiology of behavior*, 8th edn. New York: Allyn & Bacon.

Carpenter, R. H. S. and Robson, J. G. (1999). *Vision research: a practical guide to laboratory methods*. Oxford: Oxford University Press.

Graham, N. and Nachmias, J. (1971). Detection of grating patterns containing two spatial frequencies: a comparison of single-channel and multiple-channel models. *Vision Research* **11**, 251–259.

Graham, N. V. S. (1989). *Visual pattern analysers*, Vol. 16. Oxford: Oxford University Press.

Hadjikhani, N., Liu, A. K., Dale, A. M., Cavanagh, P., and Tootell, R. B. H. (1998). Retinotopy and color sensitivity in human visual cortical area V8. *Nature Neuroscience* 1(3), 235–241.

Hartline, H. K., Wagner, H. G., and Ratcliff, F. (1956). Inhibition in the eye of *Limulus. Journal of General Physiology* 39(5), 651–673.

Masland, R. H. and Tauchi, M. (1986). The cholinergic amacrine cells. *Trends in Neurosciences* 9, 218–223.

Newsome, W. T., Britten, K. H., and Movshon, J. A. (1989). Neuronal correlates of a perceptual decision. *Nature* 341, 52–54.

Rorden, C. and Karnath, H.-O. (2004). Using human brain lesions to infer function: a relic from a past era in the fMRI age? *Nature Reviews – Neuroscience* 5, 813–819.

Salzman, C. D., Britten, K. H., and Newsome, W. T. (1990). Cortical microstimulation influences perceptual judgements of motion direction. *Nature, 346*, 174–177.

Schiller, P. H., Logothetis, N. K., and Charles, E. R. (1990). Functions of the colour-opponent and broadband channels of the visual system. *Nature* 343, 68–70.

Sereno, M. I. and Tootell, R. B. H. (2005). From monkeys to humans: what do we know about brain homologies? *Current Opinion in Neurobiology* 15, 135–144.

Sereno, M. I., Dale, A. M., Reppas, J. B., Kwong, K. K., Belliveau, J. W., Brady, T. J., *et al.* (1995). Borders of multiple visual areas in human revealed by functional magnetic resonance imaging. *Science* 268, 889–893.

Tootell, R. B. H., Dale, A. M., Sereno, M. I., and Malach, R. (1996). New images from human visual cortex. *Trends in Neurosciences* 19, 481–489.

Tootell, R. B. H., Hadjikhani, N. K., Vanduffel, W., Liu, A. K., Mendola, J. D., Sereno, M. I., *et al.* (1998). Functional analysis of primary visual cortex (V1) in humans. *Proceedings of the National Academy of Sciences of the USA* 95, 811–817.

Walsh, V. and Cowey, A. (2000). Transcranial magnetic stimulation and cognitive neuroscience. *Nature Reviews – Neuroscience* 1, 73–79.

Index